AF600066

Systemic Functional Linguistics in the Digital Age

Functional Linguistics

Series Editor: Robin Fawcett, Cardiff University

This series publishes monographs that seek to understand the nature of language by exploring one or other of various cognitive models or in terms of the communicative use of language. It concentrates on studies that are in, or on the borders of, various functional theories of language.

Published

Functional Dimensions of Ape-Human Discourse
Edited by James D. Benson and William S. Greaves

System and Corpus: Exploring Connections
Edited by Geoff Thompson and Susan Hunston

Meaningful Arrangement: Exploring the Syntactic Description of Texts
Edward McDonald

Explorations in Stylistics
Andrew Goatly

Text Type and Texture
Edited by Gail Forey and Geoff Thompson

An Introduction to the Grammar of Old English: A Systemic Functional Approach
Michael Cummings

Morphosyntactic Alternations in English: Functional and Cognitive Perspectives
Edited by Pilar Guerrero Medina

Systemic Functional Perspectives of Japanese: Descriptions and Applications
Edited by Elizabeth A. Thomson and William S. Armour

Contrastive Discourse Analysis: Functional and Corpus Perspectives
Edited by Maite Taboada, Susana Doval Suárez and Elsa González Álvarez

Choice in Language: Applications in Text Analysis
Edited by Gerard O'Grady, Tom Bartlett and Lise Fontaine

Systemic Functional Linguistics in the Digital Age

Edited by
Sheena Gardner and Siân Alsop

SHEFFIELD UK BRISTOL CT

Published by Equinox Publishing Ltd.

UK: 415, The Workstation, 15 Paternoster Row, Sheffield, South Yorkshire, S1 2BX
USA: ISD, 70 Enterprise Drive, Bristol, CT 06010

www.equinoxpub.com

First published 2016.

© Sheena Gardner, Siân Alsop and contributors 2016.

All rights reserved. No part of this publication may be reproduced or transmitted in any form or by any means, electronic or mechanical, including photocopying, recording or any information storage or retrieval system, without prior permission in writing from the publishers.

British Library Cataloguing-in-Publication Data
A catalogue record for this book is available from the British Library.

Library of Congress Cataloging-in-Publication Data
Names: Gardner, Sheena, editor. | Alsop, Sian, editor.
Title: Systemic Functional Linguistics in the Digital Age / Edited by Sheena Gardner and Sian Alsop.
Description: Sheffield, UK ; Bristol, CT : Equinox Publishing Ltd., [2016] | Includes bibliographical references and index.
Identifiers: LCCN 2016010072 (print) | LCCN 2016023579 (ebook) | ISBN 9781781792384 (hb) | ISBN 9781781794784 (e-PDF) | ISBN 9781781794791 (e-epub)
Subjects: LCSH: Functionalism (Linguistics)--Data processing. | Systemic grammar--Data processing. | Computational linguistics.
Classification: LCC P147 .S989 2016 (print) | LCC P147 (ebook) | DDC 410.1/833--dc23
LC record available at https://lccn.loc.gov/2016010072

ISBN: 978 1 78179 238 4 (hardback)
978 1 78179 478 4 (e-PDF)
978 1 78179 479 1 (ePUB)

Typeset by CA Typesetting Ltd, www.sheffieldtypesetting.co.uk
Printed and bound in the UK by Lightning Source UK Ltd., Milton Keynes and Lightning Source Inc., La Vergne, TN

Contents

List of Figures ix
List of Tables xii
Acknowledgements xv

Introduction 1
Sheena Gardner and Siân Alsop

Part I
Texts that Are Born Digital: New Digital Genres

1 'There's power in stories': A Multimodal Corpus-Based and Functional Analysis of Fandom Blogs 13
Maria Grazia Sindoni

2 Digitality and Persuasive Technologies: Towards an SFL Model of New Social Actions and Practices in Digital Settings 29
Sandra Petroni

3 Digital Citizenship: Social Actors in Blog Posts to Chilean Online News Portals 45
Lésmer Montecino and María Cristina Arancibia

4 Imagined Community and Affective Alignment in Memorial Tributes to Steve Jobs on YouTube 62
Anu Harju

5 Commenting, Interacting, Reposting: A Systemic-Functional Analysis of Online Newspaper Comments 81
Mariavita Cambria

Part II
Texts that Achieve Digitality:
Professional Genres Recontextualized

6 'We're hearing from Reuters that…': The Role of Around-the-Clock News Media in the Increased Use of the Present Progressive with Mental Process Type Verbs 99
Ben Clarke

7 The Construal of Terminal Illness in Online Medical Texts: Social Distance and Semantic Space 120
Meriel Bloor

8 Moving Online to Teach Academic Writing in Science and Engineering: Theory and Practice 134
Helen Drury

9 Cut and Paste: Recontextualizing Meaning-Material in a Digital Environment 151
Daniel Lees Fryer

10 Analysis of an Online University Lecture: Multimodal Perspectives 166
Mersini Karagevrekis

11 Transitivity in Language Event Reports in an Online Corpus of Science Journalism 184
Blanca García Riaza

12 Is This the End of Hypertext? Hotel Websites' Return to Linearity 198
Martin Kaltenbacher

Part III
Texts that Have Digitality Thrust Upon Them: Super Powers in Text Analysis

13 On Negotiating the Hurdles of Corpus-Assisted Appraisal Analysis in Verbal Art 211
Donna R. Miller

14 Diachronic Change from Washington to Obama: The Challenges and Constraints of Corpus-Assisted Meaning Analysis 229
Paul Bayley and Cinzia Bevitori

15 The Role of Corpus Annotation in the SFL-CL Marriage: A Test Case on the EU Debt Crisis 246
Sabrina Fusari

16 Grammatical Metaphor through the Lens of Software? Examining 'Crisis' in a Corpus of Articles from *The Financial Times* 260
Antonella Luporini

17 A Corpus Approach to Method of Development: Discourse Markers and Presuming Reference in 32 ICE-GB Text Types 276
Michael Cummings

18 Journey of Three Digitized Texts: Entextualization and Recontextualization in a Corpus Study 296
Tom Morton and Anne McCabe

19 Annotating Cohesive Ellipses in an English-German Corpus 310
Katrin Menzel

20 Linguistic Characteristics of Schizophrenia and Mania Computationally Revealed 328
Ekaterina Shagalov and Jonathan Fine†

Subject Index 348
Author index 351

List of Figures

Figure 1.1:	Fandom can be extreme	17
Figure 1.2:	A fan's room	17
Figure 1.3:	Fandom!secrets sample entry 1	23
Figure 1.4:	Fandoms!secrets sample entry 2	24
Figure 2.1:	Fogg's Behavioural Model	33
Figure 2.2:	Fogg's Functional Triad	34
Figure 4.1:	The Appraisal system. Martin and White	67
Figure 5.1:	Comments on the article 'Celtic Tiger immigrants made us better-looking, says Mitchell'	83
Figure 5.2:	E-identity of one of the commentators	85
Figure 6.1:	Tree trunk analogy to explain language stratification	101
Figure 6.2:	Language strata as posited in Systemic Functional Theory	102
Figure 6.3:	Fifteen instances of 'hope' in the present tense drawn from the British National Corpus	104
Figure 6.4:	Present tense progressive with 'hope' in *CoHAE*	111
Figure 6.5:	Present tense progressive with 'hear' in *CoHAE*	112
Figure 8.1:	Screen from writing a report in biology showing the structural stages of the introduction section of a report	137
Figure 8.2:	Screen from writing a short lab report in biochemistry showing the stages of the discussion section of a report	138
Figure 8.3:	Screen from writing a short scientific paper in molecular biology showing the structural stages of the discussion section of a paper	140
Figure 9.1:	Figure from Bernard *et al.* (2001)	154
Figure 9.2:	Placement and relative sizing of figure in PDF (A) and HTML (B) versions of Bernard *et al.* (2001)	155
Figure 9.3:	Screenshots of selected texts in which the figure has been repurposed: A) an online presentation, B) a weblog, C) a crossword-puzzle solver, D) a hair, style, and beauty webpage	157

Figure 9.4:	Screenshots of the figure on the video-sharing website YouTube: A) thumbnail for the video, B) slide in the video	158
Figure 9.5:	Left: original figure (see Figure 9.1); right: transformed figure on YouTube	159
Figure 9.6:	From YouTube video: transformed figure (left) placed alongside an image depicting potential sepsis-related outcomes	159
Figure 9.7:	Transformed figure (and video) embedded on Global Oneness webpage	160
Figure 9.8:	Example of another video automatically embedded on the Global Oneness website	161
Figure 10.1:	The evaluative stance	172
Figure 10.2:	Negotiating with the discourse of 'others'	176
Figure 10.3:	The diagram	178
Figure 11.1:	Different reporting verbs found in the corpus studied	192
Figure 12.1:	The three dimensions of hyperlinks	198
Figure 12.2:	Screenshot of the Hotel Sacher's Rooms-webpage	204
Figure 13.1:	The overlapping semiotic systems (based on Hasan 1989[1985]: 99)	215
Figure 13.2:	*Coriolanus* appraised: Concordances of instances commented	220
Figure 14.1:	Relative frequency of *we* per 100 tokens	239
Figure 14.2:	Relative frequency of *america* per 100 tokens	240
Figure 14.3:	Relative frequency of *may* and *must* per 100 tokens	241
Figure 15.1:	Transitivity analysis of 'A disastrous failure at the summit' by M. Wolf, Halliday Centre Tagger	253
Figure 15.2:	Transitivity analysis of 'A disastrous failure at the summit' by M. Wolf, UAM Corpus Tool	254
Figure 17.1:	Text segment from *The Fellowship of the Ring*	278
Figure 17.2:	The 'Sheila' text	292
Figure 17.3:	The 'picture' text	293
Figure 18.1:	Isabel's recontextualization of the essay rubric	301
Figure 18.2:	Isabel's essay	302

Figure 18.3: Screenshot from CorpusTool with extract from Isabel's essay 303
Figure 18.4: Screenshot from CorpusTool showing comparison of Isabel's use of APPRAISAL in years 1 and 3 304
Figure 18.5: The entextualization and recontextualization cycle 307

Figure 19.1: Link between elliptical phrase and antecedent in MMAX2 320
Figure 19.2: Overall number of cohesive ellipses 323
Figure 19.3: Subtypes of cohesive ellipses in written and spoken subcorpora of original texts and translations in GECCo 324

List of Tables

Table 1.1: LJF Basic Statistics 18
Table 1.2: Positive Keyness of Lexical Items in LJF 19
Table 1.3: Main Processes in the Positive Keyness List 20
Table 1.4: Positive Keyness of Grammatical Items in LJF 21

Table 2.1: A Synoptic View of Social Networks' Target Behaviours 35
Table 2.2: Overview of the Appraisal System 36
Table 2.3: Systemic Functional Classification of Persuasive Technologies 39

Table 3.1: Ideation and Identification in the Construction of the Constitutional Action against the Chilean Minister of Education in Blog 1 54
Table 3.2: Ideation and Identification in the Construction of Profit in a Neoliberal Society in Blog 2 56
Table 3.3: Ideation and Identification in the Construction of the Chilean Social and Political Reality in Blog Comment 3 57
Table 3.4: Ideation and Identification in the Construction of the Political and Social Reality in Blog Comment 4 59

Table 5.1: Distribution of Articles on Immigration that Allowed Comments at www.irishtimes.ie in the Period July-December 2014 86
Table 5.2: Positive Keyness 88
Table 5.3: Negative Keyness in ITC 89

Table 6.1: Process-type Classification in Systemic Functional Linguistics 103
Table 6.2: Present Tense Progressive with 'hope' in *CoHAE* 105
Table 6.3: Present Tense Progressive with 'hear' in *CoHAE* 106
Table 6.4: Currency Collocates for '<BE-present> hoping that' in *UKWaC* 109
Table 6.5: Most Frequent Lemmas in *BE-hearing*, *GB-News* and *UKWaC* Corpora 114

Table 7.1: Ambiguity in a Grammatical Metaphor 125

Table 8.1: Sample of Student and Discipline Staff Comments Related to Design Challenges 147

Table 11.1: Presence of Reporting Signals in the Corpus Studied 190
Table 11.2: Position of Signals in the Reporting Clause 191

Table 13.1: 'noble' in Shakespeare according to Genre 217
Table 13.2: Comparative Raw Data and Relative Frequencies for Each Tragedy in Descending Order 218
Table 13.3: Comparative Numbers of Collocates of 'noble' with Protagonists for Each Tragedy, in Descending Order 218
Table 13.4: Who Is 'noble', How Often, and – Re Coriolanus – According to Whom? 219

Table 14.1: Keywords from 1790–1864 Segment (1) 237
Table 14.2: Keywords from 1990–2014 Segment (5) 238

Table 16.1: GM through Software: Metaphor Candidates in *Crisis* Collocate List (FT_First_page) 265
Table 16.2: GM through Software: Metaphor Candidates in *Crisis* Word Sketch (FT_First_page) 266
Table 16.3: Metaphorical Concordances in FT Corpus and Subcorpora 267
Table 16.4: GMs in FT_First_page 268
Table 16.5: GMs in FT_Leaders 268

Table 17.1: Tabulation of Reference Items and Discourse Markers in Figure 17.1 278
Table 17.2: Densities of Discourse Markers before Subject 280
Table 17.3: Percentage of NP and PRNP before, as, and after S 283
Table 17.4: Densities of NP and PRNP before and as S 286
Table 17.5: Density of DISMKs in Main CLs 289
Table 17.6: Density of NPs + PRNPs before and as S in Main CLs 290
Table 17.7: Density of DISMKs in Main CLs 291
Table 17.8: Density of NPs + PRNPs before and as S in Main CLs 292

Table 20.1: Functions of Nominal Groups 335
Table 20.2: Predictors. Classifying a New Sample 338
Table 20.3: Best Predictors: Classifying a New Sample 339

Acknowledgements

The theme for this edited collection on digitality and Systemic Functional Linguistics grew out of a conversation Sheena had with Emma Moreton on a very hot crowded train travelling from Bologna to Bertinoro in July 2012 for the European Systemic Functional Linguistics Conference. It grew through the conference at Coventry the following year, the publication of extended abstracts from that conference in 2014, and the development of the 20 full papers that were selected for their contribution to the three fields of research on digitality and Systemic Functional Linguistics identified and described in the Introduction to this volume. We are most grateful to the 24 authors for entrusting their work to us and for their patience through the editing and publishing process.

As its genesis suggests, this volume would not have been possible without the international community of scholars who congregate at conferences and interact in their teaching and research under the umbrella of Systemic Functional Linguistics. Siân attended her first Systemic Functional Linguistics conference at Bertinoro, as a PhD student in corpus linguistics. Although Sheena had encountered Halliday, Gregory, Malcolm and others at a LACUS conference in Canada when she was a PhD student in Axiomatic Functionalism, her first real introduction to Systemic Functional Linguistics was when she was working with Meriel Bloor at Warwick and attended a Systemic Functional Linguistics summer institute in Toronto. Those she remembers from the week include Robin Fawcett, David Butt, Anna Maurenen and Jonathan Fine†. She subsequently regularly referred to Fine's work in clinical linguistics as an example of the appliable nature of Systemic Functional Linguistics and was pleased to meet him again and to include here a chapter by him and one of his PhD students, which sadly he did not live to see in print.

Robin Fawcett, Emeritus Professor of Linguistics at Cardiff, has generously encouraged the inclusion of this volume in the Functional Linguistics series. Working together with Janet Joyce, Valerie Hall, Norma Beavers, Christopher Allen and colleagues at Equinox has made the whole process run smoothly. We are grateful to be part of these Systemic Functional Linguistics communities.

Finally, we would like to thank Hilary Nesi not only for her assistance with reviewing and editing this volume, but also more broadly. Since starting this project, we have each climbed another rung of the academic progression ladder with her friendship and support.

Sheena Gardner, Professor
Siân Alsop, PhD
Coventry University

Introduction

Sheena Gardner and Siân Alsop
Coventry University

> Be not afraid of greatness.
> Some are born great, some achieve greatness,
> and others have greatness thrust upon them.
> – William Shakespeare, *Twelfth Night*

> English is an assemblage of varieties of different kinds ...
> never in a state of being, always in a process of becoming ...
> while Chaucer is almost out of range, Shakespeare is not
> – Matthiesen 2014: xv

As social worlds change, we interact in different ways, and new meanings are construed through new wordings. Few could have imagined the exponential extent of the explosion in computational power or the democratizing reach of new forms of social and mass media. The aim of this volume is to explore from a Systemic Functional Linguistics (SFL) perspective the impact of these two great digital changes on our social semiotic processes, on our language systems and on our understanding of contemporary varieties of English and ways of meaning.

Part I: Texts that Are Born Digital: New Digital Genres

The international uptake in personalized digital communication devices has enabled widespread participation in new forms of communication found in online sites such as blogs, news reporting, facebook, memorial websites, and wikis. The chapters in Part I of this volume investigate genres that have been 'born digital'. They have come into existence through the changing social and mass media contexts which have enabled new meanings, new affiliations and new forms of participation in society.

These new genres challenge our traditional views of language as 'spoken' or 'written' and force us to consider not only how the ready inclusion of images and sound is nurturing a generation capable of producing with ease multimodal texts that would previously have been the province of teams of experts, but also the impact this is having on 'digital' language – language that is neither spoken nor written in the traditional senses, but is produced in a way that permits new possibilities for the spontaneity hitherto associated with spoken language in face to face contexts, and the asynchronicity hitherto associated with planned written language.

Social Media have thus afforded new forms of 'ambient affiliation' (Zappavigna, 2012, 2014) and new discourse communities, and in Chapter 1 Maria Grazia Sindoni provides insights into one such community, that of fandom bloggers. This first chapter outlines a multimodal, corpus-based and functional analysis of fandom blogs that deepens our understanding of how fans switch between different semiotic resources in these sites.

In Chapter 2, Sandra Petroni innovatively draws on Fogg's behavioural model and Martin and White's SFL appraisal model to develop a Systemic Functional Classification of Persuasive Technologies such as the 'like' button, the 'poke' button, rating systems and reminders. This makes a strong case for persuasive technologies tending to support expressions of positive attitudes and of alignment, and opens up this line of research for further development.

Chapters 3 and 4 provide insights into further specific online communities. Lésmer Montecino and Maria Cristina Arancibia uncover the world of digital citizenship through their analysis of social participation and the representation of social actors (the student movement, ordinary citizens, government officials) in online blog responses to news editorials in Chile. While the social actors in Chile are very much part of the national political sphere, Anu Harju introduces the concept of an imagined community in exploring the YouTube memorial tributes to Steve Jobs, Apple Inc's co-founder, late-Chairman and CEO. She examines the interpersonal affiliation of anonymous participation, also drawing on appraisal resources, but here to examine acts of remembrance and how communities are formed through five stages of alignment and imagined community building. Harju's explanation of how online communities are formed provides an illuminating counterpoint to Petroni's account of behavioural responses to persuasive technologies, both of which are supported by SFL appraisal analyses.

The final chapter in Part I employs transitivity analysis to better understand the lexico-grammatical choices made in online posts. Here Mariavita Cambria looks specifically at the lexical density and process choices in online newspaper comments on articles in *The Irish Times* relating to migrants and immigration in 2014. Unlike Harju's remembrance posts, which served to build two communities with little direct exchange, these tend to be more dialogic in nature, facilitating the exchange of views on news issues between the contributors.

The chapters in Part I begin to explain how new genres 'are born' or emerge in digital contexts. They also illustrate a range of participatory stances taken in online contributions by what might be called ordinary citizens.

Part II: Texts that Achieve Digitality: Professional Genres Recontextualized

In Part II, we see how more traditional forms of communication are changed through recontextualization and transduction (Kress, 2010) and how they 'achieve digitality'. Two arenas where this is particularly evident are in news reporting and education, where we now have both print and online texts with similar or complementary purposes. Here the differences in the medium and the social contexts shape the differences in language observed. For example, online news reports may be updated more frequently, can make good use of hyperlinks to related reports and sources, and may be designed to be easily consumed on small screens. Online educational materials, in contrast, may become more general, less attached to the here and now than their face-to-face counterparts, and aimed at increasingly large and unspecified audiences. Printed coursebooks (including Halliday and Matthiessen, 2014) are now regularly supplemented by websites that can be searched online and easily updated. In most cases the genres are still recognizable, and the analytical focus of the differences, or areas of change, is therefore on the registers – how the language of the genre reflects the specifics of the changing contexts of situation.

The texts analysed in Part II are drawn from the professional discourse contexts of news reporting, the medical surgery, teaching academic writing, medical textbooks, university lecturing, science journalism and hotel advertising. The focus is therefore less on which new genres are emerging in the digital age, and more on how the language of the workplace has had to respond to the ever-changing affordances and expectations of digital communication. It is also less on the emergence of new social actors in new communities, although these are present, and more on understanding the nature of changes in linguistic and communicative practices and what they bring to or detract from professional communication.

Chapter 6, by Ben Clarke, takes a diachronic perspective on present progressive forms of mental process verbs (e.g. *I am hoping; he is hearing*), and finds a clear upward trend in the general American English corpus CoHAE from 1810 to 2000. Clarke offers the introduction of the around-the-clock news as a plausible explanation for the sharp recent increase, as illustrated by '*We're hearing from Reuters that...*'.

The role of social distance is considered in Chapter 7, with a focus on how terminal illness is construed in face-to-face doctor-patient encounters compared with online medical information. Using evidence from what we know of scientific language and the construal of pain through metaphor, Meriel Bloor develops the argument that online texts are more likely to be construed as expert-expert discourse than as doctor-patient discourse, and as a result they may not only be less considerate of the feelings, history and knowledge of the patient, even to the extent of inaccuracy, but may also present a linguistic challenge to the average reader.

Chapters 8 and 9 in Part II take a useful chronological perspective. In Chapter 8, Helen Drury explains the design processes and multimodal semiotic changes involved in moving print materials online for the genre-based teaching of university student science and engineering reports, through several iterations informed by user feedback, with, among other things, the aim of compensating for the rich scaffolding that takes place in the face-to-face classroom.

From a different starting point, Daniel Lees Fryer in Chapter 9 also explores the processes of transduction from 'real world' to digital text, and the subsequent transformations and assemblages from multimodal perspectives. Lees Fryer analyses the journey of a figure in a medical research article that is re-used through cut and paste technologies. The text can be appreciated as meaning-material, available to be interpreted by readers. As he points out, the contents of many webpages do not exist as assemblages before they are activated, and the spontaneous juxtaposition of his figure alongside other texts calls into question the traditional notions of text and authorship, as well as those of reading and writing.

Chapter 10 by Mersini Karagevrekis takes us into the world of an online lecture in economics. In this multimodal analysis, we can isolate the contributions from gesture, gaze and posture, and explore the links with notes and other written media in the lecture. In Chapter 11, Blanca García Riaza considers language event reports in science journalism through the lens of transitivity, with a focus on reporting verbs and epistemic adjuncts in initial and subsequent sections. Both of these chapters produce analyses expected to benefit the English for Academic Purpose classroom.

In Chapter 12, which provides insights into digital reading paths – how webpages are designed to enable us to develop our own pathways, or to encourage us to follow an authoritative one – Martin Kaltenbacher suggests that hypertext has reached its limits, at least in the context of hotel websites, where a return to linear text and hyperlink abstinence are evidenced.

As Kaltenbacher suggests, too much freedom for the consumer may be bad for business.

The chapters in Part II have taken us beyond the creation of new social communities to a focus on how information is conveyed online, how meanings are construed, the potential influences on our language and lives, the need to understand the origins of digital texts and to critically assess our engagement with them. If they are difficult to understand, maybe we are not the intended audience; if new meanings emerge through juxtapositions or chains of hyperlinks online, maybe new texts are emerging to rebalance for felicitous meanings. In Part II we have seen the fine line between the great enabling power of digital media and the potential distortion of the messages conveyed, brought about by changes in social distance, the spontaneous creation of texts, and insufficient attention to the consequences of multiple and historic digital connections. The third and final section of this volume considers the changes digitality has brought to the tools of our profession as linguists in its presentation of examples of digitally enhanced text analysis.

Part III: Texts that Have Digitality Thrust Upon Them: Super Powers in Text Analysis

Just as the introduction of audio recording marked a step change in the study of spoken language, the ability to digitally store and interrogate increasingly large data sets has marked a step change in the study of patterns in texts, where the field of corpus linguistics is one of the fastest changing linguistic sciences. SFL can benefit greatly from corpus linguistics, for example in identifying probabilities of co-occurrence at the lexico-grammatical level and generally from the dialectal complementarity between theory and data (Halliday and Matthiessen, 2014: 53). It is noteworthy that many of the chapters here invoke systems from discourse semantics, such as appraisal, theme and cohesion, which are less amenable to corpus analysis, and where corpus evidence may require us to reconsider SFL categories (see also Hunston, 2014, 2015). The eight chapters, in Part III provide a snapshot of current practice and issues for SFL analysis.

Chapter 13 by Donna Miller introduces the work of scholars at the University of Bologna who are exploring the benefits and constraints of corpus-assisted SFL analysis. Miller usefully reviews some of the general issues – that corpus analysis is better suited to producing concordance lines of lexico-grammatical strings than discourse analysis of more extended text – before discussing the specifics of her appraisal analysis of verbal art. With a focus on 'noble' in Shakespeare's *Coriolanus*, Miller demonstrates what can usefully be done from a quantitative perspective, and the potential for this to inform more detailed and more contextualized qualitative analyses.

Paul Bayley and Cinzia Bevitori, authors of Chapter 14, are working with a diachronic corpus of 228 State of the Union Addresses delivered by US Presidents over 225 years. Interestingly for our purposes, the original texts from 1790 were delivered orally to Congress, then from 1801 many were written. With technological advances, many have been broadcast live on radio since 1923, on television since 1965, and have been available on the Internet livestream with graphics and chat since 2011. As the audience has expanded from Congress to the American people and beyond, the texts have become less informative and more persuasive. By extracting key words for five historical periods it becomes possible to identify changes in areas such as identity (increase in the use of *we* and *America*) and engagement (decrease of *must* and increase of *may*). Such changes would have been impossible to detect manually, and challenge the analyst to explore collocates and other contextual patterns together with their knowledge of the corpus in its social context to provide meaningful explanations.

Chapter 15 begins with a discussion of corpus-driven vs corpus-assisted analysis, and some of the difficulties in developing automatic parsing tools for meaningful, functionally-conflated SFL features in texts. Sabrina Fusari compares a manual analysis of transitivity in two texts from a small corpus on the European debt crisis with analyses using two widely-used SFL programmes, the UAM Corpus Tool and the Halliday Centre Tagger, considering what can and what cannot be done using each method, and the relative ease with which results can be achieved. The results indicate margins of error for each, and suggest that future trade-off will be between reliability of coding and simplification of SFL analyses.

If multi-functionality is an issue for automated annotation, then grammatical metaphor adds an additional layer of complication. In Chapter 16, Antonella Luporini uses the wordsketch facility in SketchEngine to examine the emergent metaphorical framing of the global financial crisis through an analysis of the word *crisis* in a corpus of articles from the 2008 *Financial Times*. Luporini's approach employs a judicious mix of automated searches and manual analyses, both informed by SFL concepts and knowledge. Quantitative analysis pointed to a higher incidence of ideational metaphor over interpersonal metaphor, while qualitative analysis uncovered multiple meanings.

The final four chapters pay particular attention to discourse features and cohesion in texts from very different contexts. In Chapter 17, Michael Cummings examines the method of development of texts, focusing on discourse markers in Theme position. He analyses the British Component of the International Corpus of English using the associated Corpus Utility

Programme to identify discourse markers. Although this tool works with a more formal and traditional grammar than SFL, he is able to employ a range of corpus queries to identify features such as discourse marker and Subject, thus obtaining a wealth of information about the nature of Theme and Rheme in the corpus of over a million words. This chapter reports on ten searches that enable the ranking of the 32 text types in the ICE in areas such as density of discourse markers before Subject, and density of NP and PRNP before, as and after Subject. In these rankings interactive spoken texts such as broadcast interviews and telephone calls tend to cluster at one end, while monologic, written texts such as those on skills and hobbies or academic natural science tend to cluster at the other end. This chapter shows how corpus query language working on formal properties such as Noun Phrase and Subject and informed by SFL understanding of meanings in text can be used to infer differences in SFL areas of text analysis such as method of development. Sample texts from the corpus clearly demonstrate the anticipated differences in method of development.

In Chapter 18, working with knowledge of a specific Spanish secondary school Content and Language Integrated Learning (CLIL) history lesson, Tom Morton and Anne McCabe also show the differences in meaning afforded by texts before and after they undergo corpus analysis. Morton and McCabe chart the journeys of a single student's interview, discussion and essay and reflect on the omissions and additions as new meanings are afforded through the processes of entextualization through recording, transcription and transduction, and recontextualization through corpus analysis using appraisal theory. When taken together with teacher ratings of the texts, this enables new meanings about the developing use of linguistic resources to be read into the texts.

Chapter 19 highlights the benefits and challenges of annotating a bilingual corpus, the Saarland GECCo corpus, which is a German-English multilevel annotated corpus of transcribed and written texts from a broad range of registers and text types, designed to investigate Contrasts in Cohesion from an SFL perspective. Following a review of previous research on ellipsis, Katrin Menzel clarifies her operational definitions of nominal, verbal and clausal ellipsis, then explains how she used the annotation tool MMAX2 to annotate cohesive ellipsis in the corpus. As an example, the frequency of cohesive ellipsis in translation is found to be generally lower in translations than in other texts in the same language, or in the language the texts have been translated from. As Menzel argues, corpus studies are indispensable for a comprehensive approach to features such as ellipsis. They allow us to analyse large amounts of naturally occurring language, which is particularly important in areas such as ellipsis where some subtypes that have been extensively described in the literature are relatively rare, do not occur in the GECCo corpus, and have been constructed for theoretical discussion and acceptability testing.

Where Chapters 18 and 19 have suggested how SFL-informed corpus linguistic analysis can be of value in language teaching and in translation, in Chapter 20 we turn to clinical linguistics and an examination of the linguistic characteristics of schizophrenia and mania. Ekaterina Shagalov and Jonathan Fine† explain the complexities in the search for automated methods of identifying these conditions. No one feature is key, and patients differ in symptoms, but, using computational methods, they propose combinations of features that distinguish the groups and characterize the disorders. Drawing on their previous research, they identify 46 variables under the four broad categories of dysfluency and cohesion; lexical variability and richness of description; amount of talk; and syntactic complexity. Using a linear regression analysis, they identify eight best predictor variables, and demonstrate their method of automatically classifying a new language sample as schizophrenia or mania. There are more repetitions in the language of schizophrenics and more false starts in the language of mania. Five of the best predictors relate to cohesion, and importantly are located across the four broad categories and different linguistic systems.

The chapters in Part III demonstrate the super powers of corpus linguistics when texts have digitality thrust upon them. Drawing on large 'general' corpora such as the British National Corpus, or smaller dedicated corpora such as the works of Shakespeare, State of the Union Addresses, or texts collected for specific projects, in specific classrooms or in clinical settings, the authors have all uncovered patterns in the texts that give us new understandings and answers to our research questions in ways that were not hitherto possible. While corpus building generally involves the decontextualization of texts, it is noteworthy that authors return to individual extracts in order to test their understandings of corpus findings. Future developments are beginning to suggest ways of working with multimodal and socially embedded texts on a large scale in ways that are currently hard to envisage.

The international authors of the chapters in this volume are using SFL in Australia, Austria, Canada, Chile, England, Finland, Germany, Greece, Israel, Italy, Spain and Sweden to analyse texts from an 'assemblage of varieties' across social, professional and academic research domains.

Part I, Texts that Are Born Digital, includes relatively new forms of communication, from blogs and wikis to YouTube and participatory online democracy. With its emphasis on how meanings are construed through participation in social contexts, SFL has illuminated the nature of semiotic entities in such Social Media contexts.

Part II, Texts that Achieve Digitality, provides an understanding of how the messages conveyed and the language associated with the working lives of professionals, such as university lecturers, newspaper journalists, members of the medical profession and sales personnel from the hospitality sector, are changing with the affordances and limitations of digital communication.

Part III, Texts that Have Digitality Thrust Upon Them, sheds light on how we as linguists can utilize what we might call the 'superpowers' of corpus analysis to see patterns in large bodies of text in ways that were previously not possible.

Corpus linguistics now appears regularly in research methods courses for applied linguistics, and although some areas of corpus linguistics are becoming increasingly computationally complex, it is also the case that with coding being taught in primary schools, and corpus tools increasingly freely available and easy to use, this is an area of research that has the potential to expand beyond recognition. SFL has a notoriously complex architecture, yet one which should lend itself well to computational modelling. Equally, SFL has an important role to play in maintaining the connections to the construal of meanings in 'real' texts in 'real' social contexts.

Throughout Parts I, II and III, authors have deployed Systemic Functional Linguistics and have beautifully extended our understanding. Yet in all three areas, the digital possibilities continue to expand. Building on a collection of 37 extended abstracts (Alsop and Gardner, 2014), this volume has scoped a tripartite research domain that is still sparsely populated; one where the ever-expanding possibilities can hardly be envisioned.

About the authors

Sheena Gardner is Professor of Applied Linguistics at Coventry University, Coventry, UK. Her teaching and research in Systemic Functional Educational Linguistics centre on young learner classroom discourse as well as Academic English genres and registers in the British Academic Written English Corpus of university student writing.

Siân Alsop teaches in the Centre for Academic Writing at Coventry University, Coventry, UK. Her research applies corpus linguistic and data visualization techniques to the analysis of academic discourse. She has published on the British Academic Written English Corpus of student writing and the Engineering Lecture Corpus of Engineering lectures.

References

Alsop, S. and Gardner, S. (eds) (2014) *Language In a Digital Age: Be Not Afraid of Digitality. Proceedings of the 24th European Systemic Functional Linguistics Conference and Workshop.* Coventry: Coventry University.

Kress, G. (2010) *Multimodality: A Social Semiotic Approach to Contemporary Communication.* London and New York: Routledge.

Halliday, M. A. K. and Matthiessen, C. M. I. M. (2014) *Halliday's Introduction to Functional Grammar.* 4th edn. London and New York: Routledge.

Hunston, S. (2014) 'Observing Texts Digitally: At the Interface of Grammar and Lexis'. In S. Alsop and S. Gardner (eds) *Language In a Digital Age: Be Not Afraid of Digitality. Proceedings of the 24th European Systemic Functional Linguistics Conference and Workshop,* 77–82. Coventry: Coventry University.

Hunston, S. (2015) 'Systemic Functional Linguistics, Corpus Linguistics and the Ideology of Science'. *Text & Talk* 33 (4–5): 617–640.

Matthiesson, C. M. I. M. (2014) 'Introduction'. In M. A. K. Halliday and C. M. I. M. Matthiessen, *Halliday's Introduction to Functional Grammar,* xiii–xviii. 4th edn. London and New York: Routledge.

Zappavigna, M. (2012) *Discourse of Twitter and Social Media: How We Use Language to Create Affiliation On the Web.* London: Continuum.

Zappavigna, M. (2014) 'Social Media, Ambient Affiliation, and Identity'. In S. Alsop and S. Gardner (eds) *Language In a Digital Age: Be Not Afraid of Digitality. Proceedings of the 24th European Systemic Functional Linguistics Conference and Workshop,* 146–149. Coventry: Coventry University.

Part I
Texts that Are Born Digital: New Digital Genres

1 'There's power in stories': A Multimodal Corpus-Based and Functional Analysis of Fandom Blogs

Maria Grazia Sindoni
University of Messina

> Fandom is less like being in love than like being in love with love (Michael Joseph-Gross)

> There's power in stories, though. That's all history is: the best tales. The ones that last. Might as well be mine (Varric Tethras, *Dragon Age II*)

1.1 Background Information on the Study

Blogs have been attracting scholarly interest for at least a decade, i.e. since their early beginnings (Blood, 2002; Herring *et al.*, 2004; 2005a; 2005b). As an exemplary specimen of texts that 'are born digital', they have been studied within the framework of a wide range of disciplines and from different standpoints, for example as digital artefacts that turn common users into *public intellectuals* (Park, 2003), *opinion leaders* (Delwiche, 2004), or *citizen journalists* (Gillmor, 2003; Lasica, 2002). Their role of substitute for corporate media journalism, especially in terms of their presumed ideological 'innocence' or 'neutrality', instantiated by a supposed distance from corporate interests and constraints, has been greeted as a welcome novelty in the contemporary mediascape. Ten years after their first appearance, blogs are being used both in the public and private sphere and professional blogging is today taken for granted in most media, as a huge number of blogs have now become fully incorporated in traditional and corporate media outlets. The great variability that blogs exhibit has not yet been fully explored, especially in terms of genre variation. This chapter attempts to redress this balance by undertaking a corpus-based analysis supported by a functional interpretation of lexical data in a subgenre that is still relatively unexplored:

fandom-related blogs. Fandom is a portmanteau term including *fan* and the suffix *-dom*, (as in *kingdom*) and it refers to all the social and discursive practices which fans are involved in, such as fanfiction, fansubbing, cosplay, and others.

The blog environment selected for this study is a web-based social networking platform, namely *LiveJournal* (LJ henceforth), where users can keep a blog, a diary or a journal. However, as LJ 'about us' webpage claims, the platform is 'wilfully blurring the lines between blogging and social networking' in the attempt to promote social interaction and creative self-expression. Hosting over 50 million blogs and journals to date, LJ has been selected to represent a facet of blogging in English, but not confined to the Anglo-American world. LJ is a Russian platform, which nonetheless epitomises the phenomenon of using *English as a Lingua Franca* in blog environments. Featuring such cultural and linguistic diversity, LJ lends itself to a functional analysis, exploring specifically diatypic variation through its lexicogrammar in a specific subcorpus working as a database to explore keywords (KWs) and key-keywords (KKWs henceforth).

In this chapter, Section 2 presents the theoretical background, explaining why this study can be of interest in the context of functional approaches to grammar; Section 3 outlines the rationale for the general corpus construction and annotation, giving preliminary statistics of the subcorpus used for the analysis; Section 4 discusses the corpus *aboutness* by providing a cursory exploration of the top 50 positive KWs obtained through a comparison to BNC, taken as reference corpus; Section 5 analyses in detail two examples of entries, discussing them in multimodal terms and explaining how the notion of resource-switching can be useful to analyse multimodal digital data. The last Section briefly draws some provisional conclusions.

1.2 Theoretical Framework

Systemic Functional Linguistics has traditionally used computational methods and corpus-based approaches to study texts (Teich, 2009; Wu, 2008). In SFL, the system exhibits infinite potential, but it produces a finite number of texts. It is thus possible to predict the quantity of texts that are involved in ontogenesis, i.e. how many instances a child needs to learn, in other words, 'how text becomes system where the dynamics is one of growth' (Halliday, 2005a [1991]: 45). The perspective of *growth*, intended as a means of construing a semiotic system through learning it, is complemented by the perspective of *change* in language. From the standpoint of the metastability in a semiotic system, the dynamic is thus one of evolution. According to

Halliday, 'frequency in text is the instantiation of probability in the system' (Halliday, 2005a [1991]: 45; Halliday, 2005c [1992]), as any linguistic system is probabilistic in nature. He also supported this idea by following Bernstein's principle of 'coding orientation', because if a linguistic system were not inherently probabilistic in nature, it could not display sociolinguistic effects as it does. In his view, register variation can be defined as a systematic variation in probabilities:

> *a register* is a tendency to select certain combinations of meanings with certain frequencies, and this can be formulated as the probabilities attached to grammatical systems, provided such systems are integrated into an overall system network in a paradigmatic interpretation of the grammar (Halliday, 2005b [1991]: 66).

Thus corpus studies can have important implications including for developmental, diatypic, systemic, historical and metatheoretic areas of study. Diatypic variation, i.e. variation in register, 'is the major resource for systematically construing variation in the environment (*the situation*)' (Halliday, 2005b [1991]: 73).

Analyses of register variation are particularly relevant if we consider that variation in a mono-generic corpus (i.e. including blog entries) can be explored by studying lexicogrammar of its instances (i.e. texts, or blog entries). This chapter ultimately considers language as a meaningful semiotic resource among others, such as images, music, videos and animated *gifs*.

Assuming that a lexicogrammatical approach can explain how language is used in blogging environments (i.e. LJ) to make meanings, this study reports on corpus construction and interrogation, using keyness analysis for the study of verbal data in terms of *aboutness* (Sindoni, 2013). However, a quantitative approach can provide some insights into the *aboutness* of the instances taken into consideration, but says nothing about the contribution of other resources to meaning-making events. Verbal language is in fact used in a complex semiotic environment that incorporates different resources. This study maintains that a computational analysis exclusively based on verbal data does not make justice of all that comes into play in such complex communicative events and that other semiotic resources are essential in interpreting diatypic variation. Language variation has been studied in a subcorpus extracted from a more general corpus, namely the *LiveJournal Corpus* (LJC), made up of c. 1 million words and including verbal data. The overall corpus has been explored more fully elsewhere (Sindoni, 2013), but in this chapter another subcorpus, LJF, has been created to focus exclusively on fandom-related contents. This further restriction in terms of content has been devised to explore diatypic variation. Variation has been mainly gauged with reference to a corpus of General English, namely the British National Corpus (BNC Consortium, 2001; Burnard, 2000).

Finally, another corpus section, namely the *LiveJournal Corpus with Semiotic Resources* (LJC_SR), which incorporates resources other than verbal language (visuals, videos, tags, gifs, etc.) has been used to study the integration and relative status of each resource in two relevant case studies.

1.3 Corpus Construction: Verbal Data

LJC was constructed taking into preliminary account representativeness, sampling units selection, and method of data collection, grounding the study in a problem-oriented approach to address only specific research questions.[1] After the construction, tagging and annotation of the corpus, an in-depth analysis of the two corpora subsections was undertaken, exploring: 1) variation in verbal data, and 2) variation in other semiotic resources.

With regard to verbal data, the present study investigates genre variation. To this end, some preliminary choices were necessary to define the domain of investigation which, as assumed, could produce significant results. In particular, it has been shown (Scott and Tribble, 2006: 73–88) that if a corpus is taken as a whole, keywords do not include many open-set items that are informative about the aboutness of the texts in each section of the corpus, but that the keywords distribution is similar to an average word frequency distribution. Conversely, when the corpus is segmented, following, for example, the criterion of genre, it is then possible, or very likely, that KKWs (i.e. keywords that share keyness, or that are 'co-keys') are informative of aboutness, and, to a lesser extent, of style (Scott and Tribble, 2006: 83). To this end, LJC has not been used as a whole, but five subcorpora, namely LJ1, LJ2, LJ3, LJ4 and LJ5,[2] have been selected. From these five subcorpora, only the entries loosely belonging to fanfiction and fandom have been included, further restricting the domain of analysis, assuming that by narrowing text genres scope, more revealing data could be produced. The result was the creation of one sub-subcorpus, called LJF, including *only* fan-related contents.

Fan-fiction is a typical blog-related genre emerging from the practice of manipulating already existing stories or characters by fans (it is also abbreviated as *fan-fic*). This web-based practice is currently spreading rapidly as some studies on the matter attest (cf. Coppa, 2006; Jenkins, 2007; Sindoni, 2013), involving non-traditional outlets for publication, as these works are commonly non-authorized by the original author. Figure 1.1 and Figure 1.2 show some extreme cases of contexts[3] where fans and fandom can be observed.

Figure 1.1: Fandom can be extreme

Figure 1.2: A fan's room

A preliminary analysis using basic heuristic tools from corpus linguistics has been used to extract some preliminary statistical data, with regard to LJF word count and other parameters used for understanding readability and overall complexity of the entries making up the corpus. They are shown in Table 1.1:

Table 1.1: LJF Basic Statistics

Total word count	45,948
Tokens	9,754
Complexity factor (lexical density)	21.2%
Readability (Gunning-Fog index: 6-easy 20-hard)	6.1
Average syllables for words	1.53
Average sentence length (words)	12.1
Max. sentence length (words)[4]	90
Min. sentence length (words)[5]	1

With regard to complexity factors, lexical density has been computed with a basic text analyser[6] and amounts to 21.2%, whereas readability has been computed using the Gunning-Fog index, where 6 stands for 'easy' and 20 for 'hard' to read. Both these indicators, along with other parameters shown in Table 1.1, show that fandom-related entries are easy to read and, generally, involve a simple use of language, for example favouring mono or disyllabic words, and short and concise sentences. However, further analyses are required to investigate in more detail the language used, especially in terms of lexical preferential choices.

1.4 Fandom-related Blogs' *Aboutness*

Variation of verbal data has been studied mainly via KKWs analysis, which allows insights into the most prominent and frequent linguistic features that are functionally related to the blog as a genre. Keyness is a measure of statistical unusuality, showing the most and less frequent keywords in a corpus with another, more general corpus, acting as a reference.

In previous studies on the language of blogs in English using LJC, it has been shown that the reference corpora size did not affect the results,[7] so the British National Corpus, World Edition (BNC henceforth) has been selected in this chapter as a reference corpus (RC) to explore genre variation. BNC is a 100 million word collection of spoken (c. 10%) and written texts (c. 90%) in English, and, as such, is useful for the study of written language in Standard English, especially in the context of published materials.[8] The keyword list has been generated by adjusting the pre-set limit of words to 500 and using a wordlist generated with WordSmith Tools 6 (Scott 2012) for BNC, acting as RC.[9]

Table 1.2 displays a positive keyness list for LJF with BCN acting as RC, displaying the top 50 content lexical items that have been identified. Items reported in Table 1.2 stop at the 190th occurrence. All that falls below the

190th position has been left out as it represents the threshold level for this study (more than one half of the minimum frequency list). First, it needs to be said that a high proportion of proper nouns were featured in the keyword list, as is easy to predict. Such nouns have not been incorporated in the keyness list, as they are not indicative of genre variation *tout court*. Table 1.2 is roughly indicative of diatypic variation in LJF with reference to a much larger corpus such as BNC, which furthermore includes most texts in Standard British English. As is apparent from the spelling of highly positive prominent lexical items, American English is far more represented, cf. items n. 1 (*favorite*), 29 (*coloring*), and 44 (*color*), to name but the most obvious. With regard to the *aboutness* of the entries, which represent fandom-related blog entries within LJ, a significant number of items pertaining to the virtual world is featured, for example in terms of specific social networking websites (e.g. n. 6 *facebook*, n. 20 *twitter*); general undetermined websites, platforms or web-based texts or genres (e.g. n. 10 *blog*, n. 16 *website*, n. 34 *tweet*, n. 39 *room* [i.e. *chatroom*]); specific media, web-based and digital practices and activities (e.g. n. 4 *spoilers*; n. 11 *fandom*; n. 12 *episode*; n. 23 *fiction*) or specific technical affordances typical of digital platforms (e.g. n. 36 *gifs*; n. 17 *caps* and its variant n. 41 *screencaps*).

Table 1.2: Positive Keyness of Lexical Items in LJF

N.	BNC as RC		
1	favorite	26	pretty
2	guys	27	secrets
3	boy	28	man
4	spoilers	29	coloring
5	lips	30	parenthood
6	facebook	31	smile
7	fan	32	threw
8	eyes	33	sighed
9	something	34	tweet
10	blog	35	asked
11	fandom	36	gifs
12	episode	37	characters
13	skyfall	38	kiss
14	photos	39	room
15	celebs	40	gay
16	website	41	screencaps
17	caps	42	grinned
18	said	43	started

19	like	44	color
20	twitter	45	smirked
21	head	46	sure
22	wanted	47	younger
23	awesome	48	icon
24	fiction	49	ass
25	tv	50	news

Additional concordancing search has been carried out to find out the main collocates and help clarify the context of occurrence. For example, *fiction* has been included in the category of specific media, web-based and digital practices and activities after a close inspection of L1 collocates, that turned out to be *fan-*. The complete node was thus *fan-fiction* in 38 occurrences out of 57. Another related lemma has also been incorporated in the same category, i.e. *fandom*. *Episode* is also related to fan-fiction in c. 1/3 of the occurrences in LJF.

With regard to the main processes represented in the positive keyness list generated with BNC acting as RC, we find: *said* (n. 18), *like* (n. 19), *wanted* (n. 22), *smile* (n. 31), *threw* (n. 32), *sighed* (n. 33), *asked* (n. 35), *grinned* (n. 42), *started* (n. 43), *smirked* (n. 45). However, a full concordancing of the items *like* and *smile* has been necessary to leave out all the occurrences of nouns (i.e. *smile*), adverbs, prepositions, and nouns (i.e. *like*). In the case of *like*, it has emerged that only c. 25% (25.4766%) of c. 600 occurrences are instances of verbs, whereas other occurrences must be included, respectively, in the categories of prepositions, adverbs and nouns (e.g. 'I put a like on that post'). With regard to *smile*, only one occurrence out of 80 has been identified as a verb, whereas all other occurrences are nouns. This means that both occurrences must be left out from a keyness analysis, because a more fine-grained analysis forces us to reconsider their position in the positive list, as they therefore fall below the filter threshold (i.e. 500). The remaining processes can be classified as follows:

Table 1.3: Main Processes in the Positive Keyness List

Verbal processes	**Mental processes**	**Material process**
said	wanted (desiderative)	threw
asked	sighed (emotive)	started
	grinned	(also transformative)
	smirked	
	threw (e.g. a murderous glare, a surprised look)	

A manual analysis of L1 and R1 collocates has shown that these verbs can be roughly classified in the terms sketched in Table 1.3, which nonetheless cannot be interpreted in absolute terms. However, the top 50 content words yield some interesting insights into the aboutness of blogEng, with specific reference to diatypic variation. Such findings are hardly surprising, and further concordancing analyses show that, for example, the two most prominent verbal process verbs, i.e. *said* and *asked*, are mostly introducing direct quotes instead of projections (c. 7.7031% and c. 8.1522%). The occurrence of clauses projected from verbal verbs is, quite interestingly, very low in both cases and also rather similar in terms of percentage. This seems to suggest that direct quotes are far more frequent in fanfiction entries compared to the corpus of General English, even though 'imaginative books' represent a significant amount of data (w-units c. 18%; s-units c. 27%) from the whole BNC (including bestsellers, prize winning books and the like). In other words, *said* and *asked* are more used to introduce direct speech of characters (*He said*: '...') than what is done in fiction in traditional outlets (*He said that...*) and this seems to confirm the amateur quality of fanfiction if compared to traditional fiction.

Analysing the first positive key grammatical forms, we find the items listed in Table 1.4.

Table 1.4: Positive Keyness of Grammatical Items in LJF

N.	BNC as RC		
1	his	15	just
2	he	16	like
3	him	17	himself
4	i	18	couldn't
5	you	19	out
6	did	20	what
7	does	21	so
8	me	22	why
9	her	23	maybe
10	my	24	aren't
11	wasn't	25	around
12	isn't		
13	let		
14	shouldn't		

The keywords that have been omitted fall below the threshold level of instances. Those which are reported in Table 1.4 are found up to the 190th occurrence. A full discussion of data resulting from Table 1.2, Table 1.3 and Table 1.4 goes beyond the scope of this chapter. However, a comparison with Table 1.2 allows a first generalization: prominent content words are more represented in LJF than grammatical words in a ratio of 2:1. Furthermore, observing the top 3 items in Table 1.4 (i.e. *his, he, him*), it is evident that a male world is more represented, also in comparison with other more traditional (and professional forms) of writing. This is completely consistent with previous findings (cf. Sindoni, 2013). Pronouns are highly prominent overall, and this could suggest an extreme use of characterization in fandom-related contents in blogs, also creating a distinctive male-oriented perspective. Furthermore, verbal deixis indicate a prominence of polarization, both in terms of use of Finite (mainly temporal) operators for questions (i.e. *did* and *does*, ranks 6 and 7, respectively), and in terms of negative Finite operators (both temporal and modal), such as *wasn't, isn't, shouldn't, couldn't, aren't*. Such data are revealing, because it could be preliminarily assumed that bloggers favour questions and polarization when constructing their narratives. However, further research on the matter is needed. In the next Section some considerations with regard to a multimodal analysis of entries will be presented.

1.5 Resource-switching: How Semiotic Resources are Used in Blogs

The notion of *resource-switching* has been invoked to explain the alternation of semiotic resources in blogs and other digital platforms. Participants have the possibility to deploy these resources, such as speech, writing, visuals, etc. in a number of ways and for different communicative purposes. The combination of these resources is still rather unmapped, despite the fact that the idea of a high integration of resources is very much widespread in both lay and academic discourse. To the end of exploring more systematically this phenomenon, I have devised the notion of *resource-switching* to deal with questions such as alternation, relative status and preferential use of all the semiotic resources involved in communicative exchanges and in the construction, distribution and consumption of meaning-making events (Sindoni, 2011; Sindoni, 2013). Research on the matter has shown that resources tend to aggregate more frequently with similar resources. In other words, *images tend to cluster with other images and words tend to coalesce with other words*, challenging the idea of the high integration of semiotic resources in web-based texts.

Some entries have been extracted from LJF to further illustrate this point. They are all taken from fandom-related blogs and have been randomly selected from a blog called 'Fandom!secrets', which publishes, on a weekly basis, entries from fan bloggers, who anonymously confess a 'secret' to the community. The blog is regulated by some rules, for example with regard to technical affordances (i.e. 'one secret per link') or field (i.e. 'all secrets must be fandom-related').

Figure 1.3 and Figure 1.4 show some interesting use of semiotic resources other than verbal that can be used for analysis.

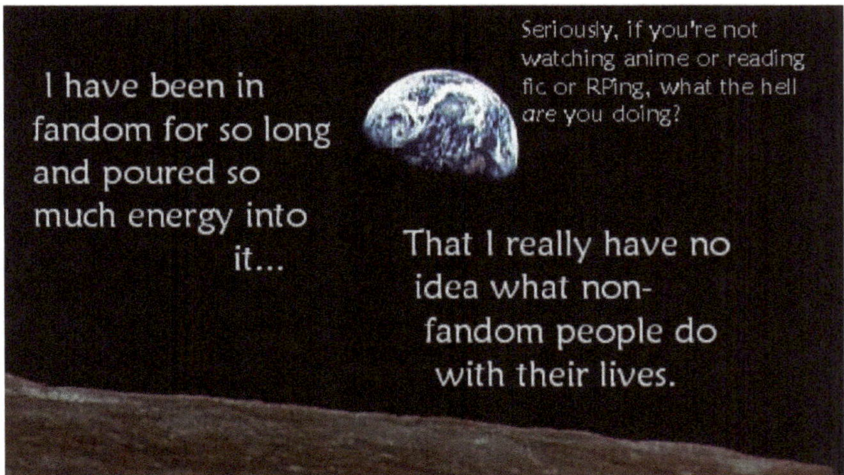

Figure 1.3: Fandom!secrets: sample entry 1

The first entry selected for analysis provides an introduction to the world of fandom, presenting interesting insights into the niche world of fans. However, it needs to be noted that such entries cannot be analysed through traditional computational methods as verbal language is *ingrained* within the visual unit that frames the 'secret'. From an experiential point of view, the image presents a naturalistic picture, where no vectors are emanated and no human participant can be detected: a conceptual process is featured instead, representing participants in terms of their class, structure or meaning, thus hinting at their generalized essence. According to Kress and van Leeuwen (2006), in a conceptual process, picture captions are often identifying clauses, with a reference to the picture as Token and the meaning of the picture as Value. However, this is not the case, as language is ingrained in the picture instead. A 'science-fiction' context can be imagined, and this hypothesis is confirmed when other entries by the same blogger are examined. From an interpersonal standpoint, modality also needs to be taken into account.

From the point of view of naturalism, reality is defined on the basis of how much correspondence there is between the visual representation of an object and what we normally see of that object with the naked eye (cf. Kress and van Leeuwen, 2001; Kress and van Leeuwen, 2006). Seen from this angle, the picture displays the highest modality. With regard to coding orientation, that has been mentioned in Section 1, the abstract coding orientation displayed in the picture represents general qualities (i.e. earth and another planet, seen from the perspective of the other planet (cf. Kress and van Leeuwen, 2001; Kress and van Leeuwen, 2006).

Finally, the compositional meaning requires careful reading, because the prevailing mode is of spatial composition with word juxtaposition, whereas the picture functions as a background. The structuring of Given and New is respected in this picture as the blogger decides to place the Given in the sentences positioned on the left and the New in the sentences positioned on the right part of the picture. Furthermore, the right part can be divided into two: the upper one gives meaning to the second, the bottom one: in other words, the ideational meaning is realized fully through a visual compositional path that the reader needs to follow to understand.

Figure 1.4: Fandoms!secrets: sample entry 2

In Figure 1.4, a specific fandom is hinted at, namely *Law and Order*. From a representational standpoint, the main characters are represented in a posed way. The image is clearly taken from the show's advertising campaign. Characters are represented as objects in a display case and are organized in terms of covert taxonomy, with the Superordinate represented by the woman in the foreground and the other participants playing the role of

Subordinates. However, they all belong to the same category: the characters of *Law and Order*. Additionally, in order to realize the stable and permanent nature of the classification, the participants are displayed in decontextualized ways, and the background is neutral.

Furthermore, an interesting semiotic modification has been realized by the blogger to operate a significant alteration of the meaning-making process realized by the picture (Sindoni, 2011): the 'secret' (that is the overall ideational meaning of the picture) is inserted in a black box containing the wording of the blogger's position (Kress, 2010). He judges the show as failing to meet her/his expectations, but he nonetheless keeps watching it. Again, the compositional meaning is instantiated visually in the ordering of the verbal language that is ingrained in the picture: the Given comes before the New. In addition to this traditional compositional feature, the blogger also operates another semiotic choice: s/he decides to erase the characters' faces by placing the black box on them (Kress and van Leeuwen, 2002). There are five different human participants in the picture and none of their faces are visible: apparently the blogger is trying to convey the low quality of the show's characterization via the ideational, interpersonal and compositional features of participants. With this strategy, s/he also reduces the modality that was originally bestowed on the characters, as it is easy to imagine that they were *all* intent on producing a *demand* image through direct viewing of the interactive participants.

1.6 Conclusion

This discussion has hinted at the potentialities that an integrated analysis could bestow upon any digital text/genre exploration. In the first part of this chapter, language has been analysed using computational tools with the aim of investigating how diatypic variation can be gauged in blogs of fandom-related topics. Some heuristic results have been presented to inform possible future lines of research. Furthermore, the question of integration of other semiotic resources that are difficult to gauge in computational terms has been addressed to show that there are cases in which the integration is so complex that a separate analysis would prove ineffective. This two-fold study has been designed to tackle the digital nature of blogs that involve many different semiotic resources that work together with written language, or spoken in the case of *vlogs*, to produce meanings.

About the author

Maria Grazia Sindoni is Assistant Professor in English Linguistics and Translation at the University of Messina, Italy. She has published in the field of Systemic Functional Linguistics, multimodality, corpus linguistics, and computer-mediated interaction. Her latest book is *Spoken and Written Discourse in Online Interactions: A Multimodal Approach* (Routledge, 2013).

Endnotes

1. Representativeness has been computed by lexical saturation, which means that the linguistic features chosen for analysis show little variation. To measure corpus variation, the corpus has been divided into several segments of equal size (i.e. LJ1, LJ2 ... LJ10), based on its tokens, and the corpus is saturated because each addition yielded approximately the same number of new lexical items. Sampling units are made up of blog entries and the overall LJ corpus includes c. 1 million words. A time-frozen analysis has been preferred in the attempt to capture a specific moment in time, namely April 2012. A further question that is seminal in any multimodal analysis is the issue of annotation, arguing the case for a problem-oriented approach, particularly flexible to address specific research questions, i.e. annotating only relevant phenomena.
2. The overall LJC has been segmented in 10 subcorpora including 150 entries each for a total of 1500 entries for a total of 160,316 running words (cf. Sindoni, 2013).
3. Source: *Arama they didn't*; Author: Colette Bennet, Date of publication: April 26, 2012, http://aramatheydidnt.livejournal.com/2012/04/26.
4. Sentence: 'There's nothing wrong with self-publishing and vanity publishing, but one of the reasons I haven't chosen that option for my own work (and one of the reasons I won't be submitting to this anthology, even though I initially thought I might) is that self-published books rarely have the level of quality that traditionally published books do with regards to editing and professionalism, and as soon as I got that vibe from the cover I wanted to know whether this publisher knows what it's doing.' Blog: *Asexuality*; Author: Swankivy; Date of publication: April 19, 2012.
5. Sentence: 'Hatred'. Blog: *Oh no, they didn't!*; Author: Anonymous; Date of publication: April 26, 2012, http://ohnotheydidnt.livejournal.com/2012/04/26/.
6. http://textalyser.net/index.php?lang=en#analysis
7. To check whether corpus size affected the results, five different wordlists have been used to create five different keyword lists with five different reference corpora, namely British National Corpus, FLOB, International Corpus of English – Great Britain component (ICE) and the latter two subcomponents, i.e. the spoken and written sections (cf. Sindoni, 2013), where specific research questions with regard to variation between speech and writing have been addressed.
8. The taxonomy of text written medium are: book, periodical, published miscellanea, unpublished miscellanea and to-be-spoken. The 'Miscellaneous

published' category includes brochures, leaflets, manuals, advertisements, whereas the 'Miscellaneous unpublished' category includes letters, memos, reports, minutes, and essays. The 'written-to-be-spoken' category includes scripted television material, play scripts, etc. See *Reference Guide for the British National Corpus (World Edition)* (Burnard 2000) and *The British National Corpus*, version 2 (BNC World) (BNC Consortium 2001).

9. Other standard default settings in WordSmith Tools 6 that have been adopted in this study are: min. keywords frequency: 3; max. p value: 0,000001; keywords procedure: log likelihood.

References

Blood, R. (2002) Introduction. In J. Rodzvilla (ed.), *We've Got Blog: How Weblogs are Changing our Culture* ix–xiii. Cambridge, MA: Perseus Publishing.

BNC Consortium. (2001) *The British National Corpus* Version 2 (BNC World). Distributed by Oxford University Computing Services. Available online at: <http://www.natcorp.ox.ac.uk/>.

Burnard, L. (2000) *The British National Corpus Users Reference Guide.* Available online at: <http://www.natcorp.ox.ac.uk/docs/userManual/>.

Coppa, F. (2006) A Brief History of Media Fandom. In K. Hellekson and K. Busse (eds), *Fan Fiction and Fan Communities in the Age of the Internet*, 41–59. Jefferson, NC: McFarland.

Delwiche, A. (2004) Agenda-Setting, Opinion Leadership, and the World of Web Logs. Paper Presented at the Annual Conference of the International Communication Association, May 2004, New Orleans, USA.

Gillmor, D. (2003) Moving Toward Participatory Journalism. *Nieman Reports,* 57 (3): 79–80.

Halliday, M. A. K. (2005a [1991]) Towards Probabilistic Interpretations. In *Computational and Quantitative Studies*, edited by J. Webster, 42–62. London and New York: Continuum.

Halliday, M. A. K. (2005b [1991]) Corpus Studies and Probabilistic Grammar. In *Computational and Quantitative Studies*, edited by J. Webster, 63–75. London and New York: Continuum.

Halliday, M. A. K. (2005c [1992]) Language as System and Language as Instance: The Corpus as a Theoretical Construct. In *Computational and Quantitative Studies*, edited by J. Webster, 76–92. London and New York: Continuum.

Herring, S. C., Kouper, I., Scheidt, L. A., and Wright, E. (2004) Women and Children Last: The Discursive Construction of Weblogs. In L. Gurak, S. Antonijevic, L. Johnson, C. Ratliff and J. Reyman (eds), *Into the Blogosphere: Rhetoric, Community, and Culture of Weblogs*.

Herring, S. C., Kouper, I., Paolillo, J. C., Scheidt, L. A., Tyworth, M., Welsch, P., Wright, E., and Yu, N. (2005a) Conversations in the Blogosphere: An Analysis 'from the Bottom Up'. *Proceedings of the Thirty-Eighth Hawai'i International Conference on System Sciences (HICSS-38)*, 107–19.

Herring, S. C., Scheidt, L. A., Bonus, S., and Wright, E. (2005b) Weblogs as a Bridging Genre. *Information Technology and People* 18(2): 142–71.

Jenkins, H. (2007) *Confessions of an Aca/Fan: Archives: Transmedia Storytelling 101.* Available online at: <http://henryjenkins.org/2007/03/transmedia_storytelling_101.html>.

Kress, G., and van Leeuwen, T. (2001) *Multimodal Discourse. The Modes and Media of Contemporary Communication.* London: Arnold.

Kress, G., and van Leeuwen, T. (2002) Colour as a Semiotic Mode: Notes for a Grammar of Colour. *Visual Communication* 1 (3): 343–69.

Kress, G., and van Leeuwen, T. (2006) *Reading Images: The Grammar of Visual Design.* 2nd edn. London: Routledge.

Kress, G. (2010) *Multimodality: A Social Semiotic Approach to Contemporary Communication.* London and New York: Routledge.

Lasica, J. D. (2002) Blogging as a Form of Journalism. *USC Annenberg Online Journalism Review.*

Park, D. (ed.) (2003) Bloggers and Warbloggers as Public Intellectuals: Charging the Authoritative Space of the Weblog. Paper Presented at Internet Research 4.0, Toronto, Canada.

Scott, M. (2012) *WordSmith Tools* Version 6.0 [Software]. Stroud: Lexical Analysis Software.

Scott, M., and Tribble, C. (2006) *Textual Patterns: Keywords and Corpus Analysis in Language Education.* Amsterdam and Philadelphia: John Benjamins.

Sindoni, M. G. (2011) *Systemic-Functional Grammar and Multimodal Studies. An Introduction with Text Analysis.* Como and Pavia: Ibis.

Sindoni, M. G. (2013) *Spoken and Written Discourse in Online Interactions: A Multimodal Approach.* London and New York: Routledge.

Teich, E. (2009) Linguistic Computing. In M. A. K. Halliday and J. J. Webster (eds), *Continuum Companion to Systemic Functional Linguistics,* 113–27. London and New York: Continuum.

Wu, C. (2008) Corpus-Based Research. In M. A. K. Halliday and J. J. Webster (eds), *Continuum Companion to Systemic Functional Linguistics,* 128–42. London and New York: Continuum.

2 Digitality and Persuasive Technologies: Towards an SFL Model of New Social Actions and Practices in Digital Settings

Sandra Petroni
University of Rome Tor Vergata

2.1 Introduction

Digital technologies are nowadays pervasive components of human social actions and practices and participate in meaning making processes. They give rise to artefacts, digital multimodal texts such as a webpage, a digital article, a Wiki page, a post uploaded on a blog or on a social network, a videochat, etc. These social media involve the simultaneous use of different devices thanks to the affordances (Gibson, 1977) of the new digital interactive and persuasive technologies.

Over the last decade, the digital domain has seen the upsurge of new representations which are strictly connected to the advent of Web 2.0. Differently from the old platform Web 1.0, where the sign maker, the content producer, was solely the conventional author, Web 2.0 has transformed the roles played by software developers and end users and the consequence has been the possibility of producing applications, and thus meaning and text, not individually but through an endless process of participatory and collaborative creation. Version 2.0 enables a form of content sharing that is totally different from, and more powerful than, the content created on the previous platform. Web 2.0 is hence the environment for the evolution of social media since this group of Internet based applications are grounded in the ideological and technological foundations of Web 2.0. They allow the production and exchange of User Generated Contents (UGCs), i.e. the several forms of media content that are free online and generated by users (e.g. collaborative projects like Wikipedia, blogs with the possibility to post personal comments, content communities like YouTube or Instagram, social networking sites like Facebook or Twitter, virtual game worlds, and virtual social worlds like Second Life). Interactivity in terms of collaboration, participation and sharing includes all these practices which entail appraisal, evaluation and persuasion.

This premise therefore gives rise to two research questions. Since interactivity technologies, typical of digital settings, affect and shape the way we negotiate mediated social actions and practices, (a) to what extent can these technologies be defined as 'persuasive'? And (b), if they are persuasive, how can they be investigated as 'evaluative meaning producers'? In order to answer these questions, it has been necessary to tackle these issues by making use firstly of two separate but complementary theoretical frameworks and secondly by combining the most significant persuasive technologies with the social practices they foster and with the appraisal resources taken from Martin and White's Appraisal System. This contribution thus benefits from the merging of Fogg's Behavioural Model (2009), focusing on the psychological and manipulating processes of technology, and Martin and White's Appraisal System (Martin and White, 2005). These two models will be presented in the paragraphs following that on digitality. Later on, a prototypical classification of the most relevant persuasive technologies in terms of appraisal resources will be proposed and commented on. This classification is in its early stage and hence does not include analyses of case studies of social media interactions representing the further development of this research. It is crucial, in fact, for the future to explore how the evaluative meaning produced by these technologies of persuasion cooperate in meaning making processes along with the other semiotic resources such as verbiage, pictures, sounds etc., which are deployed in posts, tweets, video, chat etc.

2.2 Further Insights on Digitality

What is then digitality and what does it imply in terms of meaning construction and textuality? Digital textuality lives and evolves thanks to its capability of 'remediation' (Bolter and Grusin, 1999; Bolter, 2001). It does not pertain only to digital contexts since the process of remediation is more complex because the affordances of digitality involve and manage a vast range of modes.

Traditionally, by remediation we mean a shift from an old medium, an old technology (e.g. writing), to a newer one (e.g. printing). Today 'remediation is a process of cultural competition between or among technologies' (Bolter, 2001: 23), but is not limited to technologies of writing. New media carry out their cultural significance precisely by refashioning earlier media: photography remediates painting, film remediates stage production and photography, and television remediates film, vaudeville, and radio. But a Website, a portal, a social network, for example, remediate television, radio, TV, news, journals, letters (email), and face-to-face conversation (chat) simultaneously. Furthermore, social media thanks to their networking potential augment the process of reshaping previously made texts by crossposting[1] them to different digital spaces (Adami, 2014). Multiple and interconnected settings stimulate remediation and, paradoxically, give rise to different forms of textuality by reusing an already existing text: users continuously generate and upload new texts, whether verbiage, picture, music or a multimodal ensemble, to be immediately shared again and remediated into new semiotic spaces and discourses. Via a click, they share the same text with another space. This process implies 'representation through recontextualization' (Adami, 2014: 224) where the previously made text can be forwarded, linked to other contexts or embedded into new co-texts (see also Lees Fryer this volume).

The simultaneous use of different media implies multimodality, that is to say how we encode and decode socially-situated meanings through the combination of diverse semiotic modes (Kress, 2003; Kress, 2010). The multiplicity of simultaneous modes on the Web requires a process of semiotic renegotiation since digital affordances amplify and merge the borders of each mode and its semiotic framework accordingly. A hypersemiotic approach (Petroni, 2011) is then the perspective analysts use to examine not only how many modes and resources meaning construction is based on but also why and how those resources have been deployed, and why the same meaning has been reified and materialized through different modes. Digital textuality thus goes beyond the dichotomous categories of written *vs* spoken modalities or genres (see also Sindoni and Cambria in this section), or verbal *vs* nonverbal: meaning construction in digital settings relies on new processes of production and consumption of texts where interactivity plays a pivotal and strategic role. The collaborative and participatory ideology flourished after the advent of Web 2.0 and fed by the exploitation of its affordances has further turned around the roles of producer and consumer, the conventional author and reader, and has created that of 'produser' (Bruns, 2007: 3).

These changes shape the way social actors (produsers) interact in digital settings and forge new forms of social actions and practices. Interactivity in terms of meaning potential establishes relational exchanges which inevitably entails evaluation. The user's involvement can be physical and emotional but these two facets work simultaneously and cannot be independent one from the other. When interactions occur in digital settings, interpersonal meanings are subject to manipulation deriving mainly from the affordances of the medium since they operate and are created to encage users in semiotic space, so that users are always connected. Clicking on links involves users physically, they physically have to click/tap on an icon, and affectively, they evaluate what they get by providing a feedback which moves along a gradient from appreciation to rejection. For this reason links, like many other 'apparently' technical devices, are always present and embedded in the meaning-making process on the Web and fulfil evaluative and persuasive functions.

Bruce and Hogan rightly underline that technologies should be considered as ideological tools which actualize social values. They argue that 'digital technologies can only be understood in relation to larger systems of practices. Most technologies become so embedded in daily experience that they disappear, that is, they are no longer seen as technologies. They become the ordinary [...]' (1998: 229) and hence hardly noticed.

As Kress and Pachler (2007) also claim, recent years have seen an augmentation in the social networking capability of web-based services based on online collaboration affordances, such as sharing services, constructing participatory contents (e.g. weblogs, Wikis), posting comments, and exchanging deliberative opinions, which facilitate the sharing of meaning by users. These digital actions become social and the manner in which these are performed, the actors participating in the actions, the resources needed to perform the actions constitute social practices (van Leeuwen, 2005).

For this reason, these technologies can affect people's attitude and engagement and lead them, or better, persuade them, to carry out digital social actions, such as posting, commenting on or sharing but also clicking on links, logging in, etc., which, additionally, imply evaluation.

2.3 Fogg 's Behavioural Model: the First Theoretical Framework

How, thus, are these persuasive technologies, along with the digital actions they endorse, created and used to encage users and to affect what people think and do? There is a branch of computing science called Persuasive Technology, or Captology, an odd acronym and neologism (Computers As Persuasive Technology) coined by its most authoritative scholar, B.J. Fogg at Stanford University, which has its foundations in experimental psychology, rhetoric and human-computer interaction. Persuasive technology is defined as any interactive product designed to change attitudes or behaviours by making desired outcomes easier to achieve (Fogg, 2003; 2009) and, hence, in the online world we meet persuasion attempts at every click. Potentially every digital artefact has a persuasive purpose and the creators intend to affect user attitudes or behaviours in some way: sign up for service, tell a friend about this video, enter your email address. All these actions occur thanks to a simple click.

Facebook is one of the most successful examples of persuasive technology. It has created a mechanism that motivates and persuades us to upload our photographs and divulge our personal information. We invite friends and accept their invitations. Many of us log in constantly as part of our daily actions. Mobile apps are also persuasive systems that keep engaging new people in staying connected any way and anywhere. Fogg, dealing with intentional persuasion, claims that when a designer is asked to design a new persuasive technology or app, s/he needs to select an appropriate target behaviour to be changed. But to do this, s/he has to think clearly about what leads to behaviour change. According to him, there are three elements that must converge at the same moment for a behaviour to occur: Motivation, Ability and Trigger (Figure 2.1).

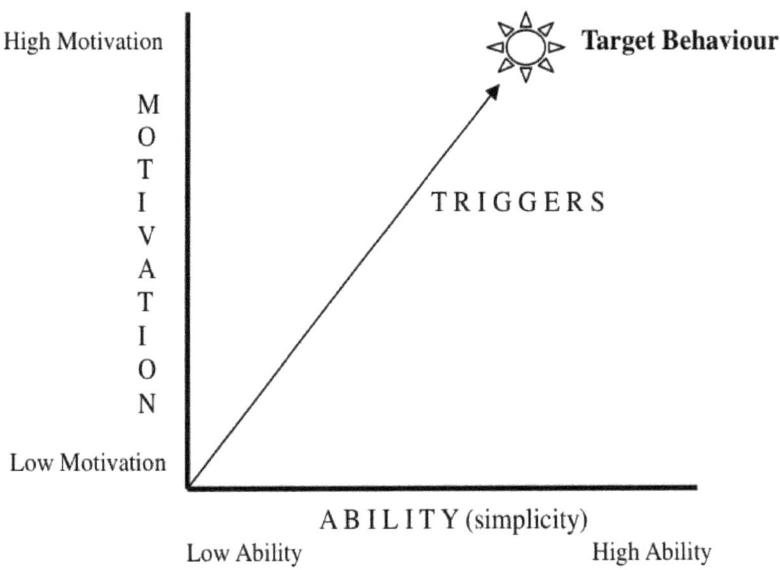

Figure 2.1: Fogg's Behavioural Model (2009, my adaptation)

A person must be sufficiently motivated to perform the target behaviour, s/he must be able to perform it, and hence this action must be simple but basically effectively triggered. Core motivators are pleasure *vs* pain, hope *vs* fear, social acceptance *vs* social rejection. They work at the Affect level and involve social attitudes since we are driven significantly, for instance, by our desire to be socially accepted, such as in Facebook communities. Simplicity factors are saving *vs* wasting time and money, preventing from *vs* providing with physical and cognitive efforts, conformity to *vs* deviance from social norms, routine *vs* non-routine actions. A trigger can be a facilitator (e.g. through 1-click action users can update a software easily) or a reminder that tells someone to 'do it now' (e.g. through a notification system or an alarm that sounds). Interactivity entails triggering and with greater reason when it is aimed at behaviour change.

According to Fogg, the ability of computing systems to be persuasive derives from how we use them. He distinguishes what he calls 'the functional triad' (Figure 2.2) of ways in which we interact with systems. Computing can be then a persuasive tool by: 1) making target behaviour easier; 2) leading people through a process; 3) performing calculations and measurements that motivate. Computing can be also a persuasive medium by: 1) allowing people to explore cause-and-effect relationships; 2) Providing people with experiences that motivate; 3) helping people rehearse a behaviour. Finally, computing can become a persuasive social actor with and through which we interact and form relationships by: 1) providing people with positive feedback; 2) modelling a target behaviour or attitude; 3) providing social support.

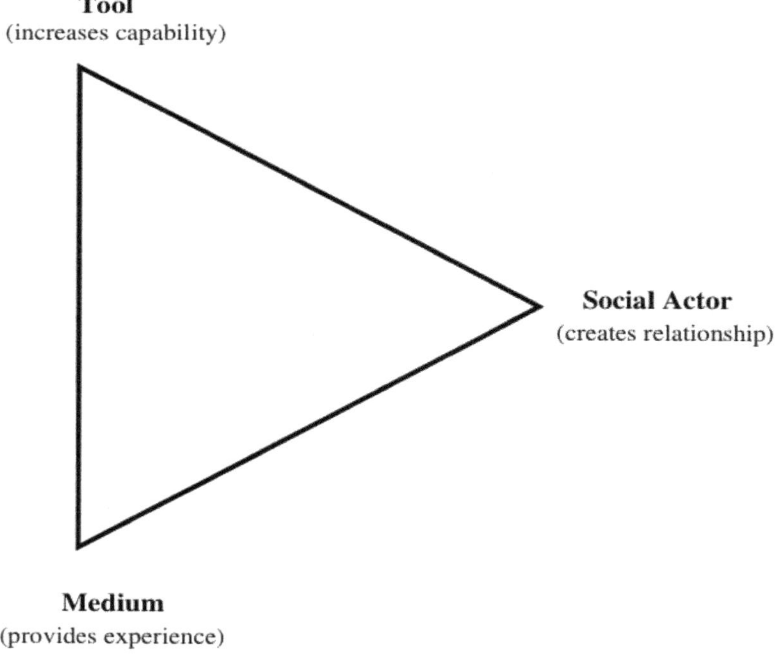

Figure 2.2: Fogg's Functional Triad (2009, my adaptation)

The concept of target behaviour is pivotal in this study since it includes the social practices and persuasive technologies used to reach the diverse targets. If, for example, we look at the socially recognized text pattern of social networks their implicit persuasive practices are clearly identifiable and can be described as in Table 2.1.

Table 2.1: A Synoptic View of Social Networks' Target Behaviours

Target Behaviour[2]	Social Practice	Persuasive Technology
Creating value and content	Creating personal profile page Presenting one's Self Preserving one's identity	Uploading tools (e.g. a post)
Involving others	Inviting friends Establishing relations Providing/asking for judgement	Notification system (e.g. 'Invite friends' button) Rating system (e.g. 'Like' button)
Creating value and content	Responding to others' contributions Constant participatory activity	Uploading/Downloading / Sharing tools
Staying active and loyal	Returning to the page frequently Maintaining relations	Poking (Facebook) Reminder Web Feed

2.4 Martin and White's Appraisal System: the Second Theoretical Framework

In 2005 Martin and White developed a system for the expression of evaluation, named Appraisal System, within the framework of Hallidayan Systemic Functional Linguistics (SFL). Before them, Hunston and Thompson used the term Evaluation and stated that:

> [...] there are three functions that evaluation is used to perform, and each of these make it an object of interest to the linguist. These functions are: 1) to express the speaker's or writer's opinion, and in doing so to reflect the value system of that person and community; 2) to construct and maintain relations between the speaker or writer and hearer or reader; 3) to organize discourse (Hunston and Thompson, 2003: 3).

Every act of evaluation manifests a communal value-system and goes towards building up the value-system that, in turn, is part of the ideology which resides behind every meaning making process. Maintaining relations implies manipulation (i.e. change of behaviours, attitudes, ideas and hence persuasion), hedging and politeness in general, typical strategies of rhetoric (e.g. power and solidarity principles, the two key tenor variables in interpersonal meaning). Evaluation creates relationships by sharing attitudes, values, and reactions and this is reflected in text and discourse organization.

According to Martin and White's Appraisal System, appraisal resources consist of attitude (for the expression of meanings of affect, judgement and appreciation), along with engagement and graduation resources aimed at 'adopting a position with respect to propositions and [at] scaling intensity or degree of investment respectively' (Martin and White, 2005: 39). Affect, judgement and appreciation are the three sub-categories of attitude which involve 'our feelings, including emotional reactions, judgements of behaviour and evaluation of things'. Engagement attends to 'sourcing attitudes and the plays of voices around opinions in discourse' and graduation deals with 'grading phenomena whereby feelings are amplified and categories blurred' (Martin and White, 2005: 35). Table 2.2 provides an overview of their appraisal system.

Table 2.2: Overview of the Appraisal System (my adaptation from Martin and White, 2005: 38)

APPRAISAL		
Engagement	Monogloss Heterogloss	Voices around opinions in discourse Relationships of alignment/ disalignment
Attitude	Affect Judgement Appreciation	Feelings, emotional relations Judgements of behaviour (Social esteem and social sanction) Evaluation of things (Reaction, Composition, Valuation)
Graduation	Force Focus	Raise Lower Sharpen Soften

Although tenor is the most relevant register variable since Appraisal works mostly on the interpersonal metafunction, there is 'no doubt that appraisal resources are sensitive to mode in a number of ways' (Martin and White, 2005: 28). Therefore, interaction makes use of a vast range of language resources for construing interpersonal meaning. In addition, the use of emoticons or prompts, such as the 'like' button or the rating box in digital texts, pushes users to display their attitude, to share their attitudinal positions without wording and to receive other's contributions. Building relations and solidarity is a necessary trait of interaction since 'when speakers/writers announce their own attitudinal positions they not only self-expressively "speak their own mind" but simultaneously invite others to endorse and to share with them the feelings, tastes or normative assessments they are announcing', as Martin and White underline (2005: 95).

Dealing with digitality entails multimodality and this means the inclusion of nonverbal meaning construction in the SFL arena. Santamaria Garcia (2014), after analysing a corpus of messages exchanged among university students and posted on Facebook, has found a massive presence of emoticons accompanying short utterances. One of these, for example, was: 'Oh, no :-(', and represented the reply to a post which had announced the destruction caused by Hurricane Irene. The sad face combined with the verbiage has been classified in her analysis as 'affect-dissatisfaction-displeasure' since it conveys an emotional reaction and mental disposition of sadness. Without the visual sign, the utterance 'Oh no' could be interpreted and classified as 'appreciation-reaction-negative impact', ignoring thus the emotional reaction. As Santamaria-Garcia has demonstrated,

> emoticons function by triggering a meaning subsumed under the core category of affect, recontextualizing meanings of judgements and appreciation as emotional reactions and giving this character even to utterances with no apparent expression of affect, such as "I'm here :-)", which adds happiness to a proposition (2014: 392).

But digitality and through it social media contents make use of a more complex multimodal ensemble than the simple combination of wording and emoticons. In addition, persuasive technologies affect how we prioritize the semiotic resources involved in meaning production. In many contexts, verbiage is backgrounded (Halliday, 1982; Martin, 2001) by the other multimodal resources codeployed in signmaking, or rather, it is remediated or reified by visuals or sounds that function as triggers. Persuasion and evaluation also reside in this process. For this reason it is necessary to explore the extent to which persuasive technologies are intertwined with meaning construction, in particular with evaluative meaning, and how they function as appraisal resources.

2.5 Persuasive Technologies as Appraisal Resources: A Systemic Functional Classification

Over the last decade there have been many speculations on the role played by conventional symbols (smiles, 'like' or 'poke' buttons on Facebook, etc.) in digital communication and, above all, on their contribution to the meaning-making process. However, they have been always considered as surrogates of and ancillary to face-to-face communication. Fogg's model for the first time looks at these technological devices as emotional triggers, motivating users' engagement through their expressions of appraisal. But how can they be investigated as evaluative meaning producers and how can they cope with the Systemic Functional Linguistics approach, considering that they are not properly linguistic?

The choice of the technologies under investigation and gathered in the first column of Table 2.3 reflects their relevance in users' daily social activities. The selection draws on those which can be considered as the most widely used such as 'like' and 'poke' buttons, two features belonging to the Facebook platform which trigger dialogic engagement of users within the heteroglossic framework of different voices; rating systems, common applications utilized to advocate evaluation by the majority of websites, applications, products sold on the Internet, etc.; notifications, reminders and RSS feeds, very short messages, or brief emails in the case of some notifications, sent automatically to a set of recipients that are members of the same group/community and aimed at informing the community about any activities carried out by a member, they are preceded by visual or sound signals which attract the attention of users and engage them in the discursive framework of alignment and rapport; uploading/downloading/sharing, three tools which allow users to be at the same time producers and consumers of contents (posts, comments, photos, videos, music etc.) and motivate interactions; clicking and logging in, two tools aimed at motivating users to be part of a community and to share the same behaviours.

The social practices and actions endorsed by these features are sketched out in the last column of Table 2.3. These two domains, persuasive technologies and social practices and actions, are classified in terms of Appraisal resources and the three interacting domains of the Appraisal Framework. Attitude, Engagement and Graduation occupy the central columns. At this stage of the analysis, only a basic articulation of these parameters has been utilized. Attitude – Affect, Judgement and Appreciation – has been evaluated simply as positive and/or negative without specifying the kind of feeling or emotion, engagement as alignment and/or disalignment, and graduation as high and/or low (see Table 2.3).

Thanks to this classification, it is possible to state that these technologies arouse mainly positive attitudes since they entail transformation of participants and processes, affective mental and behavioural processes decoded as positive (Affect). Through them, users also participate in the creation of a positive attitude to people and the way they behave (Judgement).

Table 2.3: Systemic Functional Classification of Persuasive Technologies

Persuasive technology	ATTITUDE	ENGAGEMENT	GRADUATION	Social actions and practices
'Like' button	Affect (positive) Judgement (positive) Appreciation (positive)	Alignment	High	Expressing positive opinions
'Poke' button[3]	Affect (positive/negative) Judgement (positive/negative) Appreciation (positive/negative)	Alignment/ disalignment	High/Low	Staying in contact Catching another's attention
Rating system	Affect (positive/negative) Judgement (positive/negative) Appreciation (positive/negative)	Alignment/ disalignment	High/Low	Expressing positive/ negative opinions
Notification system	Affect (positive) Judgement (positive) Appreciation (positive)	Alignment	High	Inviting friends Connecting users Being informed Recommending

Reminder	Affect (positive) Judgement (positive) Appreciation (positive)	Alignment	High	Repeating actions Catching another's attention
Web Feed (Rss Feed)	Appreciation[4] (positive)	Alignment	High	Desiring to be continuously updated
Uploading/downloading/ sharing tools	Affect (positive/negative) Judgement (positive/negative) Appreciation (positive/negative)	Alignment/ disalignment	High/Low	Posting Commenting Sending email
Clicking (1-click action) 1-click shopping 1-click address book uploader 1-click networking Join Us button, etc	Affect (positive) Judgement (positive) Appreciation (positive)	Alignment	High	Entering a social network Buying goods and services, Being part of a community
Logging in (Widgets)	Affect (positive) Judgement (positive) Appreciation (positive)	Alignment	High	Signing up to enter a community

Furthermore, they arouse in users positive reactions to things, they attract their attention, they are simple and immediate in composition, they allow users to evaluate (Appreciation). Basically, they work as motivational triggers. These technologies can be grouped under the heading of Engagement since they allow users to position their voice and hence to engage with the other voices interpreted as being in play in the communicative context in use. The technologies play the role in meaning-making processes where users negotiate relationships of alignment with the socially constituted communities of shared attitude and belief associated with those positions. When users deploy these technologies and hence unfold their own attitudinal positions, they 'not only self-expressively speak their own mind', as Martin and White claim, but simultaneously persuade others to sustain and to share feelings, actions, and assessments. Graduation, too, plays a dialogistic role in that it enables users to present themselves as more strongly aligned with the community.

Obviously, this classification is prototypical since it focuses only on the appraisal potential. Moreover, these technologies work along with the meaning potential present in the other deployed semiotic resources (verbal and/or nonverbal) and affect users' social positioning in context. For example, the 'like' button invites users to react to anything posted and works as an emotional trigger, enhancing representations of attitude and hence, when sent, it can be decoded as affect, judgement or appreciation, depending on the co-text and context of discourse. User X, for instance, can reply 'I like this' to a request to help someone or something which has been posted on Y's profile and in this case the appraisal resource can be taken as a positive judgement, evaluating the action of helping as good behaviour and contributing to building up the system of values for social sanction and social esteem in communities; but if User X replies the same to a photo just posted the action is evaluated as positive appreciation. Some technologies can be actualized iconically or verbally and acoustically but also through the combination of the three modalities. As for notifications, they are always created thanks to this multimodal ensemble, and the verbiage used for these features is worth analysing since it employs an extensive range of language resources for construing interpersonal meaning. These language resources, enmeshed within notifications, stimulate dialogue and facilitate engagement among members of the same community (e.g. 'User X invited you to Y's event').

All these speculations are necessary but are outside the scope of this contribution. However, they are undoubtedly areas of interest for further research.

2.6 Conclusion

It is possible now to answer the two research questions posed at the beginning of the chapter. It is evident that these technologies can be defined as persuasive since the application of Fogg's findings to social media has demonstrated why they act as motivational triggers and how thus they affect and shape digital social actions and practices. For this reason they *need* to be investigated as evaluative meaning producers and Martin and White's framework offers effective resources for classifying them.

The focus of this study has not been on what users, as produsers, post, comment on, share or where they click on or log in. These are instantiations of discursive practices based on linguistic resources and/or multimodal ensembles and can be broadly analysed through the Appraisal Framework in order to verify if, in comparison with face-to-face exchanges, digital settings modify their realization, as some scholars (boyd, 2010; Ellison and boyd, 2013; Page, 2012; Papacharissi, 2010; Santamaria Garcia, 2014; Sindoni, 2013; Zappavigna, 2011; 2012) have done over recent years and are still doing.

Instead, the attention here has been drawn to the effects, in terms of target behaviours and social practices, these technologies provoke in users and on their rhetorical salience. We can state that they are aimed at a further development of textuality and their designers should conceive of them as meaning potential simply because their users perceive them as meaning actuality. Therefore, to seek how the evaluative meaning embedded in these persuasive technologies endorses, reinforces, or softens the meaning produced by other semiotic resources such as verbiage, pictures, sounds, etc. will be the next step.

In 2001, talking about humour and irony, Martin argued: 'Evaluation has our theories of semiosis under pressure; add in humour and irony and the pressure becomes extreme. And that's what new frontiers of description are for' (Martin, 2001: 335). The description of persuasive technologies as potential semiotic resources for evaluation most certainly is one of these new frontiers since their impact on social positioning of users is extremely powerful. It is possible therefore to paraphrase Martin by saying that 'add in *technology and persuasion* and the pressure [on semiosis] becomes extreme *in the utmost*'.

About the author

Sandra Petroni is Senior Lecturer at the Department of Humanities of the University of Rome Tor Vergata, Italy, where she teaches on the Languages in the Information Society Degree Course. Her research fields are multimodality and specialized discourses, in particular Information and Communication Technology (ICT) discourse.

Endnotes

1. Crossposting is the ordinary social practice of posting the same content to multiple information channels such as email groups, forums, newsgroups or platforms such as Facebook, Google+, Twitter, Instagram etc.
2. These Target Behaviours are taken from Fogg and Eckles (2007).
3. The word poking derives from the verb 'to poke' which means 'to push', 'to thrust' but with a negative meaning. There are, in fact, some idioms where 'poke' reinforces the negative connotation like in 'to poke fun at' which means 'to ridicule'. Nonetheless, Facebook designers decided to borrow this term and to soften it semantically attributing the metaphorical meaning of 'to nudge' or 'to tap', metaphorical dimension that is clearly depicted by the conventional poke icon. Users poke their friends or friends of friends on Facebook just to say 'hello' or to grab their attention, to remind them of something or just for fun.
4. With the web feeds being used only for the sake of updating, Affect and Judgement have not been included.

References

Adami, E. (2014) Retwitting, Reposting, Repinning; Reshaping Identities Online: Towards a Social Semiotic Multimodal Analysis of Digital Remediation. *Lingue e Letterature d'Oriente e d'Occidente* 3: 223–243.

Bolter, J. D. (2001) *Writing Space.* Hillsdale, NJ: Lawrence Erlbaum Asssociates.

Bolter, J. D. and Grusin, R. (1999) *Remediation. Understanding New Media.* Cambridge, MA: MIT Press.

boyd, d. (2010) Social Network Sites as Networked Publics: Affordances, Dynamics, and Implications. In Z. Paparcharissi (ed.) *A Networked Self: Identity, Community, and Culture on Social Network Sites.* New York: Routledge.

Bruce, B. and Hogan, M. (1998) The Disappearance of Technology: Toward an Ecological Model of literacy. In D. Reinking, M. McKenna, L. Labbo, and R. Kieffer (eds) *Handbook of Literacy and Technology: Transformations in a PostTypographic World Vol. 1*, 296–311. London: Routledge.

Bruns, A. (2007) Beyond Difference: Reconfiguring Education for the User-Led Age. *ICE3: Ideas in Cyberspace Education: Digital Difference.* Symposium held 21-23 March at Ross Priory, Loch Lomond, Scotland. http://snurb.info/.

Ellison, N. and boyd, d. (2013) Sociality through Social Network Sites. In W. H. Dutton (ed.) *The Oxford Handbook of Internet Studies*, 151–172. Oxford: Oxford University Press.

Fogg, B. J. (2003) *Persuasive Technology.* San Francisco, CA: Morgan Kaufmann.

Fogg, B. J. (2009) A Behaviour Model for Persuasive Design. *Persuasive 2009. Pro-*

ceedings of the 4th International Conference on Persuasive Technology, Claremont CA, USA. http://bjfogg.com/fbm_files/page4_1.pdf.

Fogg, B. J. and Eckles, D. (2007) The Behaviour Chain for Online Participation: How Successful Web Services Structure Persuasion. In Y. de Kort, W. Ijsselsteijn, C. Midden, B. Eggen, and B. J. Fogg (eds) *Persuasive 2007. LNCS Vol. 4744*, 199–209. Heidelberg: Springer.

Gibson, J. J. (1977) The Theory of Affordances. In R. Shaw and J. Bransford (eds) *Perceiving, Acting, and Knowing: Toward an Ecological Psychology*, 67–82. Hillsdale, NJ: Lawrence Erlbaum Associates.

Halliday, M. A. K. (1982) The De-Automatization of the Grammar: From Priestly's an Inspector Calls. In J. M. Anderson (ed.), *Language Form and Linguistic Variation: Papers Dedicated to Angus McIntosh*, 129–159. Amsterdam: John Benjamins.

Hunston, S. and Thompson, G. (eds) (2003) *Evaluation in Text.* Oxford: Oxford University Press.

Kress, G. (2003) *Literacy in the New Media Age*. London: Routledge.

Kress, G. (2010) *Multimodality: A Social Semiotic Approach to Contemporary Communication*. London and New York: Routledge.

Kress, G. and Pachler, N. (2007) Thinking about the 'm' in M-Learning. In N. Pachler (ed.) *Mobile Learning. Towards a Research Agenda*, 7–32. London: The WLE Centre, Institute of Education.

Martin, J. R. (2001) Fair Trade: Negotiating Meaning in Multimodal Texts. In P. Coppock (ed.) *The Semiotics of Writing: Transdisciplinary Perspectives on Technology of Writing. Semiotics and Cognitive Studies*, 311–338. Turnhout, BEL: Brepols.

Martin, J. R. and White, P. R. R. (2005) *The Language of Evaluation: Appraisal in English*. New York: Palgrave Macmillan.

Page, R. E. (2012) The Linguistics of Self-Branding and Micro-Celebrity in Twitter: The Role of Hashtags. *Discourse & Communication* 6(2): 181–201.

Papacharissi, Z. (2010) *A Networked Self: Identity, Community, and Culture on Social Network Sites*. New York: Routledge.

Petroni, S. (2011) *Language in the Multimodal Web Domain*. Toronto: Legas Publishing and Rome: Aracne.

Santamaria Garcia, C. (2014) Evaluative Discourse and Politeness in University Students' Communication through Social Networking Sites. In G. Thompson, and L. Alba-Juez (eds) *Evaluation in Context*, 387–411. Amsterdam: John Benjamins.

Sindoni, M. G. (2013) *Spoken and Written Discourse in Online Interactions: A Multimodal Approach*. London and New York: Routledge.

van Leeuwen, T. (2005) *Introducing Social Semiotics*. London and New York: Routledge.

Zappavigna, M. (2011) Ambient Affiliation: A Linguistic Perspective on Twitter. *New Media & Society* 13(5): 788–806.

Zappavigna, M. (2012) *Discourse of Twitter and Social Media: How We Use Language to Create Affiliation on the Web*. London: Continuum.

3 Digital Citizenship: Social Actors in Blog Posts to Chilean Online News Portals

Lésmer Montecino and María Cristina Arancibia
Pontificia Universidad Católica de Chile

3.1 Introduction

In the last ten years, there has been a growing debate over the role that public digital media have had in social change, particularly in the creation of a public digital sphere where issues affecting local political organizations and the functioning of institutions are openly debated by citizens. The aim of this chapter is to explain from a critical discourse perspective the construction of the identity of social actors, their inclusion or exclusion in the blog comments posted by digital citizens over cases of corruption dealt with in editorials and opinion columns of Chilean online news portals.

The digital era of new media – Facebook, YouTube, online news portals' blogging, among others – is reconfiguring the political communication ecology of political elites. Communication networks in politics have been traditionally founded in the principle of political power (Wolfsfeld, 2011) which renders political elites open access to media coverage and places politicians in a superior position to get their messages across.

At present, nonetheless, the immediateness of information transmission plus its ubiquitousness provides online ordinary anonymous citizens with the possibility of being informed and contesting a variety of issues exposed in different platforms. This fact has allowed for the opening of a new arena for deliberation that contributes the construction of an e-democracy (Wright, 2012) with its own new agenda for online debate. The latter implies that digital citizens intuitively sense that representative democracy, understood in light of the principle of political power, has become obsolete.

The constant accessibility to social digital networks and the relative anonymity that social networks render to their users changed democratic participation from apathy to a growing concern over issues that affect citizens in similar ways everywhere in the globe.

Online news portals' blogging thus became an effective catalyst for raising awareness of social, political, historical and economic factors that perpetuate poverty at a local and global scale. Among one of the numerous reasons that may explain the influence that social networks are having on the political life of nations, *globalization* is considered the most influential factor. Gaventa and Tandon (2010) remark that globalization has caused the concept of authority to move beyond the traditional perspective of power limited to a nation state government. Nowadays, citizens are shifting their interest from the influence of local governments to the influence of a more globalizing force that is being built up upon worldwide conscious recognition of global human rights and universal values, both concretely expressed in collective action. During 2011, world citizens would be witness to massive parallel movements of activists in different regions of the globe. The *March of Indignant* congregated citizens from around 81 countries who took to the streets to demand changes in government policies to deal with social, economic and political conflicts that were affecting nation citizens around the world.

Global collective action in the form of marches and massive protests may be said to be the result of increasing local dissatisfaction among citizens of countries who see the rise of a global era of *soft power* (Gaventa and Tandon, 2010; Wolfsfeld, 2011; Wright, 2012) characterized by feeble accountability of political institutions and their authorities. Nowadays, the traditional equation democracy equals voting (Carpentier and Cammaerts, 2006; Mayol, 2012) fails to satisfy the critical condition that entails the practice of active citizenship. As Fairclough (2010: 397) claims: 'It is only through action that people develop the judgment, the capacity to see things not from "one's own point of view but in the perspective of all those who happen to be present", which converts mere opinions into public discourses'.

The construction of public discourses as Fairclough points out, suggests ongoing negotiations of meanings in public sphere events. In this context, online news portals' blogging constitutes an instance of digital deliberation where individuals gather in a virtual public square or café to debate/read or hear about issues of public concern. It is in the critical exploration of blog comments posted in response to editorials and opinion columns of online news portals, that we attempt to explain the identities of social actors, their inclusion or exclusion construed and negotiated by bloggers.

Our analysis will concretely focus on a corpus of blog comments retrieved from two news portals: EMOL and EL MOSTRADOR during the first half of 2013. The corpus selected shows the reaction of citizens to the impeachment of a government official, the Chilean Minister of Education at the time, for misuse and abuse of power.

3.2 Social Struggle in Chile: Education as a Consumption Good

This study mirrors the current living standards that Chile is experiencing from the perspective of everyday citizens who feel puzzled at economic figures that show the country is enjoying economic success while social policy cannot tackle the long-lasting crisis that affects hospitals, schools and universities, housing and social security, among others. For decades, progress has been based on a liberal economic model instituted by Pinochet's dictatorship. In September 1973, a military coup forced the democratically elected government of Salvador Allende out of power. During Pinochet's autocracy, the country suffered profound institutional reforms with market-oriented policies. Neoliberal practices in economy created new income flows in favour of capitalist owners, who saw in education, health and social security a fruitful business. Education, in particular, was the focus of ambitious entrepreneurs who deliberately breached the law that defines educational organizations as nonprofit institutions. Since the mid 1980s, private universities with minimum infrastructure and doubtful credited staff have been responsible for the preparation of future professionals in different skills areas, most of them former students from public schools, who had not been accepted to traditional universities via standard test. Failure to be admitted to traditional universities via standard examination is solid proof of the existence of a highly segregated schooling system that sells quality to the highest bidder (Guzmán *et al.*, 2014; Montecino, 2011). Consequently, a decentralized education system that provides municipalities with the power to manage schools triggered a divide in the quality of schooling between wealthier municipalities and poorer ones. The latter has brought about a class divide that nowadays creates anger and bitterness among Chileans.

Following Pinochet's defeat in the 1988 plebiscite, The Coalition of Parties for Democracy, a center-left party, successively stayed in office for 22 years. In 2010, however, the right wing won the elections headed by Sebastian Piñera. It was the first time in 50 years that a right wing candidate had won a democratic election in Chile. Piñera represented the opportunity for change after the country had fallen in a period of deep disenchantment with successive offices that had passively witnessed how grass root individuals struggled with an economic model that privileged market freedom to ensure sustained growth creating a profound social class gap.

In 2011, a social movement led by secondary and tertiary education students demanded the government end profit and take under its control an agonistic education system. In March 2013, Piñera's Education Minister, Harald Beyer, was accused of failing to investigate the complaints over the misuse of funds at several private universities. The news about the impeachment of the Minister of Education motivated the publication of editorials and opinion columns in online news portals. Blog comments to discuss the legitimacy of the accusations against the Education Minister constitute the object of study of this chapter.

3.3 Representation of Social Actors in Electronic Discourse: News Portals Blogging

Barton and Lee (2013) point out the fact that the world is increasingly textually mediated; written language is fundamental in vernacular activities that constitute everyday life. Progressively, new technologies provide writing spaces where meaning is negotiated. Virtual spaces that afford public debate instantiate stance rich environments where opinions are constantly negotiated and renegotiated collaboratively by a networked audience.

New media has introduced a new approach to traditional views towards oral and written modes of language, hybrid genres such as chatting, whatsapping, twittering, and news portals blogging combine the characteristics of writing with features of the oral mode of language in a phenomenon widely known as the conversationalization of discourse (Arancibia and Montecino, 2013; Fairclough, 2010; Herring *et al.*, 2005). Additionally, conventional concepts such as *author* and *reader* have also gone through substantial evolution as virtual spaces such as Wikipedia have provided users with open access to edit, post or update information of the site. Similarly, online news portals have afforded debate platforms through online blogs, a public space where the opinions of ordinary online citizens become public discourses that not only influence and constrain *political action* but also resist it.

> The blogs of online news portals are a particular instance of textual mediation; they are according to Fairclough (2010) *apparatuses of verbal interactions* that comprise the orders of discourse that result from the interactions between different discursive types. The study of online news portals blog comments involves dealing with the institution of entertainment, which is ultimately determined by the social formation of a society, in other words, the relationship between the institution, the state and the economic system. The media as an institution is considered a speech community composed of a repertoire of speech events. Blog comments to editorials and opinion columns constitute a specific type of speech event in which the struggle between the orders of discourse is clearly distinguishable in the patterns of inclusion and exclusion of social actors.

The exclusion of social actors in discourse, according to van Leeuwen (2008), is characterized by the systematic omissions and distortions in the representation of social actors. This total or partial omission of participants is realized through suppression and backgrounding (van Leeuwen, 2008). The former implies the absence of reference to social actors anywhere in the text. The following example illustrates that the control of education rests on a system that seeks inequality to maintain a state of things:

> We all want better education for our children, but in this society machiavellianly organized it exist three types of citizens: privileged education for those who can afford to pay for it, technical schools for the middle class and public schools for the working class. [Todos queremos mejor educación para nuestros hijos, pero en la sociedad maquiavélicamente organizada, existen 3 tipos de ciudadanos. Educación privilegiada para el que pueda pagarla, técnico- profesional para clase media y pública para la mayoría trabajadora]
>
> EMOL 03/27/2013

The use of nominalization in the former example indicates that the blogger takes an external stance to describe the current state of Chilean education. The exclusion of the agent of the action and the construction of education as an object confirms the existence of a rigid system of education that safeguards the strict segmentation of the population according to what the hegemonic discourse defines as individual capacity and personal effort (entrepreneurship). In backgrounding, on the other hand, the excluded social actor may appear later in the sentence, clause or text. Bortoluzzi (2010) argues that the function of backgrounding is to defocus the role of the participant in discourse to emphasize or de-emphasize its relevance. The following example presents an irritated blogger who blames the left wing for the conflicts that affect Chilean education:

> Neither education nor anything else has ever mattered to them or will ever matter to them in the future. A proof of that is that many leaders of the left are committed to private education. [La educación ni ninguna otra cosa les ha importado, ni les importa ahora y menos les importara en el futuro. Prueba de ello es que muchos de los jerarcas de la izquierda son parte comprometida en la educación privada]
>
> EMOL 04/05/2013

The previous example identifies the social actor (*many leaders of the left*) in the second clause; this can be interpreted as the will of the blogger to emphasize the identity and political participation of the social actor.

Patterns of inclusion, on the other hand, mainly involve role allocation, that is to say semantic roles assigned to participants according to the social responsibility that rests on their actions or inactions, these roles may be, namely referred to as agent, patient, and beneficiary, among others. Role allocation follows the logic of the sematic dichotomy between activation and passivation. In activation, social actors are represented as dynamic forces, the following example displays a value judgement over the moral behaviour of the Chilean Minister of Education: *The minister Beyer made a very serious mistake, he ignored evidence that accused private universities of for-profit activities* (EL MOSTRADOR, 03/21/2013).

Passivation, on the other hand, shows participants as recipients of actions (Halliday and Matthiessen, 2014). In this example, the blogger remarks that the accusation against the minister of Education is founded on Beyer's abandonment of his duties: *Beyer was alerted about the existence of profit in big universities (e.g. Saint Thomas), but he ignored the report* (EL MOSTRADOR, 03/21/2013).

In November 2014, the previous blog postings are cited in a book titled: *The Great Deception that Accuses Private Educational Institutions of Fraud against Students, their Families and the Chilean Society.*

The patterns of inclusion and exclusion of social actors in online Chilean news portals' blog comments unveil the current state of a social conflict. A conflict that begins when ordinary Chilean citizens take a public stand against the moral crisis that threatens a democratic system built on the basis of a neoliberal economic model. The voices of many groups construct a portrait of public disapproval of political corruption. Public contempt is, therefore, made visible in the semantic relations that underlie the presence of people and things connected to sequences of activities in light of what Martin and Rose (2007) label as ideation and identification, a set of resources that allow for the construction of a picture of reality as a text unfolds.

3.4 Data and Methods

As stated previously, the objective of this study is to explain the construction of the identity of social actors and the discursive patterns of their inclusion and exclusion in online news portals' blog comments to editorials and opinion columns of two online news portals. The blog discussions will be examined under the lens of the SFL theoretical-methodological framework.

The corpus used in this study consists of 160 blog comments to editorials and columns selected from the digital portals EL MOSTRADOR and EMOL that debate over the approval of the formal charges against the Chilean Minister of Education by the lower chamber of the Congress between the months of March and June of 2013. The presence of social actors in blog discussions is analysed in light of the sociosemantic perspective adopted by van Leeuwen (2008), Halliday and Matthiessen (2014) and the theoretical-methodological framework postulated by Martin and Rose (2007). The blog discussions were explored under the lens of the identification and ideation resources (Martin and Rose, 2007) present in the discourse of bloggers.

The representation of the social actors, their inclusion and exclusion in discourse is observed in this study in the construction of the ideational meaning that lies behind the grammar of the clause. Ideational meaning is realized grammatically through a configuration of core elements, namely, participants, processes (verbs) and circumstances. The analysis we propose aims to identify *taxonomic relations* realized by means of repetitions, synonymy and contrasts, among other resources and *nuclear relations* the connection established between people and things (noun phrases) with processes (verb phrases), circumstances (adverbial phrases) and qualities (adjectives and adverbs).

Both linguistic resources – *taxonomic relations* and *nuclear relations* – contribute to the construction of a picture of experience by members of a culture. In our study, the linguistic resources identified configure a portrait of reality that visualizes the social actors' terrain contestation and cultural resistance through the standpoint of Chilean grassroots *nettizens or e-citizens* (Castells and Cardoso, 2005; Yus, 2010) who debate over *ethical issues* (Arancibia and Montecino, 2013; Arancibia and Montecino, 2014; Montecino, 2011).

3.5 Identification, Inclusion and Exclusion of Social Actors in Online Blog Discussions

A global analysis of the corpus composed of 160 blog comments shows the presence of five participants introduced by the bloggers in their online discussions. The first and most frequently named is *Beyer*, the Chilean Minister of Education, considered as a fair recipient of the constitutional accusation. However, most bloggers also agree on placing at the same level of questionable accountability the Education Ministers of all the democratic governments elected in the last 20 years besides politicians of the right-center and left wings. A noteworthy fact is that politicians are construed as parasites and criminals in the totality of blog comments analysed as shown in the following example. This fact indicates that beyond the political affiliation of bloggers, corruption receives a high level of disapproval among citizens who feel their trust is being betrayed. The following posting illustrates the presence of moral judgement signalled by the lexical item *bloodsucker* to condemn the dishonesty of political leaders of all ideologies:

> WE WILL THRUST A STAKE with the greatest strength and without emotion into all these bloodsuckers from the Alliance (right wing) and the Coalition (center-left wing). [CLAVAREMOS UNA ESTACA con la máxima energía destructiva y sin emoción alguna a todos estos chupasangre de la Alianza y la Concertación]
>
> EMOL 03/27/2013

Another important participant identified in blog comments in a symbolic sense is *profit*, considered illegal under the law that regulates Chilean education. This means that any surplus universities obtain must be devoted to continue the operation of the institution. In Chile, however, loopholes in the law make its enforcement difficult. This situation has caused most private universities to continue functioning without supervision from authorities despite clear evidence that proves owners of some private entities are involved in financial activities that clearly violate the law (Guzmán *et al.*, 2014).

Profit in light of the transitive model postulated by Halliday and Mattthiessen (2014) is represented in the discourse of blog comments as token – the operative voice in the clause in which the subject is also the actor that is actively involved in a large set of activities denoted by the concept. In the following comment, profit is identified as a goal and therefore there are a number of activities associated to generating surplus implied by the use of this concept: 'Profit has been the ultimate goal of tertiary education entities' (EL MOSTRADOR, 03/21/2013). Profit is also the carrier of a quality in the following attributive clause, for instance: 'Profit is an abuse, almost a crime derived from earnings' (EL MOSTRADOR, 03/21/2013).

Finally, another two crucial social actors identified in blog comments are *the student movement* and *the ordinary Chilean citizens*. These participants are construed as long-time victims of *institutionalised theft* during the last 20 years of democracy. However, the passivity of the above social actors has undergone an evolution towards a more visible agentivity. The evolution of marches has nowadays become a sign of a construction of the future that implies real reforms not only to the education system, but also to other systems, namely: housing, health and labour, among others. The following example summarizes a widely shared view of the student and social movement as bearers of moral authority to end corruption:

> It depends on the Student and Social Movement whether this (the accusation of Beyer) is the beginning of the end of an immoral system in service of those in power. [Depende de los estudiantes y el movimiento social si esta acusación es el comienzo del fin del sistema inmoral al servicio de aquellos en el poder]
>
> EL MOSTRADOR 04/10/2014

3.5.1 It is Fine that Beyer has been Accused

A closer examination of the representation of the Chilean reality that bloggers construct through blog comments to editorials and opinion columns shows that these texts debate over the impeachment of the Chilean Minister of Education. Such opinions portray the anger and frustration of bloggers against the flagrant corruption that is affecting institutions in Chile. This country seems to have achieved an advantageous economic position in comparison to other countries in the region. However, internally Chile is a witness to the failure of a neoliberal model, the worst enemy of the Chilean middle and lower classes.

Blog comments construe impeachment as consisting of abstract entities such as *evidence* and *accusation.* These abstractions imply a large list of subordinate activities that are coherent with the social and political turmoil that Chile was undergoing at the beginning of 2013. Blog 1 illustrates the standpoint assumed by an overwhelming majority of bloggers in the corpus of 349 blog comments analysed.

> It is fine that Beyer has been accused. He just reacted when evidence proved he had not done anything against other universities that deserved thorough investigation. But, then, the accusation must be extended to the vile Minister Vitar, Mariana Elwin (misspelled on purpose), Lagos, Arrate and all those who were Ministers of Education from the dictatorship on and were accomplices in the armed robbery that implies to study in this country. [Bien que Beyer sea acusado. Reaccionó cuando la evidencia mostraba que no había hecho nada contra otras universidades que merecían ser investigadas. Pero la acusación debe luego ser extendida al Ministro Vitar, Mariana Elwin (mal escrito a propósito) Lagos, Arrate y todos aquellos que fueron Ministros de Educación desde la dictadura en adelante y que fueron cómplices en el robo armado que implica estudiar en este país]
>
> EMOL 03/10/2013

The text begins by asserting the blogger's support for the accusation against the Minister of Education. The passivation of the constitutional action against the Minister portrays Beyer as the recipient of a large set of activities that warrant impeachment such as public debate, disapproval and some others (Martin and Rose, 2007). It is interesting to notice that *evidence* is an active participant in emphasizing the passive role that the Minister assumed in regard to profit. His reaction is a consequence of the irrefutable proof that a huge number of universities were generating profit illegally. Besides, the presence of the concessive connector *but* at the beginning of the second clause indicates the blogger counters the readers' expectations created in the first part of the discussion. The variation in tenor produced by the introduction of the modal operator *must*, denotes strengthening of the obligation of including all previous public officials who had also acted unlawfully by being indifferent to an extended malpractice, protected by ambiguous laws. It is fundamental to emphasize that the lack of access to education in Chile is construed as *an armed robbery*. This critical view shows a collective portrait of the ordinary Chilean citizens as victims of these reckless criminals of the state, whose deeds are sheltered by ambiguous legislation.

Table 3.1: Ideation and Identification in the Construction of the Constitutional Action against the Chilean Minister of Education in Blog 1

It	**is** fine
Beyer	**has been accused**
He just	**Reacted**
Evidence	**proved** he had not done anything against other universities that deserved thorough investigation
The accusation	**must be** extended to Vitar, Mariana Elwin, Lagos, Arrate
All those who	**were** Ministers of Education from the dictatorship on
	were accomplices in the armed robbery
That (the armed robbery)	**implies** to study in this country
Ambiguous laws	

3.5.2 How can we not Pretend to have Profit in Education if our System is made for it?

Another issue widely debated in blogs is profit in universities, a practice forbidden by law, but pursued by private universities due to loopholes and poor supervision from the authorities. For example, Blog 2 construes profit through taxonomic relations that show that institutional fields such as the state of Chile and its economic system are pictured as a paradise for tax evasion.

> How can we not pretend to have profit in education if our system is made for it? Chile, our country, is a tax haven for corporations, for big businesses, is a haven made-to-measure for neoliberals who not only profit from education but also from health, from housing, from mass media, from natural resources, but the worst of all, the most shameful thing is that they profit from our dreams, hopes and needs. They profit from our lives. [¿Cómo pretender que no haya lucro en la educación si nuestro sistema educativo está hecho para ello? Chile, nuestro país, es un gran paraíso fiscal para el empresariado, para los grandes, es un paraíso hecho a medida de los neoliberales que así lucran no solo con la educación sino también con la salud, con el acceso a la vivienda, con el retail y con las comunicaciones; pero lo peor, lo más vergonzoso de todo, es que lucran con nuestros sueños, con nuestras esperanzas y necesidades. Lucran con nuestras vidas]
>
> EL MOSTRADOR 04/10/2014

Blog comment 2, selected from the online news portal, EL MOSTRADOR, opens with a rhetorical question, the purpose of which is to assert that profit is the result of a system that allows it to exist. The Chilean tax haven attracts the interests of *abstract entities,* namely corporations and big businesses, as well as *anonymous actors* such as neoliberals.

Chile is construed as a thematic equative in a relational identifying clause. That is to say, the country assumes the role of subject of a clause but at the same time takes up the role of an operative actor in becoming a *tax haven*. It is interesting to notice that the concept *tax haven* denotes a large set of activities related to the generation of profit. Table 3.2 presents neoliberals arising as dynamic actors involved in a single material process, in other words, *make profit*.

An analysis of nuclear relations shows that central to the process of *generating money* from a business activity, there is a long list of circumstances of means, which, according to Martin and Rose (2007) is an alternative way of involving people and things in the events. People's dreams and hopes as well as the basic rights – education and health – are construed as only having an instrumental value in the hands of neoliberals. In other words, people and their rights only bear importance in the social system, as long as they are helpful to obtain returns and profit. Altogether, Chileans are portrayed as having been robbed of their dignity and basic rights by the unrestrained ambition of a few. This is clearly observed in the peripheral role of circumstance that people's rights, dreams and hopes occupy in the message.

Table 3.2: Ideation and Identification in the Construction of Profit in a Neoliberal Society in Blog 2

We	cannot pretend that **profit** does not exist
Our system	is made for it (**profit**)
Chile, our country	is a **tax haven** for corporations for the big businesses
Neoliberals	**is a haven** made to measure for **neoliberals**
They	**not only profit** from education **but also** from health, from housing, from mass media, from natural resources
They	**profit** from our dreams, hopes and needs **profit** from our lives

3.5.3 Education must be Left in the Hands of Private Entities and Regulated by the Market

Besides constituting a means to express opinions, blog comments to editorials and opinion columns become a virtual political arena where not only individual identities are interpreted, negotiated and constructed but also the identity of the citizens of the country whose voice bloggers represent. The first outburst of student-led protests across the country began in 2006. The president, then, Michelle Bachelet promised to implement reforms to improve public education, but these reforms did not tackle the core of the problem – the high level of inequality imposed by a neoliberal system that sees education as a commodity. In 2011, the second part of the social movement was started by school and university students, and in its development, the student protests added the support of parents, teachers, workers and professionals among others. This time, the government of Sebastian Piñera acted violently repressing people's demonstration. Repression at the hands of the police and a cumulative list of corruption cases caused people to demand social recognition of their status as citizens in online news portals' blogs. Blog 3 shows how the blogger construes Chilean reality as divided into the supporters of the system – government officials and all those who believe in neoliberalism – and the great majority of citizens who oppose the marketization of all aspects of social and individual life. The blogger discursively represents the conflict as paradoxical. In this context, it is clear that a government chosen by a majority of voters must pay attention to people's mandates. Nevertheless, Piñera and his Ministers seem to be indifferent to the demands of citizens and also to the promises he made when he was running for office.

> We have arrived at a paradoxical situation in which an official is about to be removed from his position. As a citizen and expert in education, the Minister has believed and still believes that education must be left in the hands of private entities and regulated by the market. Current events show, however, that citizens, since 2011, have been expressing disagreement with the system that the Minister defends. [Hemos llegado a una situación paradójica en la cual un miembro del gobierno está a punto de ser sacado de su puesto. Como ciudadano y experto en educación, el Ministro ha creído y todavía cree que la educación debe dejarse en las manos de entidades privadas y reguladas por el Mercado. Los eventos diarios muestran, sin embargo, que los ciudadanos desde 2011, han estado expresando desacuerdo con el sistema que el Ministro defiende]
>
> EMOL 04/04/2014

A closer observation of the participants and processes involved in this comment shows that the blogger sees the accusation against the Minister as the result of a substantial antagonism between the ideology of the government and the ideology of citizens. The latter is manifested in the presence of mental processes (As a citizen and expert in education, the minister *has always believed and still believes*) that project a material consequence (education *must be left in the hands of private entities*).

Table 3.3: Ideation and Identification in the Construction of the Chilean Social and Political Reality in Blog Comment 3

we	have arrived at a **paradoxical situation**
[by The congress]	An official is about to be removed from his position
as a citizen and expert in education, the minister	has always **believed and still believes** [that education must be left in the **hands of private entities**]
private entities = Market	must regulate market
citizens	have been expressing disagreement with the system (Market)

The response of citizens, as shown in Table 3.3, is discursively realized by the behavioural process, *expressing disagreement*, which suggests a broad spectrum of activities associated with expressing discrepancy, such as protesting, marching, blogging, among others: *Current events show, however, that citizens, since 2011, have been expressing disagreement with the system.* Finally, it is interesting to observe – in the same example – how the abstraction *the system*, named in most blogs in our analysis is identified, in this blog, with the market. A market that assumes the characteristics of a person to whom Piñera's supporters feel they can trust education in its hands.

3.5.4 They Do Not Understand What Citizens Want

The last example, we will analyse is provided by blog comment 4 taken from EMOL. The blog illustrates a perspective shared in 349 blog comments. The reality is construed as a polarity between two viewpoints towards the state and the economic relations that underlie the social organization of the country. At one pole of reality, there stands the government realized by the pronoun *they* involved in a mental process that synthesizes the government's attitude to people's demands during the four years of Piñera's office, simply not understanding what people want. At the other pole, there stand the citizens who are construed as being involved in a collective struggle to claim rights despite the violent response of the government to massive demonstrations that have taken place since 2011.

> They did not understand what citizens wanted, as for example: more honesty, less corruption, more morality in their actions, professional ethics, less nepotism and above all, the serious accomplishment of promises concerning social development. This is the main cause of the current misgovernment. The situation has worsened because this government believes that repressive measures will restrain free thought, but it is impossible, history has proved it is impossible. [Ellos no comprenden lo que los ciudadanos querían, como por ejemplo: más honestidad, menos corrupción, mas moral en sus acciones, ética profesional, menos nepotismo y por sobre todo, el cumplimiento serio de las promesas relacionadas con asuntos sociales. Esta es la causa principal del mal gobierno. La situación ha empeorado porque el gobierno cree que las medidas represivas reprimen el pensamiento, pero es imposible, la historia lo ha probado así]
>
> EMOL 06/15/2013

Table 3.4 shows that failure in understanding people's hopes by Piñera government officials implies a *cognitive blindness* of these social actors to apprehend the pre-existent projections of the voters who supported his election. The desiderative nature of the following proposal: *citizens wanted more honesty, less corruption, more morality in their actions, professional ethics, less nepotism* expresses a strong inclination from citizens to seek tangible achievement of the presidential vows. It is interesting to observe the presence of the nominalization: *the serious accomplishment of promises concerning social order,* to express the one fundamental goal people expected to be materialized during Piñera's government. Nominalized processes refer to an underlying sequence of activities, that in the context of the blog comment is related to economic and social changes people trusted Piñera would implement due to his close relation to the influential world of business.

Table 3.4: Ideation and Identification in the Construction of the Political and Social Reality in Blog Comment 4

They	did not understand what
Citizens	wanted: more honesty, less corruption, more morality... Serious accomplishment of promises
This	is the main cause of the current misgovernment
The situation	has worsened
This government	believes that
Repressive measures	will restrain free thought
It	is impossible

3.6 Conclusions

This chapter has briefly explored the construction of the current political and social reality of Chile through the conflict that has affected Chilean education for over 40 years. Nowadays, thanks to the access everyday citizens have to online news portals, the digital arena has seen the birth of new patterns of democratic participation of citizens in online debates about local and global news.

The analysis of blog comments provides a nuanced account of the vertical relationship that exists between the state and citizens in Chile. This verticality perceived by a majority of bloggers construes citizenship as a *formal right* that is characterized by limited empowerment. Citizenship, interpreted as a formal right, suggests that the freedom and progress the Chilean neoliberal system guarantees to citizens is just expressed in a law written on paper. Purposeful ambiguities and omissions in laws on citizens' rights end up making their implementation and enforcement impossible. Consequently, the public's dissatisfaction with Piñera's government, as shown in blog comments, is discursively associated with a tension regarding the construal of government officials through mental processes. These portray these authorities *not understanding* citizens or *believing* that repressive measures are efficient strategies to tackle the critical situation the country was undergoing with the student strike. As Halliday and Matthiessen (2014) argue, mental processes make visible *the content of consciousness* of the senser. In the particular case of Piñera's Ministers, they all fail to project people's true mandates in their feats; instead, they obtusely focus on a conservative agenda that abandons promises made during the pre-election period.

In this context, the impeachment of the Minister of Education triggers in bloggers the deepest feelings of disappointment with politicians of all parties, and their ethical behaviour. As a matter of fact, comments portray members of the right and left wings as *parasites, bloodsuckers* and *thieves,* whose only ambition is turning every dimension of social security into a profitable business. These money driven impulses are impeccably sheltered by loopholes in laws that seek to maintain the economic model as it is. Undoubtedly, for over 40 years politicians of both parties had consciously or unconsciously contributed to the late Pinochet's intention to depoliticize society by discrediting political action. Politics is then considered a synonym of corruption, a goal carefully pursued to ensure that citizens would opt for an individualistic standpoint. This option, however, is challenged by the student movement that emerges to raise collective awareness about the crisis of a model that seeks to perpetuate social differences through an unfair educational system.

Education is discursively identified, in the comments analysed, as an armed robbery. A fragmented system largely protected by an economic system that has turned Chile into a tax haven. In other words, as we have previously stated, people and their rights bear importance as long as they mean returns and profit to entrepreneurs and capitalists. Therefore, cognitive blindness of successive offices to understand anger and dissatisfaction among Chileans is commonly condemned. Finally comments show the hope of bloggers for more honesty, less corruption, less nepotism and a more ethical attitude.

By the beginning of 2015, the student and citizen's movements had evolved from being passive witnesses to vigilant empowered citizens that observe the accomplishment of promises regarding the structural reforms that the system needs in order to provide Chilean citizens with a worthy lifestyle. Their conclusion sadly indicates that the brutal commodification of Chile's schooling system has been the cause of increasing segregation and inequality.

About the authors

Lésmer Montecino works in the Pontificia Universidad Católica de Chile, Santiago, Chile. His areas of research are pragmatics and discourse analysis. He has recently concluded a three-year research project funded by the Chilean Government. Professor Montecino is currently working on interrelational management and symbolic violence on Chilean radio programmes mediated by YouTube.

María

María Christina Arancibia works in the Pontificia Universidad Católica de Chile, Santiago, Chile. Her research areas are discourse analysis and the development of comprehension and production skills in second language.

She is currently working on an investigation about the representation of anger in websites created to condemn corruption in Chile.

References

Arancibia, M. C. and Montecino, L. (2013) El Blog De Comentarios a Textos De Opinion En Ciberperiódicos: Un Género En Constante Reconstrucción. *Lingüística Y Literatura,* 28: 121–140.

Arancibia, M. C. and Montecino, L. (2014) Recursos De Ideación E Identificación Para Representar La Corrupción Y La Crisis Ética En Comentarios De Blogs De Ciberperiódicos. *Onomázein,* Número especial IX ALSFAL: 214–229.

Barton, D. and Lee, C. (2013) *Language Online: Investigating Digital Texts and Practices.* New York: Routledge.

Bortoluzzi, V. (2010) The Agreed Decision Genre and the Recontextualization of Social Actors. *Linguagem Em (Dis)Curso,* 10(3): 511–533.

Carpentier, N. and Cammaerts, B. (2006) Hegemony, Democracy, Agonism and Journalism. An Interview with Chantal Mouffe. *Journalism Studies* 7(6): 964–975.

Castells, M. and Cardoso, G. (eds) (2005) *The Network Society: From Knowledge to Policy.* Washington, DC: Johns Hopkins Center for Transatlantic Relations.

Fairclough, N. (2010) Critical Discourse Analysis: The Critical Study of Language. Harlow: Pearson.

Gaventa, J. and Tandon, R. (2010) Globalizing Citizens: New Dynamics of Inclusion and Exclusion. London: Zed Books.

Guzmán, J., González, M., Figueroa, J. P., and Riquelme, G. (2014) *La Gran Estafa: Cómo Opera El Lucro En La Educación Superior.* Santiago: Catalonia.

Halliday, M. A. K. and Matthiessen, C. M. I. M. (2014) *Halliday's Introduction to Functional Grammar.* 4th edn. London and New York: Routledge.

Herring, S. C., Scheidt, L. A., Bonus, S., and Wright, E. (2005) Weblogs as a Bridging Genre. *Information Technology and People* 18(2): 142–171.

Martin, J. R. and Rose, D. (2007) *Working with Discourse: Meaning Beyond the Clause.* 2nd edn. London: Continuum.

Mayol, A. (2012) *El Derrumbe Del Modelo.* Santiago, Chile: LOM.

Montecino, L. (2011) Por Qué Marchan Los Estudiantes En Chile?: Discurso Electrónico Y Poder En Un Ciberperiódico Chileno. *Cadernos De Linguagem E Sociedade,* 12(2): 179–209.

van Leeuwen, T. (2008) Discourse and Practice: New Tools for Critical Discourse Analysis. New York: Oxford University Press.

Wolfsfeld, G. (2011) Making Sense of Media and Politics: Five Principles in Political Communication. New York: Routledge.

Wright, S. (2012) Politics as Usual? Revolution, Normalization and New Agenda for Online Deliberation. *New Media & Society* 14(2): 244–261.

Yus, F. (2010) Ciberpragmática 2.0: Nuevos Usos Del Lenguaje En Internet. Barcelona: Ariel.

4 Imagined Community and Affective Alignment in Memorial Tributes to Steve Jobs on YouTube

Anu Harju
Aalto University

4.1 Introduction

Technology allows the like-minded to communicate and meet in digital spaces, where we increasingly share our lives. However, our obsession with social sharing is not limited to digitally extending our lives as we record and share the everyday: digital memorials also captivate our imagination. Contemporary memorial culture is undergoing change (e.g. Lagerkvist, 2013; Walter, 2014), as new mourning practices illustrate. This is but one of the ways in which the private sphere is increasingly permeating the public sphere, mediated by, for example, social networking sites. Grief and mourning that used to be matters of the private sphere are today negotiated in public (e.g. Gibson, 2007; Walter, 2014).

There has been a growing interest in death and contemporary memorial culture (e.g. Doss, 2002; 2008; Klaassens *et al.*, 2013; Sumiala, 2013) with research on online memorial culture covering a wide range of topics from collective remembrance around tragic events such as 9/11 (Jarvis, 2011), collective remembering in the context of disenfranchized grief (Harju, 2014), parent bereavement groups on social media (Hård Af Segerstad and Kasperowski, 2015) and emotion regulation in online bereavement groups (Döveling, 2015). Klaassens *et al.* have examined temporary memorials offline and observe that the 'diversity in material forms suggests a desire for personalized places of remembrance' (2013: 155): the same applies online, where memorial tributes come in many shapes and forms.

Despite increasing research into online communities in the context of bereavement and their established importance in grief work, there is limited research on the *affiliation processes* in digital spaces, more specifically, *the linguistic mechanisms used in constructing online belonging*. It is, after all, affiliation and a sense of belonging that underlies many of the beneficial and restorative effects of social media practices of mourning.

Using the Appraisal theory (Martin and Rose, 2003; Martin and White, 2005) and drawing on the concept of 'imagined community' (Anderson, 2006), this chapter looks at the *interpersonal affiliation of anonymous participation* on YouTube in the context of celebrity death. Looking at fans' acts of remembrance on YouTube after the death of Steve Jobs in 2011, the study examines the linguistic strategies used to construct a sense of belonging. Linguistically, this translates into attitudinal alignment: alignment is understood as a form of interpersonal affiliation. Appraisal resources are generally utilized in order to invite the reader to engage in an 'attitudinal rapport' (Martin, 2004: 323).

The material is collected from YouTube, where digital commemorative artefacts, in this study the Steve Jobs video tributes, invite viewers to share in the experience and create the context. The short, anonymous user comments as acts of remembrance are analysed to see how, using appraisal resources, the community members align with each other, but also with 'the Other', as the performance of remembering unfolds and differing ideological viewpoints emerge.

The chapter is structured as follows: after a brief overview of literature and the Systemic Functional Linguistics framework and Appraisal theory, the materials and methods are described. Next, the analysis is presented of the ideational and interpersonal meanings as well as the appraisal strategies, followed by discussion of findings. The chapter concludes with a discussion and short conclusion.

4.2 Background

4.2.1 Imagined Communities Online

The term 'imagined community' was initially used by Anderson (1983/2006) to refer to nations, and it has since been used in various research fields to encapsulate communities of various kinds (e.g. Rokka and Moisander, 2009). According to Anderson, all nations (and by analogy, communities) are by nature imagined, as it is not possible for the members of a nation to all meet. Furthermore, communities are imagined as limited, in that they differ from and are separable from other nations and communities. As this chapter adopts the view that online communities are socially and discursively constructed, we can view anonymous, temporary online communities as imagined communities where a shared sense of belonging is discursively constructed in the evolving interaction. Also, communities are imagined as limited, as the community boundaries are at the same time contested and negotiated.

We all belong to multiple online communities, and while different social media platforms facilitate multiple identities (van Dijck, 2013) and performances in different ways, we all ultimately 'perform our online identities in order to connect with others' (Zappavigna, 2012: 38). In terms of participation and connecting with others, digital spaces and social media are not only enabling, but also constraining. One such constraint, according to boyd and Heer (2006), is the lack of known (and potential) audience. Marwick and boyd (2010) suggest the term 'imagined audience' to refer to potential and actual audience of digital artefacts. In linguistic terms, we may call it a 'putative audience', one written into the digital performance.

Another constraint boyd and Heer (2006) mention is the lack of readily detectable social context. To account for the lack of the physical and the related social cues, participants write themselves into the text and 'artifacts of digital performance become digital bodies' (boyd and Heer, 2006: 4). In digital spaces, these artefacts of performance provide the context and function to maintain and negotiate social relationships, build social networks, and express identities. In an anonymous online context, such as YouTube, the digital performances are initially the only source of contextual cues. Therefore, it may be useful to conceptualize the nature of an online community as *imagined*.

4.2.2 Constructing Grief on Social Media

In online commemoration the sense of belonging arises from a shared sense of loss and a joint performance of remembrance. While there are social grieving rules (e.g. Walter, 2014), online commemoration is not restricted to the loss of loved ones but has become a permanent feature of the contemporary celebrity culture, too. Walter (2014: 4) notes how '[c]ontemporary public mourning often elicits bemusement or criticism from the many who have internalised the norm that grief should be private and only for those to whom one is personally attached'. However, with the prevalence of celebrity culture in our times, public mourning over celebrity death is only ever increasing. Online shrines may be the only accessible places for celebrity commemoration. They rely for their meaning on ritual behaviour in practices of mourning. Social media shrines evoke what Pantti and Sumiala (2009: 127) categorize as 'civic rituals': they differ from religious rituals in that 'they are established by spontaneous individual action rather that through transcripts of rituals of established institutions', for example, the church.

On the social media channel YouTube, the digital artefact comes to define the emotional and ideological landscape of the space it creates and contextualizes. The video tribute pre-sets the community function as one of active remembering, memorialization, and shared affect (e.g. Harju, 2014). The social function of sharing in remembrance is the facilitation of positive emotions, and 'the online environment engenders communicative topic development that does not solely relate to death, dying, and grief' (Döveling, 2015: 12). Nonetheless, due to the nature of social media platforms, they commonly also allow for disparate voices: the difference in online and offline norms and practise of mourning can be a cause of conflict, and thus 'social media commemorations can resemble a conflict-ridden cemetery' (Walter, 2014: 11). The conflict revolving around social-media mediated celebrity shrines is often due to divergent ideologies relative to the meaning of the deceased.

4.2.3 Affective Alignment Online

Designed for participation, social media constitute a distinctive form of computer-mediated communication: according to Page (2012: 30), social media are 'collaborative, dialogic, emergent, personalized, and context rich environments'. Furthermore, as an environment, social media encourages the sharing of affect as much as it depends on it (e.g. Karppi, 2015; van Dijck, 2009). All these affordances together render social media sites opportune for commemoration and remembrance. Death and dying are among human experiences that elicit a wide range of emotions, the expression of which is governed by societal and cultural norms and practices (e.g. Walter, 2014). Moreover, the immediate environment impinges on the practices of mourning: social media, besides encouraging affective engagement with the digital memorial, offers visiting that is free from temporal and physical restrictions. Together, the affective tendencies and ease of (re)visitation facilitate ritual behaviour.

Mourning rituals have the capacity of bringing people together (Pantti and Sumiala, 2009; Walter, 2014), and as the main function of social media discourse is 'the enactment of relationships online' (Zappavigna, 2012: 192), it is easy to understand the growing popularity of social media as a site of ritualistic mourning. The community, or communality, that has its origin and orientation in commemoration differs from the 'usual' YouTube 'communities', which, according to van Dijck (2009: 45), are 'groups with a communal preference in music, movies or books' who are 'building taste together' (and form a 'taste community'): the users, as participants in the commemorative act, engage in a reconstruction of a lived life and in a reiterative process of co-construction of shared memory. In addition, the relevance of the participatory act in the fans' life outside YouTube cannot be understated.

Next, we will take a look at the theoretical framework used in this study to explore the affective alignment online.

4.2.4 Theoretical Framework – Appraisal and Alignment

The approach adopted in this article is that communities everywhere are socially and discursively constructed. Systemic Functional Linguistics (SFL) offers tools to systematically analyse which linguistic processes are employed to align (or disalign) with others, to establish communal sentiment and a sense of belonging. SFL sees language as realizing meaning potential through the system of language: language is seen as realizing meaning in three ways simultaneously, that is, ideationally, interpersonally, and textually. This study focuses on the ideational (how experience and social reality are presented) and interpersonal (enactment of social relationships, the stance toward content and audience) levels of meaning and the coupling of these: ideational content is appraised and evaluated in the enactment of interpersonal relationships. That is, attitude is interpersonal meaning toward ideation (Martin, 2004).

Appraisal theory (Martin, 2000; Martin and Rose, 2003; 2004; Martin and White, 2005) offers an interpersonal system, providing resources for enacting interpersonal evaluation, 'the semantic resources used to negotiate emotions, judgements and valuations, alongside resources for amplifying and engaging with these evaluations' (Martin, 2000: 145), and thus lends itself to the analysis of the resources of intersubjective stance. Appraisal theory is applied to examine the linguistic choices used to create affiliation, including but not limited to the positive and negative connotations in lexis.

Based on SFL, Appraisal theory has proved to be a useful theoretical framework for the examination of interpersonal affiliation. Martin (2004) showed how appraisal resources are used in constructing attitudinal alignment in newspaper texts, and Zappavigna (2011, 2012, 2014) has examined how appraisal resources are employed to create affiliation on the social media site Twitter. Appraisal analysis enables examination of the nature of affiliation by, for example, examining the types of evaluations being made, whether the attitudinal alignment is based on affect or judgement, or whether this is of positive or negative nature.

Under the Appraisal system, which falls under the interpersonal metafunction, we have Attitude, Engagement, and Graduation: this chapter focuses on attitudinal resources in establishing communal belonging. Graduation and Engagement are concerned with amplification of attitude and the sourcing of attitude, respectively, with attitude as the basic system. Martin (2000) divides Attitude further into Affect (emotional responses), Judgement (moral evaluations of behaviour), and Appreciation (valuing things). The study thus looks at how Appraisal resources are employed to create a sense of community by way of inviting the reader(s) to engage in what Martin (2004: 323) calls 'attitudinal rapport' and focuses on Attitudinal resources.

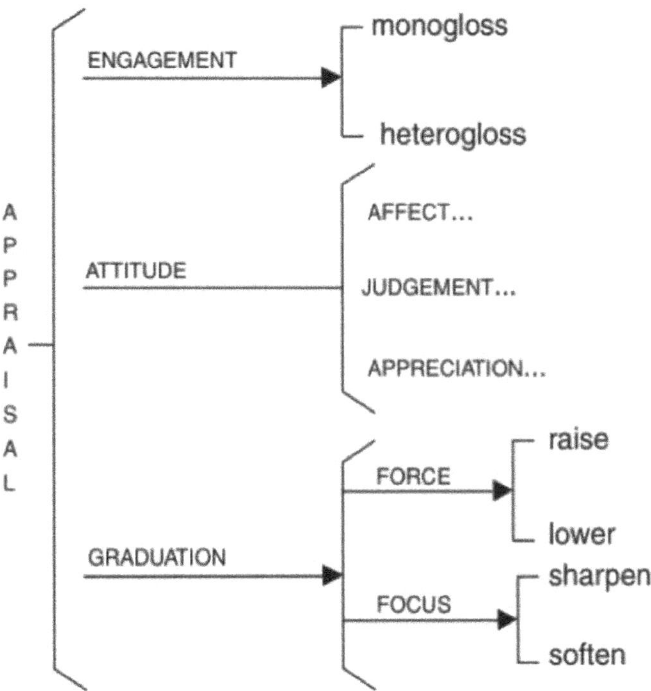

Figure 4.1: The Appraisal System. Martin and White (2005, Fig 1.18)

4.3 Material and Methods

4.3.1 Material

Video tributes to the late Apple CEO Steve Jobs are plentiful on YouTube. After choosing YouTube as the preferred channel, one video was chosen after a careful consideration as representative, that is, one that displays a memorial production (rather than documentary or a clip) and one that is widely shared with extensive commentary and discussion. The video tribute chosen for analysis has generated 362,763 views (at the time of writing) and

3,690 'likes' as well as 199 'dislikes'. Originally uploaded on October 13th, 2011, the video has been extensively shared via other social media channels, for example, Google+. The video has garnered a total of 844 user comments. The comments were manually extracted from YouTube, and transferred into an Excel file. Each comment is coded and assigned a running number as it appears on the Excel sheet (for example, User_294), and thus does not represent the order in the overall commentary (i.e. User_294 does not mean this comment is the 294th comment, as there is other information on the Excel sheet (time stamp, user ID, etc.).

The video is a collection of photos of Steve Jobs, with music sampled by the video creator using Apple sounds only (the start-up sound, the closing down sound, keyboard, etc.). There is intermittent voice-over where Steve Jobs is heard saying 'inspirational things': these are clips from his commencement speech at Stanford University, which he delivered to new graduates on June 12th, 2005. In the speech, he recounts his life, framing it retrospectively very positively: he talks of life as being full of opportunity.

The user comments represent two groups, in-group and out-group, so categorized due to the ideational meanings and evaluation arising from the user comments in relation to the 'digital context' created by the digital artefact, the video tribute, which establishes the space as a memorial site. Thus, the in-group consists of user comments indicating participation in the commemoration and construction of positive legacy and memory of Steve Jobs, whereas the out-group consist of the 'social critics' who enter the digital space with the purpose of voicing their alternative viewpoint to the effects and contribution of Steve Jobs, more often from the perspective of a capitalist critique.

4.3.2 Method

As a method for data collection a form of digital ethnography termed netnography (Kozinets, 2010) was used. Kozinets (2010: 60) defines netnography as 'participant-observational research based on online fieldwork. It uses computer-mediated communications as a source of data to arrive at the ethnographic understanding and representation of a cultural or communal phenomenon'. Time spent exploring and participating in (even if merely as an observer) online communities is thus an essential component of netnography of online communities. Kozinets (2010: 132) further points out that anonymous or pseudonymous data is 'often more honest, rather than more deceptive' than writing under one's own name in the online environment. The material collected for this study from YouTube is of the pseudonymous kind.

In the spirit of netnography, various commemorative material, fan discourse and fan productions, were observed over a two-year period, covering all of 2012–2013, and the best part of 2014, too. The video tribute selection on YouTube is vast. Other platforms in addition to YouTube were also explored and considered, but YouTube, with its multimodal affordances was selected. Apple's memorial site for Steve Jobs at www.apple.com/stevejobs was also extensively observed for the overriding fan sentiment and reaction to the loss.

The user comments were manually extracted from YouTube and organized in a temporal order to establish any potential interactive chains between users. Transitivity analysis was carried out manually to establish the ideational and interpersonal meanings in these short, anonymous messages. The material exhibits a lot of overlap, redundancy relative to meanings expressed. However, the video commentary offers rich material regarding affectual expression and alignment strategies. Ideational meanings were examined to see Steve Jobs, what he means to different people, and how his legacy is represented by different groups of people (in-group i.e. the 'fans' and out-group, the 'non-fans').

Interpersonal meanings were examined to establish what kinds of attitudes toward the late Steve Jobs, his life, career and accomplishments were prevalent. In addition, the attitudinal stance between these two groups was explored to examine the inter-group dynamic as it unfolds in the video user commentary. The Appraisal framework (Martin and White 2005) was used to explore the interpersonal stances and the attitudinal alignment in the text and how these are constructed linguistically.

This is a qualitative study, and due to the context of online celebrity commemoration as a very specific and specialized topic, the purpose of the research is to illustrate some of the ways in which attitudinal resources can be used in digital, often anonymous, contexts to create affiliation and a sense of belonging.

4.4 Analysis

The analysis is divided into three sections. First, the fan discourse is examined, focusing on the evaluation of Steve Jobs and affective alignment constructed among the fans in alignment with the video's content. Second, the discourse of the non-fans, the out-group, is examined to see how they view Steve Jobs and the stance they take towards the fans, and thereby, to the video tribute. Third, the inter-group dynamics are explored briefly, and elaborated on in the Discussion section. The ideational level is examined first, and then the interpersonal level in more detail by way of Appraisal analysis. The Mood structure is not systematically analysed in this study, as the emphasis is on the examination of evaluation and affect in building affiliation.

4.4.1 Allusional Rhetoric and Affect as Markers of In-group Status

The video tribute analysed in this study, as described earlier, consists of clips of Steve Jobs' speech in Stanford, 2005. The ideological positioning of the video tribute constructs the space as one for (positive) remembrance and idolatry. Frequent 'recycling' of Steve Jobs' quotes by the users is a sign of in-group status. Inside information has the function of building a community as the reader/viewer will recognize the quote and align either as an insider, or an outsider. This also points to the interrelation of the video's content, its ethos, and the user comments: comments as acts of reciprocal ideological confirmations build on and extend the sentiment created by the digital artefact, initially constructed by the video creator. This exemplifies the 'attitudinal rapport' Martin (2004: 323) talks about: it is also ideological rapport.

Semantically, the confirming comments are very value-laden, or 'affect-laden'. The recycled Jobs' quotes in user commentary acquire their meaning both by way of recontextualization in the new, digital environment as post-mortem reflections, but also by way of allusion to and resonance with the video tribute:

> Your time is limited, so don't waste it living someone else's life (User_11).

In their discussion of the 'popular cultural fan', Martin and White (2005: 5) point out how a seemingly 'monologic' text nevertheless constructs 'a particular set of dialogic relationships', and '[m]ost notably, it constructs an affiliation not only with the putative addressee [...] but also, through its *highly personalised use of affect*, with all those other readers who share the writer's enthusiasm (all the other "fans")'. Similarly, the video tributes on YouTube address a community by way of highly personalized use of affect, which functions by 'assuming the existence of this particular community of shared feeling' among the audience: this 'imagined audience' (Marwick and boyd, 2010) constitutes the imagined community. The example below illustrates such personalized use of affect: the fan proclaims to love something Steve Jobs is heard saying on the video tribute:

> I love 'you are already naked, there is no reason not to follow your heart!' (User_2227).

Using 'love', a verb of affect, amplifies the intensity of the emotion being expressed. Being explicitly evaluative, it expresses emotional resonance with a community who also 'love' what the phrase stands for: Steve Jobs, and individualism. Recycling the quote featured in the video effectively aligns the user with the tribute, but also, implicitly, with the wider community of Jobs' fans who recognize the origin of the phrase (the Stanford speech). The phrases evoke an attitudinal stance, which may be one of alignment or disalignment.

> Stay hungry. Stay foolish (User_2719).

Because attitude is not always explicit, the 'nature of the attitude evoked will be determined by the specific semantics of the graduated category and will also be subject to co-textual influences such as, for example, attitudinal prosodies established by inscribed attitudinal values elsewhere in the text' (2005: 139). These inscribed (that is, explicit) attitudinal values running through the fan discourse are as abundant as they are positive.

Below, a fan is poaching a part of Jobs' phrase of how to do good work, which is 'to love what you do', originally in Jobs' Stanford speech, also featured in the video. However, fans are creative users of existing texts (e.g. Booth, 2010), and the phrase is transformed into an interrogative: it acts as an engagement resource as it includes the imagined audience (referred to as 'ambient audience' by Zappavigna (2012: 64) by addressing it, thereby making other voices possible. Moreover, instead of emphasizing the addressee (you), the fan prioritizes the verbal process creating a different dialogic stance: thus, not only is the fan drawing on the power of allusion in building community, but by accentuating what already is a verb of affect the fan is upscaling the affective resources:

> Do you LOVE what you do (User_486, emphasis in original).

Upscaling is a form of graduation. Upscaling verbs is not as common or easy as that of adjectives and adverbs; however, verbs of affect tend to be more grammatically scalable (Martin and White, 2005: 145) with grammatical intensifiers, such as *slightly*, *totally*, and *absolutely*. Furthermore, upscaling of affect seems to be a frequent feature of social media discourse (Zappavigna, 2012). However, affect is not the only resource used to construct fannishness, but an identity as a fan 'is conveyed by several other objective lexico-grammatical markers of enthusiasm' (Martin and White, 2005: 5).

The transitivity selections made by the in-group and by the out-group show the ways in which the celebrity is construed. The most frequent participants are Steve Jobs and the related referents (e.g. as 'you' or 'he'), as well as the user (as 'I') or the user representing and presupposing the community (as 'we'). Such frequent use of personal pronouns indicates that the relationship is perceived as deeply personal. A relational process with Steve Jobs as the Carrier/Token is one of the most frequently used, and the assigned Attributes/Values are positive in the fan discourse (and negative in the non-fan discourse), even hyperbolic, and embedded in the evaluative rhetoric running through the whole commentary. The fans position Steve Jobs as 'the hero' and 'genius' of our times:

> He was perfect rip (User_73).

> He was a great man who changed the world. Thumbs up if you're reading this on one of his revolutionary products. We will always miss him (User_143).

Steve Jobs frequently appears as the Phenomenon in mental processes with 'I' or 'we' as the Senser. The mental processes of 'love' and 'miss' are common, indicating the reasons as to why these users watch the video tribute(s):

> We all love you Steve! Be happy wherever u are... (User_6057).

One of the most common behavioural processes is 'cry', indicating the depth of emotion the fan experiences. Being in present tense, the comment illustrates the emotional power video tributes have:

> I'm crying </3 I miss Steve's presentations and inspirational words (User_115).

The behavioural processes do not only relate to the user's own experience; addressing the imagined audience, this fan below also creates the expectation of this audience as saddened to tears by the loss of Jobs, implying that the user, too, cried over the video:

> Steve Jobs Day: This video will make you cry (User_2599).

In California, there now is a Steve Jobs Day, established after his death. Assuming there is no need to tell the audience of the existence of such a day, it is stated as a matter of fact, thereby reducing distance between the fan commentator and the audience. Reducing distance also indicates assumptions of shared ideological positioning.

The material processes describe what Steve Jobs is seen as having done, for example, he 'created products that changed the world'. Usually Jobs' innovation is translated as progress:

> lol. you are funny. Steve Jobs created products that changed the world. He helped to create computers that we now use. All of this innovation has helped society (User_1017).

The circumstantials tell us useful background information without being negotiable, that is, they are non-essential parts of the utterance. Below, the circumstantial 'of our time' functions to upscale the positive evaluation already present in the lexis ('innovator', 'one of the greatest'):

> STEVE JOBS was an INNOVATOR, one of the greatest of our time (User_1041, all emphasis in original).

Temporal circumstantials are used to reference the importance or significance of Jobs as seen from the fans' perspective, and can function as an evaluative resource.

4.4.2 Non-fans as Social Critics

Transitivity choices of the non-fans construct a bleak picture of Steve Jobs. Hyperbolic expressions in relational processes are in stark opposition to the positive appraisal of the fans. We witness a lot of polarized affect and explicit evaluation in referring terms: where the fans 'love' Jobs, the non-fans 'hate' him; where Jobs represents a 'hero' to his fans, the non-fans see him as a 'capitalist pig'.

> He was just another CEO intent on making money for his company (User_4311).

The non-fans manifest a different coupling of ideational and interpersonal meanings: mostly, the sentiment non-fans express is negative judgement (non-fans acting as social critics expressing capitalist critique of Steve Jobs' and Apple's operations) and negative affect, expressing, for example, loathing of Steve Jobs' personality:

> He was the embodiment of greed (User_464).

Also interesting is the different focus in ideation: both discussing Steve Jobs and Apple, the positive evaluation (mainly positive affect and positive appreciation) is targeted at the personality and achievements of Jobs (products), whereas the negative evaluation (mainly negative judgement) is targeted at the Steve Jobs' business ethics.

Where the fans resort to allusional rhetoric, non-fans resort to humour. While humour is an important aspect of rapport, in the material analysed in this study, sarcasm was found to be one of the strategies frequently employed by the non-fans to intrude and ridicule the object of fandom and the positive affect displayed by the fans, but also as a technique to construct solidarity among the non-fan collective. Sarcasm was often masked as a humorous comment, but with intended ridicule:

> Just before you die, you see your life pass in a Flash. Steve Jobs did not experience that. Apple does not support flash (User_3404).

In the case of humour and sarcasm, we see an incongruent coupling of the two metafunctions, ideational and interpersonal; context provides cues for recovering the intended interpretation. The role of the emoticons as resources for meaning making should not be underestimated (see also Zappavigna, 2012) and their role in providing contextual cues is significant:

> I guess an apple a day didn't keep the doctor away:((User_2137).

The example comment above is from a fan. We see, then, how the emoticon guides our interpretation in the case of humour (and in other cases) in addition to the other contextual information available. If the emoticon after this comment was a 'winking face' (i.e. ;-)), instead of a sad face :(, we would construe this comment as criticism masked in sarcasm.

4.4.3 Capitalist Pig or Hero of Our Times? Discursive Battle over Meaning

The Appraisal framework allows us to examine community dynamics as these are negotiated discursively. According to Martin:

> negotiating solidarity is a complex process that may involve feelings of different kinds and thus communities with different membership (e.g. affect inviting sympathy on the one hand, versus judgement prescribing disapproval on the other hand) (2004: 327)

Invitation to community is, at the same time, *invitation to disagree*. The ideological stance as well as the type of affective alignment separates the in-group, the fans, from the out-group. In the discursive struggles over territory, the users create different 'communities of value' (Zappavigna, 2011; 2012) within the same ideational realm.

Operating in the same field of ideation, the discourse revolves around Steve Jobs, his products and Apple. But while the fans construct Jobs as a 'genius', the evaluations generated by the out-group differ, arising from the difference in perspective and observable on the interpersonal level. The fans focus on Steve Jobs as an individual and what he means on a personal level and his 'contribution to mankind'. On the contrary, the non-fans view Steve Jobs through his role as a CEO of a multinational company. Thus, the positive evaluation (mainly positive affect and positive appreciation) is targeted at the personality and achievements of Jobs (products), whereas the negative evaluation (mainly negative judgement) is targeted at the Steve Jobs' business ethics.

The out-group acts as a social critic, condemning the very tribute as a tribute to capitalism. We see, then, the evaluation arises from different perspectives: personal, local experience versus the impersonal, global effect. Let us have another look at the example from User_1041. It typifies the discursive struggle between the opposing groups, and exemplifies also how the community boundaries are construed. The video tribute as a memorial site is defended when the user says 'STOP taking away from what's going on here…go protest somewhere else':

> @username I think its a pretty retarded point. STEVE JOBS was an INNOVATOR, one of the greatest of our time… and you faggots wanna bring up starving children and third world countries as if they are deemed "unimportant" because their death is not recognized. HOW ABOUT YOU STOP taking away from what's going on here, and appreciate what this man has done, go protest somewhere else (User_1041, all emphasis in original).

Notably, the inter-group interaction is conflict-ridden and has a tendency to escalate. In resisting the in-group ethos, the out-group, acting as a 'social critic', intervenes and constructs an alternative to what is a jointly constructed interpretation of Jobs. The discursive inter-group struggle is as much a struggle over representation of history, over meaning. However, this discursive battle only strengthens the in-group identity, as well as helping to deepen the attitudinal alignment among the members.

4.5 Findings

The linguistic analysis in the present study found the techniques used for building a community to lie with the shared intensity of positive appraisal as the commemoration unfolds mostly as a chain of positive Attitude. What on the face of it may be a surprising finding, mourning and remembrance are often positive in their tone as memorials tend to focus on the lived life rather than the loss of it (Doss, 2008). The exchanges in the user commentary are highly emotional; Döveling (2015: 9) found the predominant communicative feature in online bereavement forums to be 'emotional communication (86.0%)' and that sharing creates 'a common feeling of understanding and experience of similarity, a feeling of community understood as a common ground'.

Looking at the communicative dynamics of the two groups an interesting pattern emerges. In terms of Appraisal, we see the ebb and flow of positive and negative attitude already mentioned. Interestingly, there seems to be five distinct stages in the process of alignment and community building. First, establishing the community ethos by digital, multimodal means: visually by video, audibly by music, and also verbally: the digital artefact provides the social context (boyd and Heer, 2006), attracting like-minded fans by way of 'invitation to community' (Martin, 2004). Also, the putative reader is not only written into the text(s) produced on the site, but is digitally and multimodally included in the performance.

Second, community ideology and fan discourse is (re)created by attitudinal alignment. Neither community nor belonging are static, but dynamic processes: while the digital space allows particularized self-expression, it is these expressions of identity and acts of remembrance that create the community. In these acts, the users communicate their stance, engage in constructing the memory, and participate in the flow of positive and negative evaluation as the dialogue evolves. As noted by Jarvis (2011), creating a collective memory, the performance of remembrance creates what the community members believe was already there. Belonging is very much based on shared values and affect with positive orientation, collectively constructed in interaction. The orientation of online bereavement interaction is typically away from death and dying and toward the positive, thus having a restorative effect (e.g. Döveling, 2015). This explains the positive attitude that prevails in the fan discourse.

Third, the community is subject to ferocious discursive and ideological attack from outside and typically, the out-group discourse has negative undertones in the context. However, context plays a significant role in rendering some discourses natural while rendering others unacceptable. Regarding ideological contextualization, van Dijk (2001) notes how ideology works in indirect ways, too; through a biased representation of a social situation, some attitudes become neutralized, making them seem natural while making other attitudes seem unnatural. The video tribute itself establishes the digital space as a memorial site, casting limitations. The criticism thus seems out of place when positive evaluation and performances of idolatry are neutralized; the digital space is not neutral, but users already have a preconceived notion of its purpose. The sense of boundaries being crossed is evident in the material, as is the perceived right of the fans to express both grief and adoration.

Fourth, the community responds with equal negativity, defending their territory and their representations. Upon the clash, community boundaries are defended and negotiated, degrees of fandom drawn and representation of Steve Jobs and past events contested and negotiated.

Sense of the 'Other' is important for the establishment of the self, and this leads us to the final, fifth stage: a reinforced sense of identity, either as a fan or a non-fan, leading to increased intra-group unity. As members unite and re-align to defend their space and ideological stance, they also gain a strengthened sense of community in the process, and from the dispute, a common social identity. According to social identity theory (see, e.g. Pyysiäinen, 2011; Reicher, 2004), common social identity differentiates us from other social groups, whereas personal identity differentiates us from other individuals. Identification with a common social identity is likely to lead to inter-group behaviour (Pyysiäinen, 2011). The current study supports this as it finds that interaction takes place between different groups more than between individuals.

The intra-group interaction is scarce and is most evidently witnessed in the solidifying phase, when the attack from the outside results in an enforced sense of intra-group solidarity. The intra-group solidarity does not, therefore, arise as much from direct interaction as it does from the re-iteration of and sharing in the same ideological and attitudinal positioning. This positioning is initially constructed by the video tribute, which invites the viewers to align with the ideological and emotional landscape emanating from the video.

4.6 Discussion

Digital spaces afford identity expression and communality in new, multimodal ways. This study set out to examine anonymous affiliation on YouTube in the context of celebrity death: the focus was on the ways in which appraisal resources are employed in negotiating interpersonal relationships, and specifically, how attitudinal alignment builds community. Allusional, affective rhetoric was found to be a major aspect in building intra-group cohesion and sense of belonging. Interestingly, as the recycled material in the video tribute originates from Steve Jobs' speech (where he recounts his own life), and as these quotes are abundantly used to build communal belonging, the commemorative video tribute is, in effect, a multi-layered recontextualization of a lived life. The tribute, as a digital artefact, has the 'putative audience' digitally and multimodally included in the performance. At the same time, online memorials invite controversy and it may be argued that an 'out-group' is also constructed in commemorative performances.

In the acts of remembrance the members are (re)constructing a collective memory they can identify with, in the process forming interpersonal ties that are based on shared positive affect. This type of attitudinal alignment serves to build and strengthen the alignment within the community. We have seen how appraisal resources can be used in complex ways, to include, but also to exclude. Looking into the affiliative processes in YouTube interaction helps us understand digital spaces as sites of emotional negotiation and affectual bonding.

4.7 Conclusion

While online anonymity may in some cases increase hostility (Santana, 2013), it also encourages participation and expression of emotions traditionally excluded from the public realm. Anonymity does not necessarily stand in the way of intimacy, but rather, it may facilitate communal solidarity online. Some suggest phatic communication, as in Malinowski's phatic communion (1923), is a significant characteristic of social media discourse (e.g. Zappavigna, 2012: 28). While participation in social media sites helps create and maintain social relations, this study has shown that in addition to the management of interpersonal relationships, social media functions as a site of ideological expression. Furthermore, we need to consider the practical aspects and benefits of social media use, illustrated by the new mourning rituals online. Appraisal analysis helps us explore the attitudinal resources used to create communality in spontaneous online spaces that allow the emergence of imagined communities.

About the author

Anu Harju is a Doctoral Candidate at the Organizational Communication Unit at Aalto University School of Business, Helsinki, Finland. Her research interests include discursive and critical approaches to social media and identity, online community dynamics and consumer resistance from a cultural perspective. She has also examined mourning and commemoration online.

References

Anderson, B. (1983/2006) *Imagined Communities: Reflections on the Origin and Spread of Nationalism*. London: Verso.

Booth, P. (2010) *Digital Fandom: New Media Studies*. New York: Peter Lang.

boyd, d. and Heer, J. (2006) Profiles as Conversation: Networked Identity Performance on Friendster. *Proceedings of the Hawai'i International Conference on System Sciences* (HICSS-39). Kauai, HI: IEEE Computer Society.

Doss, E. (2002) Death, Art and Memory in the Public Sphere: The Visual and Material Culture of Grief in Contemporary America. *Mortality* 7(1): 63–82.

Doss, E. (2008) *The Emotional Life of Contemporary Public Memorials: Towards a Theory of Temporary Memorial*. Amsterdam: Amsterdam University Press.

Döveling, K. (2015) Emotion Regulation in Bereavement: Searching for and Finding Emotional Support in Social Network Sites. *New Review of Hypermedia and Multimedia* 21(1–2): 106–122.

Gibson, M. (2007) Death and Mourning in Technologically Mediated Culture. *Health Sociology Review* 16: 415–424.

Hård Af Segerstad, Y. and Kasperowski, D. (2015) A Community for Grieving: Affordances of Social Media for Support of Bereaved Parents. *New Review of Hypermedia and Multimedia* 21(1-2): 25–41.

Harju, A. (2014) Socially Shared Mourning: The Construction and Consumption of Collective Memory. *New Review of Hypermedia and Multimedia,* 21(1–2): 123–145.

Jarvis, L. (2011) 9/11 Digitally Remastered? Internet Archives, Vernacular Memories and WhereWereYou.Org. *Journal of American Studies* 45(4): 793–814.

Karppi, T. (2015) Happy Accidents: Facebook and the Value of Affects. In K. Hillis, S. Paasonen, and M. Petit (eds) *Networked Affect.* Cambridge, MA: MIT Press.

Klaassens, M., Groote, P. D., and Vanclay, F. M. (2013) Expressions of Private Mourning in Public Space: The Evolving Structure of Spontaneous and Permanent Roadside Memorials in the Netherlands. *Death Studies* 37(2): 145–171.

Kozinets, R. V. (2010) *Netnography: Doing Ethnographic Research Online.* London: Sage.

Lagerkvist, A. (2013) New Memory Cultures and Death: Existential Security in the Digital Memory Ecology. *Thanatos* 2(2): 8–24.

Malinowski, B. (1923) The Problem of Meaning in Primitive Languages. In C. K. Ogden, and I. A. Richards (eds) *The Meaning of Meaning,* 296–336. New York: Harcourt Brace.

Martin, J. R. (2000) Beyond Exchange: APPRAISAL Systems in English. In S. Hunston, and G. Thompson (eds) *Evaluation in Text: Authorial Stance and the Construction of Discourse,* 142–176. Oxford: Oxford University Press.

Martin, J. R. (2004) Mourning: How We Get Aligned. *Discourse & Society* 15(2–3): 321–344.

Martin, J. R. and Rose, D. (2003) *Working with Discourse: Meaning Beyond the Clause.* London and New York: Continuum.

Martin, J. R. and White, P. R. R. (2005) *The Language of Evaluation: Appraisal in English.* New York: Palgrave Macmillan.

Marwick, A. E. and boyd, d. (2010) Tweet Honestly, I Tweet Passionately: Twitter Users, Context Collapse, and the Imagined Audience. *New Media & Society,* 13(1): 114–133.

Page, R. E. (2012) The Linguistics of Self-Branding and Micro-Celebrity in Twitter: The Role of Hashtags. *Discourse & Communication* 6(2): 181–201.

Pantti, M. and Sumiala, M. (2009) Till Death do Us Join: Media, Mourning Rituals and the Sacred Centre of the Society. *Media, Culture & Society* 31(1): 119–135.

Pyysiäinen, J. (2011) Co-Constructing a Virtuous Ingroup Attitude? Evaluation of New Business Activities in a Group Interview of Farmers. *Text & Talk – an Interdisciplinary Journal of Language, Discourse & Communication Studies,* 30(6): 701–721.

Reicher, S. (2004) The Context of Social Identity: Domination, Resistance, and Change. *Political Psychology* 25 (6): 921–945.

Rokka, J. and Moisander, J. (2009) Environmental Dialogue in Online Communities: Negotiating Ecological Citizenship among Global Travellers. *International Journal of Consumer Studies* 33: 199–205.

Santana, A. D. (2013) Virtuous or Vitriolic: The Effect of Anonymity on Civility in Online Newspaper Reader Comment Boards. *Journalism Practice* 8(1): 18–33.

Sumiala, J. (2013) Media and Ritual: Death, Community and Everyday Life. London: Routledge.

van Dijk, T. (2001) Discourse, Ideology and Context. *Folia Linguistica* 35(1-2): 11–40.
van Dijck, J. (2009) Users Like You? Theorizing Agency in User-Generated Content. *Media, Culture & Society* 31(1): 41–58.
van Dijck, J. (2013) 'You have One Identity': Performing the Self on Facebook and LinkedIn. *Media, Culture & Society* 35(2): 199–215.
Walter, T. (2014) New Mourners, Old Mourners: Online Memorial Culture as a Chapter in the History of Mourning. *New Review of Hypermedia and Multimedia* 21(1–2): 10–24.
Zappavigna, M. (2011) Ambient Affiliation: A Linguistic Perspective on Twitter. *New Media & Society* 13(5): 788–806.
Zappavigna, M. (2012) *Discourse of Twitter and Social Media: How We Use Language to Create Affiliation on the Web*. London: Continuum.
Zappavigna, M. (2014) Enacting Identity in Microblogging through Ambient Affiliation. *Discourse & Communication* 8(2): 209–228.

5 Commenting, Interacting, Reposting: A Systemic-Functional Analysis of Online Newspaper Comments

Mariavita Cambria
University of Messina

5.1 Introduction

Newspapers have been profoundly transformed in the process of going online (Conboy, 2010). The transition from printed newspapers to online news sites has affected the entire process of producing, accessing and perceiving news, accelerating hybridization of the genres involved and raising a number of issues associated with representing, construing and experiencing news (Bednarek and Caple, 2012). A case in point is the possibility for readers to express their opinion about online articles in the comments-on-the-article section of online newspapers or via links to social networks (Facebook, Twitter etc.). This involves readers in news-making activities, empowering them in terms of opinion-making (Cambria, 2011). The web environments in which comments appear exemplify news as dialogic, heteroglossic environments that constitute a dynamic website macro-genre (Bakhtin, 1981[1975]; Baldry, 2007). News is commented on via several media and with the use of several links. Comments thus function as places where news can be questioned, commented and dialogically negotiated in an ongoing 'conversation' with members of the online community or web environment. The dialogic engagement with the reader is one reason for the foregrounding of interpersonal meanings in the comments. The user can make comments on certain articles but also on opinions already expressed by other readers. Another option is to recommend, report abuse about, share or link the article, allowing users to interact with others by commenting on previous comments.

The approach adopted in this chapter draws on Halliday's theory of social semiotics (1978, 2004) and deals with the way people use different semiotic resources to participate in, and thus produce, communicative events. A multimodal text is related to the social system via its context of situation and of culture (Kress, 2010). The aim of this chapter is twofold: firstly, to describe the participants (i.e. the people taking part in the communicative event, henceforth named 'contributors') in the comments in terms of the metafunctions they exhibit; secondly, to investigate some lexico-grammatical features of the comments, in particular lexical density and prominent processes of the experiential metafunction to pinpoint the dialogic nature of the comments. For this purpose, a corpus of comments was created, consisting of comments posted on articles published in www.irishtimes.com in the period July-December 2014 on the subject of immigration. Following a description of the contributors in Section 2, Section 3 illustrates the methodology used in the corpus construction, while Section 4 gives examples from the corpus.

5.2 Contributors in the Comments

As stated above, one of the purposes of the present study is to examine the lexico-grammatical features of written comments. Figure 5.1 shows the web environment and the organization of the comments.

There may be several people taking part in exchanges of this type: the journalist who wrote the article rarely takes part but is often mentioned in the comments, commentators who comment on the article by subscribing to the service, and readers of the article and/or the paper whose meta-comments are limited to, for example, recommending an article by sharing it or reporting abuse (Herring *et al.*, 2005). Contributors, i.e. people commenting on articles, may choose a picture, a sort of avatar to represent themselves, typically exemplifying their alter ego, and may also choose a name by which they want to be recognized within that particular community, such as 'Militantagnostic' in Figure 5.1.

Comments can be seen as a form of open forum, a computer-mediated communication genre, planned to create discussion, agreement or disagreement on what is considered the 'hottest' topic. The 'non-participating' reader (i.e. the reader who chooses not to be an explicit comment-maker) can approve or disapprove with a simple click on the desired option. From a socio-semiotic perspective, contributors and their discourse belong to the community that is generated but are also conditioned by what happens in the process. The link to the profile of each active contributor allows for a better comprehension of their 'e-identity', since their other comments can be accessed by clicking on the profile (see the profile of 'Mongo Smellybeard' in Figure 5.2).

In this chapter, the approach to Participant Analysis follows Halliday's three broad areas of meaning potential: ideational, interpersonal and

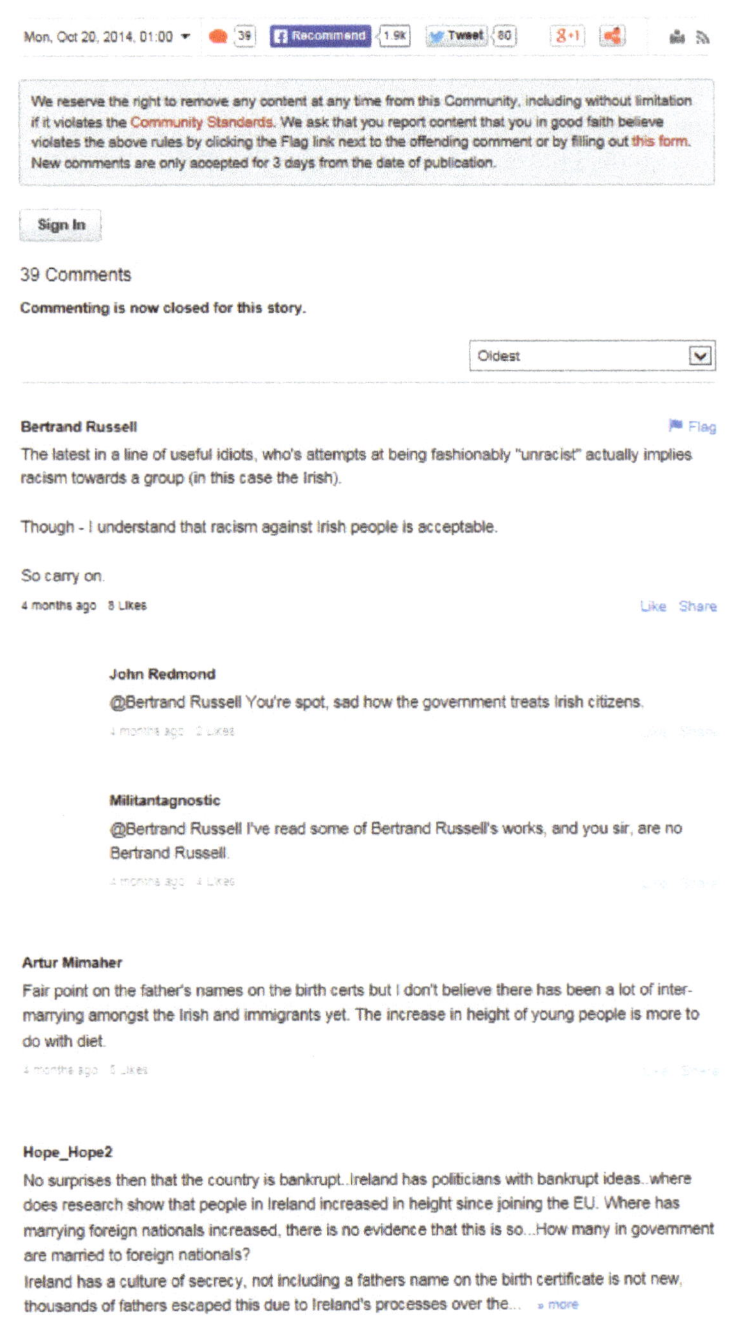

Mon, Oct 20, 2014, 01:00 ▾ 39 Recommend 1.9k Tweet 80 8+1

We reserve the right to remove any content at any time from this Community, including without limitation if it violates the Community Standards. We ask that you report content that you in good faith believe violates the above rules by clicking the Flag link next to the offending comment or by filling out this form. New comments are only accepted for 3 days from the date of publication.

Sign In

39 Comments

Commenting is now closed for this story.

Oldest

Bertrand Russell Flag

The latest in a line of useful idiots, who's attempts at being fashionably "unracist" actually implies racism towards a group (in this case the Irish).

Though - I understand that racism against Irish people is acceptable.

So carry on.

4 months ago 8 Likes Like Share

John Redmond

@Bertrand Russell You're spot, sad how the government treats Irish citizens.

4 months ago 2 Likes

Militantagnostic

@Bertrand Russell I've read some of Bertrand Russell's works, and you sir, are no Bertrand Russell.

4 months ago 4 Likes

Artur Mimaher

Fair point on the father's names on the birth certs but I don't believe there has been a lot of inter-marrying amongst the Irish and immigrants yet. The increase in height of young people is more to do with diet.

4 months ago 5 Likes

Hope_Hope2

No surprises then that the country is bankrupt..Ireland has politicians with bankrupt ideas..where does research show that people in Ireland increased in height since joining the EU. Where has marrying foreign nationals increased, there is no evidence that this is so...How many in government are married to foreign nationals?
Ireland has a culture of secrecy, not including a fathers name on the birth certificate is not new, thousands of fathers escaped this due to Ireland's processes over the... » more

4 months ago 5 Likes

Figure 5.1: Comments on the article 'Celtic Tiger immigrants made us better-looking, says Mitchell' by Mary Minihan, 20/10/2014

textual, and their correlation with register categories (Eggins and Martin, 1997; Ghadessy, 1993; Martin, 2010). Halliday's ideational meaning is interpreted in terms of the world as categories of experience. This means that the ideational metafunction is constructed as realizing a part-whole structure based on the principle of constituency (O'Halloran, 2008). One such part is the contributor's identity, an e-identity that is chosen and constructed online. Another such part is the comment, which usually refers to hot topics or issues deemed particularly relevant to the readers. Readers have a set amount of time to comment on the article (usually five to seven days), after which they still have the opportunity to read comments and look at commentator profiles. The interpersonal metafunction concerns language as interaction (speech acts, dialogic moves), the expression of attitudinal and evaluative orientation (modality) and the taking-up and negotiating of specific subjective positions in discourse. It is taken as being expressed by field-like prosodies and as scopal in character (i.e. declarative, interrogative clauses) and as attendant to the relationship between the reader and people, events and objects. The interpersonal meaning is closely related to Tenor, which refers to how people relate to one another when communicating. It should be remarked here that the interpersonal meaning potential of the linked object in the comments is also made explicit through three multimodal parameters: appeal, orientation and action (Baldry and Thibault, 2006). As such, the reader can make an appeal in the home page through a link to comments on the article. The orientation is contained in the option 'post a comment', thus realizing the potential for action by entering the community of those who comment on the article. Posting a comment and/or interacting with other commentators produces a similar path.

The textual meaning relates pieces of text to each other and to their context. It is associated with mode, the channel used to communicate and how those texts are seen in the context of culture and of situation. In the last ten years, comments have achieved a status of their own. Almost all quality newspapers offer readers the opportunity to comment on articles published, although this is usually restricted to certain articles. In www.irishtimes.ie, for example, an average of 40% of articles published provide this opportunity, while in www.theguardian.com/uk the rate is more than 60%. The comments are almost exclusively related to the context where they occur and it is not always possible to grasp the meaning of them without making reference to the context of culture and situation. In Figure 5.1, for example, 'John Redmond' addresses 'Bertrand Russell' directly and 'Militantagonist' comments on his comment. The social context is thus people commenting on articles (field) and interacting with other people (tenor), making use of a web channel of communication to do so (mode).

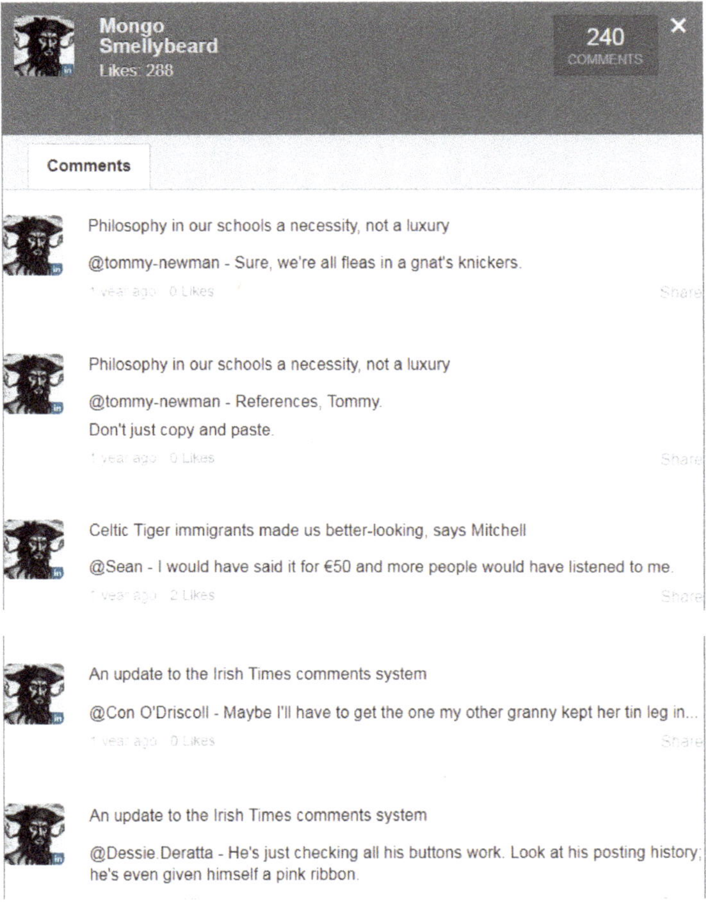

Figure 5.2: E-identity of one of the commentators

5.3 Methodology

Web texts and genres are evolving rapidly, and more and more difficult to process systematically (Cambria *et al.*, 2012). Hence the possibility of examining the web and its genres as a corpus of meaning-making units that transcend the word level and can be used to design and reshape meanings is a prerequisite for online news genre analysis and not least an opportunity for readers to contribute to the meaning-making process.

Several hurdles had to be overcome to create a corpus from online resources. The analysis had to characterize and quantify the type-token distribution and, at the same time, collect intertextual data on the comments concerned: their links to photographs, audio or video files or other hyperlinks. Finally, a check was carried out to ascertain whether a paragraph or a specific line was in any way related to a photograph, a link or any other illuminating co-text of a multimodal nature (Baldry, 2007), e.g. at its simplest the expression 'this is upsetting', supported by an ironic and co-textual emoticon. This data, which clearly puts forward the need for mini-genre analysis, requires further steps towards understanding the whole meaning-making process, i.e. taking the analysis beyond a string of words and, in this way, moving at the discourse level (Baldry and O'Halloran, 2010).

The corpus construction process went through several stages. The first was a search for the word 'immigration' or 'migrant', followed by a type-token relationship, i.e. articles that contained the word *immigration* in the headline or text in the period July-December 2014 in *www.irishtimes.com.* The latter's search engines generated a list of articles published in 2014 with the word immigration either in the headline or in the body of the text. Each item on the list indicated the title of the article, date of publication, author's name, and what Knox (2010) calls 'newsbites' (headline-plus-lead-plus-hyperlink story). As Table 5.1 clearly demonstrates, the data is highly diversified: *www.irishtimes.com* had a total of 303 articles with the word immigration or migrant in the headline or the body of the text for the period under review. Of these articles, 83 permitted comments, albeit the number of comments on the articles concerned varied according to the topic. Some articles generated only a few comments, others more than ten, while yet others were subjected to a substantial number (for instance, 690 comments on an article dealing with migration and prostitution).

Table 5.1: Distribution of Articles on Immigration that Allowed Comments at www.irishtimes.ie in the Period July-December 2014

Month	Number of articles	With comments
July	46	9
August	33	5
September	33	12
October	47	10
November	99	22
December	45	25

The second step was to create .txt files containing readers' comments (one for each month to allow for a diachronic data check) and to crosscheck frequency ratios. ICE–Ireland, the Irish section of the International Corpus of

English (ICE) project aimed at collecting material for comparative studies of English worldwide, was chosen as a reference corpus because its corpus variety is similar. A corpus is essentially a sample of language or language variety. ICE-Ireland, with its samples of written and spoken texts, was seen as the appropriate reference corpus for an in-depth investigation of the context of culture and that of the comment situation, and for analysis of the main features. A corpus of over 50,000 words was created from comments to *www.irishtimes.com* (ITC henceforth). Pictures, avatars, videos and links were analysed separately, but for purposes of space are not analysed in this chapter.

As stated in Section 1, lexical density and processes belonging to the experiential metafunction were explored in ITC.

5.4 Lexical Density and Processes in the Comments

Lexical density is a measure of the proportion of content words to the total count of words used (Eggins, 1994). Following Halliday (1985: 62–63), 'the difference between written and spoken language is one of density, the density with which information is presented. Relative to each other written is dense, spoken language is sparse'. Recent literature rightly addresses the standard division between speech and writing, and shows how the boundaries between categories usually associated with speech and writing are collapsing (Sindoni, 2013). Web 2.0 and its plethora of possibilities for comment and offer of comments on facts and events does, however, reveal a difference in their use. Lexical density in ITC is 19.6%, readability computed by the Gunning-Fox index is 9.9%, when 6 stands for 'easy' and 20 for 'hard'. The standardized type/token ratio is 51.23, the average syllable per word is 1.73 and the sentence length (words) 18.68. Readability in the 83 articles commented upon is, in contrast, 10.2% while lexical density is 40.9%, with an average syllable per word of 1.74 and sentence length of 19.04. The standardized type/token ratio is 23.15 in the articles, thus indicating a richer vocabulary in line with the article genres described.

Corpus analysis techniques such as keyness were used to check the features of the comments. The first step in the comment analysis was to observe the list of words used by the commentators with the concordance tool AntConc (Anthony, 2014). Word lists always provide interesting features to look at as they offer an ideal starting point for the understanding of a text in terms of its lexis (Scott and Tribble, 2006). In the case of ITC, the first content word in the top 100 words is *people* (28th) followed by *Irish* (37th). This is succeeded by *immigration* (43rd) and *EU* (54th). Other content words are *Ireland* (30th), *immigrants* (42nd) and *migrants* (46th).

The other corpus linguistics tool that gives hints on the nature of a text is the analysis of keyness. Keywords can be significant in text analysis and facilitate the interpretation of a text and the associated culture. In a quantitative perspective, keywords are those whose frequency or infrequency in a text or corpus are statistically significant when compared to the standards set by a reference corpus (Baker, 2004; Scott, 1997; Scott and Tribble, 2006). As argued by Bondi:

> identifying elements that are repeated to a statistically significant extent does not in itself constitute an analysis or an interpretation of the text or corpus. It does however point to elements that may be profitably studied and need to be explained (2010: 3).

In the case of the present study, a lexical-density analysis was carried out to compare the number of lexical vs. grammatical items. The ITC was compared with ICE-Ireland in order to cross check positive and negative keyness. ICE-Ireland contains two subcorpora: a spoken subcorpus (625,966 words) and a written subcorpus (426,809 words). The research questions were designed to check lexical density in terms of content and function words found in the text.

Table 5.2 and Table 5.3 show respectively the positive and negative keyness analysis of ITC with ICE-Ireland as a reference corpus.

Table 5.2: Positive Keyness

Positive Keyness			
Rank	Frequency	Keyness	Keyword
1	68	281.750	immigration
2	76	268.769	eu
3	597	229.409	you
4	41	169.879	immigrants
5	46	168.832	asylum
6	40	165.735	migrants
7	39	161.592	prostitution
8	255	154.172	people
9	48	148.251	illegal
10	65	147.444	europe
11	97	147.392	why
12	202	118.767	do
13	977	108.236	is
14	59	107.562	countries
15	438	106.253	not

16	66	104.961	uk
17	191	103.602	irish
18	24	99.441	seekers
19	254	96.111	who
20	126	93.590	us

Table 5.3: Negative Keyness in ITC

Negative Keyness			
Rank	Frequency	Keyness	Keyword
1	365	3988.890	's
2	197	360.665	was
3	110	335.026	he
4	68	330.584	know
5	597	318.404	you
6	53	216.118	she
7	677	204.215	it
8	765	145.924	that
9	28	145.366	've
10	83	145.009	well
11	48	111.872	going
12	215	106.183	there
13	25	103.759	really
14	68	101.394	now
15	72	98.498	think
16	18	94.017	mean
17	232	90.783	we
18	22	74.992	got
19	73	67.558	had
20	37	60.670	said

Positive keyness analysis confirms the main topic of the text, i.e. immigration. Words related to the area of immigration obviously have a very high keyness and rank high in the top 20 words: *immigration* (1st with 281.750 keyness), *immigrants* (4th with 169.879 keyness), *asylum* (5th with 168.832 keyness), *migrants* (6th with 165.735 keyness). *Illegal* ranks 9th and has a keyness of 148.251. Words related to the geographical area also have a high keyness: *eu* ranks 2nd (keyness 268.769) while *europe* is 10th (keyness147.444). It is worth underlining the presence of *prostitution* as one of the keywords with a high keyness (161.592). Function words deserve a separate discussion. There are six function words in the positive keyness list: *you* (3rd with 229.409), *why* (11th with 147.392), *do* (12th with 118.767), *is* (13th with 108.236), *not* (15th with 160.253), *who* (19th with 96.111) and *us* (20th with 93.590). Only *you* ranks in the top ten, which accentuates the direct address feature in the comments (either in the singular or plural form). The word *why* occurs 90 times in questions and 35 times in the cluster *the reason why. Why* is usually used to emphasize the general tone of enquiry and attempts to explain what is happening in Irish society in the comments or asks other people in the comments about their opinion.

The limited presence of function words in positive keyness is confirmed by their huge presence in negative keyness. The top ten keywords in negative keyness are: *s* (1st with 398.890 keyness), *was* (2nd with 360.665), *he* (3rd with 335.026 keyness), *know* (4th with 330.584 keyness), *she* (5th with 216.118 keyness), *it* (6th with 214.215 keyness), *that* (7th with 145.924 keyness), *'ve* (8th with 145.924 keyness), *well* (9th with 145.009 keyness) and *going* (10th with 111.872 keyness). The first negative keyword needs to be analysed separately as it seems to suggest inconsistent transcription in the two corpora, and, as such, can be left out from our analysis. Results show that there are only three content words (*know, well* and *going*). Keywords in negative keyness are in line with the results of positive keyness and suggest that the authors of the comments use many content words.

Section 2 of this chapter briefly analysed the contributors in the comments who are usually involved in processes. The experiential metafunction refers to things in the world and how these are related to each other. Language expresses how things or people are involved in actions or events. The type of processes involved in the comments may be a good indicator of the main areas of involvement in the comments. The six different kinds of processes were thus looked at in ITC to ascertain the data contained in the comments and in what type of context they were taking place. The findings from ITC are divided into six main processes.

Material processes. Most of the processes in the corpus are material. The words *happen, happening, happened* occur 45 times and are almost always accompanied by modality markers in the cluster, as in the following example where 'Johnny Bellow' is replying to a comment written by 'DessieDemona': 'Dessie, we will never know how close we came to it and it still might happen'. The same is true for *appear*, which occurs 20 times. *Give* and its variants occur 67 times, indicating transformative material processes.

Mental processes. As illustrated in Table 5.3, the verbs *think* and *mean* rank 15th and 16th respectively in negative keyness. This is an indication that mental processes are not as crucial in ITC as other processes. The verb *think* appears in sentences such as 'I honestly think it would be in the best interests of migrants to work'. This notwithstanding, several mental processes take place in the corpus. Mental processes are internal processes of human experience and can be classified as clauses of sensing. The ITC web environment is a space where people tend to express their opinion in terms of agreement or disagreement. The desiderative mental verbs *agree** and *disagree** occur 58 and 32 times, respectively. *Want** occurs 87 times and is succeeded in 50% of these cases by another verb. It is followed 22 times by a projection instantiated by material processes, as in the case of 'The reasons people want to escape to Europe' or 'If migrants want to work here they need to a have a VISA'. *Want** is preceded 13 times by its negation and in such cases followed for the most part by a projection instantiated by a verbal process, as in 'They do not want to talk about immigration'. The data also reveals a significant use of *consider** (35 times). *Suggest** is used 19 times and (60% of cases) related to what journalists have said, as in the following example: 'The author suggests asylum seekers should be allowed to work'.

Relational processes. Relational processes play the role of identifying and specifying characteristics and features. They establish a relation between two notions. The word *is* ranks 13th in Table 5.2, indicating that it constitutes a key feature in ITC. It should be noted that *is* occurs in a clause as a relational or existential process in 64% of cases (625 times out of 977), in the remaining 36% it forms the present continuous tense or other verb forms.

Existential processes. These processes represent something that simply 'is' or 'exists'. Halliday and Matthiessen (2004) maintain that although existential clauses are not frequent, they play an important role, especially in narratives and where they are often associated with *there* + simple past of the verb to be. Existential processes are also used as introductory remarks, in this case *there* + simple present of to be and when suggestions are given, as in *there* + future of to be. There are 51 occurrences of *there is* in ITC, 56 of *there are*, ten of *there was* and two of *there were*, and eight occurrences of *there will*. The data indicates that there is a prevalence of affirmative sentences in the simple present tense. Interrogative forms are rare: two occurrences of *will there*, three of *is there*, and one each of *are there* and *was there*. Existential processes in comments may well be preferred when it comes to expressing a personal point of view, as in the following comment: 'From this and previous comments, I suspected Iona-shilling. But there is absolutely nothing to confirm that this is not just a right wing view'.

Behavioural processes. Behavioural processes are usually processes of physical and psychological behaviour. They do not occur frequently in ITC. *Look** occurs 32 times and *listen** 11 times, while there are only five occurrences of *dream.*

Verbal processes. Said ranks 20th in negative keyness, while *say** appears less than 100 times. Verbs related to the area of quoting, such as *say, tell, report,* are often used to make the person's point clear, as in the following example: 'You say "So those of you advocating for the term 'illegal'"'.

Findings from the corpus show that the use of mental verbs, frequently in the first and second person, are characteristic of the interactive nature of the comments. Speakers' reference to their own and their interlocutors' mental processes is another feature of the comments as in the case of 'If you think that the word IF is the important word there'. The use of mental verbs is another sign of speakers' involvement, if the Senser coincides with the speaker/writer. It is no accident that mental verbs tend to collocate with negation (45% of times in ITC).

The entries below show exchanges started from 'Colm Gillis' and they are taken as an example of the dialogic nature of the comments (emphasis is mine).

> Colm Gillis
> That which is virtuous is what is beautiful. Celtic Tiger immigrants are not held responsible for the sharp decrease in virtue in Ireland. But virtuous behaviour has decreased in the last 25 years and therefore, an alleged increase in good looks or IQ doesn't matter. This government in particular over the last few years has made Ireland into an 'uglier' country.
>
> Andre Jacobs
> @Colm Gillis – So, dear little Colm, are immigrants to blame for the 'loss of virtue' in Irish society?
>
> Sean
> @Colm Gillis – Did Frank Dunlop give you another €500 to say that?
>
> Mongo Smellybeard
> @Sean – *I would have said it* for €50 and more people would have listened to me.
>
> Colm Gillis
> @Andre Jacobs *I did say* that 'immigrants are not held responsible'.

> Maybe *I should rephrase it and say* 'In my opinion, the influx of immigrants and asylum seekers into Ireland is not to blame …' I'm not the person to pick scapegoats for our own misdeeds.
>
> Sean Guest
> @Colm Gillis
> Yet the per capita criminal stats do show a higher per capita criminality among immigrants.

As it emerges in the entries, contributors directly address the person they refer to via the use of @ thus avoiding the repetition of some verbal processes. Expressions such as 'I did say' are used by contributors to stress their point of view. The presence of interrogative clauses is also indicative of the direct address of the comments.

5.5 Conclusion

Online newspapers merge several media into a single macro genre, an epoch-making change in terms of the quantity of news presented and ways through which it can be accessed. They have changed readers' participation in the production of news by creating opportunities to interact dialogically with news itself. They present themselves to their audience as media products created by the convergence of different means of news-making, where different genres interact in a cumulative way. They position themselves as *time* and *space machines*, allowing the reader to create a personal path that extends in many different directions and through many different periods of time. Commenting, interacting, reposting articles and comments in several spaces calls on the reader to personally engage with news/comment/opinion-making. This allows for dialogical participation in a much larger community and underscores the fluidity of web genres. Data on linguistic analysis of the comments shows that contributors are involved in several processes and co-construct comments and activities in a dialogically negotiated space. A Systemic Functional approach to the processes employed in the comments has proved extremely fruitful in highlighting the dialogical nature of those digital texts. Results from the analysis of processes of the experiential metafunction have given prominence to the construction of experience realized via the structural configuration of the contributors interacting in specific circumstances, i.e. those configured by digital environments as the space of comments to online newspapers.

About the author

Mariavita Cambria is Assistant Professor in English Linguistics and Translation Studies at the University of Messina, Italy. Her research interests include systemic-functional grammar, multimodal and discourse analysis, online genres, Irish studies and varieties of English. She has published three books, several articles on multimodality, genre and discourse analysis and has co-edited a book on web genres entitled *Web Genres and Web Tools* (Ibis, 2013).

References

Anthony, L. (2014) *AntConc* Version 3.4.3w [Software]. Tokyo, Japan: Waseda University.
Baker, P. (2004) Querying Keywords. Questions of Difference, Frequency and Sense in Keywords Analysis. *Journal of English Linguistics* 32(4): 346–359.
Bakhtin, M. (1981 [1975]) *The Dialogic Imagination: Four Essays*. trans. C. Emerson and M. Holquist. Austin: University of Texas Press.
Baldry, A. P. (2007) What are Concordances for? Getting Multimodal Concordances to Perform Neat Tricks in the University Teaching and Testing Cycle. In A. P. Baldry, M. Pavesi, C. Taylor Torsello and C. Taylor (eds) *From Didactas to Ecolingua: An Ongoing Research Project on Translation and Corpus Linguistics*, 30–50. Trieste: EUT.
Baldry, A. P. and O'Halloran, K. L. (2010) Research into the Annotation of a Multimodal Corpus of University Websites: An Illustration of Multimodal Corpus Linguistics. In T. Harris, and M. Moreno Jaen (eds) *Corpus Linguistics in Language Teaching*, 177–209. Bern: Peter Lang.
Baldry, A. P. and Thibault, P. J. (2006) *Multimodal Transcription and Text Analysis*. London: Equinox Publishing.
Bednarek, M. and Caple, H. (2012) *News Discourse*. London and New York: Continuum.
Bondi, M. (2010) Perspectives on Keywords and Keyness: An Introduction. In M. Bondi, and M. Scott (eds) *Keyness in Texts*, 1–18. Amsterdam and Philadelphia: John Benjamins.
Cambria, M. (2011) Opinions on the Move: An Exploration of the 'article-Cum-Comments' Genre. In S. Sarangi, V. Polese, and G. Caliendo (eds), *Genre(s) on the Move. Hybridization and Discourse Change in Specialized Communication*, 135–150. Napoli: Edizione Scientifiche Italiane.
Cambria, M., Arizzi, C., and Coccetta, F. (eds) (2012) *Web Genres and Tools*. IBIS: Como, Pavia.
Conboy, M. (2010) *The Language of Newspapers: Socio-Historical Perspectives*. London and New York: Continuum.
Eggins, S. (1994) *An Introduction to Systemic Functional Linguistics*. London: Pinter.
Eggins, S. and Martin, J. R. (1997) Genres and Registers of Discourse. In T. A. van Dijk (ed.) *Discourse as Structure and Process*, 230–256. London: Sage Publications.

Ghadessy, M. (ed.) (1993) *Register Analysis: Theory and Practice*. London: Pinter.
Halliday, M. A. K. (1978) *Language as Social Semiotic: The Social Interpretation of Language and Meaning*. London: Arnold.
Halliday, M. A. K. (1985) *Spoken and Written Language*. Geelong, Vic.: Deakin University Press [republished London: Oxford University Press 1989].
Halliday, M. A. K. and Matthiessen, C. M. I. M. (2004) *An Introduction to Functional Grammar*. 3rd edn. London: Hodder Arnold.
Herring, S. C., Scheidt, L. A., Bonus, S., and Wright, E. (2005) Weblogs as a Bridging Genre. *Information Technology and People* 18(2): 142–171.
Knox, J. S. (2010) Online Newspapers. Evolving Genres and Evolving Theory. In C. Coffin, T. Lillis and K. O'Halloran (eds) *Applied Linguistics Methods: A Reader*, 33–51. London and New York: Routledge.
Kress, G. (2010) *Multimodality: A Social Semiotic Approach to Contemporary Communication*. London and New York: Routledge.
Martin, J. R. (2010) Language, Register and Genre. In C. Coffin, T. Lillis, and K. O'Halloran (eds) *Applied Linguistics Methods: A Reader*, 12–32. London and New York: Routledge.
O'Halloran, K. L. (2008) Systemic Functional-Multimodal Discourse Analysis (SF-MDA): Constructing Ideational Meaning using Language and Visual Imagery. *Visual Communication* 7(4): 443–475.
Scott, M. (1997) PC Analysis of Key Words – and Key Key Words. *System* 25(1): 1–13.
Scott, M. and Tribble, C. (2006) *Textual Patterns: Keywords and Corpus Analysis in Lanugage Education*. Amsterdam and Philadelphia: John Benjamins.
Sindoni, M. G. (2013) *Spoken and Written Discourse in Online Interactions: A Multimodal Approach*. London and New York: Routledge.

Part II
Texts that Achieve Digitality: Professional Genres Recontextualized

6 'We're hearing from Reuters that...': The Role of Around-the-Clock News Media in the Increased Use of the Present Progressive with Mental Process Type Verbs

Ben Clarke
University of Portsmouth

6.1 Introduction

This chapter explores the diachronically increased use of the present progressive ('BE ... V-ing') with one group of verbs which are said to not traditionally associate with this construction, verbs variously denoting cognitive experience (Leech, 2004: 25–27; Quirk *et al.*, 1985: 200–205; Palmer, 1965). Discussed in a systemic-functional tradition (Halliday and Hasan, 1985; Halliday, 1978, 1985, 1993), the focus here is some consideration of possible semantic and particularly contextual explanations for this grammatical phenomenon; any rounded understanding of some language phenomenon requiring an account of related phenomena at neighbouring strata[1] (Barthes, 1977; Halliday, 1979, 1996). The rhetorical organization of the chapter emphasizes the importance here placed on adopting a method of language description which is suitable in this way; after an explanation of stratification as a formalization of this fundamental organizing principle of languages (§2), subsequent sections explore the use of the present progressive with verbs of cognition from the vantage point of different levels. This starts from the perspective of grammar itself (§3), where the discussion is pitched specifically in diachronic terms charting the construction's increased use across the last two centuries. Following sections move upwards to explanations at the level of context (§5) via an exploration of semantic generalizations (§4). The chapter culminates in positing the advent of 24-hour live news television media as a specific contextual explanation for one apparent semantic sense of the present progressive with verbs of cognition (Clarke, unpublished a).[2]

6.2 Levels of Language Description: Lexicogrammar – Semantics – Context

Languages, as many semiotic systems, are inherently complex, containing a range of different phenomena and relationships between these phenomena. For one thing, some phenomena within a language are very abstract and others far less so. To help conceptualize this feature of language, linguists often invoke the metaphor of levels. At other times, it is referred to by the technical label 'stratification'; language systems are 'stratified' systems, comprised of a number of levels, or 'strata', which are, then, phenomena at different orders of abstraction. These strata can be defined more strictly by, and are mostly knowable as such because of, recurring realizational patterns. Additionally, the reality of stratification – the different strata themselves – call for different units of analysis and different methods of analysis to enable their description (Barthes, 1977: 85–86; Crystal, 1997: 82–83). The aforementioned recurring patternings are highly probabilistic relationships between pairs or groups of phenomena at these different orders of abstraction; when one choice is made at one level, it has, as its consequence, a highly likely effect on choices relative to the phenomenon to which it is related at the next level.

Take, as an illustrative example, the systems of MOOD, made up of the features 'imperative', 'indicative: declarative' and 'indicative: interrogative', and SPEECH FUNCTION, made up of the features 'command', 'question', 'statement' and 'offer'. These systems – the former a lexicogrammatical one and the latter a semantic one – have a highly regular interaction. For example, the semantic feature of 'question', the demand for linguistic information, is usually formulated grammatically as an 'indicative: interrogative'. But the demand for linguistic information can be expressed by other grammatical means (e.g. 'indicative: declarative': '*It would be nice to know what you are planning for dinner*'; 'imperative': '*Tell me what you are planning for dinner*'). Although evidence for stratification are recurring realizational relationships between phenomena at different strata, by definition these relationships are non-conformal in order to postulate evidence of different strata (Hasan, 1995; Hjelmslev, 1961); cf. grammatical metaphor (e.g. Taverniers, 2004). This, then, is both the nature of and evidence for stratification.

One always has to be cautious in invoking a metaphor in an attempt to explain some phenomenon, relation or the like; in the usual case, the transfer from source to target domain imposes many more potentially misleading connections. Being careful to avoid that scenario, a metaphor which can help us come to an understanding of the stratificational organization of language systems can be found in the outward growth of a tree; looking across a cut tree trunk shows the tree's rings of growth from its earlier to later years, working from the centre outwards. As per the highly regular but non-conformal realizational relation between phenomena at neighbouring language strata, the tree's rings follow a similar, but not exact, shape. This is diagrammatically represented in Figure 6.1.

Figure 6.1: Tree trunk analogy to explain language stratification

As was mentioned in the chapter's introduction, in keeping with the wider collection this chapter is situated in the Hallidayan tradition. Figure 6.2 provides the strata posited according to Systemic Functional theory as relevant to spoken language; for written language, the expression plane is theorized as a single graphological stratum. As is standard practice in the theory, circle size symbolizes abstraction – most abstract phenomena have the largest circle – and that the circles share a tangent indicates that more abstract phenomena contextualize strata of less abstract phenomena.

In the general spirit of the Firthian dictum that linguistics causes language to be 'turned back upon itself' (Firth, 1957: 121), Halliday (1979, 1996) has argued that linguists need suitably account for the property of stratification in the method of linguistic description they develop and subsequently employ in their practice; as Barthes (1977: 87) warned, uni-stratal descriptions fail to fully account for the meaning-making processes in question. Halliday (1979, 1996) proposes that a full account of some language phenomenon requires description along 'trinocular principles' – that is, due

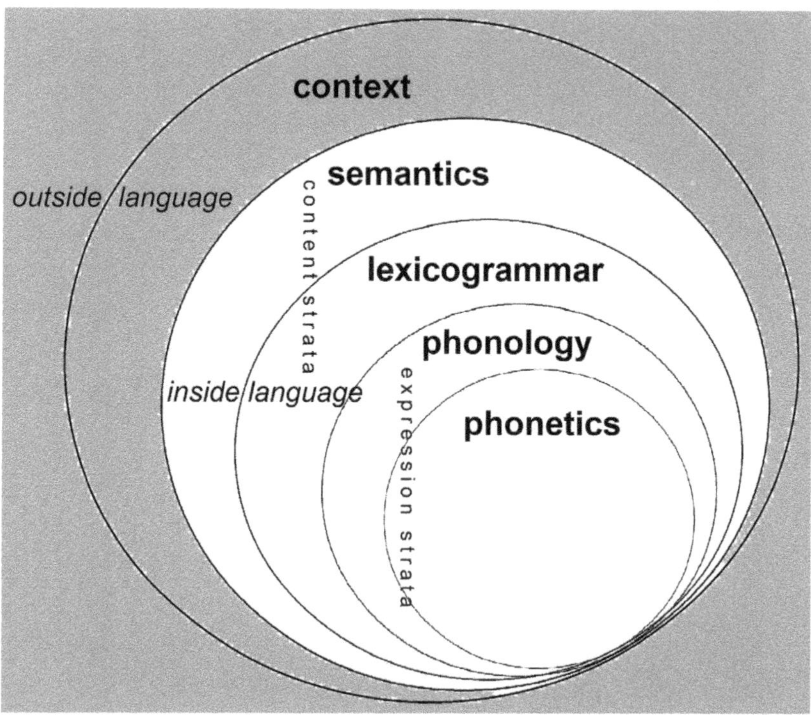

Figure 6.2: Language strata as posited in Systemic Functional theory

consideration of related language phenomenon determined 'from above' and 'from below', not only 'from round about'. Being a lexicogrammatical phenomenon, it is therefore relevant to ask both what meanings do verbs denoting cognition in the present progressive carry and what contextual factors motivate their use. After the next section which offers a diachronic, corpus-based perspective on the discussion 'from round about', the remaining sections of this chapter address the aforementioned semantic and contextual matters in turn, affording greater space to the latter given its lack of discussion in previous academic literature.

6.3 A Diachronic Approach to the Grammar of the Present Progressive with Mental Process-type Verbs

The transitivity framework proposed in Systemic Functional linguistics (Davidse, 1999; Halliday, 1967–68, 1994; Martin *et al.*, 1997: 100–164; Matthiessen, 1995: 187–380, etc.) is a semanticized approach to transitivity;

counter the 'syntax-semantics overlap' of more formal traditions (Katz and Fodor, 1963; Lyons, 1963; etc.), the Systemic Functional approach to transitivity posits that groupings based on the semantics of the verb inherently correspond with grammatical characteristics (cf. Whorf's [1956] 'reactances'). Only material (e.g. *he* ***passed*** *her*$_1$ *the list he had been looking at when she entered*$_2$)[3] and verbal (e.g. *They should* ***ask*** *two academic referees*$_1$ *to recommend them*$_2$) processes, for example, can have two grammatical Objects; mental and relational ones cannot.[4] Similarly, the possibility for the verb to 'project' – have an Object which has the form of an embedded clause, put in more traditional terms – is specific to mental (e.g. *many people still* ***believe*** *that a measure of spirits contains more alcohol than a glass of beer*) and verbal (e.g. *we'd like to* **tell** *you that this time next year you'll be Grandma and Grandpa*) process types, and is said to be impossible with material and relational ones.[5]

Table 6.1: Process-type Classification in Systemic Functional Linguistics

	Can the verb have an embedded clause as an Object?		
Can the verb have two Objects?	VERBAL I told *him*$_1$ ***I would meet him later***$_2$	MATERIAL John baked *me*$_1$ *a cake*$_2$	*yes*
	MENTAL He knew **I would meet him later**	RELATIONAL Tim is really kind	no
	Yes	No	

Theoretically, these two grammatical alternations alone allow for the cross-classification of the four primary process types (see Table 6.1), although one should offer as much evidence in support of her or his analysis as s/he can feasibly provide. Indeed, there are many other grammatical distinctions on which the Systemic Functional process-type typology is based (see Bartlett, 2014: 44–91; Fawcett, 2008: 136–149, forthcoming; Halliday, 1994: 173; Martin *et al.*, 1997: 100–164). One such further example is the unmarked present tense form of the verb phrase. For material and verbal processes, this is the progressive but it is the simple present for mental and relational processes (Bache, 2008: 36–39; Bartlett, 2014: 82; Martin *et al.*, 1997: 118); hence, with the following examples:

> *I think I missed you out* not *I am thinking I missed you out*;
>
> and
>
> *He appears confident and competent* not *He is appearing confident and competent.*

This is yet more apparent in the negative (e.g. *I do not think I missed you out* not *I am not thinking I missed you out*) and interrogative (e.g. *Does he appear confident and competent?* not *Is he appearing confident and competent?*) clause equivalents.

These general grammatical tendencies are revealed by sampling from the *British National Corpus* using the *Sketch Engine* interface (Kilgarriff *et al.*, 2014) 15 instances of 'hope', one of the two case study verbs of this chapter (see below this section), in the present tense:

[...] Busacher began to	**hope** again.
I	**hope** that many more in Hampshire and, indeed, throughout the country will follow [...]
I	**hope** you'll forgive the little deceptions I've practised on you.
we just	**hope** no-one was missed.
His sister Charlotte,	**hoping** these efforts were not in vain, wrote to a friend: `I myself, with painful
She continued clapping as long as she could,	**hoping** he'd asked her to stay.
but the 26-year-old from Hull still	**hopes** to compete in January's Commonwealth Games
I	**hope** you agree that we should show our gratitude for God's gifts in a concrete way [...]
[...] but later	**hopes** to be allowed to write an account of Elizabeth I's reign, with access to the papers
[...] until she turned the corner,	**hoping** that image would be the last she would ever have of him. Chapter Nineteen
Oh I	**hope** whoever was involved in that accident tonight was alright. Yeah so do I.
[...] and as soon as we are able to do so,	**hope** to return to that work.
the French Ocean Research Institute (FORI)	**hope** to find the wreck of his P-38 Lightning [...]
Isabella and Mortimer could scarcely	**hope** to survive long in power
Still, IBM is undeterred and	**hopes** to launch its first pen-based computer some time this quarter.

Figure 6.3: Fifteen instances of 'hope' in the present tense drawn from the British National Corpus

These instances reveal the potential of 'hope' to have an embedded clause as Object (and so be either a mental or verbal process-type) with 14 of the 15 examples attesting such an Object (e.g. *many more in Hampshire [...] will follow*, *you'll forgive the little deceptions I've practised on you*, *no-one was missed, these efforts were not in vain*, etc.). In contrast, there are no instances of 'hope' here with a second Object, which suggests it does not have the potential to be di-transitive (and so is either a mental or relational process-type). Only three of the 15 instances are in the progressive, all of which are when 'hope' is the verb of a sub-ordinating or embedded – rather than main – clause; this suggests 'hope's' unmarked present tense form is the simple present (and so it is either a mental or relational process-type). In sum, there are strong grounds to confidently analyse 'hope' as a mental process-type verb, a verb of cognition as referred to in the introduction and §2.[6]

Given that language systems are living, dynamic systems constantly in flux (Lemke, 1984), today's grammatical distinction might not be so useful in the practice of process-type dis-ambiguation tomorrow. A number of scholars (e.g. Levin, 2013; Mair and Hundt, 1995; Smith, 2002; Smitterberg, 2005 etc.) have provided a strong empirical case that verbs of cognition – mental process-type verbs in Systemic Functional terms; 'private' verbs for Leech (1987, 2004) and colleagues (e.g. Quirk *et al.*, 1985) – are used in the present progressive with increasing frequency. Their observations give reason to suggest that the usefulness of the 'unmarked present tense form' grammatical alternation for process-type distinction might at some point in the future be susceptible to eradication. In a similar way to the afore-mentioned studies, Clarke (unpublished, a), working in a Systemic Functional tradition, conducts a diachronic corpus study of the use of mental process verbs 'hope' and 'hear' in *The Corpus of Historical American English* (*CoHAE*), a 400 million word corpus of a range of popular text genres of American English from the early nineteenth century to the present day (Davies, 2012). *CoHAE*'s decade sub-corpus structure makes it possible to chart the use of 'hope' and 'hear' in the present progressive from the 1810s to the first decade of the twenty-first century (Davies, 2012); see Table 6.2 and Table 6.3.

Table 6.2: Present Tense Progressive with 'hope' in *CoHAE*

Sub-corpus	Proportional frequency (instances per 1 million words)
1810s	0.00
1820s	0.00
1830s	0.44
1840s	0.06
1850s	0.25
1860s	0.35

1870s	0.21
1880s	0.43
1890s	0.85
1900s	0.93
1910s	1.77
1920s	2.15
1930s	2.17
1940s	1.86
1950s	2.46
1960s	2.84
1970s	2.90
1980s	4.57
1990s	5.81
2000s	7.06

Table 6.3: Present Tense Progressive with 'hear' in *CoHAE*

Sub-corpus	Proportional frequency (instances per 1 million words)
1810s	0.00
1820s	0.29
1830s	0.07
1840s	0.06
1850s	0.25
1860s	0.12
1870s	0.27
1880s	0.10
1890s	0.33
1900s	0.40
1910s	0.66
1920s	0.66
1930s	1.02
1940s	1.16
1950s	1.56
1960s	1.46
1970s	2.40
1980s	2.07
1990s	2.65
2000s	2.82

As can be seen from Table 6.2 and Table 6.3, both case study verbs increase in use with the present progressive in *CoHAE*, increasingly so as time moves towards the present day. Before the turn of the twentieth century the construction is infrequent with both 'hope' and 'hear'. Based on the proportional calculations, however, its use has increased nearly ten-fold ('hope') and seven-fold ('hear') between then and the start of the twenty-first century.[7] The consistent nature of this increase, i.e. between neighbouring decade sub-corpora, is apparent with 'hope' (15 increases and three decreases moving through time towards the present day) but somewhat less so with 'hear' (12 increases and six decreases). The most marked jump in increased use between decades for both verbs involves the 1970s; this point will be returned to and discussed at greater length in §5.

Such evidence as the above provides support to the argument that where previously the present progressive construction had not typically associated with mental process-type verbs, this is less so the case. Moreover, the evidence is not limited to 'hope' and 'hear'; Levin (2013: 203–208) alone, for example, finds that 'expect', 'feel', 'think' and 'wonder', all of which would in Systemic Functional terms be classified as mental process-type verbs, increase in use in the progressive relatively steadily during the twentieth century in the 100 million word American English *TIME magazine* corpus. This trend therefore appears to be true of the mental process-type category generally, rather than particular to a few members from the category. With the claim that the present progressive is increasingly used with verbs denoting cognitive activity, the next section considers if this apparent diachronic change is motivated on semantic grounds; in other words, could it be that verbs of cognition in the present progressive are subservient in communicating some meaning, possibly one which has become focal in more recent times and societies where before then the same meaning was irrelevant or of limited value (cf. §5)? The section starts by briefly considering some of the semantic explanations offered in previous academic literature before putting an empirically-informed argument that these accounts need supplementing if all instances of the emergent present progressive with mental process-type verbs are to be sufficiently explained.

6.4 Up to Semantic Explanations for the Present Progressive with Mental Process-type Verbs

Of those studies referred to in the last section which provide evidence for the diachronically increased use of the present progressive with verbs of cognition, comparatively little has been said regarding the semantic motives for the trend. As Levin (2013: 191) remarks '[b]ecause the progressive appears to be undergoing continual change, it is difficult to define the meanings and connotations at any given point in time, let alone across time periods'. Mindt (2000), whose own corpus study of progressives is a synchronic one of present day English, has suggested that the present progressive is used with verbs of cognition to construe INCOMPLETENESS and TEMPORARINESS as meanings closely akin to that which the construction typically carries when used with the so-called dynamic verbs – material and verbal ones, in Systemic Functional terms (see §3) – with which it traditionally associates (cf. Davidse, 1999: 291). Yet Quirk *et al.*, (1985: 200–202) claim that the use of the progressive with verbs of cognition usually indexes a particular or special meaning above and beyond its semantic value when used with the dynamic verbs. Leech (2004: 26, 29–30) has claimed that some instances of the present progressive with verbs denoting cognition – 'private verbs', in his terms – such as the following[8] are not sufficiently explained by Mindt's (2000) INCOMPLETENESS and TEMPORARINESS meanings.

> I realise this is a real long-shot but I'**m hoping** you can help me. I'm looking for information on a pit accident which happened in the Doncaster/Conisbrough area of Yorkshire in (I think) 1954.
> I would like to report spam sent to me through this website. I **am hoping** that you will be able to block this or somehow stop it from happening again.
> I'm not sure I am the ideal contender for SCUBA diving but I **am hoping** you could give your opinion to settle the matter. I would be very grateful for your input.

Rather, so speculates Leech (2004: 26, 29–30), the present progressive is motivated in such instances by a desire to mitigate interpersonal pressures (cf. Brown and Levinson, 1987). Cases of the present progressive with mental process-type verbs which construe this semantic generalization typically have 'you' as the Subject of an embedded clause Object (see §3). In addition, there is often some expression of deontic modality relating to the state-of-affairs expressed in the embedded clause (e.g. *can, will …able to, could*) usually relative to some proposal for action (e.g. *help me, block this or somehow stop it from happening, give your opinion*); these tendencies are seen in all of the above examples.

Clarke (unpublished, a) in turn points to instances of the use of the present progressive with mental process-type verbs such as the following, arguing that the meaning construed by them is neither one of INCOMPLETENESS/TEMPORARINESS (Mindt, 2000) nor the special (Quirk *et al.*, 1985: 200–202) TENTATIVENESS meaning referred to by Leech (2004) and colleagues (e.g. Levin, 2013).

> Jules Verne inspired generations of travellers and explorers with his great Victorian novel *Around the World in 80 days*. Now, Horsham Museum **is hoping** to create the same sense of wonderment, awe and fascination with a stunning new costume display "Around the World in 18 Costumes".
> The Farewell brooches are due in stock this week, and they also **are hoping** that they will send the first batch sometime this week, but no promises!
> I bought a 0.5 tog off the internet and it arrive [*sic*] yesterday. Kian slept in it last night with just a nappy and he slept until 7.00am (normally awake at 5.50am). I **am hoping** this is a new trend.
> Now Mark **is hoping** to launch an innovative new lighting range in the autumn.

Instead, Clarke (unpublished, a) suggests that language users adopt the marked present progressive form for such clauses with mental process-type verbs so as to emphatically represent events under discussion as current in the here and now. As evidence, he provides the typical collocational behaviour of the construction with his case study verbs 'hope' and 'hear', following Hunston's (2002: 71–72) suggestion to recognize as having a significant relationship with the search term in question only those collocates with both a t-score greater than 2 and an MI-score in excess of 3. Prominent within such collocational profiles are words which index currency or 'present-ness', whether defined congruently as time (e.g. 'new': *they are hoping to have a* ***new*** *catalogue live as early as September*; 'now': *the College is* ***now*** *hoping to open the new facility in October 2006*; 'moment': *There are a limited number of discounts available at the* ***moment*** *and we are hoping to add to these*; etc.) or metaphorically in spatial or pseudo-spatial terms (e.g. 'here': *I am sitting* ***here*** *in my office hoping that someone said goodnight to you*; 'this': ***This*** *club is hoping to get back into the Premiership*; etc.). Table 6.4 below gives the top time collocates of 'hope' in the present progressive in *UKWaC*.

Table 6.4: Currency Collocates for '<BE-present> hoping that' in *UKWaC*

	Freq.	T-score	MI				
this	322	17.380	4.992	*continued from 'just'...*			
new	100	9.648	4.828	last	22	4.393	3.981
here	79	8.854	8.007	even	21	4.268	3.866
next	59	7.548	5.854	again	20	4.267	4.449
here	56	7.280	5.200	future	19	4.191	4.702
time	51	6.625	3.790	once	18	4.108	4.981
these	42	6.072	3.988	start	16	3.831	4.568

now	38	5.789	4.037	week	13	3.402	4.147
years	30	5.061	3.718	still	13	3.237	3.292
day	29	5.092	4.197	really	12	3.190	3.660
soon	29	5.306	6.081	continue	12	3.347	4.892
season	27	5.130	6.287	moment	11	3.234	5.324
first	24	4.336	3.120	recent	11	3.176	4.557
become	24	4.752	5.060	only	11	2.416	1.881
just	22	4.208	3.281	release	11	3.244	5.512

As corpus lexicographers and lexicologists (e.g. Moon, 1987; Stubbs, 1993) will be acutely aware, different meaning senses are often characterized by different typical lexicogrammatical characteristics. These, then, can serve as a further form of support in postulating a sense distinction. In this respect, it is worth noting that, in contrast to the TENTATIVENESS meaning (Leech, 2004), the sense seemingly in operation here typically has a non-modalized embedded clause with a Subject varied in terms of its person reference including inanimate references (e.g. *they*, *this*). In addition, the process type of the embedded clause is typically 'material: effective: creative' (e.g. *create*, *launch*) (Halliday, 1994; Matthiessen, 1995) or more infrequently 'relational' (e.g. ...*is a new trend*).

There is significantly greater complexity relative to the semantics of the present progressive with verbs of cognition than can be afforded, for reasons of space, to the discussion in this chapter. Mindt (2000) alone, for example, postulates nine different meaning senses for the progressive in his corpus-driven study. None, however, are tantamount to the CURRENCY sense just discussed; nor does any published discussion of the present progressive with verbs of cognition refer to such a sense. As such, this chapter's final section – a discussion of the potential contextual motives for the increased use of the present progressive with verbs of cognition (see §3) – is concerned only with this CURRENCY semantic sense of the construction.

6.5 Up, Up and Away: A Speculative Contextual Explanation for the Increased Use of the Present Progressive with Mental Process-type Verbs

If the charted diachronic use of the present progressive with mental process-type verbs 'hope' and 'here' in *CoHAE* (see Table 6.2 and Table 6.3 in §3) is represented graphically – see Figure 6.4 and Figure 6.5 – one particularly apparent observation is that the period between the 1960s and 1980s appears to be important; both verbs in this construction show a spiked rise in proportional frequency of use during this period, the most statistically significant jump in increased proportional use between any two decades in the *CoHAE* data with a 63.5% increase in use with 'hope' between the 1970s (2.90 instances per million words) and the 1980s (4.57 instances per million words) and a 60.8% increase with 'hear' between the 1960s (1.46 instances per million words) and the 1970s (2.40 instances per million word).

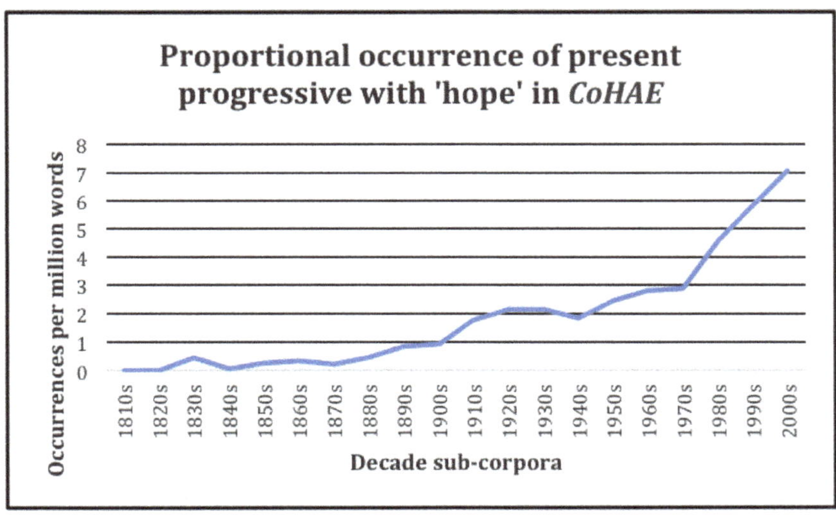

Figure 6.4: Present tense progressive with 'hope' in *CoHAE*

Amongst others, Levin (2013: 203–208) reports a similar pattern with the mental process-type (cf. §3) verbs 'expect', 'feel', 'think' and 'wonder'. In addition to the case study verbs of the present chapter, this provides a fair amount of evidence to suggest that the pattern is not just one of chance.

One plausible motive for this particularly notable upwards trend in the use of mental process-type verbs in the present progressive construction at some point during this 1960s–1980s period is the induction of the first around-the-clock, 24-hour live news media. Keeping in mind that the trends of Table 6.2 and Table 6.3 and corresponding Figure 6.4 and Figure 6.5 are from *CoHAE* – a historical corpus of American English, the first such 24-hour live news television channel was CNN, introduced in the United States of America and first aired on 1st June 1980 (Johnson and Silvia, 2001: 45). Further such channels shortly followed. In the United Kingdom, Sky News was the first around-the-clock live news channel, airing on 5th February 1989.

Why the introduction of around-the-clock live news media may – at least in part – be a plausible explanation for this diachronic change of the

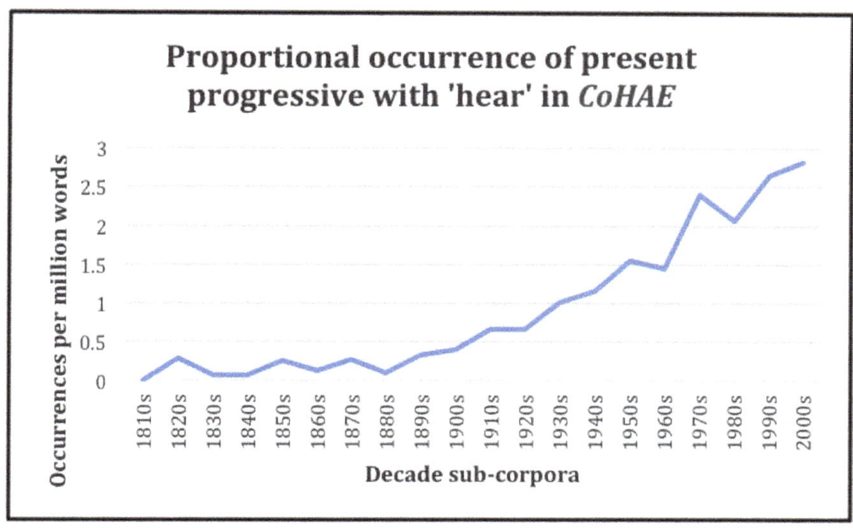

Figure 6.5: Present tense progressive with 'hear' in *CoHAE*

increased use of the present progressive with mental process-type verbs owes to the new opportunities consequently afforded to such news outlets; such technological advances have allowed them to further attend to the 'recency' value of newsworthiness, the value attached to reporting events very soon after their occurrence (Bell, 1991; Galtung and Ruge, 1965). Bell (2007) argues that fundamentally the same sort of change to the production of news was brought about by the induction of the telegraph. As he (Bell, 2007: 79) puts it in relation to the introduction of the telegraph, '[i]t established the era in which news and news work assumed its modern pattern: a quest to get the story first, before one's competitors'; not only is it a matter of technological advances like the 24-hour live platform and the telegraph affording opportunities to media organizations; at the same time, there are increased expectations to relay news stories more quickly; this situation itself likely caused in significant part by the increasing commercialization of the media and their activities (Fairclough, 1992: 109–110). As such, above and beyond actually being first is the matter of being seen to be first. Given the dialectic relationship between language and society (Fairclough, 1995: 54–55; Halliday, 1978), this is where linguistic forms such as the construction under discussion in this chapter serve a valuable purpose.

One might ask if there is any evidence to support this argument. On the basis of seemingly good logic, it could be proposed that what is needed is to work backwards from the *UKWaC* corpus output referred to above, locating the source of each text found to contain an instance of the present progressive with a mental process-type verb; text types would be noted, all the while being alert to any text-types which recurrently engender instances of the phenomenon. One could even be pseudo-scientific in the procedure by adopting a pre-existing text-type classification. The most convincing evidence for the aforementioned argument would be the return of an above chance number of instances of present progressives with mental process-type verbs in a 'news' text type. Yet this would be to advance an analysis on the basis of language-external criteria, which would be little more than to use one's common sense. How, for one thing, are 'news' texts intuitively knowable as such? Given that the corpus data in question is comprised of web-based texts, are only texts belonging to a web domain of one of the known media organizations (e.g. BBC, *The Guardian*, bSkyb, etc.) to be included in 'news'? What happens to the text which resides on, say, a charitable organization's website but is listed on their 'news' page; is this 'news' enough, or should it be excluded from a 'news' text-type? Conversely, might websites belonging to big media organizations not contain other sorts of texts – say legal terms and conditions; would it be desirable to consider such data as 'news'? Linguistics need offer more in the way of scientific method than all this implies (cf. Hasan, 2009).

The alternative approach, adopted here, is to work 'bottom-up', privileging language patterns as a determinant of text-type (Biber, 1988; Williams, 2002). The particular method for doing so in this chapter is to create a corpus which consists of the entire language of each and any text in *UKWaC* containing one or more[9] instance of the present progressive with one of the chapter's case study verbs, 'hear', comparing the language observed in this consequent BE-*hearing* corpus (8.8 million words in size) with the whole of the *UKWaC* (approximately 1.5 billion words in size, see endnote 7) as a general reference corpus and *GB-News* (a 217.3 million words corpus of news stories from the British broadsheet newspapers *The Guardian, The Observer, The Independent, The Telegraph and The Times*, circa 2004) as a news-specific reference corpus. Limits on space preclude any detailed analysis and subsequent discussion of this data (see Clarke unpublished, b for a more in depth discussion). For present purposes, limiting a consideration of language patterns only to what is revealed by a lemma-frequency-list still reveals some support for the argument that the introduction of 24-hour news media may explain the diachronic increase in use of the present progressive with mental process-type verbs. Table 6.5 below reveals the 30 most frequent lemmas for each of the three aforementioned corpora, providing their frequency as a measure 'per million word' (PMW) to aid comparability between them.

Table 6.5: Most Frequent Lemmas in *BE-hearing, GB-News* and *UKWaC* Corpora

RANK		BE-hearing			GB-News			UKWaC	
		PMW			PMW			PMW	
1		*the*	49146.24		*the*	51483.07		*the*	52056.55
2		*be*	41500.86		*be*	32612.55		*be*	31484.42
3		*to*	24462.66		*of*	23305.37		*of*	26483.77
4		*and*	24020.81		*to*	23003.40		*and*	25650.49
5		*of*	23373.72		*a*	21696.98		*to*	23196.76
6		*a*	16564.99		*and*	20185.60		*a*	18220.26
7		*in*	15832.38		*in*	16813.68		*in*	16252.82
8		*that*	15096.92		*have*	11892.03		*for*	9216.70
9		*you*	11205.82		*that*	9402.79		*have*	8660.51
10		*it*	11104.62		*for*	8258.08		*that*	7642.02
11		*have*	10809.58		*it*	8041.92		*on*	6797.42
12		*i*	9238.88		*on*	6563.82		*it*	6278.35
13		*not*	7920.46		*he*	6126.84		*with*	6178.67
14		*we*	7068.13		*with*	6104.70		*as*	5421.14
15		*do*	6807.29		*as*	5638.22		*this*	4840.18
16		*for*	6527.93		*not*	5410.45		*you*	4723.35
17		*on*	6396.80		*i*	5328.94		*i*	4617.75
18		*he*	6144.52		*at*	5030.70		*by*	4587.47
19		*with*	5372.00		*his*	4811.61		*at*	4434.40
20		*this*	5285.06		*but*	4574.99		*from*	4067.04
21		*they*	5212.37		*by*	4504.32		*or*	3689.00
22		*say*	4913.05		*from*	4150.01		*will*	3438.80
23		*as*	4692.13		*say*	3956.43		*we*	3339.14
24		*will*	4459.80		*do*	3462.70		*not*	3244.00
25		*but*	4203.25		*this*	3322.79		*an*	3140.65
26		*at*	3219.78		*they*	3317.22		*do*	3037.01
27		*his*	3252.56		*an*	3273.64		*but*	2675.12
28		*all*	3185.57		*will*	2981.41		*which*	2655.23
29		*what*	3064.42		*you*	2904.86		*they*	2467.56
30		*from*	3043.04		*we*	2700.37		*can*	2434.79

Although such a limited snapshot only shows generalized, typically grammaticized trends, the lemma-frequency-lists show a number of similarities between the language of the BE-*hearing* and *GB-News* corpora, which are not shared characteristics of the wider *UKWaC* corpus. Two such patterns are particularly relevant in the context of the current discussion, hinting at evidence of the news values of 'attribution' (quoted comment from elite sources) and 'eliteness' (reported events denote the actions of elite sources; cf. 'attribution') in the BE-*hearing* and *GB-News* corpora (Bell, 1991; Galtung and Ruge, 1965). In relation to the former, both BE-*hearing* (4913.05 times PMW, ranked 22nd) and *GB-News* (3956.43 times PMW, ranked 23rd) corpora lemma-lists have 'say' as their most frequent lexical verb, whereas this is far less frequent in *UKWaC* (ranked 58th, occurring 1296.27 times PMW) with 'use' (2005.39 times PMW), 'make' (1835.63 times PMW) and 'take' (1402.48 times PMW) more frequent lexical verbs in this corpus. In related connection to the news value of 'eliteness', it is notable that both 'he' and 'his' occur in the top 30 lemmas for both the BE-*hearing* ('he' ranked 18th occurring 6144.52 times PMW; 'his' ranked 27th occurring 3252.56 times PMW) and *GB-News* corpora ('he' ranked 13th occurring 6126.84 times PMW; 'his' ranked 19th occurring 4811.61 times PMW) but are ranked 32nd (2348.85 times PMW) and 38th (1891.72 times PMW) respectively in *UKWaC*. Despite many positive policy shifts relative to women's equality, the cultural – including discourse – reality sadly lags somewhat behind, with male elite actors dominating both the BE-*hearing* and *GB-News* corpora.

6.6 Conclusion

This chapter hopes to have added to the academic discussion regarding the progressive construction in English, particularly its increased use across time and its movement into new territory in terms of its use with verbs of cognition with which it has not traditionally associated (Leech, 2004: 25–27; Quirk *et al.*, 1985: 200–205; Palmer, 1965). A central aim of the chapter was to put the case for a previously undiscussed semantic generalization for the present progressive when used with such verbs as the aforementioned group; that is, to help construe the events under discussion as emphatically current in the here and now. Further, a tentative case has been put for changes to news production, particularly the increased potential to cater for – and subsequent demand of – attendance to recency news values as a contextual explanation for the phenomenon. At a theoretical level, it is hoped that a Systemic Functional contribution to the literature on the progressive in English has demonstrated what a stratificational and functional approach can offer in terms of linguistic method and description.

About the author

Ben Clarke is a Lecturer in English Language and Linguistics at the University of Portsmouth, UK. His research interests include functional descriptions of language and grammar, the relationship between language and semiotic context, and multimodality – particularly the relationship between language and embodied forms of communication.

Endnotes

1. Throughout this chapter, I use the terms 'stratum'/'strata' and 'level(s)' interchangeably. Doing so is in keeping with how the terms have been used in mainstream literature within Systemic Functional Linguistics.
2. I would like to thank Margaret Berry, whose comments on a related paper, delivered at the 24th European Systemic Functional Linguistics Conference and Workshop at Coventry University in July 2013, contributed to the genesis of the ideas presented in §5 here. This is not, of course, to say that Margaret would necessarily agree with how I have developed these ideas. I am also grateful to Serge Sharoff for kindly making available to me lemma and n-grams lists for the GB News Corpus referred to in §5.
3. Unless otherwise stated, examples in this chapter are drawn from the *British National Corpus* (BNC Consortium, 2007) using the Sketch Engine interface (Kilgarriff *et al.*, 2014).
4. Note that in this chapter I follow Matthiessen (1995) in recognizing four primary process types, treating Halliday's (1994) 'behavioural' type as a sub-class of 'material' and his 'existential' as a sub-type of 'relational'.
5. It should be acknowledged that characteristics here being assigned to one or other process-type category are descriptive generalizations; in the practice of authentic text analysis, it is not rare to find clauses whose instantiated lexicogrammatical features do not neatly fit one process-type category in the way these are being described at this point in the main text. Such examples instead reveal that process-type distinctions actually have many fuzzy boundaries. Even the small number of corpus examples of 'hope' in Figure 6.3 demonstrate this.
6. At this point, it is important to clarify a note on terminology. In the Introduction and in §1, reference has been made to 'verbs of cognition', 'verbs denoting cognitive experience', etc. Throughout this chapter, such labels are intended to refer to Halliday's (1967–68; 1994) 'mental process-type' verbs generally, not only the sub-type of these which, unfortunately for my present purposes, Systemic Functional scholars refer to as 'cognitive' ones (e.g. Matthiessen, 1995: 263–265, cf. 'perceptive', 'desiderative' and 'emotive' sub-types of mental process-type verbs). The reason for mention of 'verbs of cognition' (and the like) in this way is because some non-systemic literature (e.g. Palmer, 1965: 95–97; Leech, 2004: 25–27, etc.) often means by such labels what Systemic Functional Linguistics groups as 'mental process-type' verbs generally (including, but not

limited to the 'cognitive' sub-type of mental process-type verbs).

7. It is worth noting that, at a frequency of use of 7.90 times per million words, the present progressive with 'hope' in the synchronic circa 2007 *UKWaC* corpus (see endnote 8 for more details on this corpus) is closely aligned to its use in the 2000–2010 decade sub-corpus of *CoHAE* (7.09). The use of present progressive 'hear' (1.90 times per million words) in *UKWaC* is significantly less frequent than its use in the 2000–2010 decade sub-corpus of *CoHAE* (2.82).
8. All illustrative examples in the present section are from the *UK Web as Corpus* (*UKWaC*), an approximately 1.5 billion word corpus with data drawn from .uk web domains circa 2007 (Ferraresi *et al.*, 2008).
9. Any text in *UKWaC* containing multiple instances of the present progressive with 'hear' is only included in the corpus once.

References

Bache, C. (2008) English Tense and Aspect in Halliday's Systemic Functional Grammar: A Critical Appraisal and an Alternative. London: Equinox Publishing.

Barthes, R. (1977) *Image, Music, Text*. London: Fontana Press.

Bartlett, T. (2014) Analysing Power in Language: A Practical Guide. London: Routledge.

Bell, A. (2007) Text, Time and Technology in News English. In S. Goodman, D. Graddol and T. Lillis (eds) *Redesigning English*, 79–105. Oxford: Routledge.

Bell, A. (1991) *The Language of News Media*. Oxford: Wiley-Blackwell.

Biber, D. (1988) *Variation across Speech and Writing*. Cambridge: Cambridge University Press.

BNC Consortium (2007) *The British National Corpus. Version 3* (BNC XML Edition) (Distributed by Oxford University Computing Services) [online] available from <http://www.natcorp.ox.ac.uk/>.

Brown, P. and Levinson, S. C. (1987) *Politeness: Some Universals in Language Usage*. Cambridge: Cambridge University Press.

Clarke, B. P. (unpublished a) Fast Food Grammar: A New Semantic Sense of the Present Progressive with Verbs of Cognition.

Clarke, B. P. (unpublished b) The Increased Use of the Present Progressive with Verbs of Cognition in the Language of News: Support from Corpus Trends.

Crystal, D. (1997) *The Cambridge Encyclopaedia of Language*. 2nd edn. Cambridge: Cambridge University Press.

Davidse, K. (1999) *Categories of Experiential Grammar*. Nottingham: Monographs in Systemic Linguistics.

Davies, M. (2012) Expanding Horizons in Historical Linguistics with the 400-Million Word Corpus of Historical American English. *Corpora* 7(2): 121–157.

Fairclough, N. (1995) *Media Discourse*. London: Edward Arnold.

Fairclough, N. (1992) *Discourse and Social Change*. Cambridge: Polity Press.

Fawcett, R. P. (forthcoming) The Functional Semantics Handbook: Analysing English at the Level of Meaning. London: Equinox Publishing.

Fawcett, R. P. (2008) Invitation to Systemic Functional Linguistics: *The Cardiff*

Grammar as an Extension and Simplification of Halliday's Systemic Functional Grammar. 3rd edn. London: Equinox Publishing.

Ferraresi, A., Zanchetta, E., Baroni, M. and Bernardini, S. (2008) 'Introducing and evaluating ukWaC, a very large web-derived corpus of English'. In S. Evert, A. Kilgarriff and S. Sharoff (eds.) *Proceedings of the 4th Web as Corpus Workshop (WAC-4) – Can we beat Google?*, Marrakech, 1 June 2008.

Firth, J. R. (1957) *Papers in Linguistics, 1934–1951*. Oxford: Oxford University Press.

Galtung, J. and Ruge, M. H. (1965) The Structure of Foreign News. *Journal of Peace Research* 2 (1): 64–91.

Halliday, M. A. K. (1967–68) Notes on Transitivity and Theme in English, Parts 1-3. *Journal of Linguistics* 3(1): 37–81; 3(2): 199–244; 4(2): 179–215.

Halliday, M. A. K. (1978) Language as Social Semiotic: The Social Interpretation of Language and Meaning. London: Arnold.

Halliday, M. A. K. (1979) Modes of Meaning and Modes of Expression: Types of Grammatical Structure, and their Determination by Different Semantic Functions. In D. J. Allerton, E. Carney and D. Holdcroft (eds) *Function and Context in Linguistic Analysis: Essays Offered to William Haas*, 57–79. London: Cambridge University Press.

Halliday, M. A. K. (1985) Systemic Background. In J. D. Benson and W. S. Greaves (eds) *Systemic Perspectives on Discourse*, 1–15. Norwood, NJ: Ablex.

Halliday, M. A. K. (1993) Systemic Theory. In R. E. Asher (ed.) *The Encyclopedia of Language and Linguistics*, 4505–4508. Oxford: Pergamon Press.

Halliday, M. A. K. (1994) *An Introduction to Functional Grammar*. 2nd edn. London and Melbourne: Arnold.

Halliday, M. A. K. (1996) On Grammar and Grammatics. In R. Hasan, C. Cloran and D. G. Butt (eds) *Functional Descriptions: Theory in Practice*, 1–38. Amsterdam: John Benjamins.

Halliday, M. A. K. and Hasan, R. (1985) Language, Context, and Text: Aspects of Language in a Social-Semiotic Perspective. Geelong: Deakin University.

Hasan, R. (1995) The Conception of Context in Text. In P. H. Fries, and M. Gregory (eds) *Discourse in Society: Systemic Functional Perspectives*, 183–283. London: Edward Arnold.

Hasan, R. (2009) The Place of Context in a Systemic Functional Model. In M. A. K. Halliday, and J. Webster (eds) *Continuum Companion to Systemic Functional Linguistics*, 166–189. London: Continuum.

Hjelmslev, L. (1961) *Prolegomena to a Theory of Language*, trans. F. J. Whitfield. Madison, WI: University of Wisconsin Press.

Hunston, S. (2002) *Corpora in Applied Linguistics*. Cambridge: Cambridge University Press.

Johnson, T. and Silvia, T. (2001) CNN: The Origins of the 24-Hour International News Cycle. In T. Silvia (ed.) *Global News: Perspectives on the Information Age*. Iowa City, IA: Iowa State University Press.

Katz, J. J. and Fodor, J. A. (1963) 'The Structure of a Semantic Theory'. *Language* 39, 170–210.

Kilgarriff, A., Baisa, V., Bušta, J., Jakubíček, M., Kovář, V., Michelfeit, J., Rychlý, P., and Suchomel, V. (2014) The Sketch Engine: Ten Years on. *Lexicography* 1: 1–30.

Leech, G. (1987) *Meaning and the English Verb*. 2nd edn. London: Longman.

Leech, G. (2004) *Meaning and the English Verb*. 3rd edn. Harlow: Pearson.

Lemke, J. (1984) *Semiotics and Education*. Toronto: Victoria College/Toronto Semiotic Circle Monographs.
Levin, M. (2013) The Progressive Verb in Modern American English. In B. Aarts, J. Close, G. Leech and S. Wallis (eds) *The Verb Phrase in English: Investigating Recent Language Change with Corpora*, 187–216. Cambridge: Cambridge University Press.
Lyons, J. (1963) Structural Semantics: An Analysis of Part of the Vocabulary of Plato. London: Blackwell.
Mair, C. and Hundt, M. (1995) Why is the Progressive Becoming More Frequent in English? A Corpus-Based Investigation of Language Change in Progress. *Zeitschrift Für Anglistik Und Amerikanistik* 43(2): 111–112.
Martin, J. R., Matthiessen, C. M. I. M., and Painter, C. (1997) *Working with Functional Grammar*. London: Edward Arnold.
Matthiessen, C. M. I. M. (1995) *Lexicogrammatical Cartography: English Systems*. Tokyo: International Language Sciences Publishers.
Mindt, D. (2000) An Empirical Grammar of the English Verb System. Berlin: Cornelsen.
Moon, R. (1987) The Analysis of Meaning. In J. Sinclair (ed.) Looking Up: An Account of the COBUILD Project in Lexical Computing and the Development of the Collins COBUILD English Language Dictionary, 86–103. London: Collins.
Palmer, F. R. (1965) *A Linguistic Study of the English Verb*. London: Longman.
Quirk, R., Greenbaum, S., Svartvik, J., and Leech, G. (1985) *A Comprehensive Grammar of the English Language*. London: Longman.
Smith, N. (2002) Ever Moving On? Changes in the Progressive in Recent British English. In P. Peters, P. Collins and A. Smith (eds) *New Frontiers in Corpus Research*, 317–330. Amsterdam: Rodopi.
Smitterberg, E. (2005) The Progressive in 19th-Century English. A Process of Integration. Amsterdam: Rodopi.
Stubbs, M. (1993) British Traditions in Text Analysis: From Firth to Sinclair. In M. Baker, G. Francis and E. Tognini Bonelli (eds) *Text and Technology: In Honour of John Sinclair*, 1–33. Amsterdam: John Benjamins.
Taverniers, M. (2004) Grammatical Metaphors in English. *Moderna Språk* 98(1): 17–26.
Whorf, B. L. (1956) Grammatical Categories. In J. Carroll (ed.) *Language, Thought and Reality: Selected Writings of Benjamin Lee Whorf*, 87–101. Cambridge, MA: MIT Press.
Williams, G. (2002) In Search of Representativity in Specialised Corpora: Categorisation through Collocation. *International Journal of Corpus Linguistics* 7(1): 43–64.

7 The Construal of Terminal Illness in Online Medical Texts: Social Distance and Semantic Space

Meriel Bloor
University of Warwick

7.1 Introduction: The Digital Surgery

In an international survey, 87% of adults reported that they used the Internet to access health information and 10% of those people posted comments or questions on health websites (BUPA, 2012). It is not likely that there has been any decrease in such figures. One striking factor is that over 40% (49% in the United States) attempt to self-diagnose on the basis of this information without necessarily checking the reliability of the online sources they use (McDaid and Park, 2011). Other people, of course, first see a doctor in person and then turn to the Internet for more information or explanation about their medicine or their illness.

There are many online sites providing health information. Wikipedia is often used for access to information about specific illnesses, and other sites commonly used in Britain are:

- www.patient.co.uk
- www.nhs.uk
- www.macmillan.org.uk (Macmillan Cancer Support)
- www.mayoclinic.com (US)

Specialist medical sites are in the main written by expert medical practitioners, advised and edited in some cases by communication specialists. Unsurprisingly, considering the distinct context and mode of delivery, the communication strategies and even the actual language used on the Internet often differ from that which we find in face to face interaction. In particular, the non-linearity of many of the texts means that readers who follow links from useful introductory pages can find themselves lost in a dense network of incomprehensible discourse. The relatively arbitrary quality of the means of access to websites means that, without specialist advice, we can find ourselves in a community of experts, where meaning is at best elusive and at worst inaccessible.

This chapter is concerned with the lexicogrammar of death and life, focusing on the language used in online medical information on the prognosis of diseases. In it, I summarize some previous work on the language of living and dying, and then address problems the general reader may face when searching online for information about life-threatening illness. I then compare the way such information is transmitted in the traditional patient-doctor consultation, finally raising questions about how social context influences the construal of deeply sensitive human experiences.

7.2 Representations of Pain and Death

Halliday, in his work on the grammar of pain (1998), emphasized the variety of forms available in the language for the construal of pain. Using the first COBUILD corpus, he selected key lexical items (*pain, hurt, ache,* and *sore)* associated with pain and searched for their collocations including the construal of pain as a *thing* (*headache* for example), a *quality* (*sore, tender,* for example), and a *process* (*aches, hurts,* for example).

From this he listed 24 distinct structural expressions of pain, with a variety of processes and participant roles, demonstrating how pain is 'semanticised' into five representational categories: material, relational, existential, mental and verbal. Among other comments, he said, 'what is striking … is how a small number of very frequent words are deployed in such a great variety of different grammatical environments' (1992: 29).

Halliday described pain as being 'a uniquely problematic domain of human experience' and 'the most complex, and at the same time the most threatening, of all domains of human experience' (Halliday and Matthiessen, 1999: 2). Arguably, death is a good competitor for such a description. Death, however, is not as short of lexical items in English as pain, since traditional representations of death and dying in English extend far beyond the obvious use of the key lexical items identified in this section. In fact, it appears that there has been a deliberate attempt to avoid direct reference to death in normal social interaction, which is witnessed in the very many common euphemisms.

Anyone who has seen the Monty Python sketch 'The Dead Parrot' (available on YouTube) will be familiar with the following expressions used to refer to the said parrot: *it's ceased to be; it's deceased; it's retired from life; it's passed on; it's no more; it's gone to meet its maker*. Bultnick (1998) referred to such expressions as 'metaphors we die by', after Lakoff and Johnson's title *Metaphors We Live By* (1980). Other euphemistic expressions commonly replacing the verb *to die* or the noun *death* include *to pass away, to pass* (US), *to be taken from us, to lose one's life,* and many more.

Clearly some of these forms operate in specific domains, such as religious ceremonies and hymns, literary contexts or informal conversation and few of them ever appear in medical discourse. However, online digital reference to death is frequently no more direct. It is simply that alternative genres have their own distinct ways of construing what they often euphemistically refer to as *the end of life*.

Fernandez (2006) in his article on 'The language of death' reported on conceptual metaphors in references to death in Victorian obituaries. He saw euphemisms as a reaction to a death taboo in the societal framework and explained religious references as a means of relief and hope offering consolation to the living. Most of his examples have survived into the twenty-first century at least in religious contexts. He categorized his data into six groups, each with their own set of metaphors: death as a journey, a joyful life, a rest, a reward, a loss, and an end (of pain), some of which overlap (for example, *going to eternal happiness; leaving this vale of tears; being carried away from pain and care*).

A team at Lancaster University currently researching the use of metaphor in end of life care have also recorded the journey metaphor as one in use to describe living through the final stages of terminal illness. They contrast this with what they term *battle metaphors*, which present terminal cancer, for example, as a struggle where patients may see themselves fighting for life (Semino, 2010).[1]

In his article on the grammar of pain, Halliday draws our attention to the diversity of the grammatical environments in which different forms occur. He also mentions that the grammatical forms are, from one point of view, grammatical metaphors of each other, 'but that the metaphors are so deeply encrypted that no one seems more or less congruent than any other' (1998: 29). Yet the data of pain and death that we have looked at so far in this chaptergo only part way to the metaphorical complexity of medical discourse in its specialized form or even in the semi-popular form that we find in many online articles for the general reader.

7.3 Online Medical Information as Scientific Text

As far as grammatical features are concerned, medical information on the Internet often falls into the category of scientific text as described by Halliday and Martin (1993 and elsewhere). Thus we find:

- A high lexical density.
- A predominance of grammatical metaphor.
- A low frequency of personal reference.
- Relatively long or complex nominal groups.

But, as Gledhill (2000: 65), in his work on collocations in science writing, points out, the nature of scientific texts does not depend simply on individual linguistic features, which may appear in other genres and text types, but on the way their underlying meanings are 'extended and modified' by their use in specialist contexts. Gledhill illustrates this with Halliday's (1992: 70–71) example of how specialist nominal groups are gradually constructed in discourse so that collocations have their own internal coherence, a coherence that may be fully appreciated only by the specialist reader.

In the discussion that follows, I examine examples of online medical information that display some of these characteristics. The set of data in this section comes mainly from Wikipedia sites collected during 2013 and 2014 (with my underlining) but it should be noted that there is constant updating of Wikipedia and of other websites so the actual wording may not currently be precisely as quoted here. However, the grammatical and lexical features of the revised texts are similar except where an obvious attempt has been made to simplify the language as, for example, in the so-called *Simple English Wikipedia.* Even the latter, however, keeps many of the same features relating to death.

7.3.1 The Scientific Description of Disease

The first example below is a relatively straightforward opening to an explanation of a heart attack, written, I believe, for the general reader, but lacking the personal touch one would find in discourse directly addressing an ill person. The style is that of a textbook with the standard features of scientific text mentioned above. Notice that the *Themes* of the clauses do not refer to the men or women who suffer from heart attacks but are: *a/the heart attack/s; a/the section of heart muscle; blood flow; the good news; excellent treatments, these treatments.* Notice also that the general message is a positive one. We find the word *die*, but it is *the section of heart muscle* that dies – not the patient. The patient does not *die* even though the heart attack is described as *a leading killer of both men and women.* The emphasis is on the excellent treatments and saved lives.

> A heart attack occurs if the flow of oxygen-rich blood to a section of heart muscle suddenly becomes blocked. If blood flow isn't restored quickly, the section of heart muscle begins to die.

> Heart attacks are a leading killer of both men and women in the United States. The good news is that excellent treatments are available for heart attacks. These treatments can save lives and prevent disabilities.

From this site, there is a direct link to an account of Cardiac Arrest, which begins (example slightly abbreviated):

> Cardiac arrest, also known as cardiopulmonary arrest or circulatory arrest, is the cessation of normal circulation of the blood due to failure of the heart to contract effectively. Medical personnel may refer to an unexpected cardiac arrest as a sudden cardiac arrest (SCA). ...
> A cardiac arrest is different from (but may be caused by) a heart attack, where blood flow to the muscle of the heart is impaired.
> Arrested blood circulation prevents delivery of oxygen to the body. Lack of oxygen and glucose to the brain causes loss of consciousness, which then results in abnormal or absent breathing. Brain injury is likely if cardiac arrest goes untreated for more than five minutes. For the best chance of survival and neurological recovery, immediate and decisive treatment is imperative.[2]

Here there is no reference at all to the human sufferer of cardiac arrest even in the most general terms. Most of the grammatical features of scientific, expert-to-expert discourse predominate. There is no easy explanation of the difference between *heart attack* and *cardiac arrest,* and there is extended use of further technical collocations, such as *cardiopulmonary arrest, circulatory arrest* and *neurological recovery* as well as fairly long nominal groups (such as *lack of oxygen to the brain)* and examples of grammatical metaphor in most clauses.

However, lexically there is an interesting feature of this text – not unusual in current medical practice – namely that, although by implication the passage is about death, the focus is on life. The reader is only alerted to the strong possibility of death from cardiac arrest in the final sentence with the use of the words *survival* and *recovery.*

7.3.2 The Focus on Survival

As with most Wikipedia articles on serious illnesses, there is a later section headed 'Prognosis' of which this is the first, and least technical, paragraph:

> **Prognosis:** The survival rate of people who receive initial emergency care by ambulance is only 2% with 15% experiencing return of spontaneous circulation. However, with defibrillation within

> 3–5 minutes, the survival rate increases to 30%.... Although mortality in case of ventricular fibrillation is high, rapid intervention with a *defibrillator* increases *survival rate.* ... Survival is mostly related to the cause of the arrest.

Once more the text focuses on living with the words *survival rate* appearing three times. This discussion of prognosis does not explicitly mention that the vast majority of patients die. This is simply implied by the given survival rate of only 2% of those who are reached by ambulance and 30% of those who receive early defibrillation. However, the reference of the 15% is not clear and it may refer to 15% who survive without professional care. To solve the problems of understanding this text, the reader would have to follow up by finding the academic sources of the information, referenced on Wikipedia but not available online.

7.3.3 The Use of Grammatical Metaphor

Another source of ambiguity is one discussed by Halliday and Matthiessen (2006: 231). They comment that information may be lost and indeterminacy increased when a nominal group is used rather than a clause. This can happen with the use of grammatical metaphor in what they call 'objective accounts'. Their example is appropriate to much of the online data discussed in this chapter. They point out that the sentence *Lung cancer death rates are clearly associated with increased smoking* is ambiguous and they represent the ambiguity in Table 7.1:

Table 7.1: Ambiguity in a Grammatical Metaphor (Halliday and Matthiessen, 2006: 231)

Lung cancer death rates	**are clearly associated with**	**increased smoking**
[2]		[1]
people die faster of lung cancer	[1] so [2]	more people smoke
more people die of lung cancer	[2] because [1]	people smoke more
more people die faster of lung cancer	if [1], then [2]	more people smoke more

Thus, possible interpretations of the grammatical metaphor are:

- More people smoke, so more people die of lung cancer.
- People smoke more so more people die of lung cancer.
- More people die of lung cancer because more people smoke.
- If more people smoke more, then more people will die faster of lung cancer.

Since the nominal groups can be interpreted in a variety of ways, the indeterminacy of the clause is increased. If this happens in face to face interaction the speakers can question each other to determine the precise meaning of the clause. Where the act of communication takes place at a distance, such as happens when we read information online, misunderstanding is likely to occur, especially in expert-to-novice interaction.

Rare counter-examples to the general preference for life-oriented lexis are attested, but they still involve nominalization at an abstract level. When the likelihood of death is mentioned, we sometimes find the use of *fatal* as modifier of disease or illness.

> **Botulism** is, in humans, a rare but sometimes fatal paralytic illness... Foodborne botulism is an intoxication caused by consuming food contaminated with the botulinum toxin; it is not passed on from person to person when the skin is intact ...Wound botulism is found most often among substance abusers when spores enter a wound under the skin.
>
> **Prognosis**: The World Health Organization (WHO) reports that the current mortality rate is 5% (type B) to 10% (type A). Other sources report that, in the U.S., the overall mortality rate is about 7.5%, but the mortality rate among adults over 60 is 30%. The mortality rate for wound botulism is about 10%. The infant botulism mortality rate is about 1.3%.

In the prognosis section on botulism, we see an additional way of referring to death. Here there are four uses of the term *mortality rate* (the counterpart of *survival rate*). We also find reference to the source of the information in Theme position, a feature which is common in academic writing in some disciplines.

7.3.4 Enquiring about the Prospect of Death

The general reader can find rather more accessible information on the Macmillan Cancer Support website. One of the sections is headed with the direct question 'How long will I live?' Yet, since the topic concerns the prospect of death, it is surprising how much of the discourse manages to avoid explicit reference to it. In 237 words, there is no use of any word that directly specifies death or dying.

> How long will I live?
> For many people, the most obvious and important question to ask is "How long will I live?" This question is impossible for your medical team to give an exact answer to, because many things can affect life expectancy. For example, how well the cancer responds to

> treatment, the speed the cancer grows at and any changes in your general health. If the answer your doctor gives is too vague for you, perhaps because you need to make specific plans for the future – explain this to them. They may be able to give you more information, although they can only ever give you their best estimate.
>
> Many different things can affect life expectancy, so your situation and your doctor's predictions may change over time. Some people find that talking to their doctor about life expectancy is *an ongoing discussion*, rather than a one-off question.
>
> While for some people it's very important to have an idea of how long they might live, others prefer to focus on issues to do with their quality of life and choose never to ask the question. Your medical team and your loved ones may wait for you to bring up the topic of life expectancy, or they may ask you to talk with them about it. If you're not comfortable discussing this, it's fine to say so. It's important to do whatever feels best for you (Macmillan.org.uk/cancer information/end of life).

On the same website we find:

> If you've been told <u>your cancer can't be cured</u> …
> If you've been told <u>you're not going to get better</u> …
> If you fear that <u>your condition might deteriorate</u> …

Where the underlined words could be replaced by 'you're going to die'.
And one reader-contributor commented:

> I lost a friend to cancer. Eventually she was told she would have "two good months and then a swift decline." She lived for another fifteen months.

Since this website uses a much more interpersonal style and welcomes readers' comments and questions, the Macmillan Cancer Support pages are closer in some ways to the face to face doctor-patient consultation than some online sites although there are still many differences.

7.4 The Face to Face Consultation

In this section I turn to the traditional one-to-one consultation. This is presented to highlight a contrast with the lack of personal interaction when a patient consults online text. I consider the research and training that has gone into improving the success rate of these meetings and look at the similarities that exist with respect to the discussion of death.

7.4.1 Research and Training

The doctor-patient consultation has been the subject of a great deal of research resulting in many respected publications, for example Balint (1964), the classic work by Byrne and Long (1984), which reported on the analysis of 2,500 tape-recorded consultations, and the popular textbook *The Doctor's Communication Handbook* (Tate and Tate, 2014). This work is loosely now combined under the subject of 'Consultation Analysis' and forms a significant section of current specialist training for Royal College of General Practitioners' membership examinations.

The consultation has been described as 'the central act of medicine' and is seen as crucial in the first stage of diagnosis (Pendleton *et al.*, 2003). For our purposes in this chapter, the significance of this research is simply to point out that a successful consultation is seen as one that leads the doctor towards an understanding of the patient's medical problems and that a recurring theme in the description of the good consultation is the *development of the doctor-patient relationship, a relationship missing when information is read online.* Doctors are encouraged to *listen to the patient* (as explained in the Royal College of General Practitioners Trainee Portfolio and discussed in Greenhalgh and Hurtwitz (1998). Features of the good consultation are seen to be *establishing rapport, showing empathy,* and *connecting with the patient* (Neighbour, 2004). Also featured is the significance of the doctor's appreciation of the social conditions of the patient to support their continuing care, especially in the case of patients with chronic illnesses. None of these advantages of the face to face consultation are available online.[3]

7.4.2 Imparting Bad News

From time to time doctors are obliged to inform patients of the seriousness of their condition. It appears to be current practice in Britain's National Health Service (NHS) to follow a policy of complete honesty with patients about matters concerning the nature of an illness and the risks and benefits of treatment options. Thus a patient who is advised to have a total hip replacement may well be given not only details of the operation, the type and procedure of the anaesthetic, the length of recovery time, and the statistical probability of failure, which could include, appropriately worded, the statistical chance of death within a certain length of time after the operation. A patient who is about to have major heart surgery may be told the chances of death *with* and *without* the surgery. However, this does not mean that where patients have limited life expectancy they will be told immediately and directly of this fact.

A sensitive doctor may well avoid language that he feels might unnecessarily upset the patient – at least until the time comes when treatment demands it. Once a serious illness is diagnosed, the doctor or specialist nurse will invite questions and may offer leaflets or booklets on the subject.

Training for General Practitioners in the UK includes advice on how doctors can give patients and their families the bad news. It is interesting to see how conversations from the training courses avoid the use of the words 'death' and 'dying'. However, on the whole, there is no recourse to the old metaphorical expressions of religious consolation such as those still associated with funerals. Instead, we find the use of newer lexico-grammatical expressions that focus on living and affirmative action, such as:

end of life care	*for*	care of the dying
progressive conditions	*for*	conditions progressing to death
life-threatening illness	*for*	illness which is likely to cause death
life-terminating acts	*for*	allowing someone to die

The last example would include switching off a life-support system or administering a pain-killing medicine that might endanger life by affecting the heart or the breathing.

Here is a typical sample from a case study (gmc-uk.org./eGP) where a doctor is talking to the grown-up daughter of a seriously ill elderly patient (my underlining):

> **GP**: And I'm afraid that, given the severity of his current condition, even with intensive care, he might not survive, or not for very long. We think, all things considered, that it would be preferable to manage his bowel blockage with antibiotics and get an assessment from the palliative care team on how to keep him comfortable.
>
> **Patient' daughter**: That sounds to me like you're giving up on him.

The account continues with the comment that after the conversation, his daughter conceded 'that her father would probably not have wanted to be kept going at all costs, whatever she would have wanted for him' (my underlining throughout).

A less euphemistic conversation might have included the words 'he might die quickly' instead of 'might not survive … for long', and 'we cannot cure him but might be able to make him feel better'. Equally euphemistic is the daughter's final comment that her father 'would probably not have wanted to be kept going at all costs'. Note also that neither of the participants uses the word 'death' or 'die'. (Incidentally, this patient did die within a few days of this conversation).

7.5 Bureaucracy and Terminology

An understanding of when someone with a terminal illness might die is important not only for the individual and their family, but also for dealing with paperwork such as holiday insurance forms or benefit claims.

7.5.1 Terminal Illness and Median Survival Rates

A patient who submits an application to the Benefits Agency for certain allowances will find a question asking whether they are suffering from a 'terminal illness'. It is well-known that this question as well as others on the form are difficult to answer and, for this reason, applicants are often advised by their medical contacts to get help in completing the form. This question raises a number of serious issues, including linguistic ones. As we have said, there is a general inclination across the social spectrum to avoid the direct discussion of death or dying and to present the possibility of positive outcomes for disease, so a patient may not be clear in their own mind as to whether or not an illness will lead directly to death. Even if they are, they may not be familiar with the term 'terminal' and they will almost certainly not know its correct medical definition. I have asked a number of well-educated people if they know what the term means and very few have a precise understanding. Many reply something like 'the same as a fatal illness'. They may add that it is an illness that causes death.

Terms like *terminal, fatal, critical,* and *serious* are widespread online and can be easily misinterpreted when used as modifiers of *disease* or *illness.* One site, *Cancer UK*, has a page entitled 'Finding out if your illness is terminal'. This site actually discusses death and dying clearly and raises the question of how people find it very difficult to talk directly about the subject. It is an interesting and surprisingly clear site for lay people, but even here you will not, at present, find a clear medical definition of 'terminal'.

The Wikipedia entry on terminal illness explains the term inadequately since it offers no explanation of what is meant by 'a relatively short time':

> Terminal illness is a medical term popularized in the 20th century to describe a disease that cannot be cured or adequately treated and that is reasonably expected to result in the death of a patient within a relatively short period of time.

Moreover, it does not allow for the fact that many diseases that cannot be cured at present can be treated satisfactorily in ways that improve the quality of life and often prolong it.

While it is true that diseases for which there is no known cure (*incurable diseases*) are now often referred to as terminal diseases, it is these diseases for which the medical profession has established the 'median survival rate' as a guideline that is flexible enough to allow for an approximate prediction to be based on what is an historical statistical record. This explanation is from a booklet on leukaemia and lymphoma research:

> Median Survival is often misunderstood by patients and family to mean the maximum expected life span. In fact, it is the time at which one would expect half of a group of patients diagnosed at the same time to be alive. Many of those still alive will live for many more years – decades even. ... One should also remember that survival data is historical and may not reflect improvements based on newer drugs or treatments (Bloodwise, 2012: 23).

The prognosis though is changing daily, not only as a result of medical developments but also on the age and condition of individual patients, who may die at any time from other causes. It is worth noting that very few sites on the Internet that discuss terminal or fatal illness make this clear.

7.5.2 Social Distance and Semantic Space

To summarize, throughout the range of online contexts considered in this chapter, three main themes have emerged:

- The general euphemistic representation of death and dying in English cultural life.
- The current tendency to focus on living rather than dying in both spoken and written discourse about serious illness.
- The proliferation of medical information on the Internet that is written as science, with the constant use of grammatical metaphor where processes and qualities are reconstructed as participants in the clause in place of human participants.

Online medical texts are rich in both lexical metaphor and grammatical metaphor, which, it is claimed, 'expand the semantic base of the grammar' (Halliday and Matthiessen, 2006: 15, 46). They write of the construal and re-construal of experience in language as a process that happens when experience is re-categorized through the 'objectifying framework of metaphor'. This re-construal opens the possibility for even more divergence in the lexicogrammar, thus increasing linguistic potential and offering more choice to the speaker/writer. Simultaneously, however, it offers the increased possibility of discourse which is semantically ambiguous and communicatively elusive.

The social distance between the producers of digital text and the potential readers of these texts may be vast. They are often from distinct social, cultural and professional communities, sometimes with different first languages; they are likely to share little mutual knowledge of the topic of the discourse and usually have no possibility of question-answer exchange with each other. This social distance, combined with the extent of the semantic space the language potential occupies, may not facilitate successful communication.

Hence, there is a strong chance that any lay persons who look for medical information on the Internet will find texts that are more like expert-expert discourse than texts that resemble doctor-patient discourse. It is well-known that some of these texts are already out-of date and some were always inaccurate, but, in any case, they can be a considerable linguistic challenge to the average non-medical reader.

Acknowledgements

Many thanks to Thomas Bloor for his advice on an earlier draft of this chapter and to Dr Imogen Bloor for direction to appropriate online medical sources.

About the author

Meriel Bloor is an Honorary Fellow of the Centre for Applied Linguistics, University of Warwick, Warwick, UK. Her publications centre on Systemic Functional Linguistics and critical discourse analysis with applications to specialist registers and English for Specific Purposes. She is currently researching the discourse of medical communication.

Endnotes

1. Further information on this research is available at http://ucrel.lancs.ac.uk/melc/ where an extensive bibliography can be found.
2. Available at https://en.wikipedia.org/wiki/Cardiac_arrest#cite_note-IrwinRippe-6.23cite_note-IrwinRippe-6.
3. More details on the consultation process can be seen on: www.patient.co.uk/doctor/consultation.

References

Balint, M. (1964) *The Doctor, His Patient and the Illness*. 2nd edn. London: Churchill Livingstone.

Bloodwise (2012) *Leukaemia and Lymphoma Research Booklet: Myelodysplastic Syndromes (MDS)*. London: Bloodwise. [online] available from <https://bloodwise.org.uk/> [accessed 1 October 2015].

Bultnick, B. (1998) *Metaphors We Die By: Conceptualizations of Death in English and their Implications for a Theory of Metaphor*. Antwerp: University of Antwerp.

BUPA (2012) *BUPA Health Pulse 2012. Patient Power*. London: LSE and BUPA.

Byrne, P. S. and Long, B. E. L. (1984) *Doctors Talking to Patients*. London: Royal College of General Practitioners.

Fernandez, E. C. (2006) The Language of Death: Euphemism and Conceptual Metaphorization in Victorian Obituaries. *SKY Journal of Linguistics* 19(101): 130.

Gledhill, C. J. (2000) *Collocations in Science Writing*. Tubingen: Gunter Narr Verlag.

Greenhalgh, T. and Hurtwitz, B. (1998) *Narrative Based Medicine*. London: BMJ Books.

Halliday, M. A. K. (1992) Language as a System and Language as an Instance. In J. Svartvik (ed.) *Directions in Corpus Linguistics: Proceedings of the Nobel Symposium 82*, 61–77. Berlin and New York: Mouton de Gruyter.

Halliday, M. A. K. (1998) On the Grammar of Pain. *Functions of Language* 5(1): 1–32.

Halliday, M. A. K and Martin, J. R. (1993) *Writing Science: Literary and Discursive Power*. London: Routledge (formerly Falmer Press).

Halliday, M. A. K. and Matthiessen, C. M. I. M. (1999) *Construing Experience through Meaning. A Language-Based Approach to Cognition*. London: Cassell.

Halliday, M. A. K. and Matthiessen, C. M. I. M. (2006) *Construing Experience through Meaning: A Language-Based Approach to Cognition*. London and New York: Continuum.

Lakoff, G. and Johnson, M. (1980) *Metaphors We Live By*. Chicago, IL: University of Chicago Press.

McDaid, D. and Park, A. (2011) *BUPA Health Pulse 2010. Online Health: Untangling the Web*. London: LSE and BUPA.

Neighbour, R. (2004) *The Inner Consultation: How to Develop an Effective and Intuitive Consulting Style*. 2nd edn. London: Radcliffe Medical Press.

Pendleton, D., Schofield, T., Tate, P., and Havelock, P. (2003) *The New Consultation: Developing Doctor-Patient Communication*. Oxford: Oxford University Press.

Semino, E. (2010) Description of Pain, Metaphor and Embodied Simulation in End of Life Care. *Metaphor and Symbol* 25(4): 205–226.

Tate, P. and Tate, E. (2014) *The Doctor's Communication Handbook*. 7th edn. London: Radcliffe Publishing.

8 Moving Online to Teach Academic Writing in Science and Engineering: Theory and Practice

Helen Drury
University of Sydney

8.1 Introduction

Our approach to teaching academic writing in science and engineering disciplines at undergraduate level has been informed by a Systemic Functional Linguistics (SFL) theory of language and genre-based literacy pedagogy. We have used this foundation to develop teaching materials and approaches to scaffold student understandings of the genre, discourse and grammar of discipline based writing tasks (Jones, 2004). Over a ten year period, these materials and approaches have gradually been 'redesigned' (New London Group, 2000) into interactive, multimodal, online learning modules, replacing face-to-face pedagogy with digital pedagogy (Drury, 2004; Drury and Mort, 2012; Mort and Drury, 2012).

SFL and genre pedagogy can inform the 'redesign' of materials and approaches for teaching academic writing online. In addition, research in social semiotics and multimodal meaning making can contribute to the development of a digital pedagogy for academic writing. However, a key question is how students use online resources to create their own learning journey to develop successful discipline-based writing, their own 'personalised curricula' (Kress, 2003; Kress and Pachler, 2007). In monitoring these journeys, designer/teachers (or 'rhetors', Kress, 2010: 26) can further develop effective online curricula for academic writing.

This chapter will explore the cycle of design and redesign over a 10 year period of a genre pedagogy for academic writing in science and engineering, focusing in particular on the laboratory report genre. The aim is to use a social semiotic framework based on the SFL tradition using both the metafunctional meaning making principles (Halliday, 1994) and the rhetorical principles of multimodal communication (Bezemer and Kress, 2008) as a way to explore the theory and practice behind the evolution of the design of a digital pedagogy. Design begins with the move from a face-to-face pedagogy through key iterations of an online pedagogy. Additionally, the role of learners in using and transforming the online resources for their own needs and in this way contributing to further design will be discussed.

8.2 The Context of Design

8.2.1 Design Principles

The move from the classroom to an online medium involves significant redesign of pedagogic resources in terms of learning materials, tasks and the contributions of participants in the learning situation. This 'recontextualization' of these resources from face-to-face to online is a 're-presentation' of the current materials, tasks and activities in a manner suited or 'apt' for the new environment and enhanced by new affordances (Bezemer and Kress, 2008). A social semiotic approach within the SFL tradition can provide a basis for analysing and developing design. In this approach, the pedagogic resources available to teacher/designers can be categorized into three kinds of functions for making meanings, termed metafunctions, namely, ideational, interpersonal and textual. Briefly, ideational meanings comprise the content or subject matter of the site, interpersonal meanings the social relations created through interaction with this content and, textual meanings provide a unifying structure for the site. This metafunctional approach can be complemented by the four rhetorical/semiotic principles of multimodal communication provided by Bezemer and Kress (2008). These are the selection of the meaning making materials or modes, their arrangement, their foregrounding and the social relations they create. In this chapter, I am following Kress's definition of mode as 'a socially shaped and culturally given semiotic resource for making meaning. Image, writing, layout, music, gesture, speech, moving image, soundtrack and 3D objects are examples of modes used in representation and communication' (Kress, 2010: 79). In contrast, the term mode as used in the SFL 'context of situation' focuses on the role of language in 'the channelling of communication' (Martin and Rose, 2008: 14). A multimodal approach 'extend[s] the social interpretation of language and its meaning to the whole range of representational and communicational modes or semiotic resources for making meaning that are employed in a culture' (Jewitt, 2009: 1).

8.3 Re-presenting Content

In general, the ideational content of our pedagogy whether face to face or online remains the same in terms of teaching materials and to some extent the teaching activities or tasks that the teacher sets students to undertake. As the New London Group (2000: 22) has suggested 'Designing always involves the transformation of Available Designs; it always involves making new use of old materials'. The written paper-based learning materials from the classroom context still remain in a written mode on screen and also retain some elements of their arrangement, sequence, layout and foregrounding, for example, the use of capitals and bold for the headings of each section of a laboratory report genre and within each section a sequence of explanations, examples and exercises in the areas of content, structure and language (Drury, 1997). However, in transforming these materials from a page to a screen environment, new modal selections and modal combinations or ensembles have become available, and new modal arrangements have become necessary for a screen environment.

Most at risk in moving genre pedagogy online are the metafunctional meanings provided through the face to face communication of scaffolding. In this context, both teacher and students interact in spoken dialogue, accompanied by other modes of meaning making such as body language, gesture, movement, etc. and handwritten 'notes/texts' and illustrations, for example on a whiteboard, provided by both teacher and students. All these largely spoken meanings, for example, explanations, guidance and feedback, have now to be disseminated within different modes using the medium of the screen, the computer and the software available. This process termed 'transduction' (Bezemer and Kress, 2008) impacts most on the spoken mode of scaffolding, a dynamically unfolding, nuanced mode which is transduced into a largely written mode on screen.

In an online environment, the screen becomes a unit for meaning making. This imposes constraints on what can be seen at any one time. The evolution of our screen design can be seen in the sample screens in Figure 8.1 to Figure 8.3. Each presents an aspect of the deconstruction of a stage in a laboratory report. The earliest report writing programme, (Figure 8.1), was developed using Authorware in 1999/2000 to support first year students writing a laboratory report in biology. A later programme redesigned this using a template design based largely on Dreamweaver and this meant other programmes for science and engineering report genres could also be offered online as shown in Figure 8.2, a screen from a 2004/5 programme for a second year short report in biochemistry. The latest programme incorporated redesigns for all the previous report writing programmes and brought them together in one online site, WRiSE (Write reports in Science and Engineering) (WRiSE 2012) and a screen from one of the modules in this site is shown in Figure 8.3, a third year short scientific report in molecular biology designed in 2009 using HTML and Flash.

In all three figures, clearly the written mode has to be used to present the core ideational content, the structural stages and their functions of a section of a laboratory report. However, in Figure 8.1, the written mode is dominant whereas in Figure 8.3, the visual plays a much greater role in communicating this content. In all three figures, the written mode is combined with three other modes, namely layout, colour and to a lesser extent typography and these modal ensembles form the basis for the learning design. The modal arrangement or layout of the core ideational content occupies the most salient position in the centre of each screen. This layout is an abstract spatial representation of the analysis of a section of a laboratory report into its compositional stages, stages that are in numerical sequence, suggesting a linear unfolding in time as the report text is written and read. In this way, the figures are examples of the realization of a 'temporal analytical process' (Kress and van Leeuwen, 2006: 94). Linear framing of the content is used to create unity and coherence, most strongly in Figure 8.1, where an orange coloured linear, rectangular frame separates the numbered stages and their functions from each other and a bolder orange line forming the top of the rectangle separates the stages from the introductory explanatory text block.

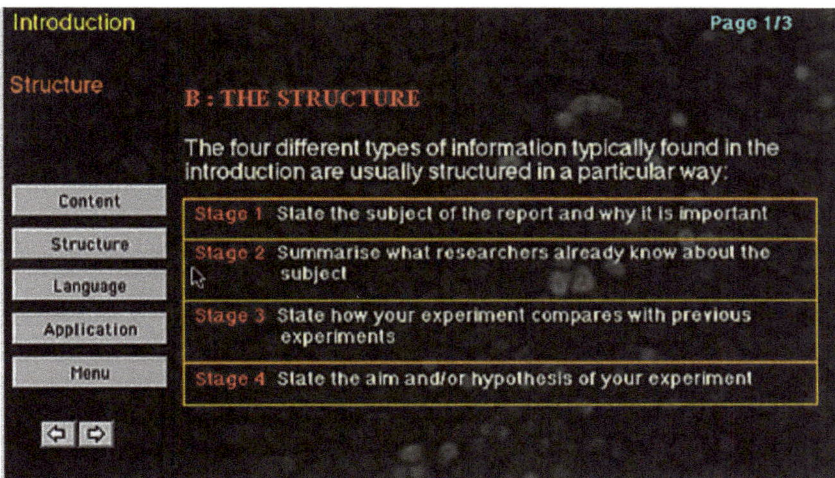

Figure 8.1: Screen from writing a report in biology showing the structural stages of the introduction section of a report.

In contrast, in Figure 8.2, the discussion stages are framed primarily through using different colour saturation for each rectangular block of text, yellow for the explanation and instructions and orange for the stages with a weaker white linear frame between each stage, indicating the closer arrangement among them. However, a stronger black, vertical, linear frame separates the content from the menu items on the left hand side of the screen and most importantly, a horizontal, linear frame, below the presentation of the stages, is used to indicate the place at the base of the screen for examples of each stage. This arrangement places the example, a 'real' text, below the abstract analysis of the stages of a typical text, the 'ideal' that students are aiming for (Kress and van Leeuwen, 2006). The layout potential is expanded in this way but it depends on students activating hypertext links embedded in each stage. Then they can simultaneously view linked examples of each stage, a key aspect of scaffolding their understanding.

The arrangement of the stages of a discussion is dramatically different in Figure 8.3 as a visual mode takes precedence over a written mode. The stages are no longer listed in a numerically, strictly linear way within a rectangular frame. Rather they are grouped, each with its own coloured semi-rectangular frame, within an 'hour-glass' frame, shaped to reflect the general to specific to general ideational meanings of the development of this section of a report. This framing comprised of a weightier grey line makes meaning in itself. The semi-linear grouping aims to show a more flexible, sequential development of the stages, namely some stages as fixed, typically in first and last position and some stages occupying more variable and recurrent positions.

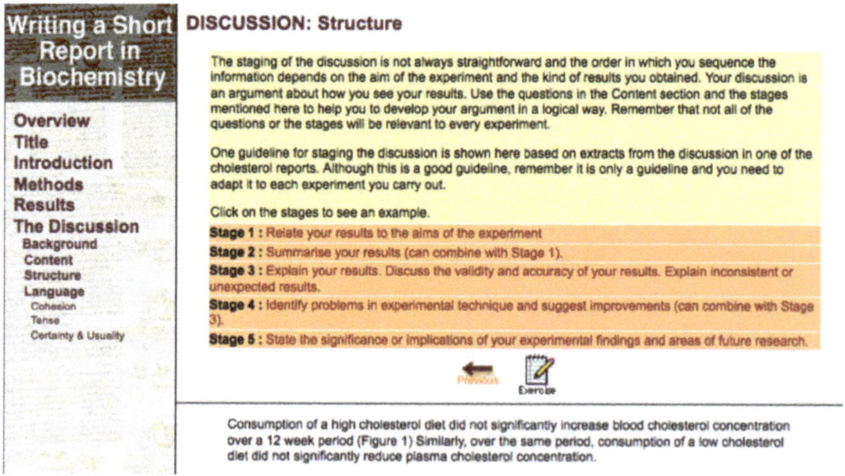

Figure 8.2: Screen from writing a short lab report in biochemistry showing the stages of the discussion section of a report.

These repeated stages are indicated by the expansion of their semi-rectangular frame and their recurrent nature is further indicated using arrows as vectors

(Kress and van Leeuwen, 2006). This visual arrangement attempts to illustrate the complexity and circular nature of writing the stages in a discussion at this level in an undergraduate degree. Furthermore, the whole arrangement can be animated to show the dynamic, unfolding nature of the text if the student chooses this option. Numbering of the stages is still retained on the left hand side of the screen alongside a vertical arrow illustrating the temporal development of the text, as well as the movement from general to specific and back to general. Whether each stage is general or specific is revealed through rolling over hyperlinks in each stage. For example, the Explain results stage, a repeated stage, is linked on roll over to the number 4, a specific stage. Layout is expanded via pop up windows which are activated through hyperlinks in each stage. These windows appear alongside their relevant stage and contain question prompts about the kind of information contained in each stage and an example text (see Figure 8.3).

This design aims to mimic the face to face, step by step, scaffolding of the classroom through the progressive presentation of the core ideational content. However, students are free to skip these steps by activating the 'Show all examples' icon at the bottom of the screen. In this case, the whole text example appears on a subsequent screen together with its stages and their colour coding. In this design, linear framing is almost absent, although a weak dotted grey line is used to create a rectangle which encloses the visual representation of the stages of the discussion and the accompanying instructional text, adding to its centrality and salience, while at the same time separating it from the explanation text.

The use of colour as a part of the modal ensemble for creating ideational meanings increases over the various design iterations of the report writing programmes. In Figure 8.1, the use of colour is minimal but nevertheless, the choice of red font for the numbered stages of the introduction foregrounds and adds salience to this list. Red font also clearly contrasts with the black-pebbled background and the white font used to explain the function of each stage. In Figure 8.2, background colours are used to differentiate between the functions of each text block, a less saturated, pure yellow for the explanation and instruction text and a brighter orange to add salience to the stages and their functions. These text block colours contrast with the overall white background colour. Typography choices are also used to distinguish the explanation and instruction text in black font from the more salient, bold, black font emphasizing the stage numbers and a bold red font, their functions. The choice of different colours for each stage of the discussion in Figure 8.3 contrasts strongly with the previous screen designs which used repetition of font colour to create cohesion among the stages and their functions. However, since these different pastel colours have a similar degree

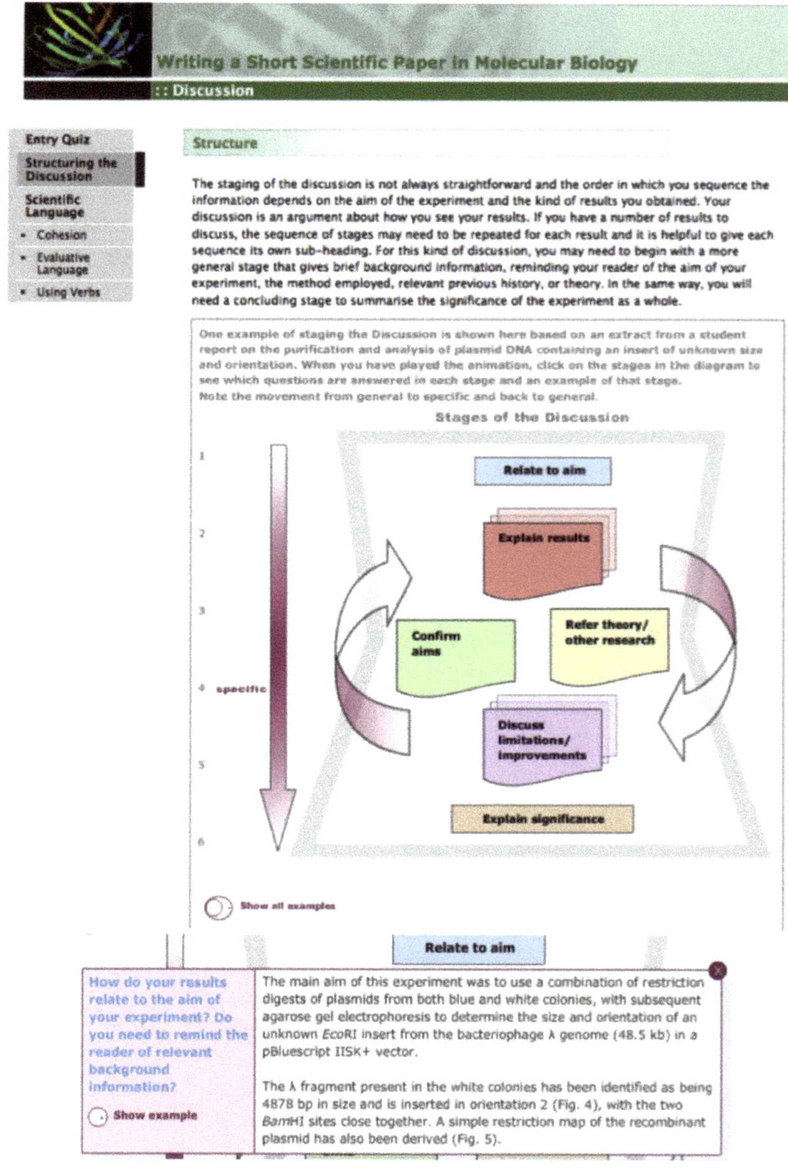

Figure 8.3: Screen from writing a short scientific paper in molecular biology showing the structural stages of the discussion section of a paper.

of saturation and purity, this creates cohesion among them (van Leeuwen, 2002). Furthermore, the choice of different colours can be said to emphasize the difference in function of each stage which is reinforced when the stage colour is used to link to the questions in the pop up windows. In contrast, the arrow vectors in the diagram have the same function and therefore share the same colour. In Figure 8.2 and Figure 8.3, the explanation text in written mode, distinguished from the instruction text in Figure 8.3 via font colour, creates related but different meanings from the presentation of the stages. In particular, the interaction of the written explanation text and the largely visual display of the location of the stages in Figure 8.3 allows for the 'multiplication' of meanings (Lemke, 1998; Unsworth and Cléirigh, 2009).

8.4 Organizing Content

A number of modes and modal ensembles have been selected to help students to understand how the website content is organized, how to navigate through the website and where they are in the website. The modal composition of banners, headings, subheadings, icons and menu items together aim to create coherence both within and across the different screens of the website. These modes, like all modes, convey ideational, interpersonal and textual meanings, but their predominant function is textual, in organizing site content as a meaningful whole. The mode of colour plays a key role in foregrounding location and navigation information so that students can easily create their own learning pathways. Colour is once again used in an increasingly sophisticated manner from Figure 8.1 to Figure 8.3. In Figure 8.1, different colours are combined in a seemingly arbitrary manner with typography, bold, upper or lower case, to create headings and sub-headings to signal the section of the laboratory report genre and within this section, the kind of content that is presented. In contrast, Figure 8.2 and Figure 8.3 suggest a more motivated use of colour combined with typography as well as layout. In Figure 8.2, the same colour is used for headings and sub-headings but typography is used to distinguish between them, upper case to draw attention to the discussion section of the laboratory report genre and capitalized lower case to signal the specific content. Both are located at the top of the screen. In Figure 8.3 the affordances of one colour, green, are used in a more sophisticated way to create cohesion between the title of the laboratory report, the section in the report and the content in this section. Different green hues are not only used for headings and sub headings but also as contrasting banner colours as background to the typography for these headings and sub headings.

A menu is essential for helping users to understand the composition of a website and menu design is critical in supporting this. In each laboratory report programme, the layout of the menu items comprises a vertical list on the left hand side of the screen, the position for locating 'given' or 'already known' information (Kress and van Leeuwen, 2006). In Figure 8.2, the main elements of this list, foregrounded through bold typography, make up the typical sections or generic stages of a laboratory report reinforcing the macro level structure of a report and its arrangement into parts. The lower levels in the menu hierarchy are clearly indicated through changes in typography, predominantly smaller font size and choice of bold/not bold (Figure 8.2). In the case of Figure 8.1 and Figure 8.3, the menu items indicate the organization of content within a section of a laboratory report, although students can access the higher levels of the hierarchy through the item 'menu' in Figure 8.1 and through a horizontal listing of other sections of the laboratory report at the base of the screen in Figure 8.3 (not shown in the Figure). Icons such as arrows can be used on their own (Figure 8.1) or combined with colour and written labels (Figure 8.2) to create cohesion among screens within a laboratory report section and suggest to users that there is a meaning relationship among screens in a given section and that moving in a more linear way at this stage will increase understanding of the content. However, students need to know how many screens are involved and where they are up to. Screen numbering is used in Figure 8.1 although this is labelled as 'Page', which is an indication of how close this design was to the original paper-based materials. In Figure 8.3 a simple numbering system, together with the word 'Next', supports students' linear movement through a section of the website (not shown in Figure 8.3).

A banner in Figure 8.2 and Figure 8.3 is highly effective in unifying a website or a module in a website by creating a distinctive and coherent identity for the content which is repeated on each screen. These banners combine a number of modes, writing, image and colour. In both Figures, the image for the banner is further used as the basis for creating cohesion through a unifying colour scheme for headings and subheadings and for menu items in Figure 8.2.

8.5 Creating Social Relations

Students are invited to engage in a more personal way with the content on the screen through a number of modal combinations. At the macro level of the whole online programme, image and banner as seen in Figure 8.2 and Figure 8.3 invite students to identify with their discipline and hence with the programme. Images were chosen by discipline lecturers as symbolic of their discipline, the extract from Leonardo's notebook for the short report in biochemistry and the image of the structure of green fluorescent protein for the short scientific paper in molecular biology. These images are located at the top left hand corner of the screen and are extended vertically in Figure 8.2 and horizontally in Figure 8.3 to form banners. Aspects of these images are repeated in the banner but the main form of extension is through different levels of colour saturation (van Leeuwen, 2002). Such image and colour laden banners aim to claim students' attention so that they will be motivated to interact with the website content to develop their knowledge and understanding of communicating in the field.

The on screen written mode largely replaces the spoken classroom mode in providing explanations about the ideational content and guidance on how to interact with this. Although the relationship is still that of student and computer as teacher, students are addressed in a personal way using the pronoun 'you' in explanations while directives using the imperative form instruct students about how to interact with the ideational content. Directives are continued in the presentation of this content, the stages of the laboratory report across all 3 examples. However, when more detail about each stage is progressively revealed through interaction with each stage as in Figure 8.3, the interrogative form is used as well as personal pronouns. This encourages students to interact by answering the questions posed as they relate to their own laboratory report. Then students can reveal an example of the stage by clicking on an icon. This sequential unfolding of content through the students' interactions with the screen is used to scaffold understanding and is carried out in two interactions for each stage in Figure 8.2 compared with four in Figure 8.3. In addition, the use of colour in Figure 8.3 is a key mode both in connecting stages, with their associated questions and examples and in encouraging students to make this connection in their own understanding.

Exercises followed by feedback provide a further way for students to interact with the site and, as in the classroom situation, are a way for students to check their understanding of the content that has been presented, typically on earlier screens. However, students are free to choose whether to do the exercises or not as well as to bypass the scaffolded checking of their answers and merely reveal the answers. Advances in technology have enabled the number of screens devoted to exercises to be reduced. For example, if students clicked on the exercise icon in Figure 8.2, they would have then been offered ten exercises on subsequent screens either radio button or check box, with feedback appearing in the frame at the bottom of the screen. In contrast, in Figure 8.3, if students choose the menu item 'Entry quiz' there is one radio button exercise, consisting of five questions on the same screen and feedback appears in a pop up window adjacent to each question. Clearly, online exercises are limited and, in the same way, feedback cannot anticipate and respond to all students' problems or questions as in the classroom situation. However, online exercises allow for more examples of the genre or genre stage to be made available for students either as good or poor examples, where feedback can identify why examples are inappropriate or how they can be improved. Also, if the online programme is fully integrated into discipline curricula in a blended way, social relations around the content of the programme can be built on as the following comment shows:

> The other day I had a normally unruly class of 2nd year Chem Eng students enthralled in a cohesion exercise from the WRiSE site.

8.6 User Practice and Evaluation: Impact on Design

8.6.1 Cycles of Design, Use and Evaluation

The success of a website design can only be gauged from how it is used and in our context whether learning has taken place as a result of user interactions with the website. Learners create their own pathways through the site to gain knowledge about how to write a laboratory report, typically while in the process of writing an assignment in their discipline. In other words they 'fashion their own knowledge, from information supplied by the makers of the site (Kress, 2005: 10) and 'design[s] a coherent complex sign that corresponds to the needs that she or he has' (Kress, 2005: 18).

In the cycle of design and redesign, user evaluation and feedback are essential for improving design for learning. In all our design iterations, student users and our team of discipline and e-learning staff, together with expert users have provided both input and feedback. Overall, our digital pedagogy has been positively evaluated by users from the very first design. Students have reported that different aspects of the programmes, such as example texts, explanations, exercises etc. have improved their learning of laboratory report genres and this has also contributed to improved performance measured through assessment grades. Each design iteration has shown a trend of improved performance for student users compared with non-users with the WRiSE site user report marks significantly higher than those of non-users ($t [323] = -2.96, p =.01$) (Drury, 2001; Drury *et al.*, 2006; Drury and Mort, 2012; Mort and Drury, 2012).

Ideally, students and expert users should be involved at the prototype stage of the design so that their insights can be included in the final version. However, this is not always easy to accomplish given development deadlines and the need to encourage and reward time-poor student volunteers. In addition, the development of effective research instruments to actually assess student learning from online environments as opposed to students' perception of their learning is a challenge. Also performance data on genre writing in the disciplines cannot be attributed solely to the intervention of an online programme to support such writing. However, over the ten year period of collecting questionnaire, focus group and performance data, in general, we can conclude that students who have used the programmes have learned from the various iterations. Over this period, we have generally used similar questionnaires to provide data on the effectiveness of the design of the programmes in such areas as user friendliness, screen layout, navigation, instructions etc. as well as student perceptions of their learning from different aspects of the programme and their pathways through the programme. Both quantitative and qualitative questionnaire data have been collected, complemented by focus groups. Pre- and post-tests using exercises from the programmes have also been used as well as the collection of performance data on the genres students have been writing supported by the online resources (Drury, 2001; Drury *et al.*, 2006; Drury and Muir, 2014).

Quantitative data for the iterations of the above programmes have been reported extensively but qualitative data less so. This kind of data can provide more nuanced insights into the relationship between learning design and learning. Open-ended comments on student and staff questionnaires as well as focus group and interview data will be discussed in two main areas, namely,

- student engagement and learning pathways
- perceptions of learning from design

8.6.2 Student Engagement and Learning Pathways

It is clear that students will only use an online programme for writing in their discipline area if it is relevant and realistic (Drury and Mort, 2012). This means that the pedagogical content, information, explanations, exercises etc. needs to be based on examples of authentic genres written by students. These can be used not only to exemplify the structure and language of a genre instance, but they also give some indication of expected levels of performance. From the beginning, we have consistently used authentic student writing to exemplify report structure and language as well as to provide content for exercises. This has led to high approval ratings even for the early website designs. For example, evaluation of the biology report writing programme (Figure 8.1) found that 80% of student users (n = 40) rated the programme highly for explanations and usefulness of exercises and feedback, as well as user friendliness, navigation and clarity of instructions (Drury, 2001).

Student comments not only refer to the usefulness of example reports but also reveal how the arrangement of the example with the analysis of its structure can aid learning.

> those examples or the example and then the structure next to it, I think was great…

> I tried to follow the content of the examples given i.e. what was written in what order…

Students have consistently asked for both more and complete example reports. For example, evaluation of the chemical engineering laboratory report programme using the template design illustrated in Figure 8.2 found that 66% of student users (n=91) requested more example texts (Drury *et al.*, 2006).

> example reports were the most helpful to know what to put in…

Including a 'whole' report has proved challenging due to the limitations of screen size and the fact that scrolling means that only part of the report is visible at any one time. However, learners not only want complete report examples but also the accompanying analysis in a more visual form.

> full examples of reports and better structural layout and diagrams of differing forms of report as different subjects want different things in forms of report…

> a data base of text examples would be great…

Student pathways through the websites strongly indicate a needs based approach. The preferred way of moving through each website iteration has been to move from screen to screen, scanning explanations and exercises and then choosing particular explanations and exercises to work through in detail (approximately 50% to 70% of survey samples). Smaller proportions of students reported moving in a linear way from screen to screen through a whole section, reading explanations, and doing exercises or checking their understanding through an entry quiz and then working through a section if they needed to. In addition, the most popular parts of the websites related to structuring sections of the report.

> I learned how to structure the report, what types of information to put in the relevant sections.

8.6.3 Perceptions of Learning from Design

Student comments can also reveal whether their learning is associated with particular aspects of the programme designs. For example, comments related to the use of colour:

> Seeing those different colours is what helped me the most … it had a sample introduction and then it highlighted each component of each part of the introduction that you needed, which was really good.

Other comments are related to layout and the use of visual diagrams:

> the explanation beside each section on the discussion provides us with a clue about how the structure of the discussion should be.

> the diagrams of content of each section … the flow diagrams and how much should be written.

And still others refer to the content contained in the written mode:

> explanations of how to write introduction, title, discussion and conclusion showing errors and giving examples that are good.

However, responses also highlighted the tensions involved in designing an online pedagogy for improving writing in science and engineering disciplines (see Table 8.1).

Table 8.1: Sample of Student and Discipline Staff Comments Related to Design Challenges

Issues	**Sample Comments**
Balancing the amount of written text on screen (examples, explanations etc.) without reducing the complexity of the genres students are expected to write.	Hard to read text on screen, more diagrams and point form layout would help students to go through more quickly to find what they are looking for.
Finding a way to present a more generic approach to genre writing while at the same time keeping a discipline specific focus.	Make a shorter more direct programme, a section on frequently asked questions or misconceptions.
Overcoming modularization so that students can see how all the parts of a report fit together.	Probably better to have all info for each section on one screen with an example at the bottom, a printable version would have also been useful.
Choosing language features to focus on for success in the genre and teaching students an appropriate metalanguage to be able to use these features.	This analysis of information structure is too detailed for my students.
Determining the level of detail, the richness of the site so that it is sufficiently comprehensive but not exhaustive.	So if there was a page that said an introduction must have this, this, this, this … let's have summary introduction page or something like that.

These comments emphasize the importance of this kind of feedback for subsequent programme design but also give some indication of the challenges for teacher/designers as they balance competing demands within contextual constraints. In addition, the rapid advances in technology not only present opportunities as can be seen in the evolution of our screen designs but also challenges in terms of how to use new media, modes and modal ensembles to achieve effective teaching and learning of academic writing.

8.7 Conclusion

As more teaching and learning moves online, it is essential to develop a principled approach to designing curricula in a medium which is very different from traditional, face-to-face classroom interactions but is inevitably influenced by these. Although the expectation is that students will develop their own online curricula, this does not mean they will 'teach' themselves. Rather, teacher/designers have an even greater responsibility to make explicit the content that needs to be learned through a conscious and informed choice among the available pedagogical resources, the multiple modes, for making meaning in an online environment. These decisions can be informed by principles developed in a social semiotic approach to meaning making and, in the case of teaching academic writing, genre and genre pedagogy in the SFL tradition. However, as in the classroom situation where teachers can monitor whether learning is taking place and if so, how and why, in an online environment, it is also essential to close the loop and assess the how, why, when and where of learning. To do this effectively is not only a matter of collecting performance data, although this is certainly useful in itself, but a much more time and resource consuming exercise of data collection on learning from design. The development of more effective online learning environments for today's diverse student population depends on this process. Perhaps the last word should be left to one of our student informants.

> I think most students don't realize how important [writing] is because it's hard. I personally tried really hard ... not for the mark ...but I want to become a good engineer and to become a good engineer you need to learn how to write reports and that's why I tried really hard ... I like the solid foundations of how to write a report and I've never learnt properly how to do it ... I've started on a really long journey on how to write a report properly. And I don't think it's a waste of time. [WRiSE] helped me.

Acknowledgments

The author gratefully acknowledges financial support from the Office for Learning and Teaching, Government of Australia in the development of the WRiSE website as well as the contributions of Learning Centre academics and discipline staff from the Universities of Sydney and New South Wales and e-learning staff from the University of Sydney.

About the author

Helen Drury is Senior Lecturer and former Head of the Learning Centre, Sydney University, New South Wales, Australia. Her research and teaching interests are in the area of academic literacy and learning and her current research involves the application of Systemic Functional Linguistics genre pedagogy to the design of online programmes for academic writing.

References

Bezemer, J. and Kress, G. (2008) Writing in Multimodal Texts: A Social Semiotic Account of Designs for Learning. *Written Communication* 25(2): 166–195.

Drury, H. (1997) *How to Write a Laboratory Report.* Sydney: University of Sydney: Learning Centre.

Drury, H. (2004) Teaching Academic Writing on Screen: A Search for Best Practice. In L. Ravelli, and R. Ellis (eds) *Analysing Academic Writing: Contextualised Framework*, 233–253. London: Continuum.

Drury, H. (ed.) (2001) Teaching Genres in the Disciplines: Can Students Learn the Laboratory Report Genre on-Screen. *Proceedings of 2001 Language and Academic Skills Conference. Changing Identities.* New South Wales: University of Wollongong.

Drury, H. and Mort, P. (2012) Developing Student Writing in Science and Engineering: The Write Reports in Science and Engineering (WRiSE) Project. *Journal of Learning Development in Higher Education Special Edition (Developing Writing in STEM disciplines)* 4.

Drury, H. and Muir, M. (2014) Using an E-Learning Environment for Developing Science Students' Written Communication: The Case of Writing Laboratory Reports in Physiology. *International Journal of Innovation in Science and Mathematics Education* 22(4): 79–93.

Drury, H., O'Carroll, P., and Langrish, T. (2006) Online Approach to Teaching Writing in Chemical Engineering: Implementation and Evaluation. *International Journal of Engineering Education* 22(4): 858–867.

Halliday, M. A. K. (1994) *An Introduction to Functional Grammar.* 2nd edn. London: Edward Arnold.

Jewitt, C. (2009) The Routledge Handbook of Multimodal Analysis. London: Routledge.

Jones, J. (2004) Learning to Write in the Disciplines: The Application of Systemic Functional Linguistic Theory to the Teaching and Research of Student Writing. In L. Ravelli, and R. Ellis (eds) *Analysing Academic Writing: Contextualised Frameworks*, 254–273. London: Continuum.
Kress, G. (2003) *Literacy in the New Media Age*. London: Routledge.
Kress, G. (2005) Gains and Losses: New Forms of Texts, Knowledge and Learning. *Computers and Composition* 22: 5–22.
Kress, G. (2010) Multimodality: A Social Semiotic Approach to Contemporary Communication. London and New York: Routledge.
Kress, G. and Pachler, N. (2007) Thinking about the 'm' in M-Learning. In N. Pachler (ed.) *Mobile Learning. Towards a Research Agenda*, 7–32. London: The WLE Centre, Institute of Education.
Kress, G. and van Leeuwen, T. (2006) *Reading Images: The Grammar of Visual Design*. 2nd edn. London: Routledge.
Lemke, J. (1998) Multiplying Meaning: Visual and Verbal Semiotics in Scientific Text. In J. R. Martin and R. Veel (eds) *Reading Science: Critical and Functional Perspectives on Discourses of Science*, 87–113. London: Routledge.
Martin, J. R. and Rose, D. (2008) *Genre Relations: Mapping Culture*. London: Equinox Publishing.
Mort, P. and Drury, H. (2012) Supporting Student Academic Literacy in the Disciplines using Genre-Based Online Pedagogy. *Journal of Academic Language and Learning* 6(3): 1–15.
New London Group (2000) A Pedagogy of Multiliteracies Designing Social Futures. In B. Cope and M. Kalantzis (eds) *Multiliteracies: Literacy Learning and the Design of Social Futures*, 9–37. London: Routledge.
Unsworth, L. and Cléirigh, C. (2009) Multimodality and Reading: The Construction of Meaning through Image-Text Interaction. In C. Jewitt (ed.) *The Routledge Handbook of Multimodal Analysis*, 151–163. London: Routledge.
van Leeuwen, T. (2011) *The Language of Colour. An Introduction*. London: Routledge.
WRiSE (2012) *WRiSE (Write Reports in Science and Engineering) Website*. Sydney: University of Sydney: The Learning Centre.

9 Cut and Paste: Recontextualizing Meaning-Material in a Digital Environment

Daniel Lees Fryer
Østfold University College, Norway, and University of Gothenburg, Sweden

9.1 Introduction

In the recontextualization of discourse, a number of choices or decisions are made with regard to the movement or translation of meaning-material across social contexts, e.g. what material should be moved from the original context, and how that material might be re-presented in the potentially different modal ensemble of the new context (Bernstein, 1975, 1996; Bezemer and Kress, 2008; Kress, 2003, 2010). Digital environments allow, and perhaps even encourage, the manipulation, reuse, and redistribution of meaning-material in diverse and potentially novel ways (see, for example, Goldsmith, 2011). In this chapter, I am particularly interested in recontextualizations that challenge or disrupt the way we understand or attempt to make sense of multimodal or composite texts.

As a case in point, I examine the creation and online recontextualization of a digital research article figure (see Figure 9.1). I compare configurations of field, tenor, and mode (Halliday and Hasan, 1985; Halliday, 1978, inter alia), looking in particular at selective appropriation, arrangement, focus, and social repositioning (Bernstein, 1996; Bezemer and Kress, 2008), as the figure is created, moved, or translated between different texts and contexts. In so doing, I ask the following questions: What elements are appropriated from the original text/context, and why? How are those elements re-presented and rearranged in the new text/context? What kinds of social relations are enacted through those new texts/contexts? And how do we make sense of texts that appear to be created through an unintentional or automated juxtaposition of semantic units?

9.2 Context and Recontextualization

In Systemic Functional Linguistics, context is typically described in terms of context of culture and context of situation (after Malinowski, 1923, 1935), with the latter usually defined in terms of the field, tenor, and mode of discourse (see, for example, Halliday, 1978; Halliday and Hasan, 1985; Martin, 1992; Matthiessen *et al.*, 2010). *Field* refers to the nature of the social action, what it is the participants are engaged in, the subject matter; *tenor* refers to who is taking part, and the relative role relations and statuses of those participants; and *mode* refers to the symbolic organization of the text, its media and channels, and its rhetorical modes.

Bernstein (1975, 1996) uses the term *recontextualization* to refer to the transmission or movement of experiences and communications from an originating or primary context to a new or secondary context. Such movement, Bernstein (1975: 28–30, 1996: 46–48) argues, implies a *decontextualization* of experiences and communications as they are selectively appropriated, relocated, refocused, and abstracted from the social base, position, and power relations of the originating context. Moreover, those appropriations, relocations, refocusings, and abstractions are ideologically motivated by the social, political, and epistemological concerns of recontextualizing agents (*recontextualizers*), i.e. those responsible for moving meanings across social contexts (Bernstein, 1996: 23, 53). As examples, Bernstein (1996) discusses the professional/scientific discourse and practices of 'carpentry' and 'physics,' and their transformations into the pedagogic discourse and practices of 'woodwork' and 'school physics'. Formal education selects, relocates, and refocuses the knowledge and practices of those professions and scientific fields, recontextualizing the *what* of the originating discourse (Bernstein, 1996: 49). It also reconfigures the social relations enacted through the discourse, from carpenters–carpenters and physicists–physicists in the originating contexts to teachers–students in the new, pedagogic context, thus recontextualizing the *how* of the originating discourses as well (see Bernstein, 1996: 48–49).

Recontextualization entails the movement of meanings made in one context, in a particular mode or modal ensemble, to another context, with a potentially different modal ensemble. Kress (2003, 2010) describes the movement of meaning as 'translation', in which meaning-material, i.e. the material realization of meaning, is either 'transformed' *within* a semiotic mode or 'transduced' *across* semiotic modes.

Based on the work of Bernstein (1996), Bezemer and Kress (2008: 184–186) propose a set of four 'rhetorical/semiotic principles' that operate during the process of recontextualization: *selection*, *arrangement*, *foregrounding*, and *social repositioning* (cf. Bernstein's selective appropriation, relocation, refocusing, and abstraction, as discussed above). *Selection* involves the choice of what meaning-material is to be moved from the originating context and how those meanings might be re-presented in the new context, bearing in mind the kinds of modal resources available and the relevance of those resources for recontextualizers. Choices also need to be made with regard to the *arrangement* of meaning-materials – such as the order in which meaning-making elements are re-presented – and with regard to what elements should be *foregrounded* (and backgrounded) in the new context. Like Bernstein (1996), Bezemer and Kress (2008: 185–186) argue that new social relations are construed and *new social positions* are enacted through the process of recontextualization.

9.3 Recontextualizing Meaning-Material: Transductions and Transformations

In this chapter, I discuss the creation and subsequent recontextualization of an image, a figure originally published in print and online in a medical research article (Bernard *et al.*, 2001) in the *New England Journal of Medicine* in 2001 (see Figure 9.1). Since its original publication, the article in which the figure appears has been widely discussed in the medical research literature and is one of the most highly cited research articles published in the *New England Journal of Medicine* in the last 20 years.[1]

The figure represents a cross-section of a blood vessel and depicts the proposed response of a certain protein, activated protein C, in regulating inflammation and coagulation in severe sepsis. The figure includes verbal resources, and is a hybrid of schematic and semi-naturalistic elements.

The figure, and the article in which it appears, is published in print and online, in full colour. Online, readers can choose between two formats: Portable Document Format (PDF) and HyperText Markup Language (HTML). The layout of the PDF version (see Figure 9.2a) is identical to that of the print version, in which the figure and its accompanying figure legend occupy an entire page. In the HTML version, the figure is presented in a separate 'media bar', at a relatively smaller size compared with other visual-verbal units in the text (see Figure 9.2b). However, the figure can be enlarged, and it is searchable and downloadable as a single unit, a standalone text, in Joint Photographic Experts Group (JPEG) format. This unit, as we shall see, can be copied, manipulated, and placed alongside other visual-verbal units to create new texts and new meanings.

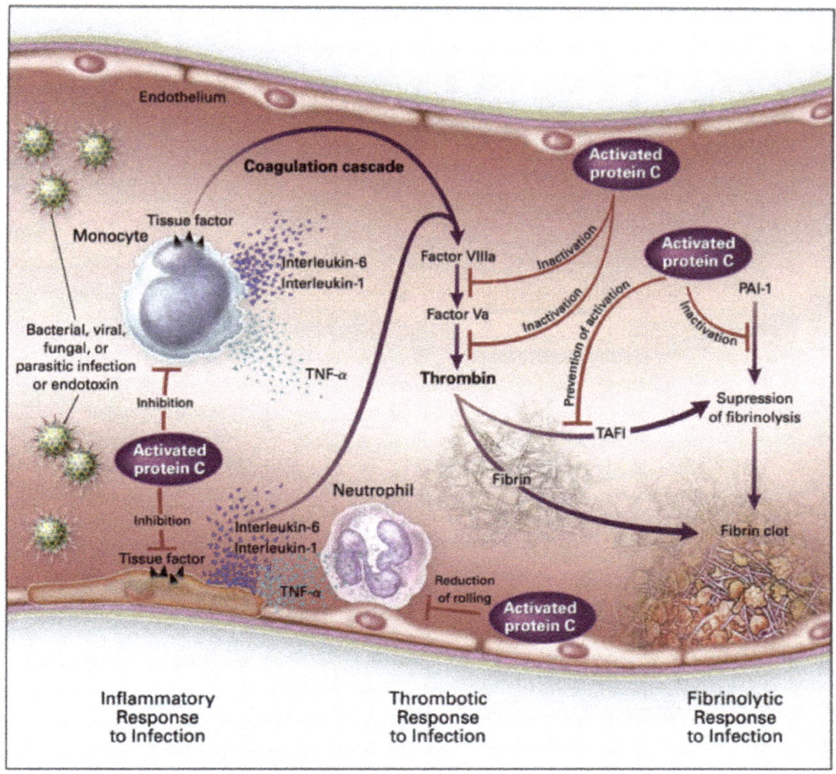

Figure 9.1: Figure from Bernard *et al.* (2001)

9.4 Transduction: Visual-Verbal Representations of Real-Life Artifacts and Actions

Before I discuss the online repurposing of Figure 9.1, it is worth noting that the figure itself is the result of a complex set of recontextualizations, or transductions and transformations (Bezemer and Kress, 2008; Kress, 2003, 2010) in which real-life, three-dimensional artifacts – for example, blood vessels, white blood cells, and bacteria – and a series of potential actions or causal pathways are reconfigured into a two-dimensional visual-verbal representation. Moving those artifacts and actions into visual-verbal modalities requires that recontextualizers – in this case, the authors of the paper and the editors and illustrator of the journal – make a number of decisions about what entities to select, or to appropriate, from the original context. They also have to consider how those entities might be represented in the new context, and how they should be arranged and refocused (Bernstein, 1996; Bezemer and Kress, 2008). For example, the

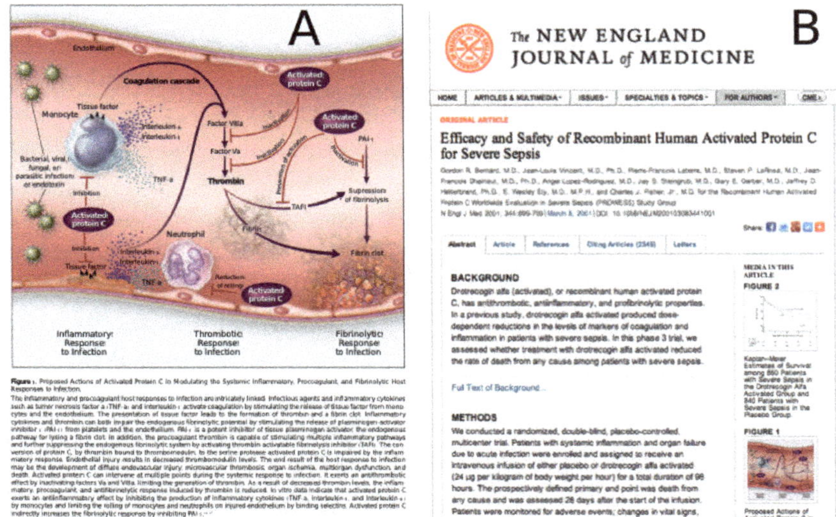

Figure 9.2: Placement and relative sizing of figure in PDF (a) and HTML (b) versions of Bernard *et al.* (2001). (HTML screenshot taken June 14, 2013)

depiction of the blood vessel in Figure 9.1 includes bacteria, a monocyte, a neutrophil, and activated protein C. It does not include red blood cells, certain types of white blood cells, or other elements that we might expect to find in a human blood vessel; nor does it attempt to represent the relative numbers or sizes of those cells typically present in blood. Some artifacts, e.g. cellular structures such as the monocyte, are represented in a 'naturalistic' style, based on their general appearance under a light or electron microscope. Other artifacts, such as proteins, are depicted as ovoid or triangular shapes, rather than in their more typical ('naturalistic') helical forms. Actions or processes, such as 'coagulation' and 'inhibition', are reconfigured visually as vectors (Kress and van Leeuwen, 1996; Kress and van Leeuwen, 2006) in the form of arrows and lines connecting different entities. And a chronology of events or actions is depicted by a left-to-right arrangement of entities in the figure – starting from the moment and type of infection, and ending in the formation of a clot. Note that most of the entities and actions represented in the figure are also labelled verbally, as a form of anchorage (Barthes, 1977: 38–41).

These and other choices are shaped by the kinds of modal resources available in the new context, as well as the intentions or motivations of recontextualizers (Bezemer and Kress, 2008). As a genre, or macro-genre (Martin and Rose, 2008), the academic research article typically and traditionally employs visual and verbal modes, with the more recent addition of sound and video in some online instances. Writing is the dominant and perhaps most highly valued mode, but visual representations in the form of figures and tables are a crucial part of the modal ensemble of the empirical research article and play an integral role in how science *means* (Lemke, 1998). For our figure, the genre-determined visual-verbal modality implies certain losses and gains (Bezemer and Kress, 2008: 177–178, see also Kress, 2005). There is the obvious loss of dimension and sensory losses such as tactility. But some entities in the originating context are also 'lost,' or chosen not to be chosen (cf. Halliday, 2013: 26), and certain qualitative and quantitative details can be overlooked (e.g. relative sizes and numbers, and variations in appearance and function) because of their limited relevance or importance for the *what* and the *how* of the new discourse (Bernstein, 1996: 49).[2] For example, entities and actions that are not involved in the regulation of inflammation and coagulation do not need to be represented in the new context if they are not explicitly relevant for the field. Also, since the medical research article can be considered the paradigmatic site for the contextualization of knowledge in modern medicine (MacDonald, 2002), and thus the primary text through which expert knowers engage (Maton, 2014), we can assume a certain amount of shared knowledge among peers (medical researchers addressing other medical researchers), which obviates the need to visualize every aspect of the process, just those parts deemed most pertinent to the purposes of the research article. Had the figure been intended for a different social context, say that of medical education, and a different genre, say that of an introductory medical textbook, different appropriations, representations, and arrangements would no doubt be necessary.

9.5 Transformation: the Rearrangement of Visual-Verbal Representations

Online, the figure from the *New England Journal of Medicine* has been repurposed a number of times, in other research articles, in weblogs, on a crossword-puzzle solver, on a hair, style, and beauty webpage, and so on (Figure 9.3). For the most part, those recontextualizations leave the figure more or less intact, with only minor transformations. However, some of those new texts suggest rather different readings from those of the original publication of the figure. Here, I focus on a particular set of interrelated recontextualizations that lead to what might best be described as an ambiguous semantic unit or *assemblage*, one that potentially challenges or disrupts the way we make sense of composite texts.

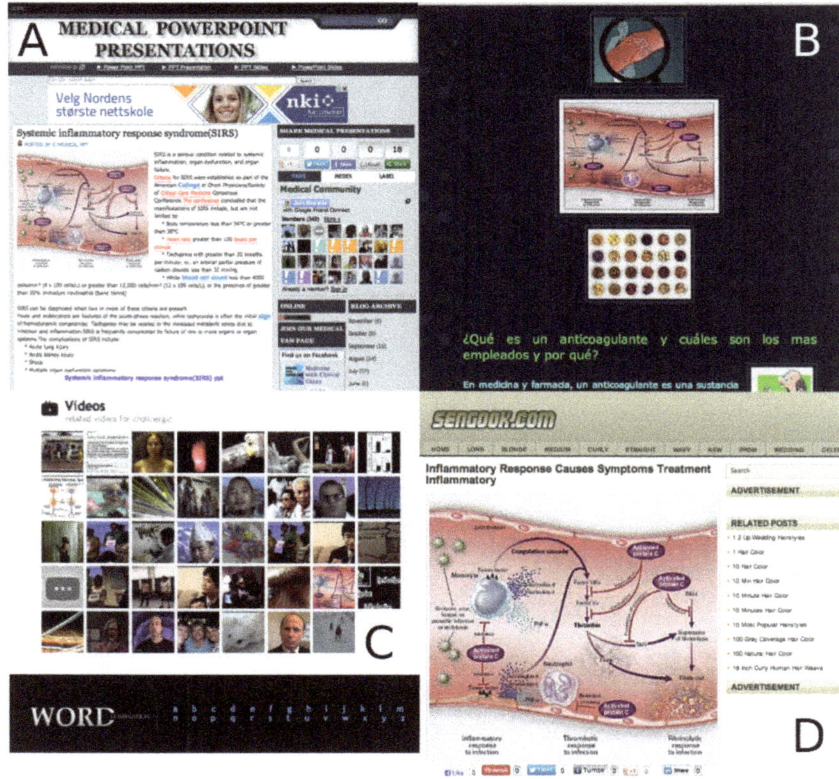

Figure 9.3: Screenshots of selected texts in which the figure has been repurposed: a) an online presentation, b) a weblog, c) a crossword-puzzle solver, d) a hair, style, and beauty webpage (all screenshots taken June 14, 2013).

Figure 9.4 shows selected screenshots from an audiovisual recording posted on the video-sharing website YouTube.com. The video is of a presentation on the regulation of leukocyte trafficking during sepsis, given by a researcher at the Feinstein Institute for Medical Research, New York, in 2007. The audio-visual recording of the presentation includes the figure from Bernard *et al.* (2001) as a thumbnail for the video (Figure 9.4a); the figure also features on a slide in the presentation as part of an approximately two-minute-long sequence (0:45-2:59) describing, visually and verbally, inflammatory response to sepsis (Figure 9.4b).

The repurposing of the figure in the video recording, as viewed on YouTube, is the result of a series of transductions and transformations. For example, the figure has been moved from the original research article, modified, inserted into a presentation programme, projected onto a screen, recorded

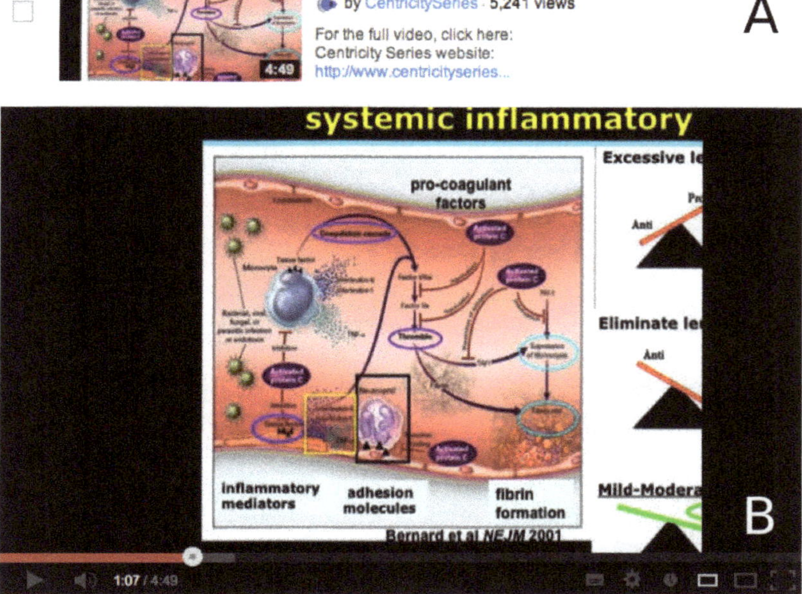

Figure 9.4a & b: Screenshots of the figure on the video-sharing website YouTube: (a) thumbnail for the video, (b) slide in the video (screenshots taken June 14, 2013).

as video, and posted on a website. As part of this process, we can see that certain verbal elements have been added to and removed from the original figure (see Figure 9.5): labels at the bottom of the original figure have been replaced, an additional label has been included at the top of the figure, and a new title and legend have been added. Also, activated protein C, one of the focal elements in the original research article, while not removed from the figure, is not otherwise mentioned in the co-text of the presentation and video recording. Because of the relabeling, the figure depicts a new, albeit relatively similar, left-to-right sequence of events. The figure is also juxtaposed with a second image, on the right side of the slide, which invites comparison and describes several potential sepsis-related outcomes (see Figure 9.6). As can be seen in Figure 9.5, coloured boxes and circles have been added to the figure in order to foreground or refocus certain elements, reducing somewhat the original saliency of activated protein C. The figure itself is also foregrounded in general in comparison to the original research article, since it is used as a thumbnail for searches on the main YouTube site (Figure 9.4a). Social positioning, particularly in terms of contact, differs from the originating context of the research article, in that the video recording presents a primary audience and presenter who are physically co-present, even though their expert status, i.e. peers interested in sepsis-related research, is likely to be similar. The tenor of discourse also includes colleagues and researchers from other institutes, as well as a potentially wider lay audience with different contact and status, since the video has been posted on a popular, publicly available video-sharing website.

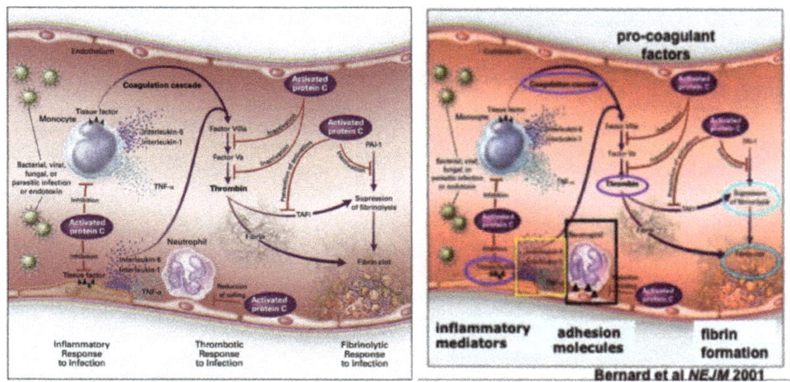

Figure 9.5: Left: original figure (see Figure 9.1); right: transformed figure on YouTube (screenshot taken June 14, 2013).

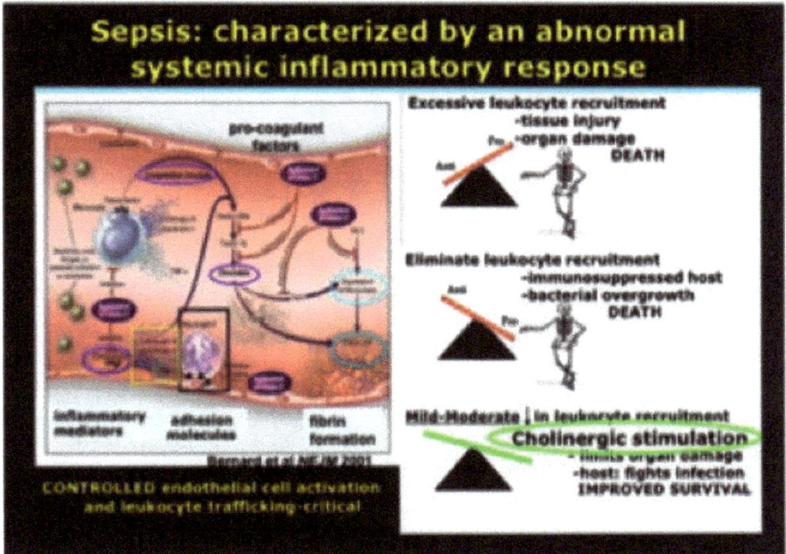

Figure 9.6: From YouTube video: transformed figure (left) placed alongside an image depicting potential sepsis-related outcomes (screenshot taken June 14, 2013).

The figure undergoes further recontextualization when the YouTube video described above is embedded on another website, Global Oneness (see Figure 9.7). Global Oneness is an online resource for 'the best articles, videos and news related to spiritual growth, personal development and alternative lifestyle' (quoted from the Global Oneness homepage at www.experience festival.com).

Figure 9.7: Transformed figure (and video) embedded on Global Oneness webpage (screenshot taken June 14, 2013).

In addition to the changes described in the previous section, the video thumbnail on the Global Oneness webpage is cropped compared to the original figure, with a visually larger, more dominant title than that of the original figure and that of the YouTube video. On the Global Oneness webpage, the image/video is arranged centrally as part of a triptych (Kress and van Leeuwen, 2006: 197–199), similar to the layout on YouTube. In addition to the foregrounding of the boxed/circled elements in the video, the terms 'trafficking' and 'stimulation' are co-textually foregrounded by their repetition in the right-hand column of the site (see Figure 9.7). These terms, however, are different from those in the sepsis video, with key words in the 'New' column (Kress and van Leeuwen, 2006: 197) referring to heroin trafficking, people trafficking, and sensory stimulation kits. In terms of tenor/social positioning and field, the webpage seems to be aimed at two main groups – those with an (academic) interest in sepsis and those with an interest in alternative lifestyles – each with characteristic, technical registers that may or may not overlap. Such a juxtaposition of compositional elements and putative readers suggests some kind of unintentional, automated placement. Indeed, as Figure 9.8 demonstrates, any YouTube video can in fact be viewed via the Global Oneness website, provided the right URL is given.

Figure 9.8: Example of another video automatically embedded on the Global Oneness website (screenshot taken June 14, 2013).

9.6 Making Sense of It All?

How might we make sense of the 'Global Oneness Sepsis' composite and similar online *assemblages*? We generally go to great lengths to interpret stretches of language and other semiotic resources as text, as a coherent passage of discourse with respect to the context of situation and with respect to itself (Halliday and Hasan, 1976: 23–24). The Global Oneness webpage (see Figure 9.7), with its particular generic structure – a familiar-looking website, with a familiar-looking layout – seems to have texture, or at least a degree of texture, even if some of the cohesive relations between verbal-visual units suggest a lack of consistency in contextual coherence. But contexts can be dynamic, and texts can project or construe new situations and new contextual configurations (see, for example, discussion in O'Donnell, 1999). Does it matter that some of the page does not seem to 'hang together', that a reader might not be able to make sense of it *all*? Does that make it a 'non-text' or 'non-sense' (Halliday and Hasan, 1976: 23–25), or just a bad, strange, complicated, obscure, or esoteric text – but a text nonetheless?

This kind of *assemblage* is not necessarily unique to the digital environment, even if the ease with which certain material can be copied, manipulated, and repurposed is arguably greater than that of other media. Visual and verbal art, for example, has often exploited the potential of found objects, found texts, or found sounds, in and across different media, to create new works that can challenge or disrupt our understandings of the original functions and cultural meanings of those appropriated objects. The artists' (or recontextualizers') intentions may be socially, politically, and/or aesthetically motivated, with some pieces created for surprising, comic, and/or subversive effect. However, the intentions or the purposes of the 'Global Oneness Sepsis' webpage may seem less obvious.

As Kress (2010: 144) notes, the 'participatory affordances' of contemporary digital environments can blur traditional distinctions between production and consumption, and between writing and reading. Existing texts can be seen as resources, as compositional elements, for new texts, and 'questions such as "Where did this come from?", "Who is the original/originating author?" seem not an issue' (Kress, 2010: 144). A similar claim is made by Goldsmith (2011: 15): 'Words very well might not only be written to be read but rather to be shared, moved, and manipulated, sometimes by humans, more often by machines, providing us with an extraordinary opportunity to reconsider what writing is and to define new roles for the writer'. These are important points with regard to the 'Global Oneness Sepsis' webpage. Authorship here lies in the design and creation of the webpage, in the layout and in the algorithms used for embedding material from other websites, but it also depends on me, the reader. The webpage designer creates a potential in the form of 'slots' that I can fill with compositional elements. The 'Global Oneness Sepsis' page does not exist until I, the reader and the searcher, bring it into being, as the example in Figure 9.8 also shows. It seems, then, that the communicative purpose or purposes of the 'Global Oneness Sepsis' webpage lie somewhere in the intentions of its various authors. These might include getting more readers to access the site, in the case of the page designers; describing and explaining various aspects of sepsis, in the case of the authors and illustrator of the original figure, and the researcher who repurposed the figure for her presentation; and finding and tracking the use of an online image, in the case of my own interests; to name a few of the possibilities.

The use of the figure from Bernard *et al.* (2001) on the Global Oneness webpage is the result of a complex process of recontextualization, a 'palimpsest', if you will, of transductions and transformations that is hard to fully appreciate. A simplified summary, though – one that barely accounts for all the appropriations, rearrangements, refocusings, and social repositionings that take place – might read as follows: the translation of artifacts and actions into a two-dimensional digital image; the placement and use of that image in a research article; the posting of the image and research article online; the downloading of the image; the modification or transformation of the image; the insertion of the image into presentation software; the projection of the image onto a screen; the discussion of the image in a lecture; the audiovisual recording of that discussion; the posting of the audiovisual recording on YouTube; and the embedding of the YouTube video on the Global Oneness website – not to mention, from this reader's perspective, the searching and finding of the image online, the viewing of the video (and the image) on a screen, the location of the screen in a particular environment, and so on. We might even add to this complex process the subsequent reproduction and discussion of the figure and 'Global Oneness Sepsis' webpage within the pages of this chapter.

Complex recontextualizations of meaning-material, like the example of the 'Global Oneness Sepsis' webpage, are not necessarily unique to digital environments – most texts are the result of a variety of transformations and transductions, some perhaps more noticeable or retrievable for the analyst than others. Similarly, as noted above, the juxtaposition of seemingly unrelated units of meaning is not a uniquely digital phenomenon – in addition to certain verbal and visual art forms, think of print magazines and the (un)intentional placement of advertisements alongside editorial content. However, the apparent prevalence of the kinds of ambiguous *assemblages* discussed above (if the examples in Figure 9.3 are anything to go by), and the role played by 'readers' in creating such texts seem to be a consequence of their digitality. In environments where mixing, sampling, and cutting-and-pasting are the text-creating techniques of choice (Goldsmith, 2011; Kress, 2010), these digital *assemblages* can challenge or disrupt our notions of text and authorship, and blur traditional distinctions between writing and reading. These are important considerations in the production and consumption of texts, especially digital texts, and they deserve further attention.

Acknowledgments

This chapter is based on a paper presented at the European Systemic Functional Linguistics Conference and Workshop (ESFLCW), July 1-3, 2013, at Coventry University. I am grateful to participants at the conference for their helpful comments and questions. I would also like to thank *New England Journal of Medicine* Graphic Arts Director Kathy Stern for taking the time to answer my questions on the process of design and creation of Figure 9.1.

Figure 9.1 is reproduced from Bernard *et al.* (2001) for the Recombinant Human Activated Protein C Worldwide Evaluation in Severe Sepsis (PROWESS) Study Group. Efficacy and Safety of Recombinant Human Activated Protein C for Severe Sepsis. *New England Journal of Medicine* 344 (10): 699–709. Copyright ©2015 Massachusetts Medical Society. Reprinted with permission from Massachusetts Medical Society.

About the author

Daniel Lees Fryer is a Lecturer at Østfold University College, Norway, and a PhD candidate at the University of Gothenburg, Sweden. His research interests include academic literacies, medical research discourse, systemic-functional linguistics, and social semiotics.

Endnotes

1. According to the Web of Science database (see URL: www.webofscience.com; accessed June 14, 2013), the article by Bernard *et al.* (2001) has been cited 3298 times since its original publication.
2. While this recontextualization entails a loss in specificity, it also implies a gain in generality, in which the figure depicts possible or probable (and not necessarily actual) sepsis-related events in a prototypical blood vessel (see Bezemer and Kress, 2008: 178). Other gains might include the relative portability and distributive potential of visual-verbal representations.

References

Barthes, R. (1977) *Image, Music, Text.* London: Fontana Press.

Bernard, G. R., Vincent, J. L., Laterre, P., LaRosa, S. P., Dhainaut, J. F., Lopez-Rodriguez, A., Steingrub, J. S., Garber, G. E., Helterbrand, J. D., Ely, E. W., and Fisher, C. J. (2001) Efficacy and Safety of Recombinant Human Activated Protein C for Severe Sepsis. *New England Journal of Medicine* 344 (10): 699–709.

Bernstein, B. (1975) *Class, Codes and Control: Towards a Theory of Educational Transmission* (Vol. III). London: Routledge.
Bernstein, B. (1996) *Pedagogy, Symbolic Control and Identity: Theory, Research, Critique*. London: Taylor & Francis.
Bezemer, J. and Kress, G. (2008) Writing in Multimodal Texts: A Social Semiotic Account of Designs for Learning. *Written Communication* 25(2): 166–195.
Goldsmith, K. (2011) *Uncreative Writing: Managing Language in the Digital Age*. New York: Columbia University Press.
Halliday, M. A. K. (1978) *Language as Social Semiotic: The Social Interpretation of Language and Meaning*. London: Arnold.
Halliday, M. A. K. (2013) Meaning as Choice. In L. Fontaine, T. Bartlett, and G. O'Grady (eds) *Systemic Functional Linguistics: Exploring Choice*, 15–36. Cambridge: Cambridge University Press.
Halliday, M. A. K. and Hasan, R. (1976) *Cohesion in English*. London: Longman.
Halliday, M. A. K. and Hasan, R. (1985) *Language, Context, and Text: Aspects of Language in a Social-Semiotic Perspective*. Geelong: Deakin University.
Kress, G. (2003) *Literacy in the New Media Age*. London: Routledge.
Kress, G. (2005) Gains and Losses: New Forms of Texts, Knowledge and Learning. *Computers and Composition* 22: 5–22.
Kress, G. (2010) *Multimodality: A Social Semiotic Approach to Contemporary Communication*. London and New York: Routledge.
Kress, G. and van Leeuwen, T. (1996) *Reading Images: The Grammar of Visual Design*. 1st edn. London: Routledge.
Kress, G. and van Leeuwen, T. (2006) *Reading Images: The Grammar of Visual Design*. 2nd edn. London: Routledge.
Lemke, J. (1998) Multiplying Meaning: Visual and Verbal Semiotics in Scientific Text. In J. R. Martin, and R. Veel (eds) *Reading Science: Critical and Functional Perspectives on Discourses of Science*, 87–113. London: Routledge.
MacDonald, M. N. (2002) Pedagogy, Pathology and Ideology: The Production, Transmission and Reproduction of Medical Discourse. *Discourse & Society* 13(4): 447–467.
Malinowski, B. (1923) The Problem of Meaning in Primitive Languages. In C. K. Ogden and I. A. Richards (eds) *The Meaning of Meaning*, 146–152. London: Routledge.
Malinowski, B. (1935) *Coral Gardens and Their Magic (Vol. II)*. London: Allen and Unwin.
Martin, J. R. (1992) *English Text: System and Structure*. Amsterdam: Benjamins.
Martin, J. R. and Rose, D. (2008) *Genre Relations: Mapping Culture*. London: Equinox Publishing.
Maton, K. (2014) *Knowledge and Knowers: Towards a Realist Sociology of Education*. Abingdon: Routledge.
Matthiessen, C. M. I. M., Teruya, K., and Lam, M. (2010) *Key Terms in Systemic Functional Linguistics*. London and New York: Continuum.
O'Donnell, M. (1999) Context in Dynamic Modelling. In M. Ghadessy (ed.) *Text and Context in Functional Linguistics*, 63–99. Amsterdam: John Benjamins.

10 Analysis of an Online University Lecture: Multimodal Perspectives

Mersini Karagevrekis
University of Macedonia

10.1 Introduction

Modern academic texts in a dynamic (electronic) form, unlike their static printed counterparts, unfold in time. This means that they involve a greater majority of semiotic resources (visual, linguistic, actional, etc.) in making meaning in specific social contexts than static texts. They are also more complex in their structure as they consist of different phases (textual sequencing units consistent in the copatterning of different resources) along with points of transition (i.e. realignments in the grouping of diverse resources) between the phases (Gregory in Baldry and Thibault, 2006: 47). Digital texts have proven particularly useful for classroom analysis within an English for Academic Purposes (EAP) context. Dynamic electronic texts, such as video texts, can capture the nonverbal expressive resources (i.e. gestures, posture, movement, gaze) and the paralinguistic features (i.e. pitch and tone of voice) that co-occur with speech but cannot be fully realized in written language. Such resources are significant in meaning making because they can modify the meaning of what is being said while at the same time alert the listeners as to how to interpret the message conveyed.

As previous work on multimodality has shown (Baldry, 2000; Baldry and Thibault, 2006; Tan, 2009), digital texts can be best analysed within a social semiotic metafunctional framework. The framework combines Halliday's (Halliday and Matthiessen, 2014) metafunctional theory and Bakhtin's (1986) views on genre and intertextuality with Gregory's notion of textual phase and transition (in Baldry and Thibault, 2006: 47). The same analytical approach is employed for the analysis of a few excerpts from an internationally available online university lecture on economic theories (Sloman, 2006: 97) for teaching EAP in this chapter. The multimodal text analysis proposed here is intended for EAP teachers who are interested in discourse analysis and thus in drawing students' attention to the way information is conveyed in the dynamic economics text rather than to what the information is. This type of analysis can be used in class with undergraduate students of English or discourse analysis who are learning EAP as one useful register. It can also be tested on nonspecialist EAP students (e.g. students of economics) who are advanced English language learners and also possess sophisticated language knowledge. To this end, short uncut sequences or selected still frames of the excerpts, accompanied by a transcription of the linguistic text, are described employing the combined analytical approach. The analysis is in the form of open-ended questions that encourage interpretation of the data according to metafunctional and genre theory. Halliday's theory of metafunctions (ideational, interpersonal and textual), extended to other semiotic resources (Halliday and Matthiessen, 2014; Kress and van Leeuwen, 2006), specifies the ways in which various semiotic resources intertwine to make meaning in its totality. Bakhtin's distinction between primary (mini-genres) and secondary genres, also applied to multimodal genres (Bakhtin, 1986; Baldry, 2000; Baldry and Thibault, 2006), shows how primary genres (prefabricated verbal, visual units) combine to form the more complex secondary genre, in our case a lecture. The relationship between phases and metafunctions is described through a frame and phase analysis, as proposed by Baldry and Thibault (2006: 47) who, following Gregory, have extended phasal analysis to multimodal dynamic texts. Baldry and Thibault's frame analysis, however, is not to be confused with Goffman's (1974) use of frame analysis which is more similar to Gregory's phasal analysis (how texts are organized 'in 'chunks' of tri-functional consistency', i.e. ideational, interpersonal and textual consistency) (Gregory in Malcolm, 2010: 14). Goffman (1974: 10) employs the term 'frame' in Bateson's sense to study the way frames ('principles of organization') structure social experience. Baldry and Thibault (2006: 187), on the other hand, use 'frame' to refer to a digital still frame image. The combined analytical approach employed in this chapter aims to enhance understanding of the way diverse semiotic modalities, with specialized functions, integrate to make meaning in the university lecture and thus further foster students' discipline specific multimodal literacy skills ('Multiliteracies' in the New London Group terminology (Cope and Kalantzis, 2000: 5).

The next three sections briefly outline Halliday's metafunctional theory, Bakhtin's views on genre and intertextuality and Gregory's notion of phase and transition.

10.2 Halliday's Theory and Its Extension to the Analysis of Other Semiotics

In Halliday's Systemic Functional Linguistics (SFL) language is analysed as social semiotic, a system of 'meaning potential' realized in use (Halliday and Matthiessen, 2014: 23). Language being a complex system is organized into two stratal planes: the content plane (further stratified as semantics and lexicogrammar) and the expression plane (phonology/graphology). The three strata are interrelated through the process of realization (i.e. meanings are realized as wordings, which, in turn, are realized as sound and writing). Each stratum is paradigmatically organized as a system of meaningful choices which are reexpressed as structural configurations. In SFL the basic unit of analysis is text, 'an instance of the semantic system, language functioning in context' (Halliday and Matthiessen, 2014: 43). Halliday's definition of text can been extended to include the multimodal text (e.g. Kress and van Leeuwen, 2006 on image, Muntigl, 2004 on gesture). In this sense all texts occur in a wider context of culture and in a more specific context of situation (the more immediate environment in which they function). Language (image, gesture, etc.) is functionally organized in such a way as to simultaneously reflect and construct the context of situation (the field/mode/tenor of discourse) along three basic dimensions of meaning or metafunctions. The ideational metafunction (representing what is going on in the world), the interpersonal ('enacting interpersonal relationships') and the textual (what makes a text into a text). The ideational metafunction is subdivided into the experiential ('construing a model of experience') and the logical ('constructing logical relations') metafunctions (Halliday and Matthiessen, 2014: 85). There is a correlation between situational features and semantic features insofar as the *field* (what is happening) is reflected in the experiential meanings of the text, the *tenor* (the personal relationships involved) in the interpersonal meanings and the *mode* (the role language is playing) in the textual meanings. It is clear, then, that a metafunctional analysis of the multimodal text can signify in a systematic way how diverse semiotic resources integrate to create an overall text meaning (Baldry and Thibault's 'resource integration principle' [2006: 17]).

Kress and van Leeuwen (2006) have extended Halliday's metafunctional theory to the visual semiotic. Let us very briefly review their 'Grammar of the Visual Design'. Ideationally/representationally Kress and van Leeuwen (2006: 74–75, 79) differentiate between narrative structures (structures of doing and happening) and conceptual structures (structures representing the world in terms of class, structure or meaning). The people, places, things that are depicted in the images are called 'represented participants'. Narrative processes distinguish between transactional and non-transactional actions or reactions, mental processes, and verbal processes. Conceptual structures differentiate between classificational, analytical and symbolical processes. Interpersonally social relations are represented through the simultaneous systems of contact/gaze (demand/offer), social distance/frame (close/middle/long shot) and attitude/perspective (frontal/oblique/high/eye level/low angle) (Kress and van Leeuwen, 2006: 149). Textually/compositionally visual composition can be structured along the following three principles: information value, salience, and framing. (Kress and van Leeuwen, 2006: 177). The composition of the whole can determine, to a large extent, the reading path that the viewer/reader will follow, i.e. circular, vertical, diagonal (Kress and van Leeuwen, 2006: 208).

10.3 Bakhtin's Views on Genre and Intertextuality

Bakhtin (1986: 60) defines genres as types of text with a particular cultural or social purpose around which clusters a specific combination of linguistic and situational characteristics. Genres, then, are closely related to considerations of ideology and relations of power. Since they are culturally defined, they vary with the times and ideological movements within society. The definition of genre, in this sense, encompasses register which is language/variety according to use and is characterized by certain linguistic forms. Bakhtin (1986: 60-2) differentiates between primary (simple) and secondary (complex/ideological) genres (oral and written). Primary genres, sometimes called 'mini-genres' (Baldry and Thibault, 2006: 42), are short spoken or written utterances such as question and answer, assertion and objection, suggestion and acceptance. Primary genres lose their immediate relation to everyday life when they are absorbed by the secondary genres (for example, novels, dramas, all kinds of scientific research).

Bakhtin's distinction between primary and secondary genres, as Baldry and Thibault suggest (2006: 43), can be extended to include multimodal texts. In multimodal texts, as they point out, pictorial (logos, photographs), linguistic and other primary genres are absorbed and recontextualized by the more complex secondary genres such as the scientific text, the web page or the school textbook. Bakhtin also refers to the concept of 'intertextuality' in language: a term introduced by Kristeva in her discussion of Bakhtin's work, according to Allen (2000: 14). Bakhtin (1986: 89) used the concept to explain that all our utterances (even the creative works) are not unique but are tinted with others' utterances 'which carry with them their own expression, their own evaluative tone'. We, in turn, 'assimilate, rework, and reaccentuate' these utterances of others. This implies, as Fairclough (1992: 102) points out, that all texts 'are inherently intertextual, constituted by elements of other texts'.

10.4 Gregory's Phasal Analysis and Its Extension to Digital Texts

Baldry and Thibault (2006: 48) have extended Gregory's frame analysis to multimodal dynamic texts. The text as a whole is segmented into a number of phases and the points of transition between them. This is done by using a post-production software programme such as Sony Vegas Pro. Transition points in a text are salient and easy to identify because they 'represent realignments' in the grouping of diverse semiotic resources (Baldry, 2000: 67). They correspond to shifts in the text thematics (e.g. ideational meaning) and by indicating when a phase or a subphase ends and another begins they can provide useful information about the textual organization of the text. Typical phase and subphase markers are words such as 'But', 'So', 'Well', 'Um'. Baldry and Thibault's frame and phase analysis provides a micro and macroanalytical examination of dynamic texts and examines the text as instance and type. Short uncut sequences of film allow a macroanalytical study of the general characteristics of the text. On the other hand, microanalytical examination of individual frames or sequences of individual frames can depict the integration of resources and how the resources relate to the metafunctions in specific phases. The same framework is used for the analysis of a few excerpts from the economics video text in this chapter. The analysis is by no means exhaustive and focuses on a few aspects of the semiotic resources employed in the production of meaning. The questions that precede the analysis are indicative of the types of questions one might have when examining the materials within a social semiotic metafunctional context. The data are presented in a three column table. The first column presents the numerical order of frames. The second column presents the most salient freeze frames of a shot in the sequence and the third column contains a simplified transcription of the linguistic text. When the excerpts are shown in the classroom the transcription need not be given to the students.

Presented in the sections below are the brief analyses of the excerpts.

10.5 A Brief Multimodal Analysis of Selected Uncut Sequences and Still Frames from the Online Economics Lecture

The lecture on 'The Marginalist Revolution' was delivered in a one week instructional programme of the Mises Institute, in Auburn, Alabama, USA. The Institute is dedicated to the promotion of Austrian Economics. The word 'Marginalist Revolution', as the lecturer explains, describes the independent but simultaneous discovery of the principle of 'marginal utility' by three nineteenth century economists who lived in different countries: Walras (a French-Swiss economist), Stanley Jevons (a British economist) and Menger (an Austrian economist and the founder of the Austrian school of economics). The lecture focuses on Menger's theory of value and of price because his theory contributed to the evolution of economic thought. According to Menger, 'marginal utility' describes the value of a unit of a good rather than the value of all units of a good. This means that the fewer units of a good you have, the higher the value.

The audience in the lecture theatre are students from all over the world with an interest in Austrian economics.

10.6 A Brief Multimodal Analysis of Evaluative Stance

The first segment under analysis is from the first subphase of a phase in which the lecturer briefly describes Walras and Jevons's approach to marginal utility.

Questions such as the following can help students better understand the role of evaluation in academic discourse and the way speakers/writers express opinions, assessments and align hearers/readers with particular views.

1. What nonverbal devices does the lecturer use to introduce the topic of discussion in this subphase?
2. What is the lecturer's stance towards Walras and Jevons?
3. How does the lecturer acknowledge the presence of the audience?
4. What role does the audience laugh play?

Let us first examine how the lecturer introduces the topic of discussion in this subphase using body language in codeployment with speech (Figure 10.1, Frame 1). The lecturer is on the podium. But his body posture (body turned towards the board), his pointing hand and gaze direct the audience's

No	Freeze Frame	TIME(02.12-02.27)LANGUAGE
1		Let us quickly dispose of Léon Walras and Leon...
2		Stanley Jevons,both of th, them
3		were pretty... odd looking.
		I have pictures of them
4		I can't ***show*** them, unfortunately.
5		But as you'd expect
		they were mathematical economists, so they were odd looking, um. [audience laugh]

Figure 10.1: The evaluative stance

attention to the economists' names on the board. The lecturer's gaze coinstantiates experiential and textual meanings. That is, the vector that emanates from the Gazer/lecturer towards the Phenomenon (the names on the board) also creates an indexical link to the board, an object in the visual field of both interlocutors. The meanings realized by gaze also tie with the textual function of the deictic hand. Indexical gestures, as Cléirigh (in Hood, 2011:

35) notes, need not co-occur with speech because they realize meanings rather than wordings. Such gestures fall into the category of Cléirigh's epilinguistic body language. The other two categories he recognizes are protolinguistic body language, which has developed out of infant protolanguage, and linguistic body language that 'only occurs during speech' (Cléirigh in Hood, 2011: 35). Body posture, gesture and gaze, then, all work together to express directionality to a referent, the written names on the board.

In the spoken language the way the lecturer expresses his point of view about Walras and Jevons reveals his stance towards them. Evaluation (Martin's 'appraisal') is an important aspect of academic discourse (spoken/written) 'contributing to the interpersonal dimension of discourse' (Hyland, 2004: 16). Speakers/writers evaluate the material they discuss, convey judgements, attitudes, and guide hearers/readers to a preferred interpretation of views and arguments. In this way they establish themselves as members of a particular discipline community and express a communal value system and the underlying ideology of this community (Thompson and Hunston, 2000: 6). Before analysing the lecturer's attitudinal stance let us briefly revise appraisal theory in SFL (Martin and Rose, 2007: 26). The appraisal system consists of the following three subsystems: *attitude* (expression of feelings, judgements), *graduation* (intensity of evaluation in terms of force and focus) and *engagement* (sources of attitude). Attitude is divided into *affect* (expression of positive/negative feelings explicitly/implicitly), *judgement* (expression of personal/moral judgements explicitly/implicitly) and *appreciation* (positive/negative evaluations of products, processes, phenomena explicitly/implicitly). *Affect* is grouped into the following three sets of emotions: un/happiness, in/security and dis/satisfaction. *Judgement* is classified as social esteem (normality, capacity and tenacity) and as social sanction (veracity and propriety). *Appreciation* is organized in terms of reaction, composition and valuation.

The lecturer's evaluative language in this excerpt indicates that the lecturer is not that positively predisposed towards Walras and Jevons. His stance is realized in the 'co-selection of functional features', i.e in the form of 'couplings' throughout the segment (Zappavigna *et al*., 2010: 219). 'Coupling' (Martin's term in Knight, 2010: 39) describes the ways metafunctional and other meanings intertwine in the logogenesis (unfolding) of a text. For example, in the first sentence the co-selection of the grading adverb 'pretty' with the tonically salient evaluative adjective 'odd looking' explicitly marks a negative value judgement as well as negative appreciation. At the same time it gives the lecturer an excuse to briefly review Walras and Jevon's approach to 'marginal utility' as the coupling of the attitudinal adverb 'quickly' with the negative evaluative verb 'dispose' indicates. Walras and Jevon's contribution to marginalism is valued as less significant than Menger's (i.e. negative appreciation). The lecturer also wanted to show pictures of the two economists to support his point of view that they were 'odd looking' but the overhead projector is not working. So he expresses his annoyance in a double hand-arm gesture with the palms turned up and sideways (Frame 5) which co-occurs with the phrase 'I can't show them' (tonic accent on 'show'). Gesture is one of the semiotic systems of body language and can 'in different ways "add" textual, interpersonal, and ideational meanings to speech' (Muntigl, 2004: 44). However, in communities in which speech is the main means of communication gesture seems to play an ancillary role, i.e. it is not that fully developed (Kress, 2010: 126). It does not have a grammar of its own like speech and writing (i.e. clearly identified constituent parts like verb or noun) (Muntigl, 2004). For this reason in terms of experiential meaning it more readily relates to a 'complete figure', i.e. a clause type (Halliday and Matthiessen in Muntigl, 2004: 36) rather than a meaningful part of the clause. In this excerpt both the lecturer's conventionalized gesture (a gesture used when the speaker feels unable to do something) and the negative form of the modal 'can' express the same experiential meaning (i.e. inability). In addition the coupling of the gesture with intonation intensifies affect. The use of the evaluative disjunct 'unfortunately' in final position as a comment on the content of the clause also construes attitudinal meaning. Since the lecturer cannot show pictures of the two economists he decides to appeal to the communal value system that he and the audience share.

In monologic events, like lectures, audience participation is minimal. As a result there is no feedback and the speaker's meanings cannot be responded and negotiated as in turntaking interactions. In this excerpt the use of the personal pronoun 'you' in the phrase 'you'd expect' explicitly acknowledges the presence of the audience. At the same time the lecturer assumes that the audience will understand his humorous comment on Walras and Jevons' appearance (i.e. they were mathematical economists and so they were odd looking) because as members of the same discourse community they all share a communal value system. Indeed, the audience respond to his humorous remark (a coupling of attitude with ideational meaning), which also seems to mitigate the tension that the lecturer's previous utterance has caused (i.e. his annoyance because the overhead projector was not working). The audience find it funny and laugh. Laughter is a semiotic system in its own right but it is confined to interpersonal metafunction (Knight, 2011: 11). It makes meaning in interaction with language and complements speech 'in the social negotiation of affiliation' (Knight, 2011: 25). The audience laugh, then, conveys attitudinal and affiliative meanings and underlines shared membership of a particular disciplinary community.

It is obvious from the analysis that evaluation is not realized only locally but spreads throughout the excerpt. Meanings intertwine within the same metafunction, across metafunctions and across modes portraying in this way 'the 'prosodic' nature of attitude, and of interpersonal meaning in general' (Martin and Rose, 2007: 36).

10.7 A Brief Multimodal Analysis of the Discourse of 'Others'

This except is from the last subphase of a phase in which the lecturer uses the mini-genre of problem and solution to explain why classical economists failed to solve the diamonds-water paradox. That is, why diamonds cost more than water although water is vital to our existence. In the segment under analysis he is concluding the section, as the use of the particle 'so' in initial position indicates (Crawford Camiciottoli, 2004: 91).

Questions such as the following can increase students' understanding of the way speakers/writers introduce alternative voices (Bakhtin's 'intertextuality' or 'social heteroglossia') into their own discourse and engage with them to express alignment or opposition.

1. Why does the lecturer introduce the discourse of 'others' into his own discourse?
2. How does he create an evaluative stance towards the text of 'others'?

Reference to previous research is an important feature of academic discourse. Speakers/writers not only introduce additional voices into their discourse but they also interact with them. They adopt an evaluative stance towards the thematics of 'others' in order to produce a convincing argument. That is exactly what the lecturer does in this excerpt. As in the previous segment, the lecturer's body posture and the pointing gesture, coarticulated with the personal pronoun 'they', direct attention to the names of the classical economists on the board (i.e. the topic of discussion) (Figure 10.2, Frame 1). He openly criticizes classical economists' failure to solve the diamonds-water paradox expressing not simply his personal value judgement but 'the generally accepted knowledge of the discourse community' he belongs to (Webber, 2004: 187). He uses negation to indicate his stance. In Appraisal theory (Martin and Rose, 2007: 49–53) negation, projection and modality are among the engagement resources that can incorporate alternative voices into a text. The negative grading adverb 'never', the emphatic use of the grading pronoun 'all' at the beginning of the clause, the negative meaning of the verb 'push to the side' (i.e. consider no more), and the tonic accent on

No	Freeze Frame	TIME(14.48-15.0.4)LANGUAGE
1		So they never solved
2		the paradox of value.
3		All they did was they,
4		they pu, pushed it
5		to the side.
6		They focused on exchange value on, on determining prices and...
7		when they ***did*** that, they said:
8		"well,
9		prices are determined by the cost of production, OK,
10		in the long run".

Figure 10.2: Negotiating with the discourse of 'others'

the verb 'did' the second time it is used, are markers of explicit (inscribed) negation. In addition the lecturer couples his spoken words 'they pushed it to the side' with a 'representational' ('iconic') gesture (Jaworski and Thurlow, 2011: 254) for extra emphasis (Frames 4 and 5). There seems to be, as

Matthiessen (2007) observes, 'a natural relationship between specific meanings and specific expressions'. Gestures, then, more readily realize figures of material processes rather than other types of processes because they can mimic the physical act they represent. It should be noted here, however, that the verb 'push to the side' is used as a mental cognitive process rather than a material process in the lecturer's spoken language. To show how flawed classical economists' reasoning was the lecturer includes a direct quotation attributed to classical economists in his monologue. This quotation is not a projection of classical economists' actual spoken words but it simply represents their viewpoint. What is interesting in this direct quotation is the gesture that couples with the spoken words 'prices are determined' (Frame 9). The gesture is the conventionalized gesture that speakers use when they do not know how or feel unable to do something. It is used again, also accompanied by a shrug, in the same utterance in codeployment with the phrase 'by the cost of production'. The attitudinal meaning of the gestures contrasts with the ideational meaning of the spoken words. The gestures evaluate the content of classical economists' proposition negatively.

It is clear from the analysis that linguistic, paralinguistic and gestural resources combine to help the lecturer create an evaluative stance towards the additional voices he brings into his monologue. These resources, however, are not always harmonized. For example, what the lecturer says can contradict what he gestures as in the case of the direct quotation of classical economists' viewpoint.

10.8 A Brief Multimodal Analysis of the Diagram

The last excerpt under analysis is the diagram the lecturer has drawn on the board to represent graphically what Menger described only verbally in his book, that is, imputation theory or cause and effect theory (i.e. a subphase in a phase that explains the imputation law). According to Menger's imputation theory all things are subject to the law of cause and effect. In other words, subjective wants cause all the objective production of goods which, in turn, causes the satisfaction of wants. Consequently factors (input) prices are determined by output prices, which is the opposite of classical economists' labour theory of value. For example, bread has a price because it causes the satisfaction of the consumer.

Questions such as the following can help students realize that diverse semiotic resources have different possibilities and limitations which are 'shaped both by the characteristics and potentialities of the medium and by the requirements, histories and values of societies and their cultures' (Kress and van Leeuwen, 2006: 35).

1. How is the cause/effect relation in the spoken discourse represented in the diagram?
2. In what way does the diagram visually address the viewer?
3. What reading path does the compositional arrangement of the diagram determine?
4. Why is the diagram a mini-genre in its own right?

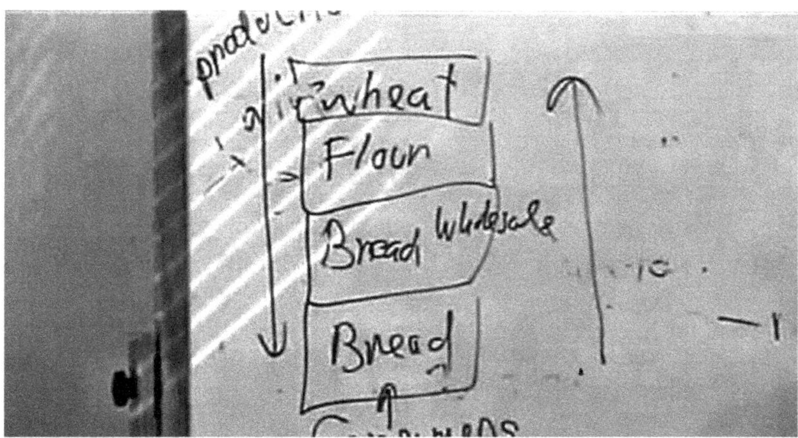

Figure 10.3: The diagram

In this excerpt the lecturer selects visual communication (Figure 10.3) as the most effective means of communicating information at the particular point in the lecture. He uses 'transduction' ('the change from one mode to another') to represent cause/effect relations in a schematic, metaphorical and economical way (Bezemer and Kress, 2008: 175). As Sloman (2006: 12) points out, economic relations that 'might take a long time to express in words can often be expressed clearly and simply in a diagram'. The lecturer is drawing on the board explaining at the same time the different stages involved in the production of bread. Pointing gestures are also used to direct attention to the ideational meaning of the diagram. In the verbal he uses the mini-genre of explanation to express 'implication sequences' temporally organized (Rose and Martin, 2012: 100). That is, events related by cause and effect with the temporal conjunction 'then' explicitly denoting the causal (if-then) relation between events (e.g. [...] and you mill the wheat into flour. Then you take the flour [...]). Visually in terms of ideational meaning the temporal sequence is realized as a conversion process. That is, 'a chain of transactional processes' with the Participant (the Relay) being the Goal of one action and the Actor of another always transforming what they receive (Kress and van Leeuwen, 2006: 68).

Interactionally the diagram is offered to the viewer objectively as an item of information. A lack of background, depth and detail also enhances objectivity. It does not involve the viewer in any way. It simply invites adoption of an attitude of acceptance in terms of the truth value of its content.

Compositionally the vertical arrangement of the boxes/participants in the diagram predetermines the reading path. The viewer has no option but to adopt a vertical reading path.

The diagram is a mini-genre in its own right and one of the typical meaning making resources of the secondary genre of economics text (Karagevrekis, 2015). The other mini-genres are tables, charts and graphs. Diagrams are highly abstract pictures and are employed for representing unfolding economic relations rather than real-life data. Diagrams cannot give accurate figures, like tables, but their ideational meaning can be perceived immediately by the viewer. They use the scientific/technological principles for the visual truth they represent (that is, the 'effectiveness' of an image as a 'blueprint') (Kress and van Leeuwen, 2006: 165). In this way they differ from the photo, which adopts the naturalistic coding orientation, i.e. the visual representation resembles what we see in real life (Kress and van Leeuwen, 2006: 165–166).

It is clear from the analysis that genres, like modes, have different potentials and limitations. The lecturer exploits the possibilities of the mini-genre of diagram to render economic relationships in a more schematic, condensed, yet clear way.

10.9 Conclusion

In this chapter I have analysed a few excerpts from an online university lecture on economic theories in an attempt to help EAP teachers who are interested in discourse analysis further develop students' discipline specific 'multiliteracies' (The New London Group term, Cope and Kalantzis, 2000: 5). The multimodal analysis proposed in this chapter can be used in class with undergraduate students of English or discourse analysis who are learning EAP as one useful register or even tested on students of economics who are advanced English language learners and possess sophisticated language knowledge. A social semiotic metafunctional framework has been used for the analysis which is in the form of open-ended questions. The combined analytical approach provides a deeper insight into the way diverse semiotic resources (e.g. verbal, visual, actional), each in its own particular way and in interaction with the others, combine to create a unified total. Since lecturing is a preferred means of instruction in higher education students need to realize that lecturers almost always when they speak simultaneously employ other semiotic resources for meaning making. The online lecture being a digital text can capture all the linguistic, paralinguistic and nonverbal semiotic resources that integrate to make meaning in the lecture. Spoken language, unlike its written co-variation, then, can more fully develop and exhibit the meaning potential of language because it constantly responds to changes in its environment no matter how small or subtle they are (Halliday, 1994: xxiii). In the excerpts under analysis, gestures with particular functions almost always co-occur with speech. For example, pointing gestures (also accompanied by posture and gaze) direct attention to the topic of discussion. Representational gestures, on the other hand, imitate the physical act they represent and enhance the meaning of spoken words whereas conventionalized gestures express affect. These gestures are often coupled with intonation (tonic accent on words) and intensify the force of spoken words. The analysis also draws attention to the rhetorical strategies and devices that are used in academic discourse and can help students 'acquire and employ a discipline-specific literacy' (Hyland, 2002: 129). For instance, evaluative language helps the lecturer adopt an attitudinal stance towards the material he discusses or when he negotiates with the discourse of 'others' in his monologue. Through evaluation (coupling of attitudinal and ideational meanings) he expresses agreement or opposition and aligns the audience with specific positions and views. In addition, changes in intonation, the 'melody' of language, as Matthiessen (2009: 12) calls it, signal attitudinal stance or affect. Transduction ('drawing' meaning from one mode to another) allows the lecturer to exploit the different potentials of modes and to represent economic relationships in a more abstract and general way than language does (i.e. visually, in a diagram) (Kress, 2010: 124). In terms of pedagogy the video text also provides a more interactive environment of teaching and learning than the static text (for student interaction in online learning programmes see Drury, this volume). Having the option to pause, start again, rewind is extremely helpful. The excerpts can also be reedited to highlight different aspects of meaning at a particular point in the text and shown again or can be used as self access materials (Baldry, 2000: 71). In the latter case the student can access the material at their own pace, stopping it, freezing it in time, watching it to pay more attention to the content or to the nonverbal communication that accompanies the lecturer's spoken language. Digital texts, then, can be profitably introduced into an EAP syllabus because they can help students engage more effectively in the specialist field of their studies which is clearly the main objective of EAP teaching and learning.

Source of Material

The Marginalist Revolution, Joseph T. Salerno. Retrieved on July 10, 2014 from http://www.youtube.com/watch?v=k5sgWFrAwnw

Acknowledgements

Thanks are due to Ludwig Von Mises Institute for permission to reuse excerpts from the online lecture, 'The Marginalist Revolution' by Joseph T. Salerno, at http://www.youtube.com/watch?v=k5sgWFrAwnw, uploaded on 11 August 2010.

Also appreciated is assistance from Fotis Sakalis, the studio technician in the department of Music Science and Art at the University of Macedonia, Thessaloniki, Greece. He provided invaluable help in the segmentation of the video text.

About the author

Mersini Karagevrekis works as an English for Academic/Specific Purposes teacher at the University of Macedonia, Greece. Her research interests include distance learning and continuing education through the use of modern technologies, multimodal and multimedial analysis of texts within a social semiotic metafunctional framework and stylistics.

References

Allen, G. (2000) *Intertextuality*. London: Routledge.

Bakhtin, M. (1986) The Problem of Speech Genres and Text Types. In C. Emerson and M. Holquist (eds) *Speech Genres and Other Late Essays*, 60–102. Austin, TX: University of Texas Press.

Baldry, A. (2000) English in a Visual Society: Comparative and Historical Dimensions in Multimodality and Multimediality. In A. Baldry (ed.) *Multimodality and Multimediality in the Distance Learning Age*, 41–89. Campobasso, Italy: Palladino Editore.

Baldry, A. and Thibault, P. (2006) *Multimodal Transcription and Text Analysis*. London: Equinox Publishing.

Bezemer, J. and Kress, G. (2008) Writing in Multimodal Texts: A Social Semiotic Account of Designs for Learning. *Written Communication* 25(2): 166–195.

Cope, B. and Kalantzis, M. (2000) Introduction. Multiliteracies: The Beginnings of an Idea. In B. Cope, and M. Kalantzis (eds) *Multiliteracies: Literacy Learning and the Design of Social Futures*, 3–8. London: Routledge.

Crawford Camiciottoli, B. (2004) Audience-Oriented Relevance Markers in Business Studies Lectures. In G. Del Lungo Camiciotti and E. Tognini Bonelli (eds) *New Insights into Evaluation*, 81–97. Bern: Peter Lang.
Fairclough, N. (1992) *Discourse and Social Change*. Cambridge: Polity Press.
Goffman, E. (1974) Frame Analysis: An Essay on the Organization of Experience. New York: Harper and Row.
Halliday, M. A. K. (1994) *An Introduction to Functional Grammar*. 2nd edn. London and Melbourne: Arnold.
Halliday, M. A. K. and Matthiessen, C. M. I. M. (2014) *Halliday's Introduction to Functional Grammar*. 4th edn. London and New York: Routledge.
Hood, S. (2011) Body Language in Face-to-Face Teaching: A Focus on Textual and Interpersonal Meaning. In S. Dreyfus, S. Hood, and M. Stenglin (eds) *Semiotic Margins: Meaning in Multimodalities*, 31–52. London: Continuum.
Hyland, K. (2002) Activity and Evaluation: Reporting Practices in Academic Writing. In J. Flowerdew (ed.) *Academic Discourse*, 115–130. Edinburgh: Pearson Education.
Hyland, K. (2004) Engagement and Disciplinarity: The Other Side of Evaluation in Academic Discourse. In G. Del Lungo Camiciotti and E. Tognini Bonelli (eds) *New Insights into Evaluation*, 13–30. Bern: Peter Lang.
Jaworski, A. and Thurlow, C. (2011) Gesture and Movement in Tourist Spaces. In J. Carey (ed.) *The Routledge Handbook of Multimodal Analysis*, 253–262. London: Routledge.
Karagevrekis, M. (2015) A Multimodal Analysis of Genres of Economics Representation in EAP/ESP. In S. Starc, C. Jones, and A. Maiorani (eds) *Meaning Making in Text: Multimodal and Multilingual Functional Perspectives*, 197–222. Basingstoke and New York: Palgrave Macmillan.
Knight, N. K. (2010) Wrinkling Complexity: Concepts of Identity and Affiliation in Humour. In J. R. Martin and M. Bednarek (eds) *New Discourse on Language Functional Perspectives on Multimodality, Identity and Affiliation*, 35–38. London: Continuum.
Knight, N. K. (2011) The Interpersonal Semiotics of Having a Laugh. In S. Dreyfus, S. Hood and M. Stenglin (eds) *Semiotic Margins: Meaning in Multimodalities*, 7–30. London: Continuum.
Kress, G. (2010) Multimodality: A Social Semiotic Approach to Contemporary Communication. London and New York: Routledge.
Kress, G. and van Leeuwen, T. (2006) *Reading Images: The Grammar of Visual Design*. 2nd edn. London: Routledge.
Malcolm, K. (2010) Phasal Analysis: Analysing Discourse through Communication Linguistics. London: Continuum.
Martin, J. R. and Rose, D. (2007) *Working with Discourse: Meaning Beyond the Clause*. 2nd edn. London: Continuum.
Matthiessen, C. M. I. M. (2007) The Multimodal Page: A Systematic Functional Exploration. In T. D. Royce and W. L. Bowcher (eds) *New Directions in the Analysis of Multimodal Discourse*, 1–62. Mahwah, NJ: Lawrence Erlbaum Associates.
Matthiessen, C. M. I. M. (2009) Multisemiosis and Context-Based Register Typology: Registerial Variation in the Complementarity of Semiotic Systems. In E. Ventola and A. J. Moya Guijarro (eds) *The World Told and the World Shown*, 11–38. Basingstoke and New York: Palgrave Macmillan.

Muntigl, P. (2004) Modelling Multiple Semiotic Systems. In E. Ventola, C. Cassily and M. Kaltenbacher (eds) *Perspectives on Multimodality*, 31–50. Amsterdam: John Benjamins.

Rose, D. and Martin, J. R. (2012) Learning to Write, Reading to Learn: Genre, Knowledge and Pedagogy in the Sydney School. Sheffield: Equinox Publishing.

Sloman, J. (2006) *Economics*. 6th edn. Edinburgh: Pearson Education.

Tan, S. (2009) A Systemic Functional Framework for the Analysis of Corporate Television Advertisements. In E. Ventola and A. J. Moya Guijarro (eds) *The World Told and the World Shown*, 158–182. Basingstoke and New York: Palgrave Macmillan.

Thompson, G. and Hunston, S. (2000) Evaluation: An Introduction. In G. Thompson, and S. Hunston (eds) *Evaluation in Text: Authorial Stance and the Construction of Discourse*, 1–27. Oxford: Oxford University Press.

Webber, P. (2004) Negation in Linguistic Papers. In G. Del Lungo Camiciotti, and E. Tognini Bonelli (eds) *New Insights into Evaluation*, 181–202. Bern: Peter Lang.

Zappavigna, M., Cléirigh, C., Dwyer, P., and Martin, J. R. (2010) The Coupling of Gesture and Phonology. In J. R. Martin, and M. Bednarek (eds) *New Discourse on Language Functional Perspectives on Multimodality, Identity and Affiliation*, 219–236. London: Continuum.

11 Transitivity in Language Event Reports in an Online Corpus of Science Journalism

Blanca García Riaza
University of Salamanca

11.1 Introduction

Nowadays, newspapers can no longer be considered as solely a paper-based media, as many also appear as digital sources of information that appeal to a general readership that uses the Internet to be updated with the latest events. Digital editions of newspapers have expanded their scope to include specialized sections that deal with new areas of knowledge, such as the case of science popularization articles, now present in national daily newspapers across Europe (Hyland, 2010: 118), such as '*The Guardian*', '*El País*', '*La Repubblica*', '*Der Spiegel*' to name but a few. The discourse of news media is now widely studied in computerized research and considered to be a productive source of information on language structure, both for discourse analysts and corpus linguists, as they reveal the distinctive features of these digital texts and thus help to characterize them.

These science popularization articles disseminate scientific findings (Giannoni, 2008: 212) and make scientific discourse and newspaper discourse merge in a new type of text that represents language events (2004: 441). These science popularization texts also create an authority that legitimizes journalists' words (Caldas-Coulthard, 1994: 303) and which is expressed through a series of linguistic and discursive choices that transmit scientific discoveries in a text (McCabe and Heilman, 2007: 139).

As Myers (2003: 265) asserts, only scientific texts that are not addressed to specialists can be considered popularizations, bearing in mind that there are other different genres of scientific discourse whose texts are written by and addressed to specialists but they do not commonly concentrate on explaining the social meaning of scientific events, as popular science texts do (Gotti, 2014: 27).

These articles report the latest national and international advances and discoveries that could result in relevant changes in our daily lives (Calsamiglia and López Ferrero, 2003: 174), and are considered in this study as a new specific register, with its own norms, patterns and styles. As Calsamiglia and Lopez Ferrero state, science popularization articles are characterized as 'Scientists having regular interaction – mediated – with the general public, [...] apparently seeking to fill the gap between the scientific community and people in general' (2003: 174), thus implying a recontextualization of scientific discourse. In addition to this, science popularization articles transform, to a certain extent, specialized knowledge into 'everyday' knowledge and try to be as informative and interesting as possible for a non-expert audience (Ciapuscio, 1997: 28; Williams, 2009: 467).

These linguistic experiences are shaped through language reports (Thompson, 1996: 501), a resource for journalists to include different voices in the story (Heritage, 2013; Martin and Rose, 2003: 23; McNamara 2013). As one of their most outstanding features, these science popularization texts include a multiplicity of authors, which are given voice through processes of attribution, in which language events are reported to provide the narration with authorial references that authorize the journalist's words (Caldas-Coulthard, 1994: 303). As a consequence, a key aspect for this study is the notion of attribution, considered as the adscription of information or opinion in a text to sources, which might be animate or inanimate (Hunston, 1999: 181). As a matter of fact, attribution is an inherent feature of newspaper discourse that gives more verisimilitude to the facts reported, detaches the journalist from the speech reported and adds a prestigious source that legitimizes the words reported. That epistemological positioning in science popularization articles is studied in this research focusing on participants and reporting verbs, signals in the reporting that identify the author of the original words, as well as the way in which the language event was originally produced. The Transitivity System within SFL, which 'specifies different types of process that are recognized in the language, and the structures by which they are expressed' (Halliday, 1985: 101) has been used as the theory of language underlying this study, due to its potential to reconstruct the world and the human experience as text, a parallelism with the recontextualization of scientific events that, as mentioned earlier, is carried out in science popularizations.

Reported speech is used in science popularization discourse as an element to introduce the scientific findings that are transmitted as new knowledge, but also as a tool for the journalist to detach him/herself from the language events presented. These are attributed to expert voices that mark the evidentiality in the text (Clift, 2006) and index aspects of the speaker's position with regard to what they are stating: their 'epistemological assessment' (Mushin, 2001: 11). Participants are 'voiced' as attributees and presented as saying or thinking, accompanied by a signal which is either an epistemic stance adjunct (*according to*) or a reporting verb. On the one hand, reporting verbs provide readers with information about how the original language event was produced (*tell/suggest/claim*), but also about the format of the original language event (*say/write*), and can sometimes be key to interpret the speaker's intention in a language report (*speculate/confirm*). On the other hand, the epistemic stance adjunct '*according to*' represents the author's comment on the source of the information provided and marks that another person's words are being reported, encoded as projection, either as direct speech (quote) or indirect speech (report) (Halliday and Matthiessen, 2004; Thompson, 1996). The interest of this study in language reports lies in the fact that they transmit, through the recontextualization of the language event produced by the journalist, the most relevant data (*who? how? what?*) that readers need to get a good account of what they are being informed about. Language reports are then an essential linguistic mechanism used by science journalists to incorporate the original information provided in a language event into the text.

11.2 Corpus and Research Methodology

Bearing all these elements in mind, the objective of this study is to analyse the occurrences and anatomy of language reports in a corpus of science popularization articles from the British newspaper *The Guardian*, focusing on the two aforementioned parameters of transitivity, participants and reporting verb as signals in the reporting clause, to obtain more information about how science popularization texts make use of projection structures to attribute language events. The ultimate aim of this study is to benefit from an SFL approach to attain a deeper level of description of the distinctive features of digital science popularization articles, and, therefore of the newspaper genre in a digital context. With this deeper knowledge, a better teaching of the phenomenon will also be possible, updating the contents taught in tertiary level classrooms with real data that allows the students to understand the most common combinations of structures and resources in a particular genre (Karagevrekis, this volume).

The fact that the texts studied are mainly designed for a digital environment made us consider two additional factors. On the one hand, we have to bear in mind that when somebody accesses a newspaper webpage, s/he is voluntarily choosing the information s/he reads, and thus selecting the section that is more interesting or better suits his/her knowledge needs with a simple click of the mouse or tap on the keypad without having to read previous pages or leaf through the whole publication as it often happens in printed publications.

On the other hand, we have to consider that the information from a digital science popularization text is shown on a computer, tablet or smartphone screen, and therefore, only the headline, the lead and possibly the first paragraphs are perceived at first sight, before dragging down the webpage and continuing reading. The text is thus not a linear construct in the sense printed publications are, but is composed as a network (Kaltenbacher, this volume) that links the reader to other sections, previous articles or occurrences of the same key terms in the newspaper. These are the reasons why a very special attention has been paid to first paragraphs (hereafter P1), initial sections of the texts with a very high degree of informativity within texts (Ho-Dac, 2008; Mahlberg and O'Donnell, 2008). We have thus considered them as initial sections that are first seen by the readers and which act as an introduction to the topic/participants and reveal the aboutness of the whole text.

For the purpose of analysing the occurrences and anatomy of language events' reports, an electronic corpus, named '*Sci_TG Corpus*', was compiled with 567 science popularization texts from the online version of the British newspaper *The Guardian* (García Riaza, 2012). The corpus has 363,636 running words, among which we have analysed 3,022 attribution cases within language events' reports. *The Guardian* newspaper is a quality broadsheet aimed at a relatively educated audience in Great Britain (Kim and Thompson, 2010: 62) and has the most numerous print run of the country with 350,000 daily copies. As a result, this publication has been frequently used in comparative studies such as Mahlberg, O'Donnell, Hoey and Scott (2007), Garcia Riaza (2012), García Riaza and Elorza (2013), Elorza (2011), Giannoni (2008) or Pounds (2010).

The corpus was annotated for the analysis with informative tags (Participant <P>, Reporting verb <RV>, According to <AC>...) that allowed us to use the computing software WordSmith Tools 5.0 (Scott, 2009) and guide the study from the perspective of Corpus Linguistics, 'A way of investigating language by observing large amounts of naturally-occurring, electronically stores discourse, using software which selects, sorts, matches, counts and calculates' (Hunston and Francis, 2000: 14–15). As a consequence, we carried out both a quantitative and a qualitative analysis of the data in the corpus from a more objective perspective and accurate analysis of the occurrences, and, accordingly, we examined the interplay between participants and reporting signals (both reporting verbs and the epistemic adjunct *according to*) in initial sections (P1, excluding the headline and the lead) and the rest of the text in the corpus of the newspaper *The Guardian* compiled for this research.

For a clearer process of analysis, a series of research questions were listed to guide the study, divided into four groups according to the studied elements they refer to, and which will also be used to present the results in the next section.

11.2.1 Research Questions, Group 1

This group of research questions aims to get information about the presence of reporting in the corpus studied, and, more specifically, the frequency of use of reporting verbs and epistemic stance adjuncts. Furthermore a deeper division was made between initial and non-initial sections of the text, differentiating occurrences in P1 and in the rest of the text:

- How many language reports are there in the corpus?/how frequent are reports in the science popularization articles studied?
- How many cases of a report with a reporting verb can be found?
- How many cases of a report with an epistemic adjuncts can be found?
- Are reporting verbs more frequent in P1 or in non-initial sections?
- Are epistemic adjuncts more frequent in P1 or in subsequent sections?

11.2.2 Research Questions, Group 2

These questions deal with the position that the reporting verb or epistemic adjunct occupy in relation to the participant to which they refer. In this sense, we focused on the preference to present the participant in the first place and then the reporting verb/epistemic adjunct, or the election of the journalist to do it the other way round. We also analysed the preference of the epistemic adjunct *according to*, to be followed by either a personal or material reference in first paragraphs. This hypothesis was based on the idea that first paragraphs are more informative sections because of occupying the initial part of the text, and also concentrate a higher proportional percentage of occurrences of this epistemic adjunct, a very overt mechanism for the journalists to present external voices and make readers aware of this inclusion by a syntactic procedure: separating the reporting signal and the participant from the information presented by means of a comma.

- Does the reporting verb prime to appear after/before the participant in P1?
- Does the reporting verb prime to appear after/before the verb in no-initial sections?

- Does the epistemic adjunct prime to appear after/before the participant in P1?
- Does the epistemic adjunct prime to appear after/before the verb in no-initial sections?
- Are epistemic adjuncts more frequently followed by a material reference rather than by a personal one?
- Is *according to* typically followed by references to material entities in P1?

11.2.3 Research Questions, Group 3

This group of questions refers to the reporting verbs found in the corpus, and intend to extract information about the repertoire of verbs that are more commonly used to introduce language reports in the science popularization articles studied. Additionally, information about the degree of evaluation of the journalist of the language event can also be extracted from the reporting verbs found:

- How many different reporting verbs can be found in the corpus?
- What is the degree of evaluation that these reporting verbs can transmit?

11.2.4 Research Questions, Group 4

The last group of questions deals with the degree of informativity that the participants named in the articles studied show. We wanted to know how detailed references to authorized voices are and if there is a typical pattern in the introduction of the participants along the texts.

11.3 Results and Discussion

With regards to research questions in Group 1, the analysis of the corpus has shown that there are 2,771 reporting verb tokens in language reports in '*Sci_TG Corpus*', among which 147 are in P1 (5.31%) and 2,624 in the rest of the text (94.69%).

Additionally, 251 cases of language reports in which there is an epistemic stance adjunct as the reporting signal (*according to*) have also been identified in the corpus. Results of the analysis have shown that there are 116 cases (46.21%) in P1 while 135 cases (53.79%) concentrate on the rest of the text.

As can be seen in Table 11.1, the total number of reporting signals is significantly smaller in P1 than in the rest of the text, mainly because first sections mean a single paragraph of the total length of the text, but is very worthwhile commenting that first paragraphs, being much shorter than the rest of the text, concentrate a very high number of occurrences of the epistemic stance adjunct. In terms of the distribution of reporting verbs, there seems, in accordance with the data on the allocation of the epistemic adjunct, to be a preference for the rest of the text, rather than being present at the initial paragraph.

Table 11.1: Presence of Reporting Signals in the Corpus Studied

	Reporting verb	Epistemic adjunct	Total
In P1	147	116	263
In the rest of the text	2,624	135	2,759
Total	2,771	251	3,022

In relation to research questions in Group 2, the reporting signals identified in the corpus were further analysed to get information about the position they occupy in reference to the participant (RS+P or P+RS). The two signals in the reporting clause, reporting verbs and participants being attributed the language events, are typically presented by the journalist either preceding the message or immediately after it, no matter if the language event is recontextualized in direct or indirect speech, as shown in Examples 1 and 2:

Example 1. **Prof Stringer added** that the Ahob project was not the end of the story for the history of humans in Britain (Sci_TG06125) [Emphasis added].

Example 2. 'The Earth would be extremely singed – the oceans will boil dry and we'll be left with a rather unpleasant rock,' **said Prof Marsh** (Sci_TG0606) [Emphasis added].

Taking these premises into account, we focus our attention on which of these two elements occupies the first position in the reporting clause, and is therefore selected by the journalist to be presented to the reader just after the words of the language event are conveyed. Reporting verbs are more commonly preceded by the participant [P+RV] rather than followed by it [RV+P]. As shown in Table 11.2, the reporting verb occurs as first element in the reporting signal in nine cases in P1 (6.12%) and in 684 cases in the rest of the articles studied (26.07%). In these cases, the journalist has chosen to state how the language event happened, before providing the readers with the information about who was the author of the words reported. Conversely, the participant appears as first element in the reporting clause 138 times (93.88%) in first paragraphs and 1,940 times (73.93%) in the subsequent sections of the text. In the light of the data obtained, it seems that the attribution to the source of information is primed to appear at the beginning of the reporting clause in science popularization texts from *The Guardian* newspaper.

Table 11.2: Position of Signals in the Reporting Clause

	RS + P	P + RS
In P1	9	138
In the rest of the text	684	1,940
Total	693	1,978

Taking a step further in the analysis, we analysed the occurrences of participants in the right position of the epistemic stance adjunct '*according to*', the typical element acting as substitute of the reporting verb in the science popularization articles studied. Three consecutive positions on the right of the adjunct (R1, R2, R3...) were thoroughly inspected using concordance lines, and found that in initial paragraphs, the epistemic stance adjunct is followed by a personal reference in the 31.9% of the cases (37), while in the 68.1% of the cases (79) the reference following according to is material rather than personal.

Example 3. 'A vast, dust-covered ocean of ice is the most likely place to discover life on Mars, **according to a team of British scientists'** (Sci_TG07259).

Example 4. Astronomers may be on the brink of discovering a second Earth-like planet, a find that would add fresh impetus to the search for extraterrestrial life, **according to a leading science journal** (Sci_TG0749).

In subsequent sections of the texts, the attributees of the epistemic stance adjunct tend to be material entities in 82 of the cases (60.74%), a higher percentage than that of personal references, which represent a 39.26% (53 cases) and establish a pattern in accordance with that of initial sections.

Example 5. 'In tests, injections of the nanoparticles formed a gel that triggered fresh growth of damaged nerves and helped restore the eyesight of 75% of animals, **according to the study published in the Proceedings of the National Academy of Sciences'** (Sci_TG06357).

Example 6. The dozen or so projects chosen each year for funding tend to be long-term, perhaps coming to fruition within 10 to 40 years, **according to Sharon Garrison, Niac's co-ordinator at Nasa** (Sci_TG06453).

Following our aim to illustrate how Systemic Functional Linguistics (SFL) can be used to describe digital texts and question the orthodox dichotomies that exist in these descriptions, and answering research questions in Group 3, we have taken into account that when language events are dealt with in English classes, typically the two verbs portrayed as reporting the speech of others, be it in a direct or indirect form, are *say* and *tell*. Some teachers at more advanced levels go beyond this simplistic presentation of the phenomenon and include verbs such as *add*, *answer*, *claim* or *describe*, but they are not yet representative of the reality found in texts. When studying '*Sci_TG Corpus*', we have found a total of 77 different verbs used in language events to show how the actual words were uttered, as can be seen in Figure 11.1.

SAY	CONCEDE	INDICATE
ADD	CONFIRM	INVITE
BELIEVE	EXPRESS	POINT
WRITE	FIND	POSE [a question]
WARN	OUTLINE	PRAISE
TELL	PROPOSE	PRESENT
SUGGEST	PUBLISH	PROMOTE
CLAIM	STRESS	PRONOUNCE
REPORT	WELCOME	[As one scientist] PUT [it]
DESCRIBE	ASSERT	RECALL
CONCLUDE	ACCUSE	RECOMMEND
ANNOUNCE	APPLAUD	REFUSE [to predict]
REVEAL	ASK	REJECT
ADMIT	ATTACK	REPEAT
ARGUE	COME OVER [the speakers]	SHOW
URGE	CONDEMN	SPECULATE
CRITICISE	CONTINUE	SUMMARISE
EXPLAIN	CONTRADICT	TALK
INSIST	DECLARE	UNRAVEL
PREDICT	DEFEND	
ADVISE	DENY	
POINT OUT	DIRECT	
AGREE	DISCUSS	
CALL	DISMISS	
CALL FOR	ENVISAGE	
COMMENT	ESTIMATE	
STATE	HAIL	
ACKWNOWLEDGE	HEAR	
CITE	HIGHLIGHT	

Figure 11.1: Different reporting verbs found in the corpus studied.

These verbs can be classified according to the degree of evaluation of the journalist towards the speaker's words (Thompson, 1994: 33–70) and although *tell* and *say* are the most frequent ones, the repertoire of options that a real writer has when building a text has unravelled as much varied and rich, as shown in these examples:

Example 7. '[This study suggests] that leisure-time exercise during pregnancy, and particularly high-impact exercise, is associated with an increased risk of miscarriage in the early stage,' the authors **wrote** (Sci_TG0761).

Example 8. Scientists **believe** that around 75% of miscarriages are caused by chromosome abnormalities (Sci_TG07256).

Example 9. Research by a team at University College London **suggests** microbes trapped in the ice could be protected against lethal ultraviolet light and intense cosmic radiation that penetrates the thin atmosphere and bleaches the surface (Sci_TG07259).

Finally, to obtain an answer to research questions in Group 4, we considered the degree of informativity of the participants present in the corpus, and further analysed the specificity of references to attributees in P1. For this purpose, we took as a basis Thompson's (1996: 507) notions of *specified other/s* and *unspecified other/s* and found that there is a vast degree of specificity in the corpus, ranging from the general reference in Example 10 to the exhaustive description of the attribute in Example 11:

Example 10. Children whose mothers smoked during their pregnancy are up to nine times more likely to develop attention deficit hyperactivity disorder, **scientists** say (Sci_TG07153).

Example 11. 'The age thing?' says Mark, a middle-aged father who spent his 30s and 40s vaguely wanting children but working and travelling and developing complicated interests instead (Sci_TG06289).

The general pattern found in first sections of *'Sci_TG Corpus'* is that of presenting a general reference to the voice included, without specifying much about who that person/entity is, and then, in the subsequent language events of the text, providing with more details that enable the reader to identify more precisely the relevance and prestige of the person/institution mentioned, as shown in Example 12:

Example 12. Children born to couples who have undergone fertility treatment are more likely to be diagnosed with autism, cancer and other disorders such as cerebral palsy and mental retardation, **researchers** claimed yesterday. [P1]
Speaking at the American Association for Reproductive Medicine (ASRM) conference in New Orleans, **Dr. Croughan** said that medical conditions more common in infertile couples may be to blame for the rise in childhood health problems [Rest] (Sci_TG0675).

11.4 Conclusion

In the light of the results obtained in this study, we can say that reporting verbs are proportionally much more frequent in language reports in subsequent sections of '*Sci_TG Corpus*' than in initial ones, in which the epistemic stance adjunct *according to*, besides also showing a higher percentage of the occurrences, has a more relevant role as reporting signal with almost half of the occurrences in these first paragraphs. *According to* can therefore be said to have a stronger preference for initial sections than reporting verbs, which prime their occurrences at subsequent sections of the science popularizations studied. The inspection of the corpus has also revealed that the verbs are the reporting signals par excellence, far more common than epistemic adjuncts in the corpus studied.

The structure 'participant + reporting verb' has unfolded as the most common organization of signals in the reporting clause. The voice to which the language event is attributed is primed to appear just after the actual words recontextualized, thus creating a strong link between the message and its author. The reporting verb is thus typically presented at the very end of the language report, a symptom perhaps of the preference of readers for the information about the source of knowledge included in the article rather than about how the language event was produced, a preference satisfied by the journalists when building science popularization texts.

Regarding the reporting verbs in the corpus, we have found that, conversely to the dichotomist and simplistic range of reporting verbs that teachers and students normally deal with when learning these structures, the reality is much more varied, and real samples of language in use, as science popularizations reveal that the journalist has a rich repertoire of reporting verbs to suit his/her needs: enabling him/her to be more/less objective in the construction of the language report, and thus add or omit his/her own evaluation on the topic. Among these common verbs, we find examples of verbs that Thompson (1996: 33–70) classifies as showing whether a report is of speech or of writing (*chat/write*); showing what the attribute thinks (mindsay) (*think/believe*); showing the speaker's purpose (*suggest/warn*); or showing the manner of speaking (*comment/mention*), just to highlight a few examples.

From the occurrences analysed, *according to* appears as the typical epistemic stance adjunct of first paragraphs, rather than of subsequent sections of the text, where the presence of this adjunct is less frequent. Regarding the participants that more frequently accompany *according to*, we find that, contrary to what is expected, in the majority of cases it refers to a material entity (*a study, a publication, a journal, an institution*) rather than to a human person, a tendency that is consistent both in initial paragraphs as well as in subsequent sections of the texts studied.

If drawing more attention to participants, we find that the first mention of the participant in initial paragraphs in '*Sci_TG Corpus*' tends to be a general reference to a collective group of people (*scientists, researchers, professors*) that transmit their discovery, whereas the presence of participants in subsequent sections of the texts have a much higher degree of informativity, and provide readers with details about their names, affiliations and relation to the discovery reported. This pattern of behaviour seems to drive the reader through a sort of 'general to specific' pattern (*study/publication – author's name*) in which more details about the attributee are revealed as the text evolves, and accordingly, reveals journalists design the structure of language reports to better suit his/her own informative needs, and those of the reader (Smirnova, 2009).

This research has aimed to shed light into the construction of language reports in science popularization articles in four publications of the British press, but further research needs to be carried out in this field, by, for example, focusing on how the different types of language reports, rephrases, quotations and 'split quotations' are distributed in the texts. In further phases of this study, we will also try to trace the first mention of participants and analyse how the entity or person is addressed in subsequent occurrences, thus tracing the participant's reference progression, and obtaining more information about how the encoding of external voices is carried out in science popularization texts.

About the author

Blanca García Riaza is Lecturer at the Department of English Studies and teaches English for educational, touristic and engineering purposes at the Escuela de Educación y Turismo, Ávila Campus, University of Salamanca, Spain. Her publications include articles on mobile devices as pedagogical tools and science popularization articles analysed within the Systemic Functional framework.

References

Caldas-Coulthard, C. R. (1994) On Reporting Reporting: The Representation of Speech in Factual and Factional Narratives. In M. Coulthard (ed.) *Advances in Written Text Analysis*, 295–308. London: Routledge.

Calsamiglia, H. and López Ferrero, C. (2003) Role and Position in Scientific Voices: Reported Speech in the Media. *Discourse Studies* 5(2): 147–173.

Ciapuscio, G. (1997) Lingüística Y Divulgación De Ciencia. *Quark* 7: 19–28.
Clift, R. (2006) Indexing Stance: Reported Speech as an Interactional Evidential. *Journal of Sociolinguistics* 10(5): 569–595.
Elorza, I. (ed.) (2011) The Encoding of Authorial Voice in Science Popularizations in the Press: A Corpus-Based Cross-Cultural Study. Paper presented at 12th International Pragmatics Conference, July 2011, Manchester, UK.
García Riaza, B. (2012) *Attribution and Thematization Patterns in Science Popularization Articles of the Guardian Newspaper*. [online] Salamanca: Ediciones Universidad de Salamanca. Colección Vítor, 310.
García Riaza, B. and Elorza, I. (2013) The Emergence of External Sources of Attribution in Science Popularizations in the Guardian. *Revista Española De Lingüística Aplicada (RESLA). Communications and Learning Context in LSP: New Perspectives on Genre Analysis* Número Extraordinario 1: 51–69.
Giannoni, D. S. (2008) Popularizing Features in English Journal Editorials. *English for Specific Purposes* 27: 212–232.
Gotti, M. (2014) Reformulation and Recontextualization in Popularization Discourse. *Ibérica* 27: 15–34.
Halliday, M. A. K. (1985) *An Introduction to Functional Grammar*. London: Edward Arnold.
Halliday, M. A. K. and Matthiessen, C. M. I. M. (2004) *An Introduction to Functional Grammar*. 3rd edn. London: Hodder Arnold.
Heritage, J. (2013) Epistemics. *Discourse Studies* 15(5): 551–578.
Ho-Dac, L. M. (2008) Discourse Organisation Though Theme Position. E. Steiner and S. Neumann (eds) *Data and Interpretation in Linguistic Analysis. Proceedings of the Nineteenth European Systemic Functional Linguistics Conference and Workshop*. Saarbrücken: Universität des Saarlandes.
Hunston, S. (1999) Evaluation and the Planes of Discourse: Status and Value in Persuasive Texts. In S. Hunston, and G. Thompson (eds) *Evaluation in Text*, 176–206. Oxford: Oxford University Press.
Hunston, S. and Francis, G. (2000) *Pattern Grammar. A Corpus-Driven Approach to the Lexical Grammar of English*. Amsterdam and Philadelphia, PA: John Benjamins Publishing Company.
Hyland, K. (2010) Constructing Proximity: Relating to Readers in Popular and Professional Science. *Journal of English for Academic Purposes* 9(2): 116–127.
Kim, C. K. and Thompson, G. (2010) Obligation and Reader Involvement in English and Korean Science Popularizations: A Corpus-Based Cross-Cultural Text Analysis. *Text & Talk* 30(1): 53–73.
Mahlberg, M. and O'Donnell, M. (2008) A Fresh View of the Structure of Hard News Stories. In E. Steiner and S. Neumann (eds) *Data and Interpretation in Linguistic Analysis. Proceedings of the Nineteenth European Systemic Functional Linguistics Conference and Workshop*. Saarbrücken: Universität des Saarlandes.
Mahlberg, M., O'Donnell, M., Hoey, M., and Scott, M. (2007) 'Exploring the Textual Positions and Functions of Lexical Items in Hard News Stories'. Paper presented at *The 4th Corpus Linguistics Conference*, July 2007, University of Birmingham, Birmingham, UK.
Martin, J. R. and Rose, D. (2003) *Working with Discourse: Meaning Beyond the Clause*. London and New York: Continuum.
McCabe, A. and Heilman, K. (2007) Textual and Interpersonal Differences between

a News Report and an Editorial. *Revista Alicantina De Estudios Inglese* 20: 139–156.

McNamara, D. S. (2013) The Epistemic Stance between the Author and Reader: A Driving Force in the Cohesion of Text and Writing. *Discourse Studies* 15(5): 579–595.

Mushin, I. (2001) Evidentiality and Epistemological Stance: Narrative Retelling. Amsterdam: John Benjamins Publishing Company.

Myers, G. (2003) Discourse Studies of Science Popularization: Questioning the Boundaries. *Discourse Studies* 5(2): 265–279.

Pounds, G. (2010) Attitude and Subjectivity in Italian and British Hard-News Reporting: The Construction of a Culture-Specific 'Reporter' Voice. *Discourse Studies* 12(1): 106–137.

Scott, M. (2009) *WordSmith Tools* Version 5.0 [Software]. Liverpool: Lexical Analysis Software.

Smirnova, A. V. (2009) Reported Speech as an Element of Argumentative Newspaper Discourse. *Discourse & Communication* 3(1): 79–103.

Thompson, G. (1994) *Collins Cobuild English Guides 5: Reporting*. London: Harper Collins.

Thompson, G. (1996) Voices in the Text: Discourse Perspectives on Language Reports. *Applied Linguistics* 17(4): 501–530.

Williams, J. (2009) Variation of Cancer Metaphors in Scientific Texts and Press Popularizations. *Proceedings of the Fifth Corpus Linguistics Conference*. Liverpool: University of Liverpool.

12 Is This the End of Hypertext? Hotel Websites' Return to Linearity

Martin Kaltenbacher
University of Salzburg

12.1 Introduction

The unpredictability of the reading paths of online texts is perhaps their most outstanding quality. This phenomenon is caused by the interlinking of verbal elements and other modalities within a website and outside of it to other websites. It is this particular feature, this linking 'in some way other than by the default sequential convention of ordinary reading' (Lemke, 2002: 300), that has shaped such texts as non-linear constructs and has created the metaphor of the Internet as a three-dimensional web. This three-dimensionality can be modelled as one dimension representing links within the same page, a second dimension epitomizing the links to other pages within the same website, and the third dimension as symbolizing the links exiting a web-domain to other sites on the world-wide-web. This model is depicted in Figure 12.1.

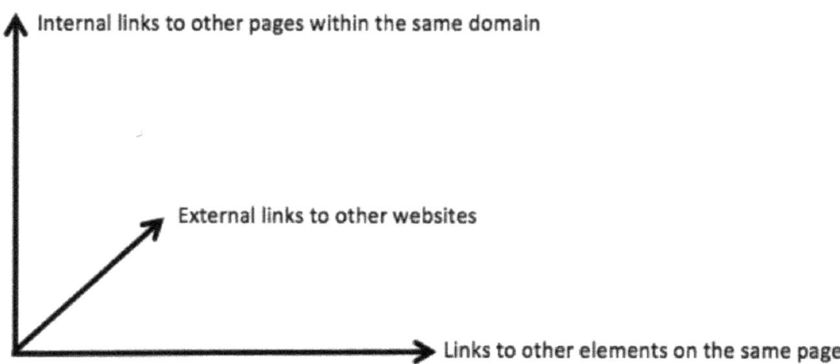

Figure 12.1: The three dimensions of hyperlinks

Without this three-dimensionality of hypertext, the world-wide-web would not have the shape it has today. The possibilities it offers to web-designers and authors in terms of textual cohesion, text expansion and content growth are virtually unlimited. These possibilities, however, do not come without risk. The larger a website grows and the more links it contains, the more consideration has to be given to the strategic planning of the website. If the links in a domain are not cleverly selected, it may well be that a user following the links may end up on a competitor's website instead. This unwanted effect can frequently be observed, e.g. in hotel websites that contain links to a town's official community website or to a regional tourist board. Community and tourist board websites invariably contain links to lists of accommodation options, so prospective guests activating a link to a tourist board may eventually be guided to an alternative hotel to the one they were originally interested in. This can happen, e.g. when surfing the website of Hotel Krallerhof in Leogang in the Province of Salzburg, Austria (http://www.krallerhof.com/en/), where several links on the bottom of the homepage redirect the reader to alternative suppliers of accommodation, such as *Saalfelden/Leogang Tourist Information, Best Wellness Hotels Austria, HolidayCheck.de* or *Tripadvisor.*

There seems to be growing awareness of such negative consequences among web designers in the hotel industry, which can be observed in the decline of the number of hyperlinks, and in particular of external links, in hotel websites. This decline goes hand in hand with a discernible return to traditional page formats and linear reading paths in such websites. This trend is clearly visible, e.g. in the 2015 version of Hotel Altstadt Radisson Blu in Salzburg, Austria (http://www.austria-trend.at/Hotel-Altstadt-Salzburg/en/). The current website (©2015) contains only five menus, each of which opens up to a single page with non-interlinked, linear text. In contrast, a similar hotel in the vicinity, Salzburg Hotel Wolf Dietrich (http://www.salzburg-hotel.at/en), hosts a complex website with seven main menus, each comprising up to seven additional submenus and each containing verbal text with up to ten hyperlinked words and phrases that take the reader outside the current page to somewhere else in the site. Although the latter website has been redesigned and relaunched several times in the past 15 years, the dense complexity of its web-structure and the high amount of hyperlinks has not been reduced. Hotel Wolf Dietrich's website, therefore, exhibits the old tradition of web-design, while the Hotel Altstadt Raddison Blu's website follows the new trend to linear design.

In the following chapter the claim that hotel websites have started to adopt a more linear text design while at the same time abstaining from the use of textual hyperlinks shall be substantiated and exemplified in the analyses of the websites of two renowned luxury hotels.

12.2 Traditional Reading Paths in Hotel Brochures

In the decades before the Internet was established, the hotel industry used professional, well-designed advertising materials to promote their enterprises. These were typically produced in the form of leaflets or glossy brochures. Such brochures were frequently the only form of promotional advertising used by the businesses, and often they did not just fulfil promotional and informative functions but could serve as a souvenir at the same time (Getz and Sailor, 1993: 112). Many hotels still use similar leaflets and brochures today. Indeed, brochures particularly have seen an upsurge in quality and usually come as fully illustrated, glossy, high–quality publications that try to give prospective guests an outlook on life in luxury and exclusivity.

As for structure, the traditional tourist brochure follows by and large the format of a magazine. This means it contains a number of related sections arranged in a logical, coherent order, with the most important information towards the beginning of the brochure and less important details following in later sections. The verbal text adheres to the rules of linear composition and can be read from top to bottom and left to right. The brochure has a clear beginning and a clear end, and though readers may of course skip certain passages and flick through others, the brochure has been written to be read in a particular order from the beginning to the end. As such, hotel brochures fairly strictly adhere to the Western writing and reading traditions of the past and can easily be read without readers getting lost or getting bored by an oversupply of irrelevant, reduplicated or redundant information.

However, as Askehave and Nielsen (2005: 126) point out, many researchers have begun to challenge this dogma of a linear reading path in traditional printed texts. When reading for gathering information rather than for pleasure, we usually flick through a text, scan the pages, skip paragraphs or whole sections in a process similar to what we do when we read on the Internet (Finnemann, 1999: 22). When doing this, we create our own reading path with even less guidance by an author, than when we search a website for a particular piece of information. This kind of browsing or speed-reading implies the risk of overlooking the very information we are seeking. Without doubt, it will take us longer to find information in print than when we turn to the web in the first place.

12.3 Hypertext

While typical Internet texts may still have a fairly clear beginning in the top left corner of the homepage of a website, they can neither be read along a pre-composed reading path, nor do they have a distinct end. In most cases, they are not even meant to be read in a particular order, nor as a whole. Instead, they are often composed as research databases providing the user with a mine of information. Where exactly the readers will look and how they will search or scan a page, will depend to a large extent on 'the importance of the performed search task and its implications for visual perception', as Hiippala (2012: 318) points out in reference to seminal work by Yarbus (1967) and Rayner (1998). In other words, the readers 'choose their own path and thereby create their "own" text in the hypertext system – becoming a kind of web author' (Askehave and Nielsen, 2005: 126). For a detailed eye-tracking study on reading paths in information websites, see Kaltenbacher and Kaltenbacher (2015).

For better orientation within such individual reading paths, most websites have integrated a search tool, which is usually replicated on each individual page of a website. This tool allows users to search for and retrieve information according to their personal needs. It also implies that users can access individual items of information in more than one way: either by searching for particular information using this tool or by following one of the many interlinked words, phrases, sentences, images, etc. provided on a page. Information that is considered important by the designers of a website is frequently interlinked several times. Baldry and Thibault (2006: 26) call this a 'semiotic cascade', by which users are enabled to come back to the same information time and again. The more important a piece of information is, the higher the number of links that navigate a user to it. Consequently, the importance of information in digital texts is not signposted by the traditional discursive tools for creating information redundancy, e.g. by repetition, paraphrase or substitution, but through multiplying the thematic links to one and the same unvaried piece of information.

12.4 Hotel Websites

Recent trends discernible in hotel websites seem to reflect a turning point in web-design which results in a return in text composition to a more traditional linear structure. This claim will be substantiated in this chapter in the analyses of two different versions of two hotel websites, the Hotel Sacher in Vienna and The Sheraton in Salt Lake City, and of their corresponding representations on the hotel reservation platform *booking.com*. The terminology used in the description of the webpages has been adopted from Kok (2004: 134) and from Baldry and Thibault's webpage genre schema (Baldry and Thibault, 2006: 115).

12.4.1 Hotel Sacher, Vienna

Hotel Sacher in Vienna, Austria, (www.sacher.com/de-hotel-sacher-wien.htm; © 2013–2015) is a famous five-star hotel with a history dating back to the nineteenth century. The world-famous chocolate cake Sachertorte is a creation by a member of the Sacher family who allegedly invented the cake for a reception given by the Austrian Chancellor, Klemens Wenzel Fürst von Metternich, in 1832 (Augustin, 2008).

The hotel website is organized in a surprisingly simple and linear form. It reproduces the format and much of the layout of traditional hotel brochures in landscape format and is quite similar to the hotel's glossy paper brochure. In fact, most of the website can be read like a printed hotel brochure. Each page in the website is identical in size and layout and fits easily into the browser's screen, which releases the reader from the necessity of having to scroll vertically or horizontally across the page. All pages are headed by the logo and the menu bar in the top banner. The different menus on the menu bar organize the website into eight sections, which are thematically arranged according to their significance, with the most important categories listed first. The eight menus are *Rooms, Dining, Conferences & Celebrations, Sacher Spa, Concierge, Petit Sacher, Impressions,* and *News*. Some of these sections contain further sub-sections, which range in number from one to nine. If existent, the subsections are visualized in table format with grids consisting of either two or three columns of three boxes each, with each box showing a thumbnail of the sub-page it indexes. This is exemplified in a screenshot produced from the Sacher's *Rooms*-webpage, presented in Figure 12.2.

The most salient item on each page is a large picture filling up the entire screen. This picture functions as an individual eye-catcher to each page. It is foregrounded in the upper two thirds of the *centre-left panel* and keeps unfolding in the background of all other *items* and *clusters* on the page. All pictures are high-quality photos either of hotel rooms or of other hotel interior. The space in the right panel, *the New* in Kress and van Leeuwen's (2006: 179) model of multimodal information structure, contains the interactive 'make a booking' cluster, which is typically one of the most important features on hotel websites. Underneath the booking interface comes a cluster with two items reporting current weather conditions and recommending current services offered at the hotel at this time of the day, such as afternoon tea or spa treatments. The *bottom banner* stretches across the whole page and contains the verbal information elaborating on the topic and the picture of each page. On some pages, there is a link labelled *More Information* underneath this text. A click on this link opens up to an extended verbal description of the information offered in the text-field. All pictures are solidly *anchored* in the verbal text, in terms of Barthes (1977: 39). This recurrent arrangement is always accompanied by a written testimonial, usually from a member of staff rather than a visitor, appraising the high quality of the service being offered. Each individual webpage within the hotel website contains a new and unique picture and a new and unique text and testimonial to describe it. In other words, there are no recycled stretches of text or visuals that would appear on various pages of the website. This comes as a surprise as such a recycled use of text would, in fact, be typical of internet texts but is usually not to be found in printed text.

The layout on more than 90% of all pages follows the canonical arrangement of information in terms of *Given* vs. *New* and *Ideal* vs. *Real*, as theorized by Kress and van Leeuwen (2006: 179). The Ideal is always represented in the form of the stylish photo, loaded with emotional appeal, followed underneath by the detailed verbal elaboration on how this ideal experience can be made real to be enjoyed by the prospective guest. As each page is pre-selected by the reader with a click on the menu bar or on a labelled thumbnail, all this information (the photo and the verbal description) is presented as the Given, while the booking interface, the cluster with current information, and the testimonials are always presented as the New. At the bottom of each page, there are two more banners containing links to internal organizational sections, such as *Press Information, Career, Imprint, the Sacher Family, Online Shop* or to the website of the sister hotel *Hotel Sacher in Salzburg*. These banners do not provide any links to external websites outside the Sacher company.

By far the most striking phenomenon in the website is that the verbal elements in the running text are not interlinked, i.e. there are no digressional nodes within the verbal descriptions that would allow the reader to navigate through the website and to jump quickly from one section to another by activating a thematic link. All verbal text is arranged in a left to right and top down reading direction. The reading experience is, therefore, similar to reading the individual pages of a landscape brochure. The only interlinked items are those in the menu bar and in the bottom banner. The menu thereby adopts the function of a table of contents as in a booklet. This low occurrence of hyperlinks is untypical of websites. In combination with the full-screen landscape format, it conveys the impression that one is reading a traditional linear text in which one can only go to a different section by browsing through the table of contents (the menu bar) and by selecting the area of content one is interested in from there. A similar strategy, though perhaps not to such extreme ends, is pursued by two other hotel-related websites: the Sheraton Hotels website and Booking.com.

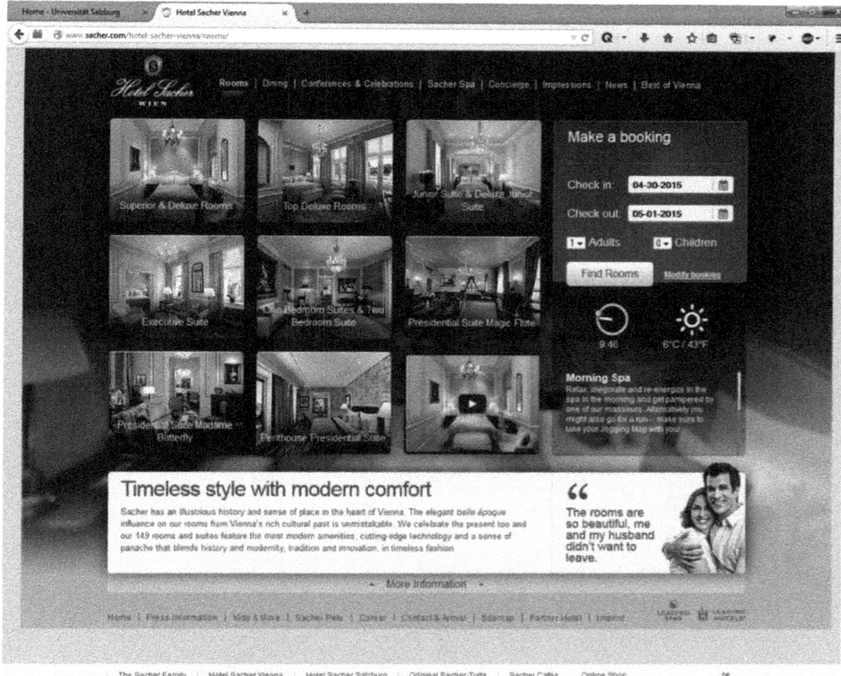

Figure 12.2: Screenshot of the Hotel Sacher's Rooms-webpage available at: http://www.sacher.com/hotel-sacher-vienna/rooms/

12.4.2 The Sheraton Hotel, Salt Lake City

Hotel Sheraton in Salt Lake City, USA, (www.sheratonsaltlakecityhotel.com; © 2009–2015) is owned and run by the international hotel chain Starwood Hotels and Resorts Worldwide Incorporation. While the Salt Lake City hotel aims to establish itself as a resort offering individual service and exclusiveness to the prospective guest, the corporate layout enforced by the mother company, nevertheless, imposes fairly rigid generic and textual restrictions onto the hotel website.

The basic generic structure of the website is similar to the one employed by Hotel Sacher. The top banner lists the hotel's name and address and contains the menu bar consisting of nine categories (*Rooms, Location & Map, Dining, Hotel Features*, etc.), which may contain up to five sub-menus. Contrary to the Sacher's website, the booking interface and some general hotel information are presented in the left panel, while the eye-catching visual is located in the centre-right panel, followed by the verbal text underneath. The individual pages are generally too large to fit onto one screen; consequently, the reader has to scroll down to be able to read an entire page. Yet, what is similar to the Sacher website is that the Sheraton website also exhibits a fairly linear reading path. This is again reflected in the low amount of lexical hyperlinks in the verbal text on the website. While the texts do contain some links, these remain few in number and usually occur at the beginning or towards the end of paragraphs or pages, where they often function as links to *Read More*-sections, expanding on what has just been offered as basic information.

In conclusion, one can say about the Sheraton website that it, too, abstains from building a complex web of interlinked pages, sections and sub-sections but tries to preconstruct a simple reading path that is both predictable as well as easily navigable for the reader.

12.4.3 Booking.com

Booking.com is an internet platform specialized in managing hotel bookings. It enforces strict genre and structure conventions onto the texts promoting the hotels listed on the platform. This is in line with Domingo, Jewitt and Kress (2015) pointing out that online platforms predetermine 'a kind of grammar that sets out potentials and constraints that in turn have effects for the possibilities of writing online'. Therefore, the *booking.com* entries for Hotel Sacher (www.booking.com/hotel/at/sacher-wien.en-us.html; ©1996–2015) and Hotel Sheraton (www.booking.com/hotel/us/sheraton-salt-lake-city.en-us.html; © 1996–2015) reflect very strict style and content constraints imposed on the writers by the operators of the booking platform.

Two outstanding features are noteworthy on *booking.com* webpages. First, the verbal text seems to be the dominant component in each individual hotel entry. While photos and other visualizations occur, they seem to play a less important role than in the Hotel Sacher and Hotel Sheraton websites described earlier. Second, as in the other hotel websites, the individual hotel entries on *booking.com* do not contain any hyperlinks that would take the reader outside each specific entry. What all hotel entries on *booking.com* do contain, however, is a cluster with bookmark links on the top of each entry and a link to the *Verified Reviews* submitted by users of *booking.com*. The bookmarks are labelled, e.g. *Available rooms, Facilities, House Rules.* They enable the reader to skip the relatively long verbal text that follows underneath each of the bookmarked sections and to leap to the next section. As an alternative to using the bookmarks, the reader can scroll down the text, which can be up to four times as long as the length of the browser window. Between the bookmark links and the verbal text comes a large eye-catching photo of the hotel described. In the main body of text there are no further items that would serve as digressional nodes or hyperlinks within or outside the text. Therefore, each individual hotel description consists of one self-contained text and is meant to be read along a prearranged, linear reading path.

Of course, every *booking.com* page contains a range of additional links, e.g. to other hotels in the same city, to other branches of the company, e.g. a car rental business, to other types of accommodation, and to other travel destinations near and far. Yet, all these links are visually set apart from the entry on an individual hotel by means of frames, space, colour, typeface, font size, etc. While these external links do reflect the typical web-character of the Internet, they are semiotically constructed as not being part of the hotel entry. The reader does not conceive of them as belonging to an individual hotel description but to *booking.com* as the host to all the individual texts.

12.5 Conclusion

In a recent publication, Domingo *et al.* (2015) point out that:

> Socially speaking, the formal/semiotic feature of *linearity* correlates with and "materializes" the social feature of *authority*: that is, it points to how the text was made and by whom; and its arrangement tells the reader how to read the text: where to start reading, how to continue reading, and, through that, tells how to "get the" meanings of the author.

In contrast to a reading path forced upon the reader through an author's authoritative design, Domingo *et al.* (2015) claim that authors of internet texts (in their study, authors of *food blogs*) have given up this authority in favour of an invitation to the readers to 'design' their own reading paths according to their personal needs and preferences. This alternative design strategy is determined by Modularity, i.e. by the offer of compositional modules of meaning for the reader to choose from. In their words, modularity 'inverts the social and power relations of maker and reader. Linearity insists that the ordering of the author has to be observed; modularity makes no such assumptions and demands' (Domingo *et al.*, 2015). While this feature of non-linear modularity still seems to be a common design principle in many hotel websites, a number of text designers in the hotel industry have realized that too much freedom for the customer may be bad for the business, and they have reverted to more traditional – in other words, to more authoritative – patterns of design.

As has been shown in the description of two individual hotel websites and their respective entries on *booking.com*, clear trends in the design of hotel websites reveal a return to a high degree of linearity in composition. It is as if web-designers have woken up to Lemke's (2002: 299) assertion that 'they [the designers] know very well that simplicity gives us welcome respite from the demanding complexity of everyday life'. Above all, hotels want to sell something. Therefore, their websites need to guide their prospective buyers to make the right decisions. Consequently, the possibilities that digital document design offers in terms of constructing a deeply interwoven system of complex net-structures are exploited to a much lesser extent than one would expect. Of course, hotel websites still contain some crucial elements of hypertextuality, in particular, the possibility for the reader to interact with the hotel through the booking interface. It is this added 'functionality' in terms of 'a user's *interaction* with the web document' (Shepherd and Watters, 1998, discussed in Bateman, 2008), that – in addition to hyperlinks – contributes much to the unique status of digital hypertexts.

Overall, it can be argued that the revival of linearity reflects a turning point in web-design. Until recently, hotel websites, like so many other websites, were constructed as three-dimensional mazes of interlinked texts, items, clusters, pages, and other webs. It was up to the readers to establish their individual but unpredictable reading paths, while hotel managements missed out on the opportunity to exploit their authority by exerting a strong steering influence on the customers. As far as hotel websites are concerned, this kind of diverting web-design with all its imponderable consequences seems to have come to an end.

About the author

Martin Kaltenbacher is a Postdoctoral Research Fellow in the Department of English and American Studies at the University of Salzburg, Austria. In his research, he applies methods of Systemic Functional Linguistics and corpus linguistics to media discourse, language of tourism and news commentary.

References

Askehave, I. and Nielsen, A. E. (2005) Digital Genres: A Challenge to Traditional Genre Theory. *Information Technology and People* 18(2): 120–141.

Augustin, A. (2008) *Hotel Sacher Wien*. London: The Most Famous Hotels in the World Ltd.

Baldry, A. P. and Thibault, P. J. (2006) *Multimodal Transcription and Text Analysis*. London: Equinox Publishing.

Barthes, R. (1977) Rhetoric of the Image. In S. Heath (ed.) *Image, Music, Text*, 32–51. London: Fontana.

Bateman, J. (2008) *Multimodality and Genre: A Foundation for the Systematic Analysis of Multimodal Documents.* London: Palgrave MacMillan.
Domingo, M., Jewitt, C., and Kress, G. (2015) Multimodal Social Semiotics: Writing in Online Contexts. In J. Rowsell and K. Pahl (eds) *The Routledge Handbook of Literacy Studies,* 251–266. London: Routledge.
Finnemann, N. O. (1999) Hypertext and the Representational Capacities of the Binary Alphabet. *Arbejdspapirer, Centre for Cultural Research, Aarhus*: 77–99.
Getz, D. and Sailor, L. (1993) Design of Destination and Attraction-Specific Brochures. *Journal of Travel and Tourism Marketing* 2(2/3): 111–131.
Hiippala, T. (2012) Reading Paths and Visual Perception in Multimodal Research, Psychology and Brain Sciences. *Journal of Pragmatics* 44: 315–327.
Kaltenbacher, M. and Kaltenbacher, T. (2015) Seeing the Unforeseen: Eye-Tracking Reading Paths in Multimodal Webpages. In J. Wildfeuer (ed.) *Building Bridges for Multimodal Research: International Perspectives on Theories and Practices of Multimodal Analysis,* 227–245. *Bern* and New York: Peter Lang.
Kok, A. K. C. (2004) Multisemiotic Mediation in Hypertext. In K. O'Halloran (ed.), *Multimodal Discourse Analysis: Systemic Functional Perspective,* 131–159. London: Continuum.
Kress, G. and van Leeuwen, T. (2006) *Reading Images: The Grammar of Visual Design.* 2nd edn. London: Routledge.
Lemke, J. (2002) Travels in Hypermodality. *Visual Communication* 1(3): 299–325.
Rayner, K. (1998) Eye Movements in Reading and Information Processing: 20 Years of Research. *Psychological Bulletin* 124(3): 372–422.
Shepherd, M. and Watters, C. (1998) The Evolution of Cybergenres. *Proceedings of the 31st Annual Hawaii International Conference on System Sciences.* Los Alanitos, CA: IEEE Computer Society Press.
Yarbus, A. L. (1967) *Eye Movements and Vision.* New York: Plenum Press.

Hotel Websites

www.austria-trend.at/Hotel-Altstadt-Salzburg/en/ [last accessed 7 May 2015].
www.booking.com/hotel/at/sacher-wien.en-us.html [last accessed 7 May 2015].
www.booking.com/hotel/us/sheraton-salt-lake-city.en-us.html [last accessed 7 May 2015].
www.krallerhof.com/en/ [last accessed 7 May 2015].
www.sacher.com/de-hotel-sacher-wien.htm [last accessed 7 May 2015].
www.sacher.com/hotel-sacher-vienna/rooms/ [last accessed 7 May 2015].
www.salzburg-hotel.at/en [last accessed 7 May 2015].
www.sheratonsaltlakecityhotel.com [last accessed 7 May 2015].

Part III
Texts that Have Digitality Thrust Upon Them: Super Powers in Text Analysis

13 On Negotiating the Hurdles of Corpus-Assisted Appraisal Analysis in Verbal Art

Donna R. Miller
University of Bologna

13.1 A Preamble: the Wider Issues Outlined

The colloquium I and my colleagues Bayley, Bevitori, Fusari and Luporini presented at the 24th ESFLCW in Coventry in 2013 was entitled 'Ticklish trawling: The limits of corpus assisted meaning analysis'.[1] Its rationale was a unified one and so I devote a few words here in section 1 to a brief account of the principles underlying our four-part contribution to this volume. Section 2 of this chapter deals with the special obstacles involved in corpus-assisted appraisal analysis, while section 3 moves to a discussion and illustration of the even knottier quandries of such analysis in 'verbal art'. The fourth section is dedicated to a report of what corpus tools can and cannot tell us about the 'noble' Coriolanus. A few words are then said in closing.

13.2 The SFL-CL Connection

As is widely recognized, the Systemic Functional Linguistics (SFL) and Corpus Linguistics (CL) relationship is not a clear-cut, trouble-free one. Often it is put in terms of divergence/convergence. For Thompson and Hunston (2006: 3–5), the two are strange, and mutually suspicious, bedfellows, which have, however, common concerns. For Tucker (2006: 76) systemic grammar and 'phraseological grammar' offer complementary viewpoints. Halliday (2006: 293) ostensibly suppresses the conflict, speaking of '[...] a natural affinity [...] a "symbiotic and synergistic relationship"' and seeing the large-scale corpus as vital to 'understanding and modelling the true complexity of a human language' (2006: 299). Thus he blesses the 'marriage', with, however, reservations, which I'll come back to presently. The point is that the relationship is problematic and so one may wonder to what degree it can be said to be worth the indisputable effort oftentimes needed to reconcile the methods.

13.3 Obstacles to Valuable Quantitative Meaning Analysis

Our group's corpus research has invariably premised that 'A corpus [...] is a treasury of acts of meaning which can be explored and interrogated from all illuminating angles, including in quantitative terms' (Halliday, 2002c: 406). In addition, we're convinced that our corpus-assisted research has indeed been profitable – but not invariably and/or consistently and/or unequivocally. In short, with time and practice we've come to realize that 'it depends'. We'd aimed to provide a brief look at just what valuable quantitative meaning analysis may depend *on*, since this allowed us to stop and take stock of what we have done, but also what we may have failed to do, and to reflect on what may be the limits of such interrogation, and why.

Firstly, it depends on whether one aims at 'volume' or 'richness'. For Halliday and Matthiessen (2004: 48–49), 'automatic analysis gets harder the higher up we move along the hierarchy of stratification', i.e. it can handle orthographic word patterns and low-ranking lexicogrammatical patterns, but not full SFL clause or semantic analysis. Comprehensive analysis of function structures and systemic features is still much harder to automate (O'Donnell, 1994, also cited in Matthiessen, 2006: 104). So, Halliday and Matthiessen sum up:

> we have a trade-off between volume of analysis and richness of analysis: low-level analysis can be automated to handle large volumes of text, but high-level analysis has to be carried out by hand for small samples of text (2004: 48–49).

Whether the 'trade-off' between volume and richness is ever a judicious and/or advantageous one will depend on research questions and chosen level(s) of inquiry. We, with Halliday and Matthiessen, posit that, if these are 'limited', 'lower' (literally, with reference to stratification/rank hierarchy), automated analyses, though not always straightforward, won't be overly constrained. But if these aim 'higher' – e.g. involving levels of semantics and context – automated analyses alone won't enable desired/required findings. Only labour-intensive manual analysis, or 'ticklish trawling', will. And the 'reservations' of Halliday (mentioned above) are analogous: at the present time and state-of-the-art, for investigating the 'higher' scales of stratum and rank, manual analysis is indeed what's needed.

Much has been done to reconcile corpus data and methods with how texts mean within specific cultural contexts (e.g. Bayley 2004; Morley and Bayley, 2009; Partington *et al.* 2003; Thompson and Hunston, 2006). But perhaps SFL corpus analysts have given too-short-shift to how they mean in extended co-text, i.e, valuable quantitative meaning analysis also depends on logogenesis, that

> unfolding of the act of meaning itself: the instantial construction of meaning in the form of a text [...] in which the potential for creating meaning is continually modified in the light of what has gone before (Halliday and Matthiessen, 1999: 18).

Perhaps we need to candidly engage with the argument that

> It is texts that mean, through their sentences and the complex of logogenetic contingencies among them – they do not mean as a selection from, or a sum of, or worse, an average of, the meanings within the clause (Martin, 2003: 177).

Or even worse, within the conventional concordance line's nine-word window.[2] This is indeed of negligible use in appraisal studies, to which I now turn.

13.4 Some Specific Snags of Corpus-assisted Appraisal Studies

If valuable quantitative meaning analysis depends on the nature of one's research questions, corpus appraisal studies are paradigmatic.[3] Evaluation analysis is 'by no means open to automation' (Hunston, 2004: 169), because it is essentially qualitative in nature, as it is aimed at a 'high' systemic/functional analysis. Identifying motivated patterns of evaluative propagation/ramification (Lemke, 1998: 49–50) is a tricky, time-consuming and largely backroom task.

A major snare of appraisal analysis, as I have found repeatedly, is that in-built interpretation fuzziness abounds. To minimize indeterminacy, one needs to probe specific situational and cultural contexts and of course extensive co-text (with an eye to at least partial logogenesis tracing) – what SFL means by 'semantic prosody', i.e. the 'cumulative groove' (Coffin and O'Halloran, 2005) of meaning patterning dynamically construed across texts. Such patterns are chosen by human appraisers, so that any variations in individual/socio-cultural subjectivity – in repertoires/reservoirs (Martin, 2010: 23) – invariably spell significant voice and value orientation distinctions. Moreover, by now it is somewhat of a truism that analysts too are biased – something that 'we can only be aware, and beware, of – and, of course, declare' (Miller, 2007: 178).

My predominant and long-ongoing corpus-assisted appraisal studies centred on register-idiosyncratic features of evaluation/stance in parliamentary debate (Miller and Johnson, 2009; cf. Miller 2010; Miller and Johnson 2013, 2014). Focus in these studies was on attitudinal function bundles (Halliday, 1985: 262) whose patterns proved statistically salient. Method involved purposefully 'shunting' (Halliday, 2002a: 45; Miller 2006) between different dimensions, using the corpus as a kind of 'echo chamber' (Thompson and Hunston, 2006: 13) Expanded concordances were analysed for APPRAISAL SYSTEMS (Martin and White, 2005), but also for the ideational meanings 'coupling' with these (Bednarek and Martin, 2010: 10). The method proved profitable. But additional snares emerged.

These included the 'Russian Doll' and 'Piecemeal Puzzle' syndromes. The former dilemma arises when one category of attitude functions as the indirect expression of a different category, which itself functions as a token of yet another category, etc. raising the question of how many of these layers, one inside the other, should be included in an analysis – and how to code them (Thompson, 2014). Corpus analysis complicates things further, as more than one concordance can belong to the same single speech: an example of what I'm calling the Piecemeal Puzzle quandary. Of course the corpus can be filtered to view speeches individually, as required, but the point is, it *must* be. This may increase the manual work involved, but it is clearly crucial to have all the pieces of the puzzle to have the full evaluative picture.

13.5 Compounding the Complications: Corpus-assisted Appraisal Analysis of the Literature Text

When dealing with verbal art, to the fact that 'high' level studies resist automation in all types of text, along with the particular thorns that appraisal analysis throws in the path of corpus studies, we now need to add the obstacles inherent in the analysis of literature, not only because the context-language connection is more intricate than for other text types, but also because literature differs from other registers by virtue of the 'special' function played by language therein (Hasan, 1989 [1985]; 2007). Indeed, these very considerations led Hasan to devise a unique model of 'double-articulation' for the analysis of what she has dubbed *verbal art*, with a semiotic system of language and a higher order semiotic system of verbal art itself (Hasan, 1989 [1985]; cf. Miller, 2010, 2012, 2013, 2016, forthcoming a, forthcoming b.

And this higher order semiotic muddies the waters even more. Undoubtedly this is a major reason why mainstream stylisticians ignore Hasan's framework. Believing, as Hasan does, that verbal art is 'special', and thus requires a special theoretical and methodological take, I espouse it.

Space constraints preclude disambiguating all but the skeleton of the model. Figure 13.1 provides a visual representation of the two overlapping semiotic systems and their different levels of abstraction.

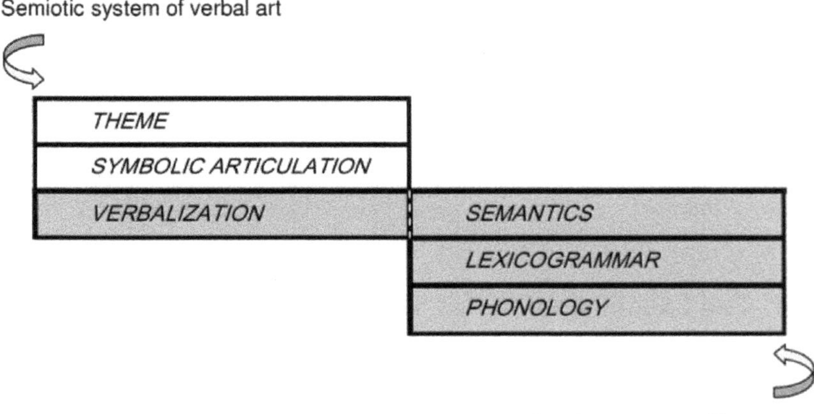

Figure 13.1: The overlapping semiotic systems (based on Hasan, 1989 [1985]: 99).

To any SFL practitioner, the first order system of language is the standard entry point for the analysis of any register. They recognize that each stratum is realized by the one below, semantics becoming accessible to us via lexicogrammar which, in turn, becomes accessible to us via phonology and/or graphology. They know that above the first level (not reproduced in the figure) is the context of situation, which tends to activate the meanings that will most likely be chosen from the total meaning potential available to the text maker (Halliday and Matthiessen, 2004: 24–31) and will then tend to be realized in the lexicogrammar of the text.

It is the second order of semiosis which sets literature apart from any other use of language. It is here that the 'art' of verbal art resides. The first stratum of the higher order system is labeled 'verbalization' and comprises all of the first order; hence the broken line in the figure. The highest stratum is that of 'theme', defined as a meaningful generalization about some aspect of human existence. The same relationship of realization within the system of language holds among the strata of the system of verbal art, so that the theme becomes accessible to us through 'symbolic articulation' – where the meanings at the first order of language are turned into signs having a deeper meaning. To arrive at the deepest meanings of the literature text, the system of language on its own is insufficient, so could the concordance line ever tell us what we need to know?

We recall Halliday's explicit caveat (2002b) that mere statistical frequency is no guarantee of significance. But Halliday did see 'counting' the linguistic options chosen by a writer as a step towards establishing the potential prominence of patterns: for determining what features deserve further investigation, '[a] rough indication of frequencies is often just what is needed' (2002b: 102–103). Indeed, as Miller and Luporini (2015) suggest, the extent to which patterns are quantifiable would seem to be inscrutable – at least in longer texts – without the at least initial assistance of CL methods.[4] My still on-going investigation into evaluation in Shakespeare's *Coriolanus* relies on such assistance.

13.6 The Case of *Coriolanus*: a Preliminary Report

My relationship with *Coriolanus* has been a long if intermittent one; for years it was confined to the 'armchair' (cf. Fillmore, 1992) – and to consulting The (cumbersome!) Harvard Concordance (Spevack, 1973). Only recently have I revisited the play, equipped with SFL and CL, focusing on the node word, 'noble', which intuitively struck me as a key clue to the paradoxical nature of the play's 'hero'.

The overarching research question, as in all verbal art analysis, is to what extent these cumulative evaluative findings may be seen to contribute to defining the pivotal 'theme' of the text – and just what that theme may be said to be. To arrive at the answer to that question, my preliminary queries – only some of which are addressed here – were, firstly, to what degree is Caius Martius (Coriolanus) appraised as being 'noble', or not. The APPRAISAL SYSTEMS used to evaluate him were also clearly an issue, but even moreso the identity of his appraisers, as not all voices in the play are equally trustworthy. Indeed, some might be qualified as 'tainted' – with reference to their own behavior and others' (more or less reliable) evaluations of them.

As 'coupling' of ideational meaning with appraisal is a vital part of the evaluative picture, I aimed to identify, in the environment of 'noble' as participant, what process types it is involved in and with what frequency, and then to assess how these choices may be seen to impact on the appraisal enacted, but also to see if there are significant differences among the experiential choices of various appraisers.

As we know, Fillmore's 'machine' provides findings, but 'armchair' musings have an ongoing role in deciding where to go, what to investigate further, and how this may be done. So, identifying what additional emerging mechanisms to be probed, and how, was an objective as well. The hunch was that, as had happened repeatedly in my past studies, these would feature evaluative elements thrown up in investigating the expanded concordances. The hunch proved yet again to be a valid one.

Although not something I'm yet qualified to adequately report on, an integral part of the project is also to probe, with reference to the intratext and context of creation of the play in particular, what meanings are comprised in 'noble', in itself, and compared to those of honourable, worthy, virtuous and so on, in the Roman (Classical) and Renaissance (Christian) world views (cf. Watson, 1960).

To answer these questions I made use principally of Wordsmith Tools (Scott, 2012), but also of the online 'Open Source Shakespeare', aiming thus to avoid succumbing to the risk of simply illustrating theoretical hypotheses conceived over my comfy-chair years.

13.6.1 Select Quantitative Data: What CL Methods Reveal

My automatic approach began with identifying occurrences of the node word 'noble' in the play – a word that emerged as figuring more significantly in the Tragedies. Marshalling occurrences by conventional genre categories with 'Open Source Shakespeare', we find a total of 609 speeches plus one poem, thus distributed:

Table 13.1: 'noble' in Shakespeare According to Genre

Comedies	Histories	Tragedies	Poems	Sonnets
90 (17 plays)	219 (10 plays)	297 (10 plays)	4	0

and, in raw numbers, mostly in *Coriolanus* (59). The findings reveal the greater significance of the concept for Shakespearean History, and especially, Tragedy. Comparing the data with the BNC is a fairly futile exercise as one would expect the frequency to be much lower there, and it is: with a 'noble' word form query with PoS = adjective, 1,315 instances emerge (11.7 per million – 0,001315 relative frequency).[5] Much more informative are the data regarding *Coriolanus* and my comparative corpora: the other nine tragedies, taken singly rather than as a whole.

Table 13.2: Comparative Raw Data and Relative Frequencies for Each Tragedy in Descending Order

Tragedy	**Raw Data 'noble'**	**Percentage of All Tokens**	**Percentage of All Types**
Coriolanus	59	0.2013	1.3122
Julius Caesar	39	0.2030	1.3742
Antony and Cleopatra	33	0.1379	0.8533
Titus Andronicus	28	0.1316	0.8438
Timon of Athens	25	0.1310	0.7805
Othello	21	0.0805	0.5636
King Lear	19	0.0703	0.4683
Hamlet	17	0.0569	0.3991
Macbeth	13	0.0783	0.3991
Romeo and Juliet	8	0.0314	0.2232

The greater reliability of the *relative* data is manifest: most strikingly, *Julius Caesar* emerges as the play in first position, despite decidedly fewer instances, as it is more than 10,000 running words fewer in length.

The first four are, interestingly, 'Roman' plays. All but *Titus Andronicus* – presumably written before Shakespeare discovered North's translation – had Plutarch as their primary source, as the fifth, another play with a 'classic' antiquity setting, had as well.[6] Could this point to a notable Shakespearean interest in the 'classical' – as well of course as in the Renaissance – notion of noble-ness? If we look at the collocates of 'noble' with specifically named protagonists, there is support for the thesis:

Table 13.3: Comparative Numbers of Collocates of 'noble' with Protagonists for Each Tragedy, in Descending Order

Tragedy	**Collocates with Protagonists**
Julius Caesar	11 (Brutus)/ 6 (Antony)
Timon of Athens	8
Coriolanus	5
Antony and Cleopatra	5 (Antony)
Titus Andronicus	5
Othello	1
King Lear	0
Hamlet	1
Macbeth	1
Romeo and Juliet	0 (Romeo)/ 2 (Paris)

An interesting concurrence at least, yet a postulate it remains. Parenthetically, with reference to the play in first position, *Julius Caesar*, the division of protagonists collocating with 'noble' provides a clear indication of the play's narrative tension.

At least in the case of *Coriolanus*, 'noble' is much more of a Shakespearean than a Plutarch-esque thing; it occurs but six times in North's Plutarch, four of which evaluate *Coriolanus* positively, plus one instance of 'nobly', also regarding *Coriolanus*.

My lemmatized wordlist for *Coriolanus* enters 'noble' as #29, with 79 instances, and a frequency of .24, but divided among: noble[59] nobler[3] nobles[9] nobly[8]. Here I focus only on the first of these.

Table 13.4 partially shows the unembellished answers to my initial Research Questions. The data, however, only emerged from close reading and manual analysis of considerably extended concordances, largely performed with Open Source Shakespeare's convenient full speech option. In short, most appraisal findings that count are simply not afforded by short concordance lines.

Table 13.4: Who Is 'noble', How Often, and – Re Coriolanus – According to Whom?

Appraisee	Number of 'noble'	Appraiser	Number of Hits
Martius/Coriolanus (or something of 'his': son, service, steed, house, nature, form, blows, deeds, mercy, memory…)	38	Menenius Agrippa Tullus Aufidius Volumnia others	8 7 5 18
Menenius Agrippa	3		
Tullus Aufidius	3		
the plebeians	1		
Tribunes	3		
senate/lords/masters	3		
Volumnia (Coriolanus' mother)	1		
the three women	4		
Coriolanus' wife and mother	1		
Valeria	1		
cunning (understanding)	1		

Coriolanus is the explicit appraisee of 64% of the 59 occurrences of 'noble'; 52% of these have three primary appraisers – his friend, his enemy and his mother – voices qualitatively analysed to some extent below. But first some additional data, with unavoidable mention of their plausible qualitative significance, most of which is further commented in section 4.2.

The predominant experiential structure is 'noble' as Epithet + Thing: 48 times; the Thing is animate/human in two-thirds of these. Once is it actually the word 'Thing', meaning, intriguingly, Coriolanus.

The bare vocatives (17) generally inscribe +appreciation: valuation of class membership. Almost invariably the *inscribed* evaluation enacted overall is appreciation: 55 times – 52 of these positive, with judgement being oftentimes contextually invoked/provoked in terms of the (repeatedly overlapping) categories of: propriety 45 times; capacity 12; tenacity 9, and veracity 5.[7] The lowest value – veracity – is also arguably the most telling. Affect figures but once. Graduation is infrequent, but crucial: 7 instances of intensified 'noble' ('right', 'all', 'most', and especially, and significantly, 'too'). Function bundle 'too + Epithet' has indeed emerged as one key to the theme of the play.

The APPRAISAL SYSTEM enacted is rarely identified without attention to how experiential meanings couple with it. Indeed, transitivity structure relevantly 'couples' with 71% of instances. Process types are relational (17: 12 attributive ('noble' as Attribute), 5 identifying, and of these 3 possessives (irrealis: wished for possession of joy, mercy and posthumous memory by Coriolanus). But they also include 14 typically abstract material Processes involving lexical and even grammatical metaphor, and 8 mental Processes, most involving projection. Research into just how these choices might impact on the appraisal enacted, as well as into potentially distinctive use of process types according to appraiser, has still to be completed.

Before passing to findings CL methods alone could not have provided, I offer the nine-word window for the concordances of the speeches analysed below.

```
<Enter Caius Marcius.> Hail,   noble    Marcius! Thanks. - What's the
   hungry plebeians would the  noble    Marcius. He's a lamb
               and out of his  noble    carelessness lets them plainly
after-meeting, To gratify his  noble    service that Hath thus
              His nature is too  noble    for the world: He
    better vantage. Well said,  noble    woman! Before he should
            can never be too  noble,   But when extremities speak.
           torn, Thou show'st a  noble    vessel. What's thy name?
            more Than thee, all  noble    Marcius. Let me twine
            see thee here, Thou  noble    thing! more dances my
                First he was A  noble    servant to them, but
              Rather to show a  noble    grace to both parts
           writ: 'The man was  noble,   But with his last
          regarded As the most  noble    corse that ever herald
             he shall have a  noble    memory. Assist. <Exeunt, bearing
```

Figure 13.2: *Coriolanus* appraised: Concordances of instances commented. [8]

It does tell us something, although, pace Louw (cf. note 2), far from all we need to know. It reveals group structure well, allowing identity of the appreciation: valuation inscribed but – apart from the final two concordances – does not provide sufficient co-text to identify experiential meanings invoking other appraisal systems. Neither is it adequate for discerning both appraisers and appraisees/appraiseds; indeed, in 7 of the 15 concordances, neither is visible. The evidence confirms the corpus as a valuable touchstone for testing theory/description and also for flagging candidates for manual probing, but, for the time being in any case, cannot do the armchair introspection entailed.

13.6.2 From Quantitative to Qualitative Data

One essential question posed was the reliability of the appraising voices. Analysis of the three dominant appraisers of appraisee Martius Coriolanus arguably reveals varying degrees of their dissembling, duplicity and even disloyalty – dishonourable behaviour and thus unreliability of voice. The following excerpts, sequenced according to the play's storyline, illustrate the ways in which the reliability of appraisers might be regarded as questionable.

Menenius Agrippa first greets our hero in Act I, 1, 163 with 'Hail, **noble** Martius!'. He next appraises him as 'noble' in a caustic repartee with one of the two Tribunes in Act II, 1, 7–10, a scene centring on the crux of the dilemma and the deceitfulness of the scheming Tribunes, mouthpieces of the people.

(1) **Men.** Pray you, who does the wolf love?
Sic. the lamb.
Men. Ay, to devour him; as the hungry plebeians
would the **noble** Martius.

The composite lexical metaphor construes Coriolanus as the Goal of the savage, if irrealis, material Process 'devour' with the 'hungry plebeians' as the alleged Actors, provoking Menenius' -judgement:social sanction:propriety on the people, and their Tribunes.

In Act II, 2, 38–41, Menenius evaluates the service for which Coriolanus should be given the consulship:

(2) it remains,
As the main point of this our after-meeting,
To gratify his [Coriolanus'] **noble** service that
Hath thus stood for his country:

Where 'noble service [...]' functions as Scope of the abstract material Process 'gratify', i.e. recompense, Coriolanus himself being implicit Recipient.

Appraisal enacted includes inscribed +appreciation:valuation of said service but also invoked +judgement:social esteem:capacity/tenacity of the doer of the service, as well as +judgement:ss:propriety of so-gratifying. Such 'propriety' is acknowledged by all sides, but Coriolanus is adamant against petitioning the people for their customary consent.

In Act III his determination not to pander to the Tribunes/people's demands steadily precipitates the crisis. In Act III, 1, 254–257, Menenius tellingly notes:

(3) His nature is too **noble** for the world:
He would not flatter Neptune for his trident,
Or Jove for's power to thunder. His heart's his mouth:
What his breast forges, that his tongue must vent [...]

According to the Renaissance concept of honour, neither flattery nor dissembling is virtuous/noble behaviour (Watson, 1960: 257–258). One of the five significant instances of +judgement:ss:veracity is invoked here. The judgement:ss:propriety seems positive, yet that 'too' intensifying 'noble' must give us pause. Here we have an echo of concordance #11, in Act II, 2, 11–15, in which a minor character, the Second Officer, foreshadows Menenius' insight:

(4) Therefore for Coriolanus neither to care whether they love or hate him manifests the true knowledge he has in their disposition; and out of his **noble** carelessness lets them plainly see't.

Here Coriolanus' indifference is Instrument of [making] manifest a Phenomenon – his 'knowledge' of the plebeians – evaluated as 'true'. Beyond the surface appreciation:valuation of 'noble carelessness', judgement on veracity is again enacted with the causative VGC that follows: 'lets them plainly see't'. But are these evaluations positive or negative? Their value seems to be tied to the theme of the play, and is, like the theme, ambivalent. 'Carelessness' here is 'artlessness', candour, and 'plainly' is honestly, and thus the judgement is positive, but as with most virtues participating in the play, if exaggerated, then they are adulterated.

In Act III, 2: Martius' mother Volumnia counsels Coriolanus to abandon the inopportune principles *that she herself instilled in him*. Menenius, a staunch defender of Coriolanus' position up until now, dithers (31–34):

(5) Well said, **noble** woman.
Before he should thus stoop to the herd, *but that*
The violent fit o' the time craves it as physic
For the whole state, I would put mine armour on,
Which I can scarcely bear.

Volumnia resumes her entreaty with a comparable subtractive clause:

(6) You are too absolute;
Though therein you can never be too **noble**,
But when extremities speak. (39–41)

Arguing – sophistically – that the extreme situation makes it *less* noble to be *too* absolute, 'too' once again construing pivotal if equivocal meanings.

In Act IV, 5, Coriolanus is banished for refusing to humble himself. He bonds with his former enemy the Volscian warrior, Aufidius, against Rome. In speeches rich with invoked +judgement:se:capacity and ss:propriety re Coriolanus, Aufidius repeatedly calls him 'noble'. Here we get the one previously signalled instance of affect: a peculiarly intense inscribed happiness at seeing – and holding – Coriolanus, explicitly compared to his heterosexual experience of passion (115–118).

(7) I loved the maid I married; never man
Sigh'd truer breath; but that I see thee here,
Thou **noble** thing! more dances my rapt heart
Than when I first my wedded mistress saw
Bestride my threshold.

And note too Coriolanus as 'noble thing', also signalled above: meaning more, or less, than a man?; semantically echoing Menenius' 'too noble for the world'?

It is Aufidius, in Act IV, 7, 35, who ruminates perceptively on Coriolanus' possible failings, on why

(8) First he was
A **noble** servant to them; but he could not
Carry his honours even [...]

The co-text is rife with invoked judgement:se:capacity/tenacity and ss:propriety re Coriolanus – ultimately ambiguous once again re polarity, Aufidius' intratextual mood swings frustrating interpretation.

In Act V, 3, 121–122, Volumnia gains admittance to try to convince her son,

(9) rather to show a **noble** grace to both parts
Than seek the end of one [...]

– that is, spare Rome and bring about a peace; many are her arguments invoking the propriety of doing so, among them an alarming prediction of his final,

(10) ... chronicle thus writ: "The man was **noble**,
But with his last attempt he wiped it out;
Destroy'd his country, and his name remains
To the ensuing age abhorr'd" (145–148).

The 33 hits of 'name' also emerge as candidates for further study. Coriolanus succumbs, knowing it means his death, which Aufidius is fast to arrange in scene 6. The final two instances of 'noble' evaluate, respectively, his corpse and his memory. A 'First Lord' commands he be a superlative Phenomenon Sensed:

(11) let him be regarded
As the most **noble** corse that ever herald
Did follow to his urn (142–144).

And Aufidius, his rage at the 'traitor' he's had slain now spent, or satisfied, with the final words of the play proclaims:

(12) he shall have a **noble** memory. Assist.

Evaluating with inscribed +appreciation:valuation that memory, thus invoking +judgement:ss:propriety of his life's deeds, expediently, even perhaps fittingly, but unreliably.

The words of a minor character appraising Coriolanus seem an apt epilogue to this report of partial findings to date regarding the ambivalently 'noble' Coriolanus:

(13) You have deserved **nobly** of your country, and you
have not deserved **nobly**.

13.7 Conclusion

A modest assessment of what one has done and/or failed to do, and/or might have done and/or will continue to do, is standard practice in winding up a chapter. Shortcomings figure largely in this space-constrained case, as regarding *Coriolanus* I've not been able to comment explicitly further evaluative elements that only emerged in expanded concordances investigation: among these, the 23 occurrences of intensifier 'too' in the play, as they lend substantial credence to the findings regarding Coriolanus' 'too noble' nature seen above. Moreover, related lemmas are also significant, especially the eight occurrences of 'nobly'. These await reporting at another time and place, as do our intricate Russian Dolls (within at least separate speeches, only hinted at above) and the complexities of the Piecemeal Puzzle quandary (requiring full text scrutiny). Neither have I been able to present the amount of findings needed to systematically marshal the mechanisms symbolically articulating the theme in the play, let alone link this adequately to its context of creation and so, finally, formulate it. In short, the overarching research question still remains to be answered – perhaps in terms of something like 'the relativity of the concept of "noble"'.

The chapter, however, has provided an accurate delineation of the issues involved in meaning analysis – and in particular appraisal analysis of verbal art – assisted by corpus tools/methods, and a good number of these have been adequately illustrated. It has documented the usefulness of CL as a remarkable quantitative tool in the service of qualitative linguistic analysis. For now, this will have to suffice.

About the author

Donna R. Miller is Professor and Chair of English Linguistics at the Department LILEC of the University of Bologna, Italy and heads its Centre for Linguistic-Cultural Studies (CeSLiC). Her research in Systemic Functional Linguistics focuses on institutional register analysis, corpus-assisted investigations into the grammar of evaluation, and expanding the Hasanian framework of 'verbal art'.

Endnotes

1. After Miller (2000).
2. Cf. Louw (2007: 159): 'Sinclair (1991: 175) has always made it plain that collocative power is concentrated within a nine word window [...]'. Louw's article may be seen as a resolute attempt to prove this assertion with reference to verbal art. My dissent will be evident below.
3. Martin's (2003) insistence on meaning made through a 'complex of logogenetic contingencies' appeared in the introduction to an appraisal publication, not fortuitously.
4. The chapter presents the pilot study results of an ongoing project. The first experiential findings were not unpromising and we've now moved on to appraisal analysis – with findings presented at the 42nd International Systemic Functional Congress, in Aachen in 2015.
5. Interestingly, in a bigger and more diachronic corpus, frequency increases: in the 1810 to 2000 Google British corpus (34 billion words – ngrams) the relative frequency is 0,00844.
6. For further particulars, cf. http://internetshakespeare.uvic.ca/Annex/Texts/Plutarch/intro/Intro/default/;jsessionid=7D95AEF5F89147614BFE32FB2BFE34C7 (last accessed 03/01/2015) and http://internetshakespeare.uvic.ca/Library/

SLT/reference/sources/sourcetragedies.html#tit (last accessed 30/12/2014. Also see the Gutenberg Etext Project's *Lives of the noble Grecians and Romans by Plutarch*, at http://www.gutenberg.org/ebooks/674 (last accessed 27/04/2015).

7. Most instances of 'noble' are coded firstly as appreciation despite the appraisee being human, or a metonymic part of a human, the first inscribed value being as a socially significant member of the 'nobility'. The fuzzy border between appreciation and judgement is well-known; hence one often finds invoked judgement as well, of behaviour responsible for the evaluation as 'noble'.
8. The spelling of Marcius in these concordances is that of the Shakespeare Corpus for WordSmith Tools at http://www.lexically.net/wordsmith/support/shakespeare.html (last accessed 14/01/2015). My Open Source speeches and most other sources have Martius. See www.opensourceshakespeare.org/ (last accessed 12/01/2015). Program code and database © 2003–2015 George Mason University. All texts are public domain.

References

Bayley, P. (ed.) (2004) *Cross-cultural Perspectives on Parliamentary Discourse*. Amsterdam and Philadelphia: John Benjamins Publishing Company.

Bednarek, M. and Martin, J. R. (eds) (2010) *New Discourse on Language: Functional Perspectives on Multimodality, Identity, and Affiliation*. London and New York: Continuum.

Coffin, C. and O'Halloran, K. A. (2005) Finding the Global Groove: Theorising and Analysing Dynamic Reader Positioning using Appraisal, Corpus and a Concordance. *Critical Discourse Studies* 2(2): 143–163.

Fillmore, C. (1992) Corpus Linguistics or Computer-aided Armchair Linguistics. In J. Svartvik (ed) *Directions in Corpus Linguistics*, 13–38. Berlin: Mouton de Gruyter.

Halliday, M. A. K. (1985) *An Introduction to Functional Grammar*. London: Edward Arnold.

Halliday, M. A. K. (2002a [1961]) Categories of the Theory of Grammar. In J. J. Webster (ed.) *The Collected Works of M. A. K. Halliday, Vol 1: On Grammar*, 37–94. London and New York: Continuum.

Halliday, M. A. K. (2002b [1971]) Linguistic Function and Literary Style: An Inquiry into the Language of William Golding's the Inheritors. In J. J. Webster (ed.) *The Collected Works of M. A. K. Halliday, Vol. 3 Linguistic Studies of Text and Discourse*, 88–125. London: Continuum.

Halliday, M. A. K. (2002c [1996]) On Grammar and Grammatics. In J. J. Webster (ed.) *The Collected Works of M. A. K. Halliday, Vol 1: On Grammar*, 384–417. London and New York: Continuum.

Halliday, M. A. K. (2006) Afterwords. In G. Thompson and S. Hunston (eds) *System and Corpus: Exploring Connections*, 293–299. London: Equinox Publishing.

Halliday, M. A. K. and Matthiessen, C. M. I. M. (1999) *Construing Experience through Meaning. A Language-Based Approach to Cognition*. London: Cassell.

Halliday, M. A. K. and Matthiessen, C. M. I. M. (2004) *An Introduction to Functional Grammar*. 3rd edn. London: Hodder Arnold.

Hasan, R. (1989 [1985]) *Language, Linguistics and Verbal Art*. Oxford: Oxford University Press.

Hasan, R. (2007) Private Pleasure, Public Discourse: Reflections on Engaging with Literature. In D. R. Miller and M. Turci (eds) *Language and Verbal Art Revisited. Linguistic Approaches to the Study of Literature*, 13–40. London: Equinox Publishing.

Hunston, S. (2004) Counting the Uncountable: Problems of Identifying Evaluation in a Text and in a Corpus. In A. Partington, J. Morley and L. Haarman (eds) *Corpora and Discourse*, 157–188. Bern: Peter Lang.

Lemke, J. (1998) Resources for Attitudinal Meaning: Evaluative Orientations in Text Semantics. *Functions of Language* 5(1): 33–56.

Louw, B. (2007) Collocation as the Determinant of Verbal Art. In D. R. Miller, and M. Turci (eds) *Language and Verbal Art Revisited. Linguistic Approaches to the Study of Literature*, 149–180. London: Equinox Publishing.

Martin, J. R. (2003) Introduction. *Text* 23(2): 171–181.

Martin, J. R. (2010) Semantic Variation – Modelling Realisation, Instantiation and Individuation in Social Semiosis. In M. Bednarek and J. R. Martin (eds) *New Discourse on Language: Functional Perspectives on Multimodality, Identity, and Affiliation*, 1–34. London and New York: Continuum.

Martin, J. R. and White, P. R. R. (2005) *The Language of Evaluation: Appraisal in English*. London: Palgrave Macmillan.

Matthiessen, C. M. I. M. (2006) Frequency Profiles of some Grammatical Systems: An Interim Report. In G. Thompson, and S. Hunston (eds) *System and Corpus: Exploring Connections*, 103–142. London: Equinox Publishing.

Miller, D. R. (2000) 'On Computing Appraisal in a Corpus of Parliamentary Debate, Or, Ticklish Trawling'. Unpublished paper delivered to the Euro Systemic-Functional Workshop, Glasgow, 19–22 July.

Miller, D. R. (2006) From Concordance to Text: Appraising 'giving' in Alma Mater Donation Requests. In G. Thompson and S. Hunston (eds) *System and Corpus: Exploring Connections*, 248–268. London: Equinox Publishing.

Miller, D. R. (2007) Towards a Typology of Evaluation in Parliamentary Debate: From Theory to Practice – and Back Again. *Textus* 20(1): 159–180.

Miller, D. R. (2010) The Hasanian Framework for the Study of 'Verbal Art' Revisited… and Reproposed. *Textus XXIII* (1): 71–94.

Miller, D. R. (2012) Slotting Jakobson into the Social Semiotic Approach to 'verbal Art': A Modest Proposal. In F. Dalziel, S. Gesuato and M. T. Musacchio (eds) *A Lifetime of English Studies: Essays in Honour of Carol Taylor Torsello*, 215–226. Padua: Il Poligrafo.

Miller, D. R. (2013) Another Look at Social Semiotic Stylistics: Coupling Hasan's 'Verbal Art' Framework with 'the Mukarovský-Jakobson Theory'. In C. A. M. Gouveia, and M. F. Alexandre (eds) *Languages, Metalanguages, Modalities, Cultures: Functional and Socio-Discoursive Perspectives*, 121–140. Lisbon: BonD.

Miller, D. R. (2016) A Jakobson's Place in Hasan's Social Semiotic Stylistics: 'pervasive Parallelism' as Symbolic Articulation of Theme. In W. Boucher and J. Liang (eds) *Society in Language, Language in Society: Essays in Honour of Ruqaiya Hasan*, 59–80. London: Palgrave Macmillan.

Miller, D. R. (forthcoming a) Language and Verbal Art. In T. Bartlett and G. O'Grady (eds) *Routledge Handbook of Systemic Functional Linguistics*. Abington: Routledge.

Miller, D. R. (forthcoming b) Language and Literature. In G. Thompson, W. L. Bowcher, L. Fontaine and J. Yameng Liang (eds) *The Cambridge Handbook of Systemic Functional Linguistics*. Cambridge: Cambridge University Press.

Miller, D. R. and Johnson, J. H. (2009) Evaluation, Speaker-Hearer Positioning and the Iraq War: A Corpus-Assisted Study of Congressional Argument. In J. Morley and P. Bayley (eds) *Corpus-Assisted Discourse Studies on the Iraq Conflict: Wording the War*, 34–73. New York: Routledge.

Miller, D. R. and Johnson, J. H. (2013) 'Register-Idiosyncratic' Evaluative Choice in Congressional Debate: A Corpus-Assisted Comparative Study. In L. Fontaine, T. Bartlett, and G. O'Grady (eds) *Systemic Functional Linguistics: Exploring Choice*, 432–452. Cambridge: Cambridge University Press.

Miller, D. R. and Johnson, J. H. (2014) Evaluative Phraseological Choice and Speaker Party/Gender: A Corpus-Assisted Comparative Study of 'register-Idiosyncratic' Meaning in Congressional Debate. In G. Thompson and L. Alba-Juez (eds) *Evaluation in Context*, 346–366. Amsterdam and Philadelphia, PA: John Benjamins Publishing Company.

Miller, D. R. and Luporini, A. (2015) Social Semiotic Stylistics and the Corpus: How do-Able is an Automated Analysis of Verbal Art? In A. Duguid, A. Marchi, A. Partington and C. Taylor (eds) *Gentle Obsessions: Literature, Linguistics and Learning. In Honour of John Morley*, 235–250. Rome: Artemide.

Miller, D. R. and Turci, M. (eds) (2007) *Language and Verbal Art Revisited. Linguistic Approaches to the Study of Literature*. London: Equinox Publishing.

Morley, J. and Bayley, P. (eds) (2009) *Corpus-Assisted Discourse Studies on the Iraq Conflict: Wording the War*. New York: Routledge.

O'Donnell, M. (1994) 'Sentence Analysis and Generation: A Systemic Perspective'. Unpublished PhD thesis: Sydney University.

Partington, A., Morley, J., and Haarman, L. T. (eds) (2004) *Corpora and Discourse*. Bern: Peter Lang.

Scott, M. (2012) *WordSmith Tools* Version 6.0 [Software]. Stroud: Lexical Analysis Software.

Spevack, M. (1973) *The Harvard Concordance to Shakespeare*. Cambridge, MA: Belknap Press of Harvard University Press.

Thompson, G. (2014) AFFECT and emotion, target-value mismatches, and Russian dolls: Refining the APPRAISAL model. In G. Thompson and L. Alba-Juez (eds) *Evaluation in Context*, 47–66. Amsterdam and Philadelphia: John Benjamins Publishing Company.

Thompson, G. and Hunston, S. (eds) (2006) *System and Corpus: Exploring Connections*. London: Equinox Publishing.

Tucker, G. (2006) Systemic Incorporation: On the Relationship between Corpus and Systemic Functional Grammar. In G. Thompson, and S. Hunston (eds) *System and Corpus: Exploring Connections*, 83–102. London: Equinox Publishing.

Watson, C. B. (1960) *Shakespeare and the Renaissance Concept of Honour*. Princeton, NJ: Princeton University Press.

14 Diachronic Change from Washington to Obama: The Challenges and Constraints of Corpus-Assisted Meaning Analysis

Paul Bayley and Cinzia Bevitori
University of Bologna

14.1 Introduction

This chapter will present some findings of an ongoing project analysing a domain specific, diachronic corpus of political texts, namely the State of the Union corpus, made up of 228 State of the Union addresses (henceforth SoUs) delivered by US Presidents over a period of 225 years, and it will respond to three interrelated questions set out below.

Firstly, the most general of these regards methodology; it has been claimed that – and the principle underlying the project assumes that – the methods and procedures of corpus linguistics can be successfully and fruitfully combined with discourse analysis, or the analysis of meanings in texts, by shifting back and forth between the data made available in a corpus through concordance software (such as WordSmith Tools [Scott, 2005], which was used for this study) and a manual analysis of the individual texts that go to make up such a corpus (see, for example, Baker 2006; Baker *et al.*, 2008; Baker 2011; Bayley and Williams, 2012; Gabrielatos and Marchi, 2012; Morley and Bayley, 2009; Partington *et al.*, 2004). However, as Miller has pointed out in this volume, the feasibility of conducting a rich meaning analysis of a large corpus, especially within such a complex framework as Systemic Functional Grammar, cannot be taken for granted and that, citing Halliday and Matthiessen (2004: 48–49), there has to be 'a trade-off between volume of analysis and richness of analysis'. This chapter will identify some of the constraints and limitations to our approach; however, as a primary and rather obvious premise, a necessary condition of tackling such a project is that the analyst needs to have a clear idea of the context (of culture and of situation) of the texts and of the register to which they belong.

Secondly, after identifying constraints and limitations to corpus-assisted meaning studies, we consider what level of meaning analysis can be aimed at. Work with specialized corpora, depending on what kind of tagging and mark-up they contain, if any, tends inevitably to focus on single lexical items, frequencies, clusters of lexical items, co-selection of lexical items, collocations, colligations and semantic associations. On the one hand it is argued that corpus analysis provides not just quantitative data but also semantic information on lexical items. For example, and famously, *cause* is associated with negative meanings and *provide* with positive ones (Stubbs, 1996: 173–174), and that corpus data can suggest an entry point into the texts and thus lead to richer analyses. On the other hand, however, a word, a cluster or a chunk of text only means what it does because of what precedes it and, therefore the 'shifting back and forth' mentioned above must foresee great attention to entire texts. Moreover, specialized corpora lend themselves well to analyses of 'aboutness', or the ideational meanings of words and clusters in texts (see, for example, our work on instances of *security* in the SoU corpus, Bayley and Bevitori [2015]), while the analysis of interpersonal and textual meanings is far more complex (but see the work on appraisal systems by Miller [2006, 2007] and Miller and Johnson [2009]).

Finally, we will test whether a corpus of this nature can reveal diachronic meaning shifts over quite a long period of time, going beyond the more simple analysis of the 'aboutness' of the texts. Because they were made evident by corpus analysis, we will look at aspects of clause structure and lexical density, the construal of speaker and addressee identity, and engagement, in particular modalization and modulation.

14.2 The State of the Union Address

14.2.1 SoU: Practice, Purpose and Contextual Configuration

SoUs are one of the canonical forms through which presidential power takes shape. Presidents have few formal powers but they have acquired 'the power to persuade' (Neustadt, 1990). Persuasion and negotiation are the means through which U.S. Presidents exercise their authority and influence decisions. Congress, on the other hand, as well as having more formal powers than the President, is often in conflict with the Administration; as a consequence, SoUs can constitute a discursive site of this conflict.

The delivery of a message to the joint houses is an obligation imposed on the President by Article II, Section 3 of the Constitution of the United States, which affirms that:

> He [*sic*] shall from time to time give to the Congress Information of the State of the Union, and recommend to their Consideration such Measures as he shall judge necessary [...]

The Constitution gives no indications as to the frequency of these communications, but convention has established them to be annual events. An address has been made to a joint session of Congress every year since 1790, with the exception of 1841 and 1933, and two were made in 1790, 1953, 1961, and 1981. Neither does the Constitution establish the medium through which the information and recommendations should be given; from 1790 until 1800, all SoUs were delivered orally, while from 1801 to 1912 they were written texts. From 1913 to 1932 there was an alternation between spoken and written texts. Since 1934 they have all been oral with the exceptions of 1945, 1946, 1956, 1961, 1973 and 1981. Overall, 129 have been written messages and 99 spoken addresses.[1] The address has been broadcast live on radio since 1923, on television since 1947, and on prime time television since 1965. Since 2011 the address has been available on the Internet in a livestream 'enhanced' form, with graphics and a chat.[2]

The mediatization of the SoU has, in our opinion, led to significant shifts in the field and the tenor of discourse. While on the one hand the Constitution establishes the role and status of both speaker and addressee, the media have added a new, albeit secondary, addressee: the general public. In fact this has become discursively explicit and since 1959, with a few exceptions, the President has opened the SoU with a greeting along the lines of Eisenhower's 1959: *Mr. President* [pro tempore of the Senate] *Mr. Speaker, Members of the 86th Congress, my fellow citizens [...].* Moreover, the Constitution also specifies the nature of what is to be exchanged in the discourse, the speaker is to give information and request goods and services. In terms of the field of discourse and the eight 'semiotic processes' that Matthiessen proposes as 'activities' (see Matthiessen *et al.*, 2010; Matthiessen and Teruya, 2016), those of a SoU should be 'reporting' and 'recommending'. However, a closer reading of the texts indicates that some Presidents do not merely 'report' but they also 'expound' and 'assess', and, especially since 1961, Presidents have also been 'recreating' (narratives) and 'sharing' (experiences and values). In short, SoUs have become less 'informative' and more 'persuasive'.

14.2.2 The Corpus

At the time of writing, the SoU corpus is composed of the complete set of the transcriptions or the texts of the addresses or messages delivered to joint sessions of Congress between 1790 and 2014 and is composed of 228 texts and about 1,800,000 running words, or tokens.[3] The corpus is not annotated (see Fusari in this volume on potential problems of annotation) but each file has been numbered sequentially so that, using the default settings of Wordsmith Tools 4 (Scott, 2005), results are initially displayed in chronological order. Moreover, in order to facilitate diachronic analyses, the corpus has been broken up into segments; this could have been done in many ways but we chose to use major wars as socially and politically significant watersheds and so the segments are as follows:

1. 1790–1864 – up to the last Civil War address; 76 texts, 551,000 tokens.[4]
2. 1865–1916 – before entering WWI; 52 texts, 684,000 tokens.
3. 1917–1945 – up to the end of WWII; 28 texts 153,000 tokens.
4. 1946–1989 – the Cold War; 47 texts 293,000 tokens.
5. 1990–2014 – end of Cold War to the present day; 25 texts 152,000 tokens.

For a more detailed overview of the corpus see Bayley and Bevitori (2015). We do not, however, suggest that shifts in discursive patterns have taken place at the borderlines of these historical eras; language change normally takes place gradually and for a variety of reasons.

14.2.3 Exploring the Corpus

The starting point of our diachronic analysis of the corpus was to make five keyword searches comparing each individual segment of the corpus with the remainder of the corpus, through the keywords function of WordSmith Tools and choosing the log likelihood option (or LL) to calculate 'keyness'.[5] Keywords, in the sense that is being used here, are words that have an unusually high relative frequency in one corpus or sub-corpus compared to a reference corpus; in our case, to identify the keywords in segment one, the reference corpus was made up of segments two to five, and so on. The resulting list of keywords may provide indications of diachronic shifts in wording patterns and meaning pattern.

However, a few points need to be made. This kind of procedure inevitably omits many things. For example, it does not show what the texts have in common, for which one would need to use a word list derived from a general corpus of American English. Secondly, as we shall see in the following section, it does not reveal semantic areas that are frequent but highly lexicalized, for example, in the SoU corpus the notion of 'God'. Thirdly, many keywords in any corpus of political language are intuitively obvious to any observer with a basic knowledge of the historical and cultural context. For example, that *mexico* and *texas* have a high keyness ranking (according to LL) in the 1790–1864 segment should be of no surprise; the same goes for *war* in the 1917–1945 segment and *soviet* in the 1946–1989 segment. Very often, what is more interesting are features that are unexpected and thus not necessarily searched for. Moreover, 'unusually high relative frequency' is not the only criterion for deciding whether a feature is 'meaningful' or not. From our point of view, as observers, the keyword analysis constitutes one heuristic device to provide a potentially useful entry point in the corpus and a guide to where to start to look in the texts. However, we would conclude by saying that such a procedure is not a substitute for reading texts from beginning to end; it is complementary to it.

14.3 Some Results

14.3.1 (Some of) What Cannot Be (Easily) Seen with Concordance Software

This section will consider those features of meaning-making that are not readily discernible through the use of concordance searches and which have been identified by reading the corpus.

One of the principal textual features that is difficult, if not impossible, to discern through software (unless the reading work has already been done and the corpus annotated) is the way in which a text unfolds in different stages. Although it is simple to produce large chunks of text from a concordance line, the full meaning of the chunk derives from what precedes it and from what the speaker is 'doing'. The 11 SoUs of the eighteenth century have a fairly linear structure:

> Greetings (to members of Congress) > Thanks (to God) > Report on past events –domestic policy actions > Report on past events – foreign policy actions (for example international relations, treaties, defence, navigation, etc.) > Announce –possible future proposals for executive action > Recommend – future legislative action > Summarize – share (with Congress) one's good intentions.

These staging structures are subject to variation; for example, the thanks may be very brief and embedded in a report or they may be extended and constitute an autonomous stage; reports on foreign and domestic policy may be inverted; occasionally recommendations may precede reports. The summary is sometimes omitted; moreover, it may take the form of a report or it may be a process of sharing highly charged values, as in the case of Washington's 1794 closure:

Example 1. Let us unite, therefore, in imploring the Supreme Ruler of Nations to spread his holy protection over these United States; to turn the machinations of the wicked to the confirming of our Constitution; to enable us at all times to root out internal sedition and put invasion to flight; to perpetuate to our country that prosperity which his goodness has already conferred, and to verify the anticipations of this Government being a safeguard of human rights.

The recommendation stage can be worded in terms of higher or lower intensity of compulsion. For example, *It rests with the wisdom of Congress to...* (Washington, 1793) gives Congress ample space for manoeuvre, while *they will not omit to inquire ...* (Washington, 1794) has a peremptory meaning.

Using this as a model, these features remain fairly constant throughout the nineteenth and twentieth centuries with some variations; the lexis relating to policy issue areas obviously changes over time, and changes radically in moments of crisis, such as major wars; for example, in the years leading up to the Civil War, the Constitution became an important topic and *constitution* was a key word. Between Greeting and Thanks there is occasionally a metatextual passage explaining what an SoU is. For example:

Example 2. In obedience to the command of the Constitution, it has now become my duty "to give to Congress information of the state of the Union and recommend to their consideration such measures" as I judge to be "necessary and expedient" (Buchanan, 1857).

Conclusive summaries have tended to become more evaluative. Stages of narration (of self, of the nation, of individuals used as metonyms of values and policy aims) appeared in the mid nineteenth century (Taylor, 1849) and have been a constant since 1961. Presidents do not always merely report but they also explain, or 'expound' (see, for example Van Buren, 1839; Pierce, 1856; T. Roosevelt, 1901). The 'Thanks' stage acknowledging God's providence was a regular feature until 1881 (with some exceptions, such as –1809, 1810, 1811 – Monroe; 1819, 1820, 1821, 1822, 1823, 1824 – Madison; 1855, 1856 – Pierce), and then all but disappeared. See Example 3.

Example 3. No country has been so much favored, or should acknowledge with deeper reverence the manifestations of the divine protection. An all wise Creator directed and guarded us in our infant struggle for freedom and has constantly watched over our surprising progress until we have become one of the great nations of the earth (Polk , 1847).

The 'Thanks to God' cannot easily be picked up through a concordance search because then Presidents used numerous names for God – to give just two examples *Author of all Good*, or *the Sovereign Arbiter of All Human Events* – and for the works of God – *the gracious indulgence of Heaven*. In fact, a simple search for *God* would produce distorted results since 80 of the 157 occurrences in the entire corpus date from the years between 1982 and 2014.

Similarly, the Recommend stage cannot be easily identified through automated procedures because, although a search for *recommend** shows that it is a very frequent lexical item, a perusal of the texts demonstrates that there are very many ways of asking for legislative action (it would be necessary to run searches for *attention, consideration, suggest*, require*, necess*, expedient*, urge** and many more besides). However, what can be achieved through corpus searches is the demonstration that over time requests for action have taken on a greater intensity. For example, the verb *urge* has a relative frequency of 0.005 per 100 tokens in segment 1 and 0.037 during the 1946–1989 segment. On the other hand, the frequency of *recommend** diminished from 0.097 in the 1790–1864 segment to 0.009 in the post-Cold War one.

For much of the nineteenth century and the early part of the twentieth century (let's say between 1829 and 1912), SoUs were rather lengthy texts, most of them composed of more than 10,000 running words and reaching a peak of over 27,000 in 1910 (and this is obviously a feature that the software can easily identify). In 1913 Wilson reintroduced the practise of making an oral address directly to the two houses and consequently texts became, with some exceptions, much shorter (around 5,000 running words), and also less detailed. Although the State of the Union address has maintained its characteristic as a political report and a request for political action, and the presence of technical lexis related to politics is still a feature of the texts, there is also a higher presence of more general lexical items related more closely to 'shared values' than to precise political actions. This was acknowledged specifically by Wilson in his introduction to the 1916 address:

Example 4. I shall continue the practice, which I hope has been acceptable to you, of leaving to the reports of the several heads of the executive departments the elaboration of the detailed needs of the public service and confine myself to those matters of more general public policy [...] (Wilson, 1916).

But the switch to spoken mode also had other consequences on the grammar. While the typical dialogic positioning of Presidents in the written mode is the monoglossic bare statement, Wilson engages with his addressees heteroglossically by entertaining different points of view (Martin and White, 2005: 99–102); for example, *it seems to me, I think, I venture to say, I think you may agree with me, may I say a few words*, and his discourse had greater variation in Mood, with interrogatives and imperatives, than his predecessors.

In later Presidents the shift towards an informal style led to the use of extended lexical metaphors, such as:

Example 5. We have plowed the furrow and planted the good seed; the hard beginning is over. If we would reap the full harvest, we must cultivate the soil where this good seed is sprouting and the plant is reaching up to mature growth (F.D.R. Roosevelt, 1934).

Example 6. We are not lulled by the momentary calm of the sea or the somewhat clearer skies above. We know the turbulence that lies below, and the storms that are beyond the horizon this year. But now the winds of change appear to be blowing more strongly than ever (Kennedy, 1963).

It is certainly not possible through automated procedures to pinpoint when discursive changes actually took place, although the last three Presidents that have been cited, Wilson, F.D.R. Roosevelt and Kennedy, represent significant turning points leading to where we are today. But that profound lexicogrammatical change has taken place is (not surprisingly) undeniable. Examples 7 and 8, which we will comment on briefly in the next section, are taken from the conclusions of the first and the penultimate SoUs.

Example 7. The welfare of our country is the great object to which our cares and efforts ought to be directed, and I shall derive great satisfaction from a cooperation with you in the pleasing though arduous task of insuring to our fellow citizens the blessings which they have a right to expect from a free, efficient, and equal government (Washington, 1790).

Example 8. That's just the way we're made. We may do different jobs and wear different uniforms and hold different views than the person beside us. But as Americans, we all share the same proud title: We are citizens. It's a word that doesn't just describe our nationality or legal status. It describes the way we're made. It describes what we believe. It captures the enduring idea that this country only works when we accept certain obligations to one another and to future generations; that our rights are wrapped up in the rights of others; and that well into our third century as a nation, it remains the task of us all, as citizens of these United States, to be the authors of the next great chapter of our American story (Obama, 2013).

14.3.2 (Some of) What Can Be Seen Through a Keyword Search

14.3.2.1. *Analysing Key Words.* Table 14.1 and Table 14.2 illustrate ten key words chosen from the 1790–1864 segment (1) and the 1990–2014 segment (5) calculated and ranked by WordSmith Tools 4.0 on the basis of log likelihood. In each case, one segment was compared to a reference corpus composed of the other four segments; the first column is the rank attributed by WordSmith, the third column displays relative frequency per 100 tokens in the segment while the fourth column displays relative frequency in the reference corpus. For reasons of space we have chosen a mere ten words from among the top 50 in the attempt to illustrate that the presence of most items can be explained by historical events; but not all of them.

What is immediately evident in Table 14.1 is that the first three entries would never be expected in a key word search; in general, key words tend to be nouns. Similarly in Table 14.2, while most examples can be explained by political and historical reasons, items like *children* and *families* reflect the simplification of lexical choices (issue areas such as education and unemployment are explained through simple examples). That *we*, and *you* are attributed a high keyness value is a surprising result, although the relative frequency difference is extremely clear; the same can be said of *america*. We will briefly make some considerations on the presence of *the*, *which* and *of* as top-ranking items, in terms of written and spoken modes of meaning making, and then consider *we* and *america* in terms of construction of collective identity, and then *may* and *must* in terms of engagement.

Table 14.1: Keywords from 1790–1864 Segment (1)

	Key word	**%**	**% ref**
1	the	9.403	7.881
2	which	0.984	0.563
3	of	6.125	5.069
5	mexico	0.111	0.019
6	states	0.522	0.283
7	may	0.296	0.142
9	constitution	0.104	0.027
27	british	0.057	0.015
28	territory	0.079	0.027
35	citizens	0.154	0.079

Table 14.2: Keywords from 1990–2014 Segment (5)

	Key word	**%**	**% ref**
1	we	1.936	0.529
2	you	0.524	0.079
3	america	0.389	0.050
6	tonight	0.190	0.011
7	children	0.214	0.017
9	jobs	0.157	0.010
16	iraq	0.070	0.000
18	families	0.126	0.011
22	health	0.168	0.025
37	must	0.402	0.160

That a determiner, a relative pronoun and an extremely high frequency preposition figure as the highest ranking key words in segment 1 compared to the remainder of the SoU corpus can be seen as a reflection of the 'nominal' style, displaying 'crystalline complexity', of written language, evident in Example 7 (even though Washington actually delivered the address orally) compared to the 'clausal' style, characterized by 'choreographic complexity', of Example 8 (Halliday, 1987: 147). However, looking at the difference in relative frequency of *the* (9.403 vs 7.881 per 100 tokens) it would seem that the determiner has a higher than average frequency in the entire corpus (in the Corpus of Contemporary American English (COCA)[6] the relative frequency of *the* is 5.569). But an examination of the individual segments of the corpus shows that *the* was extremely frequent from 1790 until 1917, after which its frequency gradually declined, arriving at 4.874 in the 1990–2014 segment. So we might summarize this by saying that the frequency of nominal groups that are intended as 'identifiable' in this particular register of political discourse has declined over time.

14.3.2.2. *Identity.* Table 14.2 shows that the item with the highest keyness value in a comparison between the post-Cold War segment and the remainder of the SoU corpus is the personal pronoun *we*. Similarly to the keyness of *the* in segment 1, this is another surprising finding, since *we* is a frequent word in political language and spoken language. However, the difference between the relative frequencies in the segment and those in the remainder of the corpus leave little room for doubt: 1.936 versus 0.529 (the relative frequency of *we* in the COCA is 0.464). Figure 14.1 shows how this has been a continuous and consistent trend. Enough has probably been said on the importance of the item *we* in the literature on political discourse and so it need not be belaboured here other than to point out that this is a clear index of the construction of a collective identity since a large number of the instances point to an 'inclusive' meaning (*we* as nation, see Example 11), even though *we* is always a rather slippery reference word.

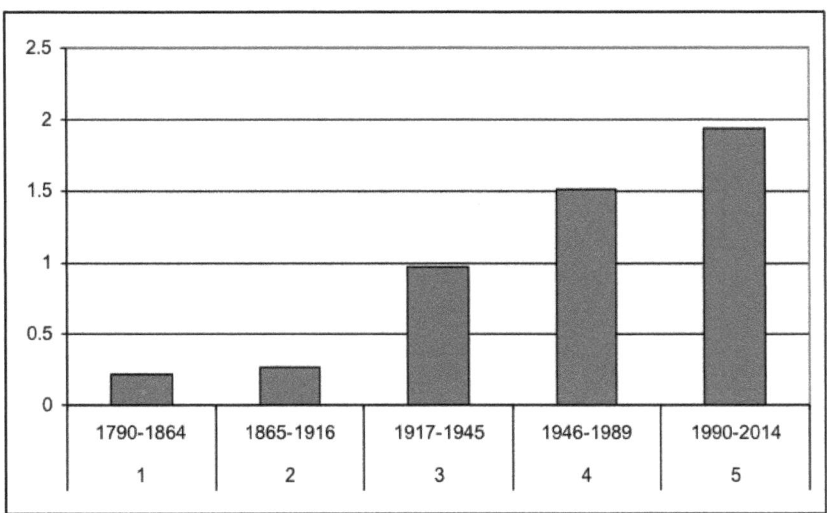

Figure 14.1: Relative frequency of *we* per 100 tokens

The third ranking key word, with an unequivocally high frequency difference, is *america*, and yet another time it is an item that we had not expected to be 'key', although Figure 14.2 shows a very clear pattern of constant increase in frequency over time. If we turn this around and look at the 1790–1864 segment, there are only 119 instances (corresponding to a frequency of 0.022 per 100 tokens) and although *united states* is a frequent cluster, *united states of america* occurs but eight times. On the other hand there are 380 instances of *the union*, 63 of *our union* plus one instance of *24 sovereign States and 12,000,000 happy people* (Jackson, 1829). Evidently America was not used as a term of national identity but rather as a geographical space; in fact of the L1 collocates of *america,* 51 are *central*, 14 *south* and 8 *north*. On the other hand, in the 1990–2014 segment, although the meaning of geographical space does not entirely disappear, the meaning of America is also construed as a political space, in particular as a set of values, as a sentient symbol of collective identity and as a protagonist of a narrative:

Example 9. America, not just the nation, but an idea alive in the minds of the people, everywhere (Bush,1990).

Example 10. I thank you. America is very, very proud of you (Clinton, 1996).

Example 11. From the earliest days of our founding, America has been the story of ordinary people who dare to dream. That's how we win the future. We're a nation that says, "I might not have a lot of money, but I have this great idea for a new company." "I might not come from [...]" (Obama, 2011) .

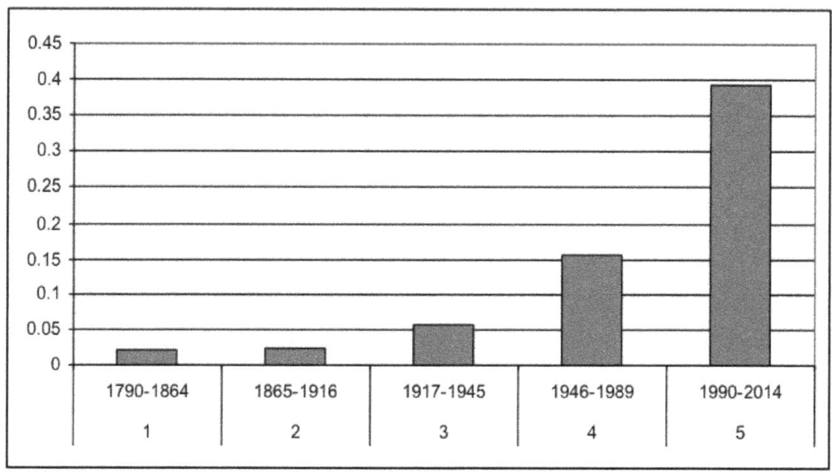

Figure 14.2: Relative frequency of *america* per 100 tokens

14.3.2.3. *Engagement – may and must*. In this section, we will deal with interpersonal meanings realized by the two modals *may* and *must*, in order to examine one of the ways that SoUs have shifted to a more persuasive style over time.

A preliminary quantitative analysis shows that their relative frequencies in the corpus as a whole are quite similar: 0.191 per 100 tokens for *may* and 0.181 for *must*. However, a diachronic investigation of their distribution reveals two very different trends. In fact, referring to Table 14.1 and Table 14.2, *may* figures as a key word in the 1790–1864 segment and *must* in the 1990–2014 segment. Moreover, as Figure 14.3 shows, the relative frequency of *may* steadily and constantly decreases over time, from 0.296 in the first segment to 0.043 in the fifth, with a sharp drop in the fourth and fifth segments. On the other hand the frequency of *must* gradually increases, from 0.075 to 0.401, with a sharp rise in the fourth and fifth segment.

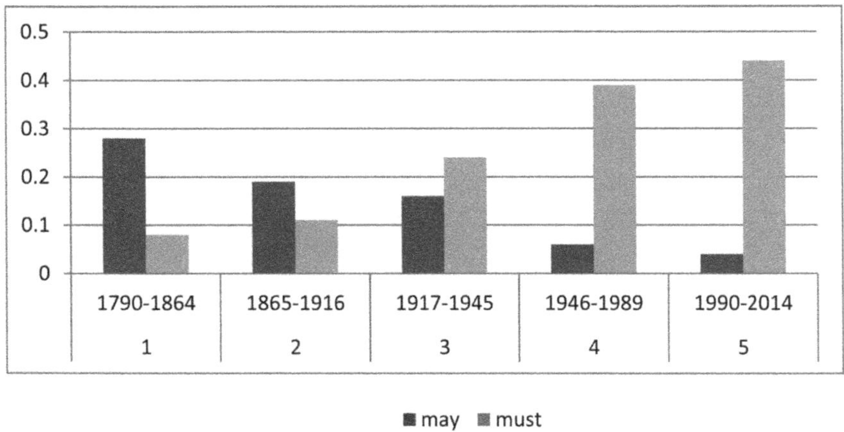

Figure 14.3: Relative frequency of *may* and *must* per 100 tokens

From the perspective of the appraisal system of engagement (Martin and White, 2005), a close examination of these two interpersonal resources of 'heteroglossic' engagement thus suggests that there has been a steady decrease in the use of discursive resources that 'expand' the speaker's/writer's intersubjective position, and an increase of resources that 'contract' this position. This can also be confirmed by comparing instances of *may* across segment 1 and segment 5; in fact, in the latter, instances of *may* are typically found in two distinctive patterns. The first is the formulaic *may God bless America*, and its variants, which accounts for 15% of all occurrences of *may* in this segment and expresses a desire, rather than probability or possibility. We pointed out in section 3.1 that up until the 1880s, most SoUs began with a 'Thanks to God'. From 1953 onwards God's assistance begins to be invoked at the very end of SoUs, and it has been a standard discursive feature since the 1980s.

The second pattern is the expanding/contracting pair *may [...] but/yet*, which is a typical pattern in persuasive discourse in institutional/political domains (see Bayley, 2007). The expanding/contracting pair *may...but /yet* covers one third of all instances of *may* in segment 5. In spite of its 'entertaining' and opening function, the role played by the modal *may* combined with a resource of counter-expectancy (*but/yet)* acts to construe a reader to align with the speaker's point of view; the possibility that is opened in the first clause is denied or countered in the second, as illustrated in examples (12) and (13).

Example 12. Just saying no to everything may be good short-term politics, but it's not leadership (Obama, 2012).

Example 13. In a complex and challenging time, the road of isolationism and protectionism may seem broad and inviting – yet it ends in danger and decline (Bush, 2006).

In contrast, instances of the low-intensity modalizing locution *may* in the first segment reveals that this 'expanding' resource is typically co-selected with the word 'Congress'. Moreover, a close reading of the enlarged co-text and context shows that *may* is typically associated with words indicating legal instruments such as *measure, provisions, convention*, as well as meanings of necessity (*i.e. necessary, required, deemed, advisable* etc.) through which these legal instruments are enacted:

Example 14. I shall submit this convention to the Senate for its advice and consent as to the ratification, and, if obtained, shall immediately bring the subject before Congress for such provisions as may require the interposition of the Legislature. (Monroe, 1822).

Example 15. As it is presumed that those documents will be essential for the correct disposition of the claims, it may become necessary for Congress to extend the period limited for the duration of the commission (Fillmore, 1850).

In contrast to segment 5, instances of *may* and their patterns of co-occurrence in this segment function rhetorically to open up the dialogic space to alternative points of view; at the same time, however, they hint at a deferential attitude towards the Congress and this, in turn, may explain why the frequency of this modalizing locution is higher in the eighteenth century and nineteenth century presidential addresses.

As far as *must* is concerned, Table 14.2 shows that it has been calculated as a key word in the fifth segment and Figure 14.3 demonstrates that its relative frequency has increased consistently over time. However, a word of warning; to interpret findings drawn from segments of a corpus, it is necessary to check the distribution of the item within the segment. In this particular case, a look at frequency in the discourse of individual Presidents shows that in Clinton relative frequency is 0.549 while in Obama it is 0.174 and it could be argued that Clinton's idiolect skews the data (even though, frequency was very high in both G.H and G.W. Bush's speeches). For this reason, we have focused on the Cold War segment (1946–1989), where the difference between relative frequencies (0.393 compared to 0.140 in the remainder of the corpus) is greater than that relative to segment 5. In fact we argue that this contractive modal typically characterizes the language of Cold War Presidents.

A first glance at its collocates shows that the personal pronoun *we* is the strongest left collocate of *must*, co-occurring in more than half of all instances

(612 out of 1.147). A close analysis of the phrase 'we must', which indeed provides a clear strategy of speaker-hearer alignment, reveals that the modal locution is typically followed by material processes in the semantic domains of 'taking action' and 'maintaining strength (*act, continue to support/to strengthen, improve/expand/increase, protect*). Indeed, the analysis shows that *must* is co-selected with *strong/strength** 54 times in 46 speeches in this segment (compared to only one single occurrence in the remainder of the corpus, i.e. in Roosevelt's 1938 address). The use of 'we must' is typically contractive and foregrounds an assessment of obligation on the part of the speaker, obviously including the Congress, but also the whole nation. Patterns of co-selection, moreover, show that its use is related to military duties and defence, which suggests that 'we must', within this political domain and in this particular historical period, is an index of political priorities. This can also be regarded as a clear pointer to 'aboutness'. The following two extracts exemplify this:

Example 16. We cannot do all we want to in times like these – we have to choose the things that will contribute most to defense – but we must continue to make progress if we are to be a strong nation in the years ahead (Truman, 1952).

Example 17. We must continue to strengthen our mutual security efforts. Most people now realize that our programs of military aid and defense support are an integral part of our own defense effort (Eisenhower, 1958).

14.4 Concluding Remarks

The aim of this chapter was to discuss some of the challenges and limits of a corpus-assisted meaning analysis and to see whether the analysis of a diachronic corpus can reveal changes in meanings over time. Our analysis has necessarily been very brief and it has picked out very few features. However, we think it has shown that some things can be achieved, although we cannot emphasize enough that without actually reading the texts we only obtain a piecemeal and fragmentary picture. In short, if you don't know your corpus, you're not going to go very far. On the other hand, if you don't have a corpus, you might miss important parts of the picture.

About the authors

Paul Bayley is Professor of English Language and Linguistics at the Department of Political and Social Sciences of the University of Bologna, Italy. He has recently co-edited *European Identity: What the Media Say*, with Geoffrey

Williams (Oxford University Press, 2012) and *Corpus-assisted Discourse Studies on the Iraq Conflict*, with John Morley (Routledge, 2009).

Cinzia Bevitori is Senior Lecturer and Researcher of English Language and Linguistics at the Department of Social and Political Sciences at Bologna University, Forlì, Italy. Her research interests are in the field of corpus-assisted discourse analysis within the framework of Systemic Functional Linguistics, focusing in particular on political and media discourse.

Endnotes

1. To make this situation still more complex, in 1911 and 1912 Taft broke up his written messages into three and four different sections and delivered them on different dates; in 1944 and 1956 Roosevelt and then Eisenhower delivered written messages but also broadcast summaries of them on the radio; in these cases we have included only the written message in the corpus. Nixon in 1972, 1974, and Carter in 1978, 1979 and 1980 gave oral addresses to Congress but also submitted written versions. In these cases the corpus contains only the oral. In 1973 Nixon delivered six written messages to Congress over a period of five weeks. The first was an overview and the remainder covered specific topics. The corpus contains the first of these.
2. Available from https://www.youtube.com/watch?v=arhBRouSmWs (last accessed January 2015).
3. The texts have been downloaded from State of the Union pages of the website of The American Presidency Project of the University of California at Santa Barbara: http://www.presidency.ucsb.edu/sou.php (last accessed January 2015).
4. Figures have been rounded up or down to the nearest 1000 tokens.
5. We are aware that this particular metric has been criticized (see for example Gabrielatos and Marchi, 2012) and alternatives proposed; space does not permit a discussion here. Suffice to say that we will cite, where necessary, differences in relative frequency.
6. The Corpus of Contemporary American English (COCA) is a freely available corpus containing over 450 million words of texts between 1990–2012. Available from http://corpus.byu.edu/coca/ (last accessed January 2015).

References

Baker, P. (2006) *Using Corpora in Discourse Analysis*. London: Continuum.

Baker, P. (2011) Times May Change but We'll Always Have Money: A Corpus Driven Examination of Vocabulary Change in Four Diachronic Corpora. *Journal of English Linguistics* 39(65): 88.

Baker, P., Gabrielatos, C., KhosraviNik, M., Krzyzanowski, M., McEnery, T., and Wodak, R. (2008) A Useful Synergy? Combining Critical Discourse Analysis and Corpus Linguistics to Examine Discourses of Refugees and Asylum Seekers in the UK Press. *Discourse and Society* 19(3): 273–306.

Bayley, P. (2007) Perhaps ... but: Expanding and Contracting Alternative Viewpoints. *Textus* 20(1): 117–136.
Bayley, P. and Bevitori, C. (2015) Two Centuries of 'Security': Semantic Variation in the State of the Union Address. In A. Duguid, A. Marchi, A. Partington and C. Taylor (eds) *Gentle Obsessions: Literature, Linguistics and Learning. In Honour of John Morley*, 59–80. Rome: Artemide.
Bayley, P. and Williams, G. (eds) (2012) *European Identity: What the Media Say.* Oxford: Oxford University Press.
Gabrielatos, C. and Marchi, A. (2012) Keyness: Appropriate Metrics and Practical Issues. *CADS International Conference* 13-15/09/2012, Bologna, Italy.
Halliday, M. A. K. (1987) Language and the Order of Nature. In N. Fabb, D. Attridge, A. Durant and C. MacCabe (eds) *The Linguistics of Writing: Arguments between Language and Literature*, 135–154. Manchester: Manchester University Press.
Halliday, M. A. K. and Matthiessen, C. M. I. M. (2004) *An Introduction to Functional Grammar*. London: Arnold.
Martin, J. R. and White, P. R. R. (2005) *The Language of Evaluation: Appraisal in English*. New York: Palgrave Macmillan.
Matthiessen, C. M. I. M. and Teruya, K. (2016) Registerial Hybridity: Indeterminacy among Fields of Activity. In D. R. Miller and P. Bayley (eds) *Hybridity in Systemic Functional Linguistics: Grammar, Text and Discursive Context*, 205–239. Sheffield: Equinox Publishing.
Matthiessen, C. M. I. M., Teruya, K., and Lam, M. (2010) *Key Terms in Systemic Functional Linguistics*. London and New York: Continuum.
Miller, D. R. (2006) From Concordance to Text: Appraising 'Giving' in Alma Mater Donation Requests. In G. Thompson, and S. Hunston (eds) *System and Corpus: Exploring Connections*, 248–268. London: Equinox.
Miller, D. R. (2007) Towards a Typology of Evaluation in Parliamentary Debate: From Theory to Practice – and Back Again. *Textus* 20(1): 159–180.
Miller, D. R. and Johnson, J. H. (2009) Evaluation, Speaker-Hearer Positioning and the Iraq War: A Corpus-Assisted Study of Congressional Argument. In J. Morley, and P. Bayley (eds) *Corpus-Assisted Discourse Studies on the Iraq Conflict: Wording the War*, 34–73. New York: Routledge.
Morley, J. and Bayley, P. (eds) (2009) *Corpus-Assisted Discourse Studies on the Iraq Conflict: Wording the War.* New York: Routledge.
Neustadt, R. E. (1990) *Presidential Power and the Modern Presidents. The Politics of Leadership from Roosevelt to Reagan*. New York: The Free Press.
Partington, A., Morley, J., and Haarman, L. (eds) (2004) *Corpora and Discourse.* Bern: Peter Lang.
Scott, M. (2005) *WordSmith Tools* Version 4.0 [Software]. Oxford: Oxford University Press.
Stubbs, M. (1996) *Text and Corpus Analysis: Computer-Assisted Studies of Language and Culture*. Oxford: Blackwell.

15 The Role of Corpus Annotation in the SFL-CL Marriage: A Test Case on the EU Debt Crisis

Sabrina Fusari
University of Bologna

15.1 Introduction

This chapter discusses the role of annotation in the interplay between Systemic Functional Linguistics (SFL) and Corpus Linguistics (CL), with a view to analysing its potential and drawbacks for the depth and reliability of linguistic insight, especially as concerns the processing of grammatical data. As the title suggests, and based on the existing literature (Bednarek, 2010; Butler, 2004; Halliday and Matthiessen, 2004; Thompson and Hunston, 2006), this study starts from the assumption that the relation between SFL and CL is, by now, well established and enduring over time – a 'marriage', so to speak, within which both partners give and receive, affirm their individual and joint identity, share and work towards a common life goal, and sometimes have to work in the art of compromise. What annotation can bring to this marriage, and to what extent it can contribute to making this relationship thrive, is the question I will try to address.

This chapter has four sections: firstly, I provide a brief survey of the state of the art in the annotation of electronic language corpora for SFL studies; secondly, I illustrate some problems in Systemic annotation, which are at least partially responsible for its greater difficulty in comparison with other grammatical formalisms; thirdly, I present a test of two widely available corpus programmes, the UAM Corpus Tool (O'Donnell, 2009a) and the Halliday Centre Tagger (Wong *et al.*, 2014), performed on two fairly long texts taken from a set of corpora on the news and institutional discourse of the European sovereign debt crisis (Fusari, 2016); finally, I present some conclusions on the advantages of corpus annotation for systemicists, its disadvantages and areas that call for improvement. Although a number of technical issues will be touched upon, my main focus is not on the technicalities of corpus annotation, but on the overall capacity of annotation (including automatic annotation) to enhance the power of corpus analysis, especially within the framework of a theory rich model of grammar like the one put forth by systemicism.

15.2 Theoretical Background

The endeavour to find a common ground between SFL and computational approaches to linguistics has over the years spanned from text generation grammars, to dialogue systems, to machine translation (O'Donnell and Bateman, 2005), and has found what is perhaps its most fruitful expression in CL. This is clearly demonstrated by the manifold aspects of SFL which have recently been investigated with corpus methodologies, ranging from lexical cohesion (Flowerdew and Mahlberg, 2009), to evaluative language (Bednarek, 2006, 2008; Coffin and O'Halloran, 2006), inquiries into the ideologies and rhetoric of news discourse (Bednarek, 2006; Bevitori, 2010; Haarman and Lombardo, 2009), congressional and parliamentary debates (Bayley, 2004; Miller, 2007; Miller and Johnson, 2009) language education (Flowerdew, 2003, 2009), genre analysis (Gardner, 2008) and corpus assisted meaning analysis (Miller *et al.*, 2014).[1]

The fact that CL and SFL have interacted for most of their existence (Halliday, 1966; Sinclair, 1966), however, does not mean that their relationship has always been a bed of roses – in fact, despite numerous points of contact, perhaps most crucially the idea that lexis and grammar should be seen as just one object of analysis, there are still some key theoretical issues on which SFL and CL largely disagree.[2] One of the most fundamental differences is, indeed, the role of theory itself in language studies: while SFL is renowned for its theoretical depth, including – among other aspects – a three-tiered model of grammar, CL, especially its corpus-driven strand, firmly believes that the theoretical 'burden' of grammatical formalism should be minimized, giving rise to what has sometimes been described as a 'theory neutral stance'. While the whole idea of theory neutrality may sound quite impressionistic, and has in fact been discarded by one of the lead proponents of corpus driven linguistics, Tognini Bonelli (2001: 178), it bears clear testimony to the attempt by at least some corpus linguists to 'jettison many of the categories and distinctions made in traditional and functional grammars' (Butler, 2004: 160).

To 'trust the text' (Sinclair, 2004a), however, does not mean to dispense with theory entirely, but to try and derive it systematically from language data, relying on the identification of corpus patterns and their mapping into what have been described as 'local grammars' (Hunston and Francis, 2000).

This radically empirical approach accords grammar the power to provide generalizations, largely through the detection of repeated patterns in and across corpora, but it crucially strips it of its power to explain meaning (Hunston and Francis, 2000: 260), in contrast with SFL's fundamental tenet that grammar and meaning are one.

Corpus-driven linguistics' mistrust for any preconceived theoretical ideas extends, at least in part, to corpus annotation. Sinclair famously believed that annotation should be approached with caution, as 'used without understanding of its limitations it is a hazardous practice' (2004b: 56). More specifically,

> because they [tags] impose one particular model of language on the corpus, they restrict the kind of research that can be done [...] Because the models imposed by current conventions of annotation are unlikely to be informed by corpus evidence, I believe researchers who use them are likely to make unnecessary problems for themselves (Sinclair, 2004b: 54).

According to Sinclair, annotation should also be kept distinct from mark-up, the former encoding less objective information, derived from the researcher's intuition rather than from the nature of the text itself.[3] Sinclair also mentioned the use of annotation as one of the key differences between corpus-based studies, for which he deemed annotation 'indispensable', and corpus driven studies, in which tags played a minor, possibly even 'obfuscating', role. Any SFL annotation, therefore, would certainly be understood by Sinclair as being a strictly corpus-based, rather than a corpus-driven endeavour.

The fundamental problem with SFL annotation, which would have corpus-driven linguists frown, is therefore the fact that, on top of having *digitality* thrust upon them, as in any corpus research, texts annotated with SFL tagsets also have a *formalism* thrust upon them, and this formalism inevitably channels the answers researchers can elicit from their texts in a particular direction. It is clear that this problem is much more philosophical than technical, and it pertains to the different role of introspection[4] in SFL and CL: according to SFL, CL's 'being "atheoretical" disguises a particular theoretical conviction' (Halliday and Matthiessen, 2004: 35), so that even the most extreme corpus-driven stances, which tend to see all grammatical parsing as a 'misplaced effort' (Tognini Bonelli, 2001: 90), constitute, in fact, a theory. CL, for its part, while recognizing that introspection cannot be simply shut out of the mind of researchers, or indeed of any human being, still believes the use of introspection to be hazardous, as it lends leeway to less than objective views of language, based on the 'model or theory of language through which we perceive linguistic events and with which we interpret them' (Sinclair, 2004b: 43).

In short, while the yet uneventuated possibility to parse a large scale corpus using a full SFL formalism would certainly be hailed by systemicists as a praise worthy achievement, it would probably leave many corpus linguists unimpressed, especially those who have more faith in the corpus- driven approach and shun the practice of annotation as 'stretching the evidence to fit the categories' (Tognini Bonelli, 2001: 90).

15.3 Problems of SFL Annotation: Technical and Cultural

'Misplaced' or not, devising parsing models is certainly a formidable effort, even more so for the grammar of SFL than for others. The reason for this greater complexity lies essentially in the richness of the Systemic Functional formalism in terms of its emphasis on meaning, as reflected in the three metafunctions of language (Ideational, Interpersonal and Textual), leading to frequent conflation of functions in a single element. In addition, since each metafunction has more than one SYSTEM working within it, each allowing for a range of alternative and simultaneous choices, illustrated through sometimes very articulated System networks, the complications of parsing are much greater for Systemic Functional Grammar than for more structurally oriented ones.

This has led to the conclusion that some kind of simplification is needed for the development of computational tools that will strike a reasonable compromise between the level of detail required by SFL and the constraints of computer processing. Perhaps the main strategy used to make headway towards a simplified, yet usable and reliable SFL parsing system is the reduction of conflation (O'Donnell, 2005; O'Donnell and Bateman, 2005), which has recently led to significant improvements in the user friendliness and potential of SFL aware corpus tools (O'Donnell, 2013).

Technical issues, however, are only partly responsible for the problems involved in SFL annotation. SFL has traditionally been seen as a qualitative approach to language, and it is known to prioritize the paradigmatic, whereas much segmentation required in corpus annotation procedures is largely syntagmatic.[5] In addition, many scholars who have been raised in heavily theoretical milieus prioritizing the close reading of texts, and the *integrity* of texts, may fail to see the potential of corpus tools beyond their capacity to provide a source of examples which then need to be extracted and approached manually in any case. And even when they do see this potential, scholars are preoccupied that annotation systems, especially automatic ones, will never be able to account for logogenetic issues (Miller *et al.*, 2014: 104; Miller in this volume). As Butler notes:

> the results of studies on large corpora present very serious challenges which can strike at the very heart of traditional assumptions about language patterning and how we should describe it. This is clearly highly uncomfortable for many linguists, as it appears to require a radical rethinking of the ways in which we approach linguistic description and theorising. This sense of discomfort, compounded by the "mechanical" nature of the initial analysis by computer, the "messiness" of corpus data, and the sense of loss of control in the face of numbers of words running into the hundreds of millions, is probably one of the most important factors which is still holding some functional linguists back from using corpus analysis (2004: 168).

These objections may not be dismissed as yet another case of scholars in the humanities showing distrust for computing, but they need to be approached as a cultural dilemma pertaining to the nature of language data, to the role of SFL in the broader arena of studies on language, and ultimately to what it means, practically, to work with a grammar that prioritizes meaning over form. The argument that automatic annotation cannot (or, indeed, *should* not) replace manual tagging entirely[6] is also not easily dismissed, and is actually taken into account by compilers of parsing systems, who currently use manually annotated corpora as gold standards (O'Donnell, 2009a: 1424) for the training sets of their systems.

The most important challenge, therefore, is not the technical complication of corpus annotation projects, nor is it the expensiveness of these undertakings in both money and time, although these are very real problems: the central issue is what simplifications the SFL community is prepared to accept and agree upon as a reasonable standard to reconcile its deep, meaning centred qualitative approach with the quantitative power, statistical reliability and processing speed offered by corpus methodologies.

At this point, however, one question inevitably arises: if SFL annotation is so problematic, and some degree of manual work and constant improvement are still required, is the effort worthwhile? The answer is largely positive, for a variety of reasons, most importantly the fact that raw text corpora make it complicated, and sometimes even impossible, to test a number of assertions in the literature that have so far remained unproven on representative samples of data. This in turn may limit the capacity of SFL to address many of its own fundamental questions with the full power of existing technology, reducing the scope, reliability and effectiveness of these studies (Honnibal, 2004). In addition, the practical applications of SFL annotation extend beyond the community of systemicists, to include scholars interested in Natural Language Understanding, Critical Discourse Analysis (Costechi, 2013) and even military intelligence services (Kappagoda, 2009).

15.4 A Test on Two Taggers

This section presents a test on the potential for annotation offered by two widely available corpus programmes, the UAM Corpus Tool and the Halliday Centre Tagger. The programmes were selected due to their wide availability, and as a follow-up to a previous study (Fusari, 2016) I concluded by promising to explore their potential to enhance Systemic analysis. The two programmes are not comparable *stricto sensu*, because they are aimed to meet different needs and levels of expertise: the UAM Corpus Tool is more suitable for research, and 'more oriented towards the doctoral student than to the beginner' (O'Donnell, 2009b: 223), whereas the Halliday Centre Tagger is more designed to 'facilitate SFG based text annotation and analysis' (Wong *et al.*, 2014: 1664) and is definitely suitable for students, including beginners. What these two programmes have in common, in addition to their being freely available online, and the product of extensive research in the interplay between SFL and CL, is that they both provide an answer to the rising demand for Systemic corpus analysis at varying degrees of complexity.

The UAM Corpus Tool (O'Donnell, 2005, 2009a), perhaps the best known software to assist systemicists in the annotation of texts, is not only a tagger. It is, as its name suggests, a corpus tool, so a system that will do most of the work one can ask of a corpus, including concordances, lists of keywords (calculated against everything else in a given project, against a specific subcorpus, or against another project), phrases and statistical analysis. It also includes a Subjectivity tab, based on a list of 16,000 words, each indicated as positive or negative, which the programme can find in any given text, thus offering an aid to Appraisal analysis. It also calculates lexical density and other general statistics automatically, for each text in a corpus, for a subcorpus, or for a whole corpus. At the time of writing, the UAM Corpus Tool is in its third version, providing automatic annotation for Parts of Speech, following either the Stanford Tagger or Tree Tagger, and Grammatical Structure, for Transitivity, Mood, and Theme. For manual annotation, in addition to schemes designed *ad hoc* by the user, four different built-in schemes may be used (Clause Grammar, Appraisal, Rhetorical Structure Theory and Error Analysis). Layers of annotation, again defined by the user, are kept separated within the same project, allowing the analyst to keep annotation to a minimum, or to increase its complexity as needed.

The Halliday Centre Tagger (Wong *et al.*, 2014) is a genuine tagger, as its name says, which allows users to store their texts online and annotate them either with the inbuilt predefined set of Systemic labels, or with a tagset of their own. Statistics related to the occurrences of annotated features are also automatically provided. Although the tagging process is essentially manual, this online platorm can perform a semiautomatic identification of some grammatical features, more specifically relating to Process types. The Halliday Centre Tagger is a new project, whose earliest prototype was put online for internal test in May 2011, and is still being developed, but it is of great interest because of its extremely intuitive interface, user friendliness and portability.

The test was performed on two texts taken from a set of small corpora representing the discourse of the European sovereign debt crisis as it appears in the business press and in official statements published on the website of the European Union (EU) (Fusari, 2016). The texts are the transcript of the speech in which Mario Draghi coined the term 'fiscal compact' (2,174 words)[7] and a *Financial Times* editorial in which Martin Wolf evaluates its pros and cons (1,068 words).[8] The texts were chosen due to their importance from the ideational point of view, as they both contributed to the discursive instantiation of an ideology, that of the 'fiscal compact', which has since become common currency in the rhetoric of EU policy. The test, therefore, concentrated on the Ideational metafunction, and more specifically on Transitivity, with a closer focus on Process types, but also including Participants and Circumstances. Both texts were first annotated manually, then using the UAM Corpus Tool's Autocoder and the semiautomatic facility integrated into the Halliday Centre Tagger.

Figure 15.1 and Figure 15.2 illustrate the typical screenshot of a Transitivity analysis in the Halliday Centre Tagger and UAM Corpus Tool respectively, with the beginning of Wolf's text taken as an example.

The greater delicacy of the Halliday Centre Tagger's output is obviously a result of the much greater amount of manual work required on this programme, as the labels to be attached to each textual segment are selected by the users themselves from the menu provided in the Step Selection window. Although more basic, and at times imprecise, the UAM Corpus Tool's output was obtained automatically, and can still be edited to meet the users' needs.

In the UAM Corpus Tool, the margin of error for manual and automatic annotation was, respectively, 8.4% and 18.8%. While all the mistakes made in manual analysis resulted from distraction or issues related to the hybrid nature of certain Processes (Banks, 2016), most errors in automatic annotation arose from Verbal Group Complexes being counted by the Autocoder as two Processes. Other errors occurred in the Autocoder's recognition of relational Processes instantiated by verbs other than 'to be' and 'to have' (e.g. 'the ECB stands ready' and 'banks have come under pressure' were recognized as material; 'this means' was recognized as mental), and with modal Adjuncts including a verb (e.g. 'as far as I'm concerned' was recognized as a mental Process).

In the Halliday Centre Tagger, the margin of error for semiautomatic annotation was slightly lower (18%), but this is probably connected with the fact that the interface 'remembers' the previous choices made in the user's manual annotation, in what may be considered to be a form of 'on the job training'. The tagging process is still more time consuming, as all the text must be gone through manually by swiping each segment, including semi-automatically tagged ones, with the mouse. However, the fact that it does not require installation, and that projects can be accessed any time online, makes manual annotation more user friendly on the Halliday Centre Tagger than on the UAM Corpus Tool.

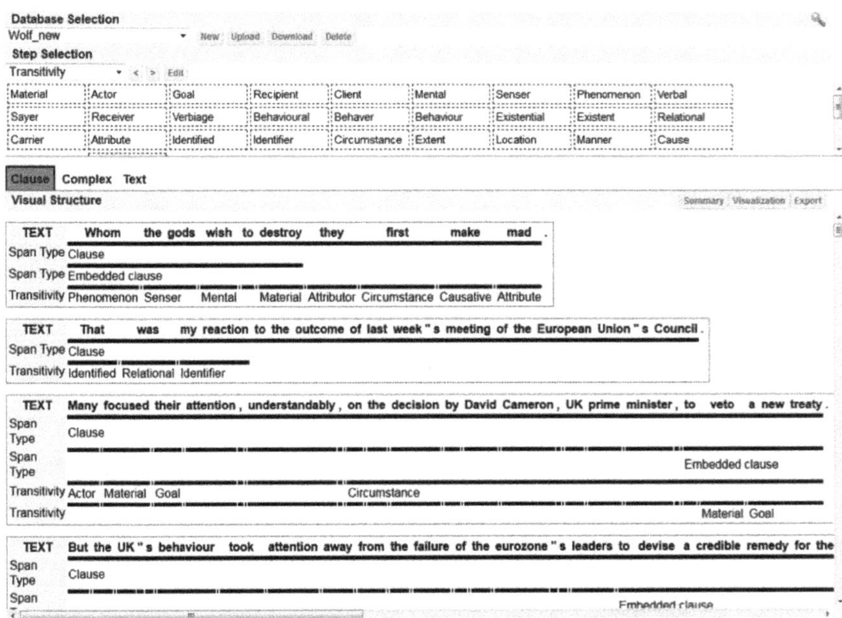

Figure 15.1: Transitivity analysis of 'A disastrous failure at the summit' by M. Wolf, Halliday Centre Tagger.

To summarize, the advantages of the UAM Corpus Tool emerging from this test are: the general statistics, offered even without annotation, for text, corpus and subcorpus; concordancing, including various forms of the same lemma, and other corpus facilities, which are numerous and very effective;

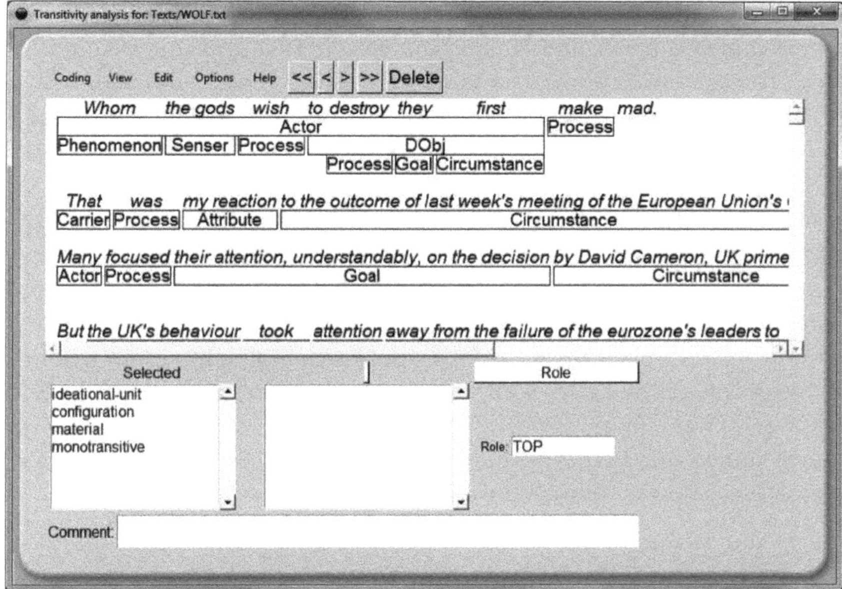

Figure 15.2: Transitivity analysis of 'A disastrous failure at the summit' by M. Wolf, UAM Corpus Tool.

the Autocoder, whose user friendliness has improved with version 3. The disadvantages are: the need for manual double-checking on the Autocoder's output, unless the analyst is prepared to accept a near-20% error margin; the need for more computer skills and expertise than required for the Halliday Centre Tagger, making the UAM Corpus Tool less suitable for students. The possibility for users to define their own tagset and/or restrict automatic annotation to POS tagging, without bringing SFL annotation into the picture, makes the UAM Corpus Tool a flexible instrument meeting the needs of scholars outside the field of SFL. The current version does not support any text encoding standard, but as this development is on the agenda (O'Donnell, 2009a: 1437), the software has the potential to eventually come to represent a valuable, more stable and user- friendly alternative to current corpus tools designed to analyse TEI-conformant documents, like XAIRA.

The Halliday Centre Tagger's advantages can be summarized as follows: it works online without installation, on any computer; it offers a set of preloaded SFL tagging schemes based on the three metafunctions, while still permitting customization; it can export tagged texts easily by copying and pasting them on a text editor, proving a valuable resource for students, including SFL beginners and the 'computer challenged'. Its disadvantages, as highlighted by my test, are: the lack of a fully automatic annotation tool and, perhaps most importantly, the fact that tagged texts cannot be saved in a format directly readable by a corpus concordancer, so the platform cannot be used to generate and/or explore concordances.

15.5 Conclusion

This test shows that SFL annotation, at various degrees of complexity, can be used for a variety of purposes, from building language corpora, to keeping track of Systemic analyses, eliciting quantitative data, testing qualitative hypotheses against those data, or simply enhancing SFL teaching to include computer tasks in which students can put their hands on texts and tag them for various Systemic features they have learned. The main objections to SFL annotation, as we have seen, are directed at automatic annotation, which is seen by many scholars as chaotic, incomplete and depriving the analyst of control over the data. However, without some form of automatic annotation, SFL tagging of large scale corpora will continue to be impossible, or simply not done (Honnibal, 2004), causing this model of language to lag behind others that have espoused the computational approach more passionately. A valuable guiding principle would be to rely on annotation for whatever positive results it may yield, without swearing by it in any dogmatic way, or expecting unrealistically revolutionary results. This has been, by the way, the inspiring principle of all the interplay between CL and SFL, for which,

> corpus linguistic investigation is not a panacea for all the problems of linguistic theorising and description. It is unquestionably a valid point of departure and a sound basis, upon which to develop it, and against which to test theoretical and descriptive statements (Tucker, 2001: 212).

Corpus annotation itself may be seen as a point of departure towards the possibility to analyse much larger volumes of data more quickly and reliably, testing SFL hypotheses against a wider array of texts of a size that would be unthinkable with fully manual approaches.

The cultural reservations that exist against SFL annotation may also be largely overcome as the power and user friendliness of SFL computational tools constantly increase, as has been the case in recent years. To this end, a flexible, open mind is needed to engage in an ambitious research programme, not so much to try and produce the ultimate SFL parser that will allow researchers to tag multiple layers of meaning to a near-perfect degree of reliability, but more importantly to agree on the 'simplifications', especially in terms of conflation and delicacy, that can be accepted in exchange for the advantages of corpus analysis.

About the author

Sabrina Fusari is Researcher of English Linguistics at the Department of Modern Languages, Literatures and Cultures of the University of Bologna, Italy. Her research in Systemic Functional Linguistics focuses on the use of electronic language corpora for the analysis of institutional and news registers, with particular focus on patterns of Transitivity.

Endnotes

1. Butler (2004: 169) notes that, in some SFL literature, 'the role of the corpus is merely ancillary, in that it is used merely as a source of examples to illustrate and support the claims being made'.
2. A detailed account of these differences is in Butler (2004).
3. On this and other distinctions, e.g. tagging vs. parsing, see Aguilera Carnerero (2008).
4. By 'introspection' here is not meant native speaker intuition, which is dismissed by both SFL and CL as an unreliable measure of functional adequacy. I refer to introspection as 'the analyst's own introspective judgements [...] play[ing] a part in linguistic description and theorising, if only because the evidence from corpora still needs to be interpreted, and this activity inevitably brings in what the linguist already knows and believes about language' (Butler, 2004: 150).
5. The combination of elements is particularly important for correct tagging, as highlighted in a discussion in the online group Sysfling (15-16 December 2014), where the automatic annotation of Projection was said to involve not only the tagging of the verb carrying the Process function, but also of the Verbiage following it, to avoid clauses like 'The doctor admitted the problem' and 'The doctor admitted the patient' being both recognized as Verbal.
6. The complementary nature of manual and automatic corpus annotation for SFL is illustrated in Teich (2009) and Degaetano-Ortlieb, Teich and Lapshinova-Koltunski (2012).
7. Speech by Mario Draghi, President of the European Central Bank, Ludwig Erhard Lecture, Berlin, 15 December 2011.
8. 'A disastrous failure at the summit', *Financial Times*, 13 December 2011.

References

Aguilera Carnerero, C. (2008) (Dis)Advantages of Working with a Parsed Corpus: Looking for Indirect Objects in the ICE-GB. In A. Linde López, J. Santana Lario, and C. M. Wallhead Salway (eds) *Studies in Honour of Neil Mclaren*, 289–404. Granada: Universidad de Granada.

Banks, D. (2016) On the (Non)Necessity of the Hybrid Category Behavioural Process. In D. R Miller and P. Bayley (eds) *Hybridity in Systemic Functional Linguistics. Grammar, Text and Discursive Context*, 21–40. Sheffield: Equinox Publishing.

Bayley, P. (ed.) (2004) *Cross-Cultural Perspectives on Parliamentary Discourse.* Amsterdam and Philadelphia, PA: John Benjamins Publishing Company.

Bednarek, M. (2006) *Evaluation in Media Discourse. Analysis of a Newspaper Corpus.* London: Continuum.

Bednarek, M. (2008) *Emotion Talk across Corpora.* Basingstoke and New York: Palgrave Macmillan.

Bednarek, M. (2010) Corpus Linguistics and Systemic Functional Linguistics: Interpersonal Meaning, Identity and Bonding in Popular Culture. In M. Bednarek and J. R. Martin (eds) *New Discourse on Language: Functional Perspectives on Multimodality, Identity, and Affiliation*, 237–266. London: Continuum.

Bevitori, C. (2010) *Representations of Climate Change. News and Opinion Discourse in UK and US Quality Press: A Corpus-Assisted Discourse Study.* Bologna: Bononia University Press.

Butler, C. S. (2004) Corpus Studies and Functional Linguistic Theories. *Functions of Language* 11: 147–186.

Coffin, C. and O'Halloran, K. A. (2006) The Role of Appraisal and Corpora in Detecting Covert Evaluation. *Functions of Language* 13: 77–110.

Costechi, E. (2013) A Method to Generate Simplified Systemic Functional Parses from Dependency Parses. *Proceedings of the Second International Conference on Dependency Linguistics.* Prague: Publishing House of the Faculty of Mathematics and Physics.

Degaetano-Ortlieb, S., Teich, E., and Lapshinova-Koltunski, E. (2012) Domain-Specific Variation of Sentiment Expressions: A Methodology of Analysis for Academic Writing. *Empirical Methods in Natural Language Processing. Proceedings of the 11th Conference on Natural Language Processing (KONVENS).* Vienna: Eigenverlag ÖGAI.

Flowerdew, L. (2003) A Combined Corpus and Systemic-Functional Analysis of the Problem-Solution Pattern in a Student and Professional Corpus of Technical Writing. *TESOL Quarterly* 37: 489–511.

Flowerdew, L. (2009) Applying Corpus Linguistics to Pedagogy: A Critical Evaluation. *International Journal of Corpus Linguistics* 14: 393–417.

Flowerdew, L. and Mahlberg, M. (2009) *Lexical Cohesion and Corpus Linguistics.* Amsterdam and Philadelphia, PA: John Benjamins Publishing Company.

Fusari, S. (2016) The Permeable Context of Institutional and Newspaper Discourse: A Corpus-Based Functional Case Study of the European Sovereign Debt Crisis. In D. R. Miller and P. Bayley (eds) *Hybridity in Systemic Functional Linguistics. Grammar, Text and Discursive Context*, 306–333. Sheffield: Equinox Publishing.

Gardner, S. (2008) Integrating Ethnographic, Multidimensional, Corpus Linguistic and Systemic Functional Approaches to Genre Description: An Illustration through University History and Engineering Assignments. In E. Steiner, and S. Neumann (eds) *Data and Interpretation in Linguistic Analysis. Proceedings of the Nineteenth European Systemic Functional Linguistics Conference and Workshop*. Saarbrücken: Universität des Saarlandes.

Haarman, L. and Lombardo, L. (2009) Evaluation and Stance in War News: A Linguistic Analysis of American, British and Italian Television News Reporting of the 2003 Iraqi War. London: Continuum.

Halliday, M. A. K. (1966) Lexis as a Linguistic Level. In C. E. Bazell, J. C. Catford, M. A. K. Halliday and R. H. Robins (eds) *In Memory of J. R. Firth*, 168–205.

London: Longman.
Halliday, M. A. K. and Matthiessen, C. M. I. M. (2004) *An Introduction to Functional Grammar*. 3rd edn. London: Hodder Arnold.
Honnibal, M. (2004) Converting the Penn Treebank to Systemic Functional Grammar. *Proceedings of the Australasian Language Technology Workshop*. Sydney: Association for Computational Linguistics.
Hunston, S. and Francis, G. (2000) *Pattern Grammar. A Corpus-Driven Approach to the Lexical Grammar of English*. Amsterdam and Philadelphia, PA: John Benjamins Publishing Company.
Kappagoda, A. (2009) *The Use of Systemic-Functional Linguistics in Automated Text Mining*. Edinburgh, South Australia: The Defence Science and Technology Organisation of the Australian Government.
Miller, D. R., Bayley, P., Bevitori, C., Fusari, S., and Luporini, A. (2014) Ticklish Trawling: The Limits of Corpus Assisted Meaning Analysis. In S. Alsop and S. Gardner (eds) *Language in a Digital Age: Be Not Afraid of Digitality. Proceedings of the 24th European Systemic Functional Linguistics Conference and Workshop*, 103–114. Coventry: Coventry University.
Miller, D. R. (2007) Towards a Typology of Evaluation in Parliamentary Debate: From Theory to Practice – and Back Again. *Textus* 20(1): 159–180.
Miller, D. R. and Johnson, J. H. (2009) Strict Vs. Nurturant Parents? A Corpus-Assisted Study of Congressional Positioning on the War in Iraq. In J. Morley and P. Bayley (eds) *Corpus Assisted Discourse Studies on the Iraq Conflict. Wording the War*, 34–73. London: Routledge.
O'Donnell, M. (2005). The UAM Systemic Parser. *Proceedings of the 1st Computational Systemic Functional Grammar Conference*, 16 July 2005, Sydney, Australia.
O'Donnell, M. (2009a) The UAM Corpus Tool: Software for Corpus Annotation and Exploration. In C. M. Bretones Callejas, J. F. Fernandez Sanchez, J. R. Ibáñez, M. E. Garcia Sanchez, M. E. Cortes de los Rios *et al.* (eds), *Applied Linguistics Now: Understanding Language and Mind/La Lingüística Aplicada Hoy: Comprendiendo El Lenguaje Y La Mente*, 1433–1447. Almeria: Universidad de Almeria.
O'Donnell, M. (2009b) Resources and Courses. In M. A. K. Halliday and J. J. Webster (eds) *Continuum Companion to Systemic Functional Linguistics*, 215–228. London and New York: Continuum.
O'Donnell, M. (2013) Exploring Identity through Appraisal Analysis: A Corpus Annotation Methodology. *Linguistics and the Human Sciences* 9: 95–116.
O'Donnell, M. and Bateman, J. (2005) SFL in Computational Contexts: A Contemporary History. In J. J. Webster, R. Hasan and C. M. I. M. Matthiessen (eds), *Continuing Discourse on Language: A Functional Perspective*, 343–382. London: Equinox.
Sinclair, J. (1966) Beginning the Study of Lexis. In C. E. Bazell, J. C. Catford, M. A. K. Halliday, and R. H. Robins (eds) *In Memory of J. R. Firth*, 410–430. London: Longman.
Sinclair, J. (2004a) *Trust the Text: Language, Corpus and Discourse*. London: Routledge.
Sinclair, J. (2004b) 'Intuition and Annotation – the Discussion Continues'. *Advances in Corpus Linguistics. Papers from the 23rd International Conference on English Language Research on Computerized Corpora* (ICAME 23), 22-26/05/2002,

Göteborg, Sweden. Amsterdam and New York: Rodopi.
Teich, E. (2009) Linguistic Computing. In M. A. K. Halliday and J. J. Webster (eds) *Continuum Companion to Systemic Functional Linguistics*, 113–127. London and New York: Continuum.
Thompson, G. and Hunston, S. (2006) Introduction. System and Corpus: Two Traditions with a Common Ground. In G. Thompson, and S. Hunston (eds) *System and Corpus. Exploring Connections*, 1–14. London: Equinox.
Tognini Bonelli, E. (2001) *Corpus Linguistics at Work.* Amsterdam and Philadelphia, PA: John Benjamins Publishing Company.
Tucker, G. (2001) Possibly Alternative Modality. *Functions of Language* 8: 183–216.
Wong, B. T. M., Chow, I. C., Webster, J. J., and Yan, H. (2014) The Halliday Centre Tagger: An Online Platform for Semi-Automatic Text Annotation and Analysis. *Proceedings of the Ninth International Conference on Language Resources and Evaluation (LREC 14).* Reykjavik: European Language Resources Association.

16 Grammatical Metaphor through the Lens of Software? Examining 'Crisis' in a Corpus of Articles from *The Financial Times*

Antonella Luporini
University of Bologna

16.1 Introduction

This chapter reports on research into the metaphorical framing of the current global financial/economic crisis as it emerges from a purpose-built corpus of articles from *The Financial Times* 2008, focusing on interpersonal and ideational grammatical metaphor (GM) within Systemic Functional Linguistics (SFL). The aim of the chapter is two-fold: on the one hand, select results are discussed with a view to highlighting patterns of use and effects of GM in news discourse; on the other, 'pros and cons' of corpus-assisted research on metaphor are taken into account. The rest of this introductory section is dedicated to an overview of the notion of GM, also in relation to lexical metaphor (LM). For reasons of space, I only touch upon aspects relevant to this study, drawing upon the in-depth accounts provided by Taverniers (2003), Halliday and Matthiessen (1999, 2014) and Thompson (2014). I then proceed in the following sections to describing the methodology and discussing select results.

16.1.1 Lexical Metaphor and Grammatical Metaphor

Without going into the details of an age-old debate, the most straightforward definition of metaphor comes from the etymology of the word itself. As already stated by Aristotle in the *Poetics* (1457b; 1997: 7–30), metaphor implies a *transfer* of meaning from the linguistic element that is most naturally associated with it to a different one, on the basis of some shared property. In recent years, and especially after the inception of Conceptual Metaphor Theory (CMT, Lakoff and Johnson, 1980), this has been the focus of massive research. For most scholars working in this field, metaphor is by definition *lexical*: it involves the use of a lexeme (word, group/phrase) within a non-standard domain. Classic examples are expressions like *my lawyer is a shark* or *man is a wolf*, where a subset of relevant features, commonly considered typical of a wild animal, is mapped onto a human being, foregrounding certain behavioural traits.[1]

From the viewpoint of SFL, however, 'metaphorical variation is lexicogrammatical rather than simply lexical' (Halliday, 1985: 320): it goes beyond the selection of single lexemes, affecting entire lexicogrammatical structures. The basic principles are the same: semantic transfer and functional contrast between standard and non-standard use. In fact, in the same way as lexical units have literal meanings, so grammatical structures can be said to have *congruent*, 'default' functions within the linguistic system: they tend to be naturally associated with the expression of certain interpersonal, ideational and textual meanings.[2] Thus, a non-congruent grammatical configuration creates a tension between wordings and semantics that is comparable to the one caused, at the opposite end of the lexicogrammatical cline, by LM. As a consequence, GM and LM can be thought of as two complementary perspectives on semantic variation (Taverniers, 2006): two complementary strategies thanks to which we can expand our meaning-making potential.

16.1.2 Types of Grammatical Metaphor

The linguistic system provides speakers with more or less congruent options to construe different kinds of meaning: from the viewpoint of SFL, these correspond to as many metafunctions played by language in context.[3]

The *interpersonal* metafunction accounts for the fact that speakers use language to enact social relationships; the main lexicogrammatical systems involved are those of MOOD, MODALITY and APPRAISAL. The MODALITY SYSTEM includes options for expressing degrees of probability, usuality (modalization) obligation, willingness, and ability (modulation). Modal operators (Example 2a) and modal adjuncts (Example 2b) are congruent options to construe the speaker's modal assessment within the clause. However, this can also be expressed metaphorically by a separate clause, making it explicitly subjective or objective (i.e. realizing explicit subjective or objective orientation: Halliday and Matthiessen (2014: 182), as in Example 2c and 2d:

Example 2a. Tomorrow may be too late.
Example 2b. Tomorrow is probably too late.
Example 2c. I think that tomorrow will be too late.
Example 2d. It is likely that tomorrow will be too late.

GM also interacts with the MOOD SYSTEM, generating metaphors of mood: these, however, play a key role in oral communication and are not taken into account in the case study presented in the following sections (the notion is discussed in, e.g. Halliday and Matthiessen 2014: 704–707; Thompson, 2014: 246–247).

The *ideational* metafunction accounts for the fact that speakers use language to represent extra-linguistic reality, through *figures*: configurations of Processes (congruently realized by verbal groups, VGs) and the participants therein (congruently realized by nominal groups, NGs), with optional circumstantial information. Here too GM plays an important semogenic function. Its most productive form in this area is *nominalization*, whereby Processes or Qualities are metaphorically portrayed as 'things' through NGs, as in Example 3b (examples taken from Halliday, 2004 [1998]: 34).

Example 3a. Glass cracks more quickly the harder you press on it.
Example 3b. <u>Cracks</u> in glass grow faster the more <u>pressure</u> is put on.

One of the main features of ideational metaphor, which also contrasts with metaphors of modality, is its tendency to 'compress' meanings, downgrading the domain of realization: typically, sequences of figures (congruently realized by clause nexuses) are 'packed' into metaphorical clauses, and figures (congruently realized by clauses) are 'packed' into groups/phrases. As a consequence, logico-semantic relations between events and experiential relations between elements in an event shift towards implicitness (Halliday and Matthiessen, 2014: 719).

Finally, the *textual* metafunction accounts for the fact that speakers enact social relationships and represent extra-linguistic reality by building cohesive and coherent texts. It is debatable whether GM can be said to occur at the level of textual semantics. Several scholars (e.g. Martin, 1992; Thompson, 2014) include textual metaphor in their surveys. Thompson, for instance, analyses special thematic structures as metaphorical realizations of textual meanings. Given here are examples (taken from Thompson 2014: 251–252) of a thematic equative (Example 4a) and a predicated Theme (Example 4b); more congruent wordings are provided in brackets.

Example 4a. What you need to do is to write me a letter.
(You need to write me a letter).
Example 4b. It's not the technology which is wrong. (The technology isn't wrong).

However, Halliday (e.g. 1985) and Halliday and Matthiessen (e.g. 1999, 2004) have always limited their accounts to interpersonal and ideational metaphor, and have recently re-affirmed their position: 'While some scholars have explored the possibility of grammatical metaphor within the textual metafunction, we do not see any evidence that the textual metafunction engenders metaphor' (2014: 731). Since textual metaphors are not involved in the corpus study presented in this chapter, the notion and the surrounding debate will not be dealt with further.

16.2 The Case Study: Background and Methodology

16.2.1 Metaphor and Corpus

Corpus techniques are widely employed in metaphor analysis, at both ends of the lexicogrammatical continuum, and on different languages (e.g. Charteris-Black, 2004; Deignan, 2005 on LM; Holtz, 2009; Yanning, 2011 on GM). Yet, just like other 'high-level' studies, addressing semantics and context (Bayley and Bevitori, this volume; Miller, this volume; Miller and Luporini, 2015), metaphor studies largely resist automation: metaphor identification in corpora remains a highly complex task, for which the analyst's contribution is essential (McEnery and Hardie, 2012).

As stated in the Introduction, metaphor is by its very nature a second-order phenomenon, implying a transfer of meaning and a resulting functional contrast with the corresponding non-metaphorical alternative. Thus, it requires engaging with multiple and delicate layers of analysis, incompatible with automation. Indeed, despite recent attempts to implement automatic extraction of metaphors from corpora (especially in the field of LM and CMT, e.g. Berber Sardinha, 2010), at present extensive manual analysis and a close reading of at least part of the texts are always required. Yet manual analysis itself comes at a cost, being time-consuming, and subject to bias and inconsistency. In the case of GM, a further obstacle to quantitative/qualitative corpus-assisted research is the lack of specifically annotated, would-be reference corpora, whose creation remains a demanding task in the absence of fully automated SFL-based annotation software (Fusari, this volume).

At the same time, it is undeniable that corpus techniques enable researchers to process large quantities of real linguistic data and carry out analyses that would be impossible otherwise, making research more rigorous, replicable, and retrievable (Simpson, 2014: 4). Furthermore, a major advantage of using corpus methodologies is the possibility of collecting data according to the research needs, compiling ad hoc corpora that aim to be representative of a given phenomenon, period, or text type, such as the one used for this study.

16.2.2 Corpus Construction and Methodology of Analysis

Being interested in examining the metaphorical representation of the financial/economic crisis in the specialized press, I built an ad hoc corpus collecting articles from all the issues of *The Financial Times* (FT, London edition) published in 2008.[4] The year was chosen for the significance of its financial events: among them, the collapse of Lehman Brothers, after which concerns about the global size of the crisis spread throughout the world. *The FT* was chosen for its importance and circulation, being one of the most authoritative financial newspapers worldwide, with several international editions, and a paying readership of 720,000 across print and online as of 2014.[5] The sampling was based on the type of article: for each issue, the main first page article and the leader were retrieved and stored in electronic format. Another possible criterion for choosing the texts was to look for all the occurrences of the lemma *crisis* in the electronic version of the newspaper, and select all and only the relevant articles. However, my original intention was to take into account the section of the newspaper where the GMs appeared: headline news are interesting because they reflect the editorial board's perception of what can be considered the main event of the day, and are likely to be read by a larger group of people (possibly including non-specialists), while leaders are expressions of the newspaper's stance, and typically show a more creative use of language. The corpus in its final form amounted to 307,181 words, including two subcorpora: FT _First_page and FT_Leaders (310 articles each).

The lexeme *crisis* was selected as search word for the study, and Key Word In Context (KWIC) concordances for it were retrieved and analysed for instantiations of GM, as described below. I should hasten to say that the term concordance in this work does not refer to the classic nine-word window used to assess collocational trends (Louw, 2007: 159). Since GM is a wide-ranging phenomenon, often going beyond clause boundaries, a wider window was selected, corresponding to the entire sentence in which the core lemma *crisis* occurred. Obviously, focusing on *crisis* meant narrowing down the scope of research, and acknowledging 'that patterns of potential interest may be missed, a risk which is difficult to avoid completely' (Deignan and Potter, 2004: 1234). Yet, especially when working on metaphor, an initial choice has to be made, even if the data set may seem small in comparison with a general corpus.

In the preliminary phase of the study, the corpus was uploaded to the online corpus query system Sketch Engine (Kilgarriff *et al.*, 2004) and tagged using the available tree-tagger for English. A query for *crisis* initially yielded a total of 414 results (203 in FT_First_page and 211 in FT_Leaders); indeed, a look at the lemmatized wordlists from the two subcorpora, where *crisis* ranked 39th and 23rd respectively, seemed to confirm the centrality of this topic in the year under analysis. Irrelevant occurrences (not directly referring to the field of finance/economics, e.g. mentions of the Georgian crisis) were subsequently discarded by scanning collocates and word sketches,[6] leading to a final set of 357 hits to be further investigated (180 in FT _First page and 177 in FT_Leaders).

The analysis initially exploited the fact that several automatically or semi-automatically identifiable lexicogrammatical elements could be taken as pointers to the presence of GM within the environment of *crisis*. For instance, Banks (2003) identifies three main categories of options for creating nominalized Processes in English, which can be (more or less readily) tracked down using software tools. These are: nouns that are morphologically identical to the agnate verb, like *change* (conversion); nouns that are morphologically different from the agnate verb, like *identification* (suffixation); nouns that have no agnate verb, but still indicate a Process, like *trend*. In the area of interpersonal metaphor, lexical units like *probable* or *possible* and verbs representing mental Processes are primary candidates for closer scrutiny if the focus is on metaphors of modality. Thus, the first step of analysis involved looking for potential metaphor markers in the collocate lists (lemmatized and part-of-speech-tagged) and word sketches for *crisis* in the two subcorpora. Table 16.1 shows, by way of example, a number of lemmas that were marked as potentially relevant instantiations of GM by looking at the collocate list for *crisis* in the FT _First_page, in the range from five items to the left to five items to the right of the node word.

Table 16.1: GM through Software: Metaphor Candidates in *Crisis* Collocate List (FT_First_Page)

Lemma	**Raw Frequency**	**Metaphorical Shift (Congruent → Metaphorical)**
response	6	Ideational metaphor (Process → Thing)
fear (N)	6	Ideational metaphor (Process → Thing)
deepen	5	Ideational metaphor (Quality → Process)
repeat (N)	4	Ideational metaphor (Process → Thing)
possible	2	Interpersonal metaphor of modality: explicit objective orientation (*it is possible that*)

Table 16.2, by contrast, illustrates potentially relevant information as it emerges from a word sketch for *crisis* in FT_First_page. For reasons of space, the table only reports select grammatical relations between node word and collocates (e.g. in the first column, *crisis* functioning as Object of the verbs that follow), and, in the case of long lists of collocates, the top ten results ordered by logDice (a measure of collocation strength, Rychlý, 2008).

Table 16.2: GM through Software: Metaphor Candidates in *Crisis* Word Sketch (FT_First_Page)

		Crisis (noun)	FT_First_Page		Total Freq = 203		
OBJECT_OF	logDice	SUBJECT_OF	logDice	MODIFIER	logDice	PP_OBJ_OF	logDice
tackle	11.09	**deepen**	9.61	credit	11.52	**repeat**	11.00
avert	10.63	prompt	9.36	financial	10.56	wake	11.00
address	10.32	face	8.31	subprime	10.31	casualty	10.78
quell	10.14	have	6.52	global	9.93	effect	10.22
discuss	10.12	be	6.10	economic	9.37	scale	10.07
combat	10.12			Northern	9.19	bad	8.66
solve	10.07			**banking**	9.16		
prevent	9.51			recent	9.09		
deepen	9.43			mortgage	8.66	PP_OBJ_TO	logDice
trigger	9.40			Rock	8.66	**response**	11.09
[...]				[...]		**solution**	10.83
						respond	10.51
						PP_OF	logDice
						confidence	10.01

Potential metaphor candidates (all of the ideational type) are marked in bold. One of them is the verb *deepen* ('Object_of' and 'Subject_of' columns), which also appears in Table 16.1. As already noted, this implies a metaphorical shift from Quality to Process; however, the word sketch also provides colligational information, showing that the verb occurs both with *crisis* as Object and as Subject. Other relevant items, all instantiating a Process →

Thing shift, include *banking, repeat* (N), *response* and *solution*. While *banking* occurs in the corpus as a pre-modifier (Classifier) of *crisis*, the other three function as Head within NGs featuring *crisis* as part of an embedded Qualifier (e.g. *repeat of crisis*). Finally, a further noteworthy entry is *confidence*, which post-modifies *crisis* in the expression *crisis of confidence*, and may be thought of as instantiating an almost 'crystallised' ideational metaphor of the Process → Thing type.

At the end of this preliminary stage, a first set of relevant concordances was selected for qualitative analysis, which, as stated above, cannot be but manual. Still, since the risk of overlooking meaningful patterns by relying exclusively on software was too high, after this pilot survey all the remaining concordances were also manually searched. The combination of corpus-driven and manual analysis led to the full picture described in the following section.

16.2.3 Select Results

The first thing to notice is the number of metaphorical concordances for *crisis* (i.e. containing at least one GM), markedly high in both subcorpora, as shown by Table 16.3.

Table 16.3: Metaphorical Concordances in FT Corpus and Subcorpora

Subcorpus	Number of Analysed Concordances	Number of Metaphorical Concordances	Per cent of Metaphorical Concordances
FT_First_page	180	94	52.2
FT_Leaders	177	88	49.7
Total in FT corpus	357	182	51

Through qualitative analysis, each instance was assigned to one of the two classes of GM taken into account for the study and, within these, to a specific subclass. Metaphors of modality were classified according to the type and orientation of modality encoded; no evidence was found of metaphors involving modalization: usuality and modulation: inclination. Ideational metaphors were classified according to the type of lexicogrammatical downgrading involved (Halliday and Matthiessen, 2014: 719–726): *sequences of figures* realized as simple clauses rather than clause nexuses, or *figures/parts of figures* realized as groups/phrases rather than as individual clauses. Table 16.4 and Table 16.5 below provide a snapshot of the classes/subclasses, with number of occurrences and corpus examples.

Table 16.4: GMs in FT_First_Page

Subcorpus: FT_First_Page	**Total Number of GMs: 134**
a. Interpersonal (8)	
Modalization: probability (6)	
Subjective explicit orientation (5)	'I don't think we would get rid of the crisis with just monetary tools,' he said.
Objective explicit orientation (1)	The move to extend the credit facility is likely to soothe Wall Street, by confirming Fed support [...] through the credit crisis.
Modulation: obligation (2)	
Subjective explicit orientation (2)	'I intend the Bank to contribute to the design of regulatory and incentive structures... to try to curb the excessive build-up of risk-taking [...] which was seen ahead of the recent crisis,' Mr King said.
b. Ideational (126)	
Involving sequences of figures (72)	
Expansion nexus → simple clause (52)	[...] the draft report was written a month ago, before the global financial crisis deepened after the collapse of Lehman Brothers.
Projection nexus → simple clause (20)	Mr Darling also used the crisis to stage a series of tactical retreats [...], announcing a rethink of his plans to reform air passenger taxes.
Involving figures/parts of figures (54)	
E.g. Process as Participant	The participation of Mr. Buffett's Berkshire Hathaway group [...] underlines the instrumental role of cash-rich investors during the crisis.

Table 16.5: GMs in FT_Leaders

Subcorpus: FT_Leaders	**Total Number of GMs: 110**
a. Interpersonal (1)	
Modalization: probability (1)	
Objective explicit orientation (1)	He, and it appears most likely it will be a he, will need to take the lead in fighting the most serious financial crisis since the 1930s.
b. Ideational (109)	
Involving sequences of figures (50)	

Expansion nexus → simple clause (40)	After a clumsy start, the ECB has effectively responded to the credit crisis too.
Projection nexus → simple clause (10)	If the Treasury were able to declare a crisis and order injections of cash it would violate the independence of monetary policy.
Involving figures/parts of figures (59)	
E.g. Process as Participant	Central banks have co-ordinated their supply of liquidity remarkably well since the credit crisis began in August 2007.

Ideational metaphors were by far the most frequent class of GMs. Within the subclass of metaphors affecting sequences of figures (downgrading the domain of realization from clause nexus to simple clause), qualitative analysis also unveiled a higher frequency of metaphorical realizations of Expansion nexuses.[7] Good reasons for this can be found in the discourse type under analysis: these GMs are convenient ways of encoding logical relations between events, as they condense longer strings of text into a single clause, thus meeting the newspaper's tight space constraints. This is evident in titles, which typically aim to be both concise and eye-catching. The following example from FT_First_page is a case in point:

Example 1. Banks face closer scrutiny. Rule changes seek to prevent repeat of crisis

Let us focus on the second clause: a more congruent re-wording would turn it into a clause nexus, linked by Enhancement (Cause: Purpose): 'someone is changing (*has changed? will change?*) rules to prevent the crisis from repeating'. Several meaningful points emerge from this attempt to go back to the congruent version and its comparison with the original. One of them is the textual role played by the GM, whereby the nominalized element can be chosen as Theme and function as a rhetorical foundation for what follows (in this case, the body of the article: (Halliday, 2007[1996]: 108). Connected to this is the fact that GMs of this kind are frequently used to *encapsulate* complex meanings that have been expressed elsewhere in clause form (Thompson, 2014: 244). Indeed, as Thompson notes, encapsulation is an important textual and argumentative strategy: encapsulated propositions can be made thematic to indicate different steps in the unfolding of an argument. Secondly, information concerning time and doers gets lost in the semantic compactness brought about by the metaphor: Processes become atemporal and de-personalized (Thompson, 2014: 245), i.e. less open to negotiation; background knowledge is required to fill-in the informative gaps. Thirdly, figures are *reified*, and this has consequences on the reader's interpretation:

for instance, in Example 1, the fact that the crisis may 'repeat' is metaphorically portrayed as a concrete entity, i.e. something whose existence cannot be denied, thus also increasing apprehension towards it.

The observations made so far are also valid for ideational metaphors affecting figures/parts of figures, in which the domain of realization is downgraded from clause to group/phrase level. In particular, being non-negotiable, a metaphorical NG can be used to 'establish' certain meanings in a text. In the concordance below, from FT_First_page, a figure, which would be congruently realized by a clause ('the subprime crisis is spreading') is 'nouned', i.e. condensed into a NG which in turn becomes part of an embedded prepositional phrase; thus, it is presented as a fixed, unquestionable truth:[8]

Example 2 The Peloton ABS fund [...] is the latest victim of the spread of the subprime crisis into high-quality mortgage securities.

Another essential function which, by contrast, emerged from analysis as being typical of GMs affecting figures is the creation of technical terms (e.g. *recession, securitization*). Of course, ideational metaphor always comes at a price, and its use in the development of technical vocabulary is no exception. To borrow Thompson's words again: 'the reader needs to be able to identify the uncondensed wording that the nominalization relates to' (2014: 245). From this viewpoint, ideational metaphor is a fundamental tool in the creation of a jargon that tends to marginalize uninitiated readers. The patterns highlighted so far also suggest that ideational metaphor can be considered a *register-idiosyncratic* feature (Miller and Johnson, 2013) of the language of financial journalism.

Turning now to metaphors of modality, their low incidence precludes meaningful generalizations: in this case, the analysed concordances highlighted a strong tendency towards congruent realizations (i.e. implicit subjective/objective orientation: cf. Section 1.2). Still, some interesting patterns, to be further investigated, can be identified. Metaphors of modalization (probability) outnumber metaphors of modulation (obligation) in the analysed concordances (seven *vs.* two; no occurrences of metaphors of modulation in FT_Leaders), with a preference for subjective explicit orientation. Interestingly, relying on statistics would have been misleading in this case. A look at the wider co-text shows that subjective explicit metaphors invariably appear within quoted/reported locutions or ideas from external sources, usually well-known financial institutions or authorities (as in the example in Table 16.4, a quotation from a public speech given by the then head of the IMF, Strauss-Kahn). Thus, perhaps unexpectedly, these GMs do *not* function as explicit markers of the writer's modal attitude towards the proposition, in line with the objective style characterizing hard news reporting, but also editorial comments, in English (Pounds, 2010). Indeed, the only instance of a metaphor of modalization in FT_Leaders (cf. Table 16.5) is located at the objective explicit end of the orientational cline:

> Example 3. He, and it appears most likely it will be a he, will need to take the lead in fighting the most serious financial crisis since the 1930s.

Here, the topic is the appointment of the Treasury Secretary in Obama's Administration (November 2008): as can be noticed, the metaphor is used as a strategy to distance authorial voice from the opinion of probability being expressed, which is objectified (i.e. made objective, presented as a fact).

Similar observations can be made with reference to the two metaphors of modulation (both with subjective explicit orientation) in FT_First_page. The example in Table 16.4 is part of a quoted locution from a speech given by the Governor of the Bank of England; the other instance (below), occurs within a reported locution from the then President of the European Commission:

> Example 4. In Europe, José Manuel Barroso [...] said the crisis made it imperative to strengthen banking supervision and develop "a truly European response".

In Example 4, a modal clause is 'experientialised' through a metaphorical attributive relational clause, where the source of the modulated judgement is indicated as the Attributor ('the crisis'). Yet, readers are not told exactly who will be in charge of taking action. The lexicogrammatical structure is inherently opaque: while being apparently more informative than its congruent counterpart, in that the assessment of modulation is explicitly entrusted to a source, it leaves the actual doers of the modulated Processes implicit. Here too qualitative analysis proved necessary to disambiguate the effects of GM on the text's construction and reception, and to reveal its power in 'diluting' modal responsibility.

16.3 Conclusion

In this chapter I have attempted to shed light on the applicability of corpus linguistics techniques to metaphor analysis by relating my own experience of looking for GMs in a specialized, purpose-built corpus, taking a 'hybrid' approach that merged computational tools with a close reading of parts of the texts.

Several aspects of the use of GM in the business press emerged from this combination of automated and manual analysis. Quantitative data highlighted a wide presence of ideational metaphors, as opposed to the low frequency of interpersonal metaphors of modality. Qualitative logogenetic analysis revealed the multi-functional nature of ideational metaphor, which emerged as a fundamental argumentative and textual strategy, but also as a tool enabling writers to condense and de-personalize complex events, making them less negotiable and less accessible to uninitiated readers. Quantitative and qualitative data also pointed towards the register-idiosyncratic nature (Miller and Johnson, 2013) of ideational metaphor in the discourse-type under scrutiny. In the case of metaphors of modality, qualitative analysis of extended concordances proved essential to correctly identify their function in context, which was found to be consistent with the objective style characterizing news reports and editorial comments in English.

Overall, with reference to the question posed by the chapter's title, the results suggested a positive answer: metaphor, GM in particular, can indeed be studied through the lens of software, provided that we do not lose sight of the inherently *instrumental* role played by the lens, as a magnifying tool. In fact, it is undeniable that corpus techniques smooth the way for the analyst, making it much easier to process data, compute statistics and retrieve potentially meaningful patterns, thus adding to the rigour and the general quality of research. Yet, as the (albeit partial) discussion of data in the previous pages suggests, the analyst's contribution remains essential on both the quantitative and the qualitative plane: quantitatively, to avoid the risk of overlooking meaningful occurrences, which is particularly high when working on metaphor (grammatical and lexical); qualitatively, to examine the functions played by the relevant instances in context, and link them to the general features of the register in which they appear. Against this background, corpus-assisted metaphor studies, as semantics-oriented and context-oriented studies in general, certainly qualify as a *ticklish* task (Miller, 2000); yet, as this case study has hopefully shown, a rewarding one.

About the author

Antonella Luporini is Lecturer in English language and linguistics at the School of Foreign Languages and Literatures, Interpreting and Translation of the University of Bologna, Italy. Her research interests include corpus-assisted metaphor analysis, computer-mediated student/faculty interaction, and application of corpus techniques to the study of 'verbal art'.

Endnotes

1. It would go beyond the scope of this chapter to mention the many and varied streams of research carried out on this type of metaphor in the last decades: comprehensive accounts can be found in, e.g. Deignan (2005) and Gibbs (2008); a historical overview is also provided in Luporini (2013).
2. The fact that congruent structures are primary in *phylogenesis* (i.e. in the evolution of language) is confirmed by studies on language acquisition (*ontogenesis*: e.g. Painter, Derewianka and Torr (2007). Congruent structures also tend to be *logogenetically* primary, i.e. to occur earlier in the unfolding of discourse (Halliday, 2007[1996]: 106).
3. In SFL, congruency and metaphoricity are thought of as two ends of a cline: different realizations can be *more* or *less* congruent, or metaphorical, depending on where exactly they can be located in the continuum (Halliday, 2004[1998]: 34).
4. This study is part of a larger PhD research project, in which I examined the metaphorical representation of the crisis in the British and the Italian specialized press, taking into account both GMs and LMs. To this end, I built a comparable Italian corpus, collecting first page articles and leaders from all the issues of *Il Sole 24 Ore*, 2008. Due to space constrictions, the discussion here focuses on the FT corpus; the whole set of results is discussed in Luporini (2013).
5. Source available at: http://aboutus.ft.com. Last accessed 13 May 2015.
6. Sketch Engine's Word Sketch tool generates a one-page summary of a word's collocational/grammatical behaviour, grouping collocates according to their grammatical relation with the node word.
7. The lower frequency of GMs affecting Projection nexuses may be motivated by the tendency to quote/report wordings from public speeches or interviews.
8. Here we come to the border between GMs and LMs as realizations of conceptual metaphors: in this example, the internal coherence of the underlying conceptual metaphor THE CRISIS IS A PHYSICAL ENTITY is guaranteed by the nominalization *the spread*, with its 'objectifying' effect (in the sense of 'making like an object'). A discussion of this finding would indeed deserve a chapter of its own.

References

Aristotle. (1997) *Poetics*, trans. G. Whalley. Montreal: McGill-Queen's University Press.

Banks, D. (2003) The Evolution of Grammatical Metaphors in Scientific Writing. In A. M. Simon-Vanderbergen, M. Taverniers and L. Ravelli (eds) *Grammatical Metaphor: Views from Systemic Functional Linguistics*, 127–148. Amsterdam and Philadelphia, PA: John Benjamins Publishing Company.

Berber Sardinha, T. (2010) A Program for Finding Metaphor Candidates in Corpora. *The ESPecialist* 31(1): 46–67.

Charteris-Black, J. (2004) *Corpus Approaches to Critical Metaphor Analysis*. Basingstoke: Palgrave Macmillan.

Deignan, A. (2005) *Metaphor and Corpus Linguistics*. Amsterdam and Philadelphia, PA: John Benjamins Publishing Company.
Deignan, A. and Potter, L. (2004) A Corpus Study of Metaphors and Metonyms in English and Italian. *Journal of Pragmatics* 36: 1231–1252.
Gibbs, R. W. (ed.) (2008) *The Cambridge Handbook of Metaphor and Thought*. Cambridge: Cambridge University Press.
Halliday, M. A. K. and Matthiessen, C. M. I. M. (2014) *Halliday's Introduction to Functional Grammar*. 4th edn. London and New York: Routledge.
Halliday, M. A. K. (2007 [1996]) Literacy and Linguistics: A Functional Perspective. In R. Hasan and G. Williams (eds) *Literacy and Society*, 339–376. London: Longman. Reprinted in J. J. Webster (ed.) (2007) *Language and Education. Volume 9 in the Collected Works of M. A. K. Halliday*, 97–132. London and New York: Continuum.
Halliday, M. A. K. (2004 [1998]) Language and Knowledge: The 'unpacking' of Text. In D. Allison, L. Wee, B. Zhiming and S. A. Abraham (eds) *Text in Education and Society*, 157–178. Singapore: World Scientific. Reprinted in J. J. Webster (ed.) (2004) *The Language of Science. Volume 5 in the Collected Works of M. A. K. Halliday*, 24–48. London and New York: Continuum.
Halliday, M. A. K. and Matthiessen, C. M. I. M. (2004) *An Introduction to Functional Grammar*. 3rd edn. London: Hodder Arnold.
Halliday, M. A. K. and Matthiessen, C. M. I. M. (1999) *Construing Experience through Meaning. A Language-Based Approach to Cognition*. London: Cassell.
Halliday, M. A. K. (1985) *An Introduction to Functional Grammar*. London: Edward Arnold.
Holtz, M. (2009) Nominalization in Scientific Discourse: A Corpus-Based Study of Abstracts and Research Articles. *Proceedings of the Corpus Linguistics Conference CL 2009*. Liverpool: University of Liverpool.
Kilgarriff, A., Rychlý, P., Smrz, P., and Tugwell, D. (2004) The Sketch Engine. *Proceedings of the Eleventh EURALEX International Congress, EURALEX 2004*. Lorient: Université de Bretagne Sud.
Lakoff, G. and Johnson, M. (1980) *Metaphors We Live By*. Chicago, IL: Chicago Press.
Louw, B. (2007) Collocation as the Determinant of Verbal Art. In D. R. Miller and M. Turci (eds) *Verbal Art Revisited. Linguistic Approaches to the Study of Literature*, 149–180. London: Equinox Publishing.
Luporini, A. (2013) Metaphor in Times of Crisis: Metaphorical Representations of the Global Crisis in *The Financial Times* and *Il Sole 24 Ore* 2008. PhD thesis, University of Pisa, Italy. Available at: https://etd.adm.unipi.it/t/etd-05132013-001020/.
Martin, J. R. (1992) *English Text: System and Structure*. Amsterdam and Philadelphia, PA: John Benjamins Publishing Company.
McEnery, T., and Hardie, A. (2012) *Corpus Linguistics*. Cambridge: Cambridge University Press.
Miller, D. R., and Luporini, A. (2015) Social Semiotic Stylistics and the Corpus: How do-Able is an Automated Analysis of Verbal Art? In A. Duguid, A. Marchi, A. Partington and C. Taylor (eds) *Gentle Obsessions: Literature, Linguistics and Learning. In Honour of John Morley*, 235–250. Rome: Artemide.
Miller, D. R., and Johnson, J. H. (2013) 'Register-Idiosyncratic' Evaluative Choice in Congressional Debate: A Corpus-Assisted Comparative Study. In L. Fon-

taine, T. Bartlett, and G. O'Grady (eds) *Systemic Functional Linguistics: Exploring Choice*, 432–452. Cambridge: Cambridge University Press.
Miller, D. R. (2000) *On Computing Appraisal in a Corpus of Parliamentary Debate, Or, Ticklish Trawling.* Unpublished paper delivered to the Euro Systemic-Functional Workshop, 19-22 July 2000, Glasgow, UK.
Painter, C., Derewianka, B., and Torr, J. (2007) From Microfunction to Metaphor: Learning Language and Learning through Language. In R. Hasan, C. M. I. M. Matthiessen and J. J. Webster (eds) *Continuing Discourse on Language: A Functional Perspective. Volume 2*, 563–588. London: Equinox Publishing.
Pounds, G. (2010) Attitude and Subjectivity in Italian and British Hard-News Reporting: The Construction of a Culture-Specific 'Reporter' Voice. *Discourse Studies* 12(1): 106–137.
Rychlý, P. (2008) A Lexicographer-Friendly Association Score. *Proceedings of the Second Workshop on Recent Advances in Slavonic Natural Language Processing, RASLAN 2008*. Brno: Masaryk University.
Simpson, P. (2014) *Stylistics*. 2nd edn. London and New York: Routledge.
Taverniers, M. (2006) Grammatical Metaphor and Lexical Metaphor: Different Perspectives on Semantic Variation. *Neophilogus* 90: 321–332.
Taverniers, M. (2003) Grammatical Metaphor in SFL: A Historiography of the Introduction and Initial Study of the Concept. In A. M. Simon-Vanderbergen, M. Taverniers and L. Ravelli (eds) *Grammatical Metaphor: Views from Systemic Functional Linguistics* 5–34. Amsterdam and Philadelphia, PA: John Benjamins Publishing Company.
Thompson, G. (2014) *Introducing Functional Grammar*. 3rd edn. London and New York: Routledge.
Yanning, Y. (2011) Grammatical Metaphor in Chinese: A Corpus-Based Study. *Functions of Language* 18(1): 1–28.

17 A Corpus Approach to Method of Development: Discourse Markers and Presuming Reference in 32 ICE-GB Text Types

Michael Cummings
York University

17.1 Introduction

'Method of development' is a term introduced into Systemic Functional Linguistics (SFL) by Peter Fries to describe the roles played by the Themes and Rhemes of clauses in the logogenetic development of information in discourse (1981/1983: 116, 119, 121, 125, 135). The language of Themes is predicted to be rich in markers of topical continuity, for example, presuming reference items, and also rich in markers of discoursal variation, for example, conjunctive Adjuncts. Rhemes are predicted to be rich in lexical variation, serving the development of successive points in the discourse. This theory has had both supporters – particularly in its development by Jim Martin in *English Text* (1992: 434–460) and Christian Matthiessen in *Lexicogrammatical Cartography* (1995: 575–590) – and some detractors. The purpose of this chapter is to test the theory by tabulating the distribution of continuity and variation markers within the clauses of various text types in a large corpus: the *British Component* of the *International Corpus of English* (Survey of English Usage, 2006). Comparison of different proportions of continuity and variation markers in Themes and Rhemes through a whole spectrum of text types will permit the identification of some texts which are really contrastive in their respective methods of development.

17.2 Theme and Rheme

Let's begin by reviewing the basic principles of the Theme/Rheme distinction. Theme for Halliday is 'the point of departure of the message ... that which locates and orients the clause within its context' (Halliday and Matthiessen, 2014: 89). It is realized in classical SFL by all the elements in clause from the beginning through to the first element which plays a role in the experiential grammar of the clause. In the unmarked case in declarative mood this is the Subject, and the Theme stretch may therefore include before the Subject one or more textual elements, that is, continuatives, conjunctions, or conjunctive Adjuncts; and one or more interpersonal elements, that is, vocatives or modal Adjuncts. In a marked case, the Theme stretch may end with a Complement, a circumstantial Adjunct or even a Predicator occurring before the Subject, and thus as the first experiential element (Halliday and Matthiessen, 2014: 97–101). Matthiessen in particular stresses the wave-like descending-ascending contrast between the Theme and the New Information mapped onto Rheme (1995: 513–519). For some systemicists this permits taking the Theme stretch through to the Subject even when preceded by another experiential element (Downing, 1991: 127). This turns out to support the connection between Theme and method of development in its continuity aspect.

The meaning which Theme represents relates to the local method of development of the text. The development relates to the rhetorical organization of the text, its structure. The Themes in successive clauses are said to realize the method of development in the sense that they together signal topical continuity, and at the appropriate time, variation either from or within that continuity. The signal of continuity is frequently the repetition of the same referent item in proforms, or by deictic nominal groups. The signal of variation from or within continuity is frequently by conjunctions, continuatives, or conjunctive Adjuncts. The Rheme on the other hand is a meaning, realized by the rest of the clause, that relates to the accumulated information goals of the text. The Rheme stretch is the typical locus of the new information offered by successive clauses, and the Rhemes taken together constitute the 'point' of the text (Fries, 1981/1983: 116, 119, 121, 124–135; Fries, 1994: 230–234). An example is in Figure 17.1, a paragraph from *The Fellowship of the Ring* (Tolkien, 1999: 372–373). The Themes of all finite clauses (always including supplied Subject) are in bold, and the terminal elements in Rhemes carrying the New information (Fries's 'N-rheme' [1994: 234]) are italicized. Continuity markers in the Themes indicate that the major structural division is between the first seven lines focusing on the naive Hobbits, Dwarves and Elves, and the second seven lines focusing on the more experienced Aragorn. This is reinforced by the parallel time Adjuncts in lines 1 and 9, and the transitional hyper-Theme of line 8 (Martin, 1992: 437). All the N-rhemes except that in line 9 convey lexically, or more often, symbolically, either of the two contrasting attitudes of relaxation or vigilance. Table 17.1 is a simple tabulation of continuity-forming presuming reference items (items which signal that the identity of the participant can be recovered from the context, including proforms, demonstratives, possessives, definite articles, proper nouns: Martin (1992: 98–102, 109–115) in nominal groups and discourse markers in Theme and Rheme respectively (for a more detailed analysis, see Cummings, 2004: 346–348).[1]

01 **That morning they** lit a fire in a deep hollow shrouded by great bushes of holly,
02 **and their supper-breakfast** was merrier
03 **than it** had been
04 **since they** set out.
05 **They** did not hurry to bed afterwards,
06 **for they** expected to have all the night to sleep in,
07 **and they** did not mean to go on again until the evening of the next day.
08 **Only Aragorn** was silent and restless.
09 **After a while he** left the Company
10 **and** wandered on to the ridge;
11 **there he** stood in the shadow of a tree, looking out southwards and westwards, with his head posed
12 **as if he** was listening.
13 **Then he** returned to the brink of the dell
14 **and** looked down at the others laughing and talking.

Figure 17.1: Text segment from *The Fellowship of the Ring*

Table 17.1: Tabulation of Reference Items and Discourse Markers in Figure 17.1

	in Theme	in Rheme	
		in Other	in N-rheme
reference items	13	1	6
conjunctions (7), conjunctive Adjuncts ('Then')	8		

17.3 Quantificational Analysis

In some previous studies (2004, 2005, 2006, 2009a, 2009b) I have attempted to quantify the distribution of continuity markers like presuming reference between Theme and Rheme based on an analysis of particular short texts. The method was to identify chains of presuming reference items all having or being connected with the same referent. For example, in the Figure 17.1 passage there is a chain for the Company, realized by pronouns and a deictic in most of the first seven lines, and its extension in a sub-chain for Aragorn, realized by his name, pronouns and a deictic in most of the last seven lines. Of the 12 items in this long chain, only one lies outside of the Theme stretches. There are also three items in short chains referring to features of the landscape that fall only within the N-rhemes, and two chained deictic time or place references in the Themes. This makes for a disproportionate 76% of chain items within the Themes, and a 92% distribution of the long chain into the Themes (Cummings, 2004: 349–350).

A quantificational analysis of the language of Theme and Rheme based on a computational analysis of a large corpus could not hope to distinguish reference chains, but could measure simple distributions of different language features between the two clause functions. The work of Douglas Biber offers a multidimensional analysis of the distributions of associated language features through a variety of different text types. Information about presuming reference can be interpreted from his results for the relative distributions of deictics and proforms. However his studies permit only comparisons among whole registers, not between contrasting parts of clauses within different register types (Biber, 1988, 1995; Biber and Conrad, 2009). A more applicable approach has been taken by a method-of-development sceptic, Peter Crompton. In his study of two related text types, student essays and newspaper editorials, a corpus of 1100 sentences comprising 23,000 words was coded by a systemic-functional clause analysis, and the coded clauses analysed for the distribution of definite nominal groups and indefinite nominal groups between Themes and Rhemes. His results purport to show that while there is a strong statistical significance in the disproportion of definite nominal groups within Themes, nevertheless there is no complementary association of indefinite nominal groups within Rhemes. These results are seen to support his conclusion that the theory of the method of development is at least partially invalid and that teaching Theme and Rheme to students will do nothing to help their essay writing skills (2008: 315–326).

17.4 A Corpus Approach

My approach here is to attempt to broaden this kind of analysis to include an entire standard corpus, and to tabulate both presuming reference items and discourse markers, the latter including conjunctions, conjunctive Adjuncts, and continuatives. The *British Component* of the *International Corpus of English* (ICE) includes 32 different text types grouped in various categories, 15 from spoken-English transcriptions and 17 from written English, all from the period 1990–1993, comprising 500 separate texts containing over 1 million words (Nelson *et al.*, 2002: 4–5; Nelson *et al.*, 2006). The corpus is searched with an engine named 'Corpus Utility Program' (CUP). Unfortunately it is not coded on systemic-functional terms. Instead it is tagged with part-of-speech labels and grammatical structure labels, and the sentences or sentence fragments are parsed as logical tree structures.

One search procedure is to use the ICE-CUP software to edit a generalized tree-diagram template termed 'fuzzy tree fragment' (FTF) matching some desired structure, and inspect the matches in the output. For example one might construct an FTF designed to return all parsing units which have a non-interrogative mood main clause in which some immediate constituent (IC) element occurring before an IC Subject element is realized by a noun phrase realized by a pronoun Head which is demonstrative, personal or possessive, but not anticipatory 'it'. The task then is to utilize this kind of corpus and search procedure to emulate the terms and approaches of Systemic Functional Linguistics.

17.4.1 Densities of Discourse Markers

Another example of such a search is intended to establish the number of thematic 'discourse markers' (which is a named structural element in the corpus) per clause in all the different text types. This category includes realizations like 'OK', 'um', 'to begin with' (continuatives), 'therefore', 'then', 'instead' (conjunctive Adjuncts), 'and', 'but', 'yet' (conjunctions), and so forth. The number of discourse markers falling within Theme and Rheme respectively would seem to be a more basic question, but in fact the disproportion in favour of Themes is so great that it is a trivial issue (in the whole corpus approximately 85%). The FTF search is limited to non-interrogative main clauses, and to discourse markers occurring before the Subject element, taking that as the terminal Theme element. The number of instances in each text type is shown in Table 17.2, together with the number of such clauses in each text type. The number per clause, i.e. the density, is calculated in the last column of the spreadsheet.

Table 17.2: Densities of Discourse Markers before Subject

	Query: DISMK^S		**CLs**	**Density**
ICE-GB		19050	63334	0.301
spoken		17011	40342	0.422
dialogue				
private				
	direct conversations	6778	14727	0.460
	telephone calls	941	1763	0.534
public				
	broadcast discussions	1135	2327	0.488
	broadcast interviews	748	1390	0.538

	business transactions	633	1348	0.470
	classroom lessons	1258	2356	0.534
	legal cross-examinations	511	1226	0.417
	parliament debates	188	565	0.333
mixed				
	broadcast news	495	2389	0.207
monologue				
scripted				
	broadcast talks	433	2473	0.175
	non-broadcast speeches	195	937	0.208
unscripted				
	demonstrations	642	1264	0.508
	legal presentations	493	1027	0.480
	spontaneous commentaries	949	3207	0.296
	unscripted speeches	1612	3343	0.482
written		2039	22992	0.089
non-printed				
correspondence				
	business letters	75	1368	0.055
	social letters	256	2137	0.120
non-professional				
	student exam scripts	173	1053	0.164
	untimed student essays	114	978	0.117
printed				
academic				
	humanities	118	942	0.125
	natural sciences	81	1101	0.074
	social sciences	88	903	0.097
	technology	59	963	0.061
creative				
	novels/stories	262	3287	0.080
instructional				
	admin/regulatory	31	1011	0.031
	skills/hobbies	52	1319	0.039
non-academic				
	humanities	114	1227	0.093
	natural sciences	107	1095	0.098

	social sciences	102	1050	0.097
	technology	108	1139	0.095
persuasive				
	press editorials	142	1051	0.135
reportage				
	press news reports	157	2368	0.066

17.4.2 Presuming Reference

A more complicated set of searches seeks to establish the proportions of presuming reference items between Theme and Rheme. The method was limited to ten separate searches for each of the 32 text types. The first six searches were for six variations on presuming reference noun- or pronoun-headed nominal group realizations before or as the Subject, and four more for after the Subject. The search for one kind of pronoun-headed presuming reference noun phrase before the Subject element is represented by the FTF in Section 4 above (read the first Query label 'PP_NP^S' below as 'prepositional phrase with IC noun phrase before Subject', etc. so that the Section 4 FTF is Query 'PRNP^S'). The results for all the searches are in spreadsheet form in Table 17.3, which shows in the last two columns of line 1 that for the whole corpus, more than 80% of such items occur before or as the Subject element.[2]

17.4.3 Densities of Presuming Reference

The same output data can also be used to calculate the density of presuming reference items before or as the Subject element, that is, the number of such items per clause, for each of the text types. These results are shown in Table 17.4. For example, the last column implies that the density of thematic presuming reference items for telephone calls (line 7) is about 83 for every 100 main clauses, whereas the density for press editorials (line 3 from the bottom) is about 43 for every 100 main clauses.

The numerical results in Table 17.2, Table 17.3, and Table 17.4 can now be reorganized to show rankings of the different text types in terms of densities. This is shown in Table 17.5 and Table 17.6. Each of these tables shows the density or percentage figure, the ranking, the name, and the spoken/written register type for each of the text types.

Table 17.3: Percentage of NP and PRNP before, as, and after S

	Query:	PP_NP^S	NP^S	S_NP	PP_PRNP^S	PRNP^S	S_PRNP	total	S^PP_NP	S^NP	S^PP_PRNP	S^PRNP	total	% Th	% Rh
ICE-GB		897	118	6177	143	52	33002	40389	2839	2883	1029	3056	9807	80.5	19.5
spoken		488	81	2898	85	40	25590	29182	1751	1952	821	2403	6927	80.8	19.2
dialogue															
private															
	direct conversations	57	18	471	11	19	11514	12090	479	673	316	1151	2619	82.2	17.8
	telephone calls	4	3	47	4	1	1401	1460	48	78	65	153	344	80.9	19.1
public															
	broadcast discussions	31	6	111	6	1	1571	1726	105	101	69	109	384	81.8	18.2
	broadcast interviews	11	3	56	2	1	1045	1118	49	62	48	92	251	81.7	18.3
	business transactions	12	1	51	2		1019	1085	42	63	40	104	249	81.3	18.7
	classroom lessons	33	4	151	5		1528	1721	104	117	47	94	362	82.6	17.4
	legal cross-examinations	20	2	72	1	6	916	1017	62	71	32	78	243	80.7	19.3
	parliament debates	5	1	83	1		320	410	41	23	4	20	88	82.3	17.7
mixed															
	broadcast news	58	17	464	5		780	1324	117	115	10	50	292	81.9	18.1
monologue															
scripted															

	Query:	PP_NP^S	NP^S	S_NP	PP_PRNP^S	PRNP^S	S_PRNP	total	S^PP_NP	S^NP	S^PP_PRNP	S^PRNP	total	% Th	% Rh
	broadcast talks	69	8	354	10	2	890	1333	110	124	32	91	357	78.9	21.1
	non-broadcast speeches	21	1	145	3	1	311	482	40	41	17	15	113	81	19
unscripted															
	demonstrations	23		139	6	2	710	880	44	69	17	58	188	82.4	17.6
	legal presentations	35		140	2	1	529	707	48	36	27	69	180	79.7	20.3
	spontaneous commentaries	51	11	258	8	1	1240	1569	302	219	43	199	763	67.3	32.7
	unscripted speeches	58	6	356	19	5	1816	2260	160	160	54	120	494	82.1	17.9
written		409	37	3279	58	12	7412	11207	1088	931	208	653	2880	79.6	20.4
non-printed															
correspondence															
	business letters	29	4	121	3		790	947	53	42	22	46	163	85.3	14.7
	social letters	18	6	155	10	3	1330	1522	85	90	30	107	312	83	17
non-professional															
	student exam scripts	20	1	155	5	2	229	412	55	34	6	18	113	78.5	21.5
	untimed student essays	32		150	3		186	371	52	45	1	12	110	77.1	22.9
printed															
academic															
	humanities	24	1	156	2		214	397	33	36	9	18	96	80.5	19.5
	natural sciences	30		192	1		124	347	52	26	1	6	85	80.3	19.7

	Query:	PP_NP^S	NP^S	S_NP	PP_PRNP^S	PRNP^S	S_PRNP	total	S^PP_NP	S^NP	S^PP_PRNP	S^PRNP	total	% Th	% Rh
	social sciences	19		146	2		132	299	36	15	4	8	63	82.6	17.4
	technology	21	1	195	2		110	329	45	22	2	8	77	81	19
creative															
	novels/stories	38	9	317	10	2	1840	2216	184	165	66	213	628	77.9	22.1
instructional															
	admin/ regulatory	3		143	2		268	416	71	47	8	35	161	72.1	27.9
	skills/hobbies	12	1	203	2		218	436	54	34	3	18	109	80	20
non-academic															
	humanities	41	3	222	5	2	365	638	72	57	11	40	180	78	22
	natural sciences	23		190	2		200	415	61	38	10	17	126	76.7	23.3
	social sciences	22	5	162	2	1	371	563	47	37	9	25	118	82.7	17.3
	technology	25		266	2	1	193	487	48	51	7	11	117	80.6	19.4
persuasive															
	press editorials	17	1	176	4	1	255	454	35	57	12	25	129	77.9	22.1
reportage															
	press news reports	35	5	330	1		587	958	105	135	7	46	293	76.6	23.4

Table 17.4: Densities of NP and PRNP before and as S

	Query:	PP_NP^S	NP^S	S_NP	PP_PRNP	PRNP^S	S_PRNP	total	CLs	density
ICE-GB		897	118	6177	143	52	33002	40389	63334	0.638
spoken		488	81	2898	85	40	25590	29182	40342	0.723
dialogue										
private										
	direct conversations	57	18	471	11	19	11514	12090	14727	0.821
	telephone calls	4	3	47	4	1	1401	1460	1763	0.828
public										
	broadcast discussions	31	6	111	6	1	1571	1726	2327	0.742
	broadcast interviews	11	3	56	2	1	1045	1118	1390	0.804
	business transactions	12	1	51	2		1019	1085	1348	0.805
	classroom lessons	33	4	151	5		1528	1721	2356	0.730
	legal cross-examinations	20	2	72	1	6	916	1017	1226	0.830
	parliament debates	5	1	83	1		320	410	565	0.726
mixed										
	broadcast news	58	17	464	5		780	1324	2389	0.554
monologue										
scripted										

	Query:	**PP_NP^S**	**NP^S**	**S_NP**	**PP_PRNP**	**PRNP^S**	**S_PRNP**	**total**	**CLs**	**density**
	broadcast talks	69	8	354	10	2	890	1333	2473	0.539
	non-broadcast speeches	21	1	145	3	1	311	482	937	0.514
unscripted										
	demonstrations	23		139	6	2	710	880	1264	0.696
	legal presentations	35		140	2	1	529	707	1027	0.688
	spontaneous commentaries	51	11	258	8	1	1240	1569	3207	0.489
	unscripted speeches	58	6	356	19	5	1816	2260	3343	0.676
written		409	37	3279	58	12	7412	11207	22992	0.487
non-printed										
correspondence										
	business letters	29	4	121	3		790	947	1368	0.692
	social letters	18	6	155	10	3	1330	1522	2137	0.712
non-professional										
	student exam scripts	20	1	155	5	2	229	412	1053	0.391
	untimed student essays	32		150	3		186	371	978	0.379
printed										
academic										
	humanities	24	1	156	2		214	397	942	0.421

	Query:	PP_NP^S	NP^S	S_NP	PP_PRNP	PRNP^S	S_PRNP	total	CLs	density
	natural sciences	30		192	1		124	347	1101	0.315
	social sciences	19		146	2		132	299	903	0.331
	technology	21	1	195	2		110	329	963	0.342
creative										
	novels/stories	38	9	317	10	2	1840	2216	3287	0.674
instructional										
	admin/regulatory	3		143	2		268	416	1011	0.411
	skills/hobbies	12	1	203	2		218	436	1319	0.331
non-academic										
	humanities	41	3	222	5	2	365	638	1227	0.520
	natural sciences	23		190	2		200	415	1095	0.379
	social sciences	22	5	162	2	1	371	563	1050	0.536
	technology	25		266	2	1	193	487	1139	0.428
persuasive										
	press editorials	17	1	176	4	1	255	454	1051	0.432
reportage										
	press news reports	35	5	330	1		587	958	2368	0.405

Table 17.5: Density of DISMKs in Main CLs

Density	Rank	Text Type	Spoken/Written
0.538	1	broadcast interviews	sp
0.534	2	telephone calls	sp
0.534	2	classroom lessons	sp
0.508	4	demonstrations	sp
0.488	5	broadcast discuss	sp
0.482	6	unscripted speeches	sp
0.480	7	legal presentations	sp
0.470	8	business transactions	sp
0.460	9	direct conversations	sp
0.417	10	legal cross-examinations	sp
0.333	11	parliament debates	sp
0.296	12	spontaneous commentaries	sp
0.208	13	non-broadcast speeches	sp
0.207	14	broadcast news	sp
0.175	15	broadcast talks	sp
0.164	16	student exam scripts	wr
0.135	17	press editorials	wr
0.125	18	academic humanities	wr
0.120	19	social letters	wr
0.117	20	untimed student essays	wr
0.098	21	non-academic natural sciences	wr
0.097	22	non-academic social sciences	wr
0.097	22	academic social sciences	wr
0.095	24	non-academic technology	wr
0.093	25	non-academic humanities	wr
0.080	26	novels/stories	wr
0.074	27	academic natural sciences	wr
0.066	28	press news reports	wr
0.061	29	academic technology	wr
0.055	30	business letters	wr
0.039	31	skills/hobbies	wr
0.031	32	admin/regulatory	wr

Table 17.6: Density of NPs + PRNPs before and as S in Main CLs

Density	Rank	Text type	Spoken/Written
0.830	1	legal cross-examinations	sp
0.828	2	telephone calls	sp
0.821	3	direct conversations	sp
0.805	4	business transactions	sp
0.804	5	broadcast interviews	sp
0.742	6	broadcast discussions	sp
0.730	7	classroom lessons	sp
0.726	8	parliament debates	sp
0.712	9	social letters	wr
0.696	10	demonstrations	sp
0.692	11	business letters	wr
0.688	12	legal presentations	sp
0.676	13	unscripted speeches	sp
0.674	14	novels/stories	wr
0.554	15	broadcast news	sp
0.539	16	broadcast talks	sp
0.536	17	non-academic social sciences	wr
0.520	18	non-academic humanities	wr
0.514	19	non-broadcast speeches	sp
0.489	20	spontaneous commentaries	sp
0.432	21	press editorials	wr
0.428	22	non-academic technology	wr
0.421	23	academic humanities	wr
0.411	24	admin/regulatory	wr
0.405	25	press news reports	wr
0.391	26	student exam scripts	wr
0.379	27	untimed student essays	wr
0.379	27	non-academic natural sciences	wr
0.342	29	academic technology	wr
0.331	30	academic social sciences	wr
0.331	30	skills/hobbies	wr
0.315	32	academic natural sciences	wr

In Table 17.5, the highest density of thematic discourse markers belongs to broadcast interviews at almost 54 discourse markers per 100 clauses, whereas the lowest density, for administrative and regulatory prose, is just over 3 per 100 clauses. Every spoken text type outranks every written text type. In Table 17.6, the highest density of thematic presuming reference belongs to legal cross-examinations, at 83 items per 100 clauses. The lowest belongs to academic writing in the natural sciences, with less than 32 items per 100 clauses. In the middle ranks, some written text types outrank some spoken text types, but most spoken text types outrank most written text types.

17.4.4 Density and Method of Development

These two indices were selected in hopes that they might reveal text types that are consistently very contrastive in thematic features, and thus, perhaps, in types of their methods of development. One good bet would seem to be 'skills and hobbies' which is second from the bottom in each table and Table 17.5: Density of DISMKs in Main CLs. At the high ends of each scale, one might pick out at least two or three types with similarly consistent rankings, such as 'telephone calls' and 'broadcast interviews' – the latter was chosen as potentially more interesting. An arbitrary selection of text from each of these two text types was made, and the beginnings of each of these two texts are set out as Figure 17.2 and Figure 17.3. These texts preserve the numbering of the parsing units from the corpus and separate clauses are placed on separate lines; clause elements with presuming reference are bolded and the discourse markers are underlined.

The text selected from broadcast interviews is a transcription of a November 1, 1990, BBC 4 broadcast. The other text is from *The Complete Book of Video*, c. 1990. Table 17.7 and Table 17.8 show the same kind of information as do Table 17.5 and Table 17.6, but just for these two texts, referred to here as 'Sheila' and 'picture'. The numbers in the 'rank' columns in each table are in reference to the ranks in the previous two tables respectively: thus the Sheila text hits the jackpot with a higher density of thematic discourse markers and a higher density of thematic presuming reference than the average of any of the text types, including its own, while the picture text has a discourse marker density just higher than the average for its own text type, but a presuming reference density which is significantly higher than that of its own text type.

Table 17.7: Density of DISMKs in Main CLs

Density	Rank	Text	Spoken/Written
0.628	< 1	Sheila	Sp
0.050	> 28	Picture	Wr

1. A: Sheila Mottley **you** 've spent the past twenty-eight years caring for **your children** and in particular **your eldest daughter Jeanette who was born with no arms or legs,**
2. B: Yes
3. B: **That** is correct,
4. B: Uhm **Jeanette**, unfortunately
as **I** found out later
was the result of thalidomide
but there again **she** 's not on **her own**
5. B: There 's about four hundred and twenty of **these children**,
6. B: But from what **I** can gather **Jeanette** is one of the worst,
b because
like **you** 've just said
she 's got no arms,
and **she** 's got h hardly any lower limbs whatsoever,
7. B: But saying **that it** 's not stopped **Jeanette** getting on in life
8. A: How soon was it that **you** knew
there was something wrong with **your baby**,
9. B: Well actually uhm **I** was told
when **I** was
when **I** was pregnant,
much to **my alarm**
uhm that **I** was carrying a child with no upper limbs,
and **they** didn't know
to what extent **the lower limbs** had been damaged,
but not to sort of look forward to a great deal
because **they** didn't think
she 'd live,
10. B: And uhm **they** said
well **I** 'd just have to proceed with the pregnancy
and uh get **it** over and done with
and go and start again, on **the next one** like a baby machine,
11. A: But **it** didn't turn out like **that**
12. B: No,
13. B: Twenty-eight years later **she** is still with **us the person** that everybody

Figure 17.2: The 'Sheila' text

Table 17.8: Density of NPs + PRNPs before and as S in Main CLs

Density	Rank	Text	Spoken/Written
0.861	< 1.	Sheila	Sp
0.425	> 22.	Picture	Wr

The general organization of the Sheila text is governed by the interventions and reactions respectively of speaker 'A', the interviewer, and speaker 'B', the interviewee. 'A' prompts the discussion in numbered Unit 1, refocuses it in Unit 8, and again in Unit 11. 'B' essentially monologues in response to these prompts. The discourse keeps tightly focused on a narrow range of persons, mainly speaker 'B' herself and her eldest child, less so on other children and the unfeeling medical 'they'. The method of development in the monologue sections is characterized by explicit marking of micro-stages with abundant conjunctions, conjunctive Adjuncts and continuatives introducing short

1. *GETTING THE BEST PICTURE*
2. Assuming that **you** have found the receiver that suits your present and future needs (including the variety of ways in which **it** can fit into the rest of your audio-visual system),
the next stage is to install **it**
so that **it** will give the best results that it can deliver.
3. **You** should begin with **the most fundamental and most frequently overlooked item - the aerial or antenna.**
4. *Reception*
5. With regular television (cable and satellite have different problems), reception quality can vary from country to country, and even from house to house in the same street.
6. One large building can reflect visual echoes
(known as "ghosting ");
7. **other forms of interference** can create "snow "in darker areas of the image.
8. **The list of possible causes for poor reception** is virtually endless,
but **the remedies** are simple.
9. Employ a properly qualified installer
to put a large antenna on **the roof**
(not in **the attic**,
unless **you** live next to **the transmitter**),
and make sure
that **the incoming signal** is free of extraneous visual or sonic noise.
10. If **you** live in a remote valley or a complex of high-rise buildings
you may need some form of booster near **the antenna**.
11. Do not even consider an indoor antenna -
12. **they** are a simple way of throwing money down the drain.
13. There is no point in wasting expensive television equipment on an unsatisfactory signal.
14. European televisions use 75 ohm co-axial cable as an input for UHF broadcasts,
whereas in the USA and some other countries VHF broadcasts are received via 300 ohm unbalanced inputs.
15. UHF is much more refined than VHF though more directional,

Figure 17.3: The 'picture' text

clauses; and by a topical continuity through very long reference chains – mainly realized with proforms and deictics – for the speaker herself and her daughter, the former mainly distributed into Themes, and the latter roughly divided between Themes and Rhemes. This kind of development seems to be reflected in the data of Table 17.7 and Table 17.8.

The picture text is partly organized under headlines and subheadlines, as in numbered Units 1 and 4. Units 2 and 3 lead into the discussion of the first main topic, the antenna and its accessories, which begins in Unit 5. Subtopical transitions are usually not signalled with discourse markers, but are often simply lexical, with new subtopics sometimes introduced in Rheme, sometimes in Theme. Another type of transition signal is an imperative or a modalized directive of the 'you should' or 'you may have to' sort. Presuming reference is relatively sparse, and often of a bridging rather than a direct reference type. The longest presuming reference chain is the 'you' chain with five items in the first 15 parsing units; other chains have only two or three items, and are mostly bridging, with only one being pronominal. The relatively low number of grammatical items serving as discourse markers or as items in reference chains, and the brevity of reference chains lends the discourse a feeling of brisk informational efficiency and density. Again the method of development seems consonant with the data of Table 17.7 and Table 17.8.

17.5 Conclusion

In sum then, we have now tabulated the distribution of continuity and variation markers within the clauses of various text types in a large corpus. The findings support the notion that grammatical items marking topical continuity and variation preponderate in Themes. We have also measured the different densities of continuity and variation markers in Theme through a range of text types and used this method to identify texts which are really contrastive in their respective methods of development.

About the author

Michael Cummings is Professor Emeritus and Senior Scholar in the English Department of York University, Toronto, Canada. His research interests include Systemic Functional Linguistics approaches to discourse and lexicogrammar in Old English and Modern English.

Endnotes

1. Thus these items do not include presuming reference by comparison and by ellipsis (Martin, 1992: 100). The definite article does not always imply developmental continuity; it may simply realize a cultural given (homophora, Halliday and Matthiessen, 2014b: 631), as in 'the moon', or anticipate a nominal group postmodifier (esphora, Martin, 1992: 123), as in 'The Man Who Came to Dinner'.
2. Prepositional phrases in FTF searches are limited to those with Adverbial function in ICE parsing. Presuming reference in noun-headed NPs is represented in FTFs by Modifier elements realized by definite articles, or by demonstrative or possessive pronouns; NPs with postmodifier elements were excluded to avoid esphoric reference. Homophoric references however could not be excluded. Search results in Table 17.3 have been adjusted for instances produced or omitted because, unlike SFL, ICE-parsed existential 'there' is not labelled as a Subject.

References

Biber, D. and Conrad, S. (2009) *Register, Genre, and Style*. Cambridge and New York: Cambridge University Press.
Biber, D. (1995) *Dimensions of Register Variation: A Cross-Linguistic Comparison*. Cambridge: Cambridge University Press.
Biber, D. (1988) *Variation across Speech and Writing*. Cambridge and New York: Cambridge University Press.
Crompton, P. (2008) Definiteness and Indefiniteness in Theme: A Corpus-Based Analysis. In B. Lewandowska-Tomaszczyk (ed.) *Corpus Linguistics, Computer Tools, and Applications – State of the Art*, 309–328. Frankfurt am Main: Peter Lang.
Cummings, M. (2009a) Theme and Topic in Written French and English: A Perspective on Comparative Discourse Analysis. In P. Sutcliffe, L. Stanford, and A. Lommel (eds) *LACUS Forum XXXV*, 3–19. Houston, TX: Linguistic Association of Canada and the United States.
Cummings, M. (2009b) The Theme/Rheme Distinction and the Method of Development in Written French Text. In D. Banks, J. Ormrod and S. Eason (eds) *La linguistique systémique fonctionnelle et la langue française*, 43–66. Paris: L'Harmattan.
Cummings, M. (2006) Measuring Lexical Distributions across Theme and Rheme. In S. J. J. Hwang, W. J. Sullivan and A. R. Lommel (eds) *LACUS Forum XXXII*, 289–299. Houston, TX: Linguistic Association of Canada and the United States.
Cummings, M. (2005) The Role of Theme and Rheme in Contrasting Methods of Organization in Texts. In C. S. Butler, Gómez M. d. l. A. González and S. M. Doval-suárez (eds) *The Dynamics of Language Use: Functional and Contrastive Perspectives*, 129–154. Amsterdam and New York: John Benjamins.
Cummings, M. (2004) Towards a Statistical Interpretation of Systemic-Functional Theme/Rheme. In G. Fulton, W. J. Sullivan and A. R. Lommel (eds) *LACUS Forum XXX: Language, Thought, and Reality*, 343–354. Houston, TX: Linguistic Association of Canada and the United States.
Downing, A. (1991) An Alternative Approach to Theme: A Systemic Functional Perspective. *Word* 42: 119–144.
Fries, P. H. (1994) On Theme, Rheme and Discourse Goals. In M. Coulthard (ed.) *Advances in Written Text Analysis*, 229–249. London: Routledge.
Fries, P. H. (1981/1983) On the Status of Theme in English: Arguments from Discourse. *Forum Linguisticum* 6: 1–38.
Halliday, M. A. K. and Matthiessen, C. M. I. M. (2014) *Halliday's Introduction to Functional Grammar*. 4th edn. London and New York: Routledge.
Martin, J. R. (1992) *English Text: System and Structure*. Amsterdam: Benjamins.
Matthiessen, C. M. I. M. (1995) *Lexicogrammatical Cartography: English Systems*. Tokyo: International Language Sciences Publishers.
Nelson, G., Wallis, S., and Aarts, B. (2006) *The British Component of the International Corpus of English*. Release 2 (Software CD-ROM). London: Survey of English Usage.
Nelson, G., Wallis, S., and Aarts, B. (2002) *Exploring Natural Language: Working with the British Component of the International Corpus of English*. Amsterdam and Philadelphia: John Benjamins Publishing Company.
Tolkien, J. R. R. (1999) *The Fellowship of the Ring: Being the First Part of the Lord of the Rings*. London: Harper Collins.

18 Journey of Three Digitized Texts: Entextualization and Recontextualization in a Corpus Study

Tom Morton
Birkbeck, University of London

Anne McCabe
Saint Louis University, Madrid Campus

18.1 Introduction

In this chapter, we chart the journey of a single student's written and spoken texts which had 'digitality thrust upon them' by being included in a corpus study which aimed to show how learners of English as an additional language used the resources of APPRAISAL systems to develop appropriate 'voices' in secondary history. The aim of the chapter is to show how, through processes of 'entextualization' (Bauman and Briggs, 1990; Urban, 1996) and 'recontextualization' (Lees Fryer, this volume; Linell, 2009; Wodak and Iedema, 1999), the original fragments of spoken and written discourse took on a range of new meanings as they were transcribed, loaded into corpus analysis software (O'Donnell, 2013) and subjected to quantitative analyses. In documenting this process, we describe the affordances that these entextualization and recontextualization processes allowed in providing for successive rereadings of the texts. We show how this process can be recursive and cyclical, in that these new readings, when taken back to practitioners, can increase their agency in producing new discursive acts, which in turn may also be en- and recontextualized.

The chapter is organized as follows. In the next section, we outline the context of the study, its aims, methods, participants and key findings. We then briefly introduce the concepts of 'entextualization' and 'recontextualization', using them in the subsequent section as a guiding framework to track the 'journey' of three texts produced by one student, in which we show how they took on new meanings as they were digitized and analysed. The discussion and conclusion sections bring into focus what can be gained from this process as the successive re-readings increase researchers' understandings of the phenomena addressed by the research questions, along with the potential benefits of taking these new understandings back to the producers of this type of text. We argue that entextualization and recontextualization are important conceptual tools which allow SFL researchers to perceive the affordances and constraints of digitization when working with texts which are transductions (Kress, 2003) of discursive acts produced in real time through the modes of sound, image and movement (Nicholas and Starks, 2014).

18.2 Context: Corpus-based Appraisal Analysis of Student Texts in a Bilingual Education Programme

The texts which are the focus of this chapter were produced as part of a corpus-based study[1] of secondary students' use of evaluative language in a Bilingual Education Programme in Spain, in which curricular content (in this case history) was taught through the medium of English as an additional language. This study was part of the ongoing Content-and-Language-Integrated Learning (CLIL) project carried out by researchers at the Universidad Autónoma de Madrid (UAM-CLIL), which seeks to gain insights into the nature of the language that students produce in secondary CLIL classrooms, and how their language use changes/develops over time. For data collection purposes, the researchers worked with the teachers to generate prompts about topics studied in the classroom and based on the established school curriculum. The prompts were used for classroom discussions, in-class essays, and interviews with several of the students. The discussions and interviews were video-recorded and subsequently transcribed, and the hand-written essays were digitized in order to be loaded into the UAM Corpus Tool software.

In the most recent phase of the project, we focused on the students' use of language to express interpersonal meanings, using the framework of APPRAISAL (Martin and White, 2005) to analyse evaluative language in written and spoken data (see McCabe and Whittaker, forthcoming, for results on the written data). To briefly summarize the results, it was found that, for the most part, in both spoken and written texts, the APPRAISAL resources used were appropriate to the tasks set in the prompts. The students showed development overall from the use of APPRAISAL resources to express more everyday meanings in the earlier years to, in the final year, more discipline-appropriate use of these resources, for example by presenting countries as Emoters, (e.g. *most countries were afraid of Germany*), which then become targets of positive or negative moral judgement through expressions of SOCIAL SANCTION. Overall, the results provided evidence that, in spite of variation among individual students, there was overall progress in their ability to use APPRAISAL systems to produce the different voices – interpreter, adjudicator and recorder – identified by Coffin (2006) as important for school history.

At the same time, as part of the study, we asked an expert CLIL history teacher to rate the students' texts holistically by simply classifying the texts into one of three categories, higher, average and lower. We found differences in the results between texts that were rated higher and those that were rated average and lower, which suggests that differences in the way APPRAISAL resources were being used by the students were contributing to the teachers' implicit assessments of the texts. Thus, the processes that these texts went through as part of the corpus study yielded insights that we argue can be taken back to participants to help them increase their control and agency in producing new texts as part of their educational practices. However, in order for these insights to become available, the students' texts needed to undergo a journey in which digitality was thrust upon them, as they were initially pulled out of their original contexts of production through a process of entextualization, and re-read at successive stages in a process of recontextualization.

18.3 Entextualization, Recontextualization and Digitality

Entextualization refers to the process by which a piece of discourse, for example, a stretch of talk-in-interaction, is ripped out of its original context and treated as a textual object, something to be studied, analysed, and re-related to its original or to a new context. Bauman and Briggs (1990) define entextualization as 'the process of rendering discourse extractable, of making a stretch of linguistic production into a unit – a text that can be lifted out of its interactional setting' (1990: 73). Silverstein and Urban (1996) used the concept of entextualization as part of what they described as 'the natural history of discourse', and Blommaert (2005) glosses this process as one in which 'original' pieces of discourse, which took place as socially, culturally and historically unique events are 'lifted out of their original context and transmitted, by quoting or echoing them, by writing them down, by *inserting them into another discourse*, by using them as "examples" (or *as data for scientific analysis*)' (2005: 47, italics added). Once a stretch of discursive action is entextualized, taking on new life as a 'text', it has inevitably been decontextualized, and is open to being recontextualized. As Bauman and Briggs put it, 'If we now consider what becomes of text once decontextualized, we recognize that decontextualization from one social context involves recontextualization in another' (1990: 74). As Baumann and Briggs point out, recontextualization is linked to issues of control, power, access and legitimacy of access to texts. This links with Bernstein's (1996) view of recontextualization as the removal of a (pedagogic) discourse from its original production site in one field to another where it takes on new meanings. Wodak and Iedema (1999) point out that different 'technologies' can be involved in recontextualization, including such means as grammatical nominalization, writing, and, of relevance to this study, electronic communication (see also Lees Fryer, this volume). Linell (2009) identifies three kinds of recontextualization: intratextual, intertextual and interdiscursive. Here, we focus on interdiscursive recontextualization as the original pieces of discourse are re-read through the lenses of different discourses and genres relating to the tools and concepts used in the analyses.

The concepts of entextualization, decontextualization and recontextualization help us to understand the processes that the student texts in the APPRAISAL study underwent: they took on new meanings as they became examples of data for scientific analysis and were inserted into a very different discourse from the school history ones they were originally part of. In this process, digitality played a very important role, as the data moved from the analogue into the digital world. In a process of transduction (Kress, 2003), the sound mode mediated by the body (Nicholas and Starks, 2014) in real-time interaction became recorded digital video images with accompanying word-processed transcripts; hand-written texts were typed into a word processor and fed into the CorpusTool software, or scanned for display in research reports and presentations. Also, in this interdiscursive process, other texts, belonging to different discourses and genres, were overlaid on the originals, producing new readings of them. For example, the APPRAISAL framework (Martin and White, 2005) gave the digitized texts new meanings as words, phrases and clauses produced by the students were assigned to the different categories in the system. In the next section, we track this process by describing the journey of three texts produced by one student.

18.4 The Journey of Three Texts

In this section, we chart the journey of three texts which were incorporated into the corpus to be analysed using the APPRAISAL framework. All three texts were produced by the same student, Isabel (a pseudonym). They were extracted from video recordings of a class discussion in which she participated, a one-to-one interview with one of the researchers on the project, and an essay she wrote (along with the instructions for the writing task and her underlinings of various parts). To provide some context regarding the tasks, the students in the 9th grade history class (14-15 years old) were asked to prepare to write an essay based on the following prompt:

> Write a composition about "The Modern State: strong and weak Monarchs; Economy and Society". Make sure you include the following ideas: Describe the evolution of Philip II and whether you think he was a good or a bad monarch and why. Focus on how mercantilism influenced economic activity and compare the way rich and poor people lived at that time and how they live today. Evaluate the impact of European nations on indigenous civilizations.

Prior to writing the essay, the class prepared in groups for, and then held, a classroom discussion on the same topic. As the researchers were also interested in comparing the students' ability to express their ideas on the topic in both spoken and written modes, individual students, chosen by their teachers to represent ranges in ability, were interviewed individually following the same prompts as in the classroom discussion.

The first step in the journey, the 'natural history' of the texts, can be seen as the conversion of real-time interaction into a set of moving video images. Already, by producing video recordings, the flow and the dynamics of the real-time interaction have been frozen and converted into a 'text', an object of study, repeated perusal and analysis. The further move of producing transcripts of the interactions portrayed in the video creates a set of new texts, at least one other step removed from the original situated event. The choices involved in making these transcripts are already part of a process of creating new meanings, as transcribers take decisions on what to include or leave out guided by their own 'theory' (Ochs, 1979). Thus, in extract 1, which shows part of Isabel's participation in the classroom discussion, there is no information on communication in non-linguistic modes (e.g. gaze, gesture), interactional features such as timed pauses and overlaps which may have had communicative significance, or translation of the code-switched utterances in Spanish. There is only minimal information on silent and filled pauses in Isabel's turns.

Extract 1. Part of Isabel's participation in the classroom discussion

I: He called the Spanish Armada eh *la armada invencible*
T: Hm mm
I: Because anyone can eh win the ... armada of Spain
T: Anyone or no one?

I: No one
T: Aha
I: But the English eh did it
T: But the English did it

In the extract from the interview, there is a similar 'theory' of transcription, with perhaps slightly more features of the interaction included, such as the micro-pauses in Isabel's turn and filled pauses such as 'eh' and 'erm'.

Extract 2. Part of Isabel's participation in the interview

R: Do you think that he was a good or a bad monarch, and why?
I: I think both because he.. he was a bad monarch monarch because he ... he ...he left a lot of people eh... fighting against the... England but ... and also because he don't let the Spaniards erm ... study in foreign universities.

Both cases, however, are examples of how what was 'entextualized' by being lifted out of its original context is now 'recontextualized' by being filtered through 'theories' of transcription which assign to the text a new set of meanings, while erasing other meaning potentials. These texts are now firmly in the domain of 'data for scientific analysis' and their readings are constrained not just by the theories of transcription that produced them, but the other theories which are overlaid on them to produce new readings of their meanings.

A similar process of entextualization and recontextualization takes place with Isabel's written text. Even before producing this text, Isabel demonstrated agency by recontextualizing the original rubric of the essay instructions by adding her own images to it, in the form of underlinings of the most salient (to her) aspects of the task (Figure 18.1):

B) Write a composition about "The Modern State: strong and weak Monarchs; Economy and Society". Make sure you include the following ideas: Describe the evolution of Philip II and whether you think he was a good or a bad monarch and why. Focus on how mercantilism influenced economic activity and compare the way rich and poor people lived at that time and how they live today. Evaluate the impact of European nations on indigenous civilizations. (20 minutes)

Figure 18.1: Isabel's recontextualization of the essay rubric.

Such acts of agency are inevitably erased as the only texts of interest to the research project are the student's oral and written linguistic productions. Thus, the text that eventually is incorporated into the corpus is Isabel's handwritten essay, reproduced as Figure 18.2.

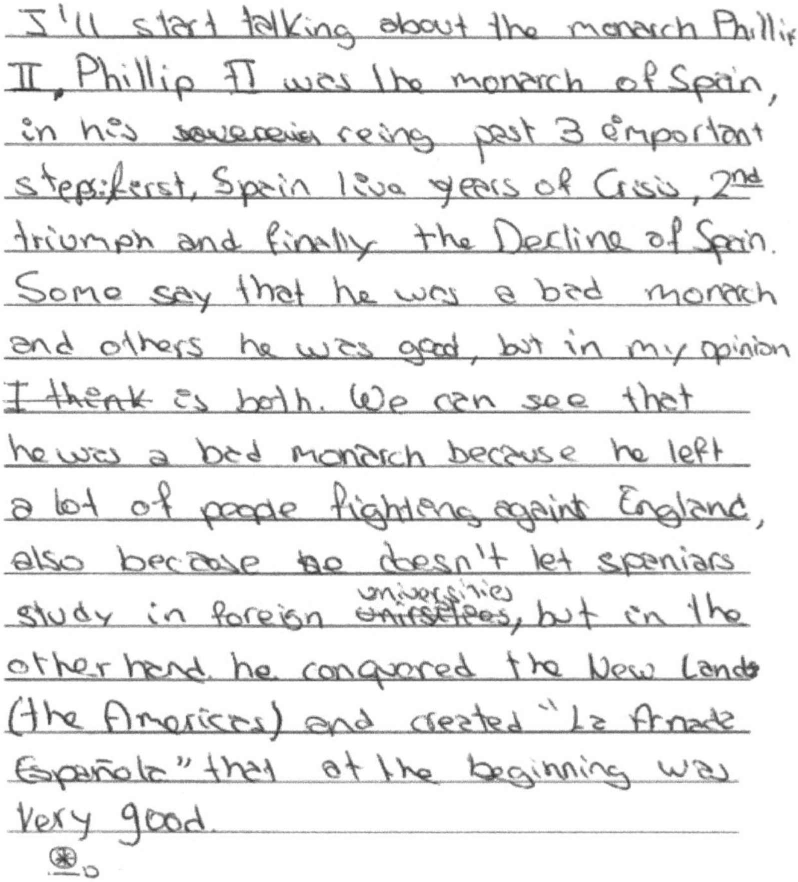

I'll start talking about the monarch Phillip
II, Phillip II was the monarch of Spain,
in his ~~soverein~~ reing past 3 important
steps: ferst, Spain live years of Crisis, 2nd
triumph and finally the Decline of Spain.
Some say that he was a bad monarch
and others he was good, but in my opinion
~~I think~~ is both. We can see that
he was a bad monarch because he left
a lot of people fighting againt England,
also because ~~he~~ doesn't let spaniars
study in foreign ~~unirsities~~ universities, but in the
other hand he conquered the New Lands
(the Americas) and created "La Armada
Española" that at the beginning was
very good.

Figure 18.2: Isabel's essay.

In converting this analogue text into a digital version for inclusion in the corpus, again, certain decisions have to be made. For example, Isabel's strikethrough of 'soverein' and its replacement with 'reing' is lost as is her correction of the spelling of 'universities'. Also, there is ambiguity, in that it is not clear that, in spite of the strikethrough, 'I think' (line 8) is meant to be included in her text. Of course, these can be seen as minor or marginally relevant points if the focus of the research is on linguistic representations of choices from the APPRAISAL systems. However, more recent approaches to the acquisition of literacy in additional languages place emphasis on how learners draw on features across a wide range of modes and mediational means as they build their communicative repertoires (Nicholas and Starks, 2014). In this context, it may be rash to leave out as irrelevant to the analysis any feature(s) or agentive acts that may be contributing to that repertoire.

In continuing their journeys, both Isabel's spoken and written texts lose more contextual information as they are stripped down to simple text files for uploading to the corpus software, CorpusTool. Thus, even though the texts are labelled as 'spoken' and 'written' for retrieval and searching in the corpus, almost all remaining features, apart from lexico-grammatical ones, that could have identified them as such, have been removed. All that is left to distinguish 'spoken' and 'written' texts is the appearance of labelled turns in the texts representing the classroom discussions and interviews, but at a later stage in the process, even these were removed in order to focus on the students' linguistic production. Figure 18.3 is a screenshot from CorpusTool which shows an extract from Isabel's essay as it appears in the window, and the analysis that is being carried out on it. As can be seen, Isabel's text has now taken on a new identity, as a number (CA-T4-7). Not only has it been stripped of features which might have shown Isabel's agency, but it now has overlaid on it another text, the scheme for APPRAISAL analysis, which has been added to CorpusTool. Her text, then, is further recontextualized as it takes on a new set of meanings, with concepts such as ATTITUDE, APPRECIATION and SOCIAL VALUATION being used to categorize words and phrases that she had written with her own purposes and interests in mind as she responded to the task she was set.

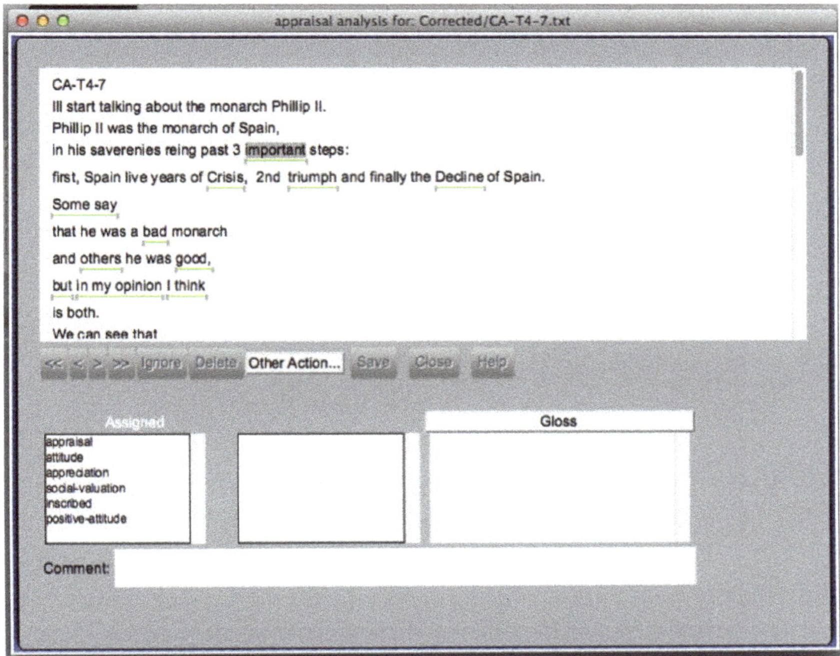

Figure 18.3: Screenshot from CorpusTool with extract from Isabel's essay.

By this stage in its natural history, Isabel's discourse has had 'digitality thrust upon it' in various ways. Pieces of discourse that were produced in very different situated contexts using different modes (sounds, images) and analogue mediational resources (the body, a pen) have now been merged into a 'corpus' of new texts, with not only digitality, but new meanings, thrust upon them. But, at least, in some ways, they are still recognizable as the discourse that Isabel produced. If we see meaning-making as a purely linguistic endeavour in which speakers and writers deploy the resources of languages as discrete systems, we can still use these texts to recover some of the co-text in order to make inferences about how Isabel deploys these parts of her communicative repertoire.

However, the next stage in the journey of Isabel's texts takes us further from any contextual information, as what was produced in the dynamic flow of interaction or written with pen and paper becomes a set of numbers. Figure 18.4 shows a screenshot from CorpusTool in which Isabel's use of APPRAISAL across the different modes in years 1 and 3 is compared. This screenshot is a new multimodal text in which resources of image (numbers, words and graphs) and spatial organization are used to create new meanings about Isabel's discourse. All other information apart from the numbers of examples of APPRAISAL which were coded by the researchers has been stripped away.

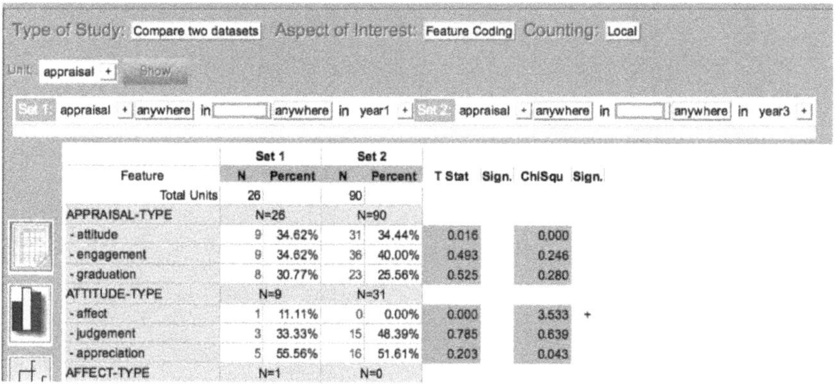

Feature	Set 1 N	Set 1 Percent	Set 2 N	Set 2 Percent	T Stat	Sign.	ChiSqu	Sign.
Total Units	26		90					
APPRAISAL-TYPE	N=26		N=90					
- attitude	9	34.62%	31	34.44%	0.016		0.000	
- engagement	9	34.62%	36	40.00%	0.493		0.246	
- graduation	8	30.77%	23	25.56%	0.525		0.280	
ATTITUDE-TYPE	N=9		N=31					
- affect	1	11.11%	0	0.00%	0.000		3.533	+
- judgement	3	33.33%	15	48.39%	0.785		0.639	
- appreciation	5	55.56%	16	51.61%	0.203		0.043	
AFFECT-TYPE	N=1		N=0					

Figure 18.4: Screenshot from CorpusTool showing comparison of Isabel's use of APPRAISAL in years 1 and 3.

This recontextualization creates new affordances for making meaning, in that it allows the researchers to make statements about putative changes or development in Isabel's performance over three years. However, the distance traversed in the process of entextualization, recontextualization and digitization means that it is ever more difficult to see ways in which these new texts are 'quotes' or 'echoes' of the originals, in Blommaert's terms. Perhaps they are faint echoes of the agentive decisions Isabel took as she confronted the tasks of participating in a class discussion, an interview with a researcher, and writing a timed essay. By the end of this process, the texts have indeed come a long way, and along the way the new meanings they yielded allowed the team of researchers to make statements about how the use of evaluative language resources may develop under the conditions of studying content in an additional language.

18.5 Closing the Circle: Back to Qualitative Analysis

The journey of the three texts can be seen as a process similar to social constructivist views of translation, where a piece of discourse is, as Gouanvic (2002: 100) puts it, 'decontextualized from the source field and re-historicized in the target field.' In this sense, then, the source field is the unique situations in which the original pieces of discourse were produced, with the participants' stake and interests, and the target field is that of Systemic Functional Linguistics research in language education. It is not that the new texts lack a 'natural history', it is rather that they have been re-historicized as part of a different field. By re-historicizing the texts as part of the field of Systemic Functional Linguistics, as researchers we were provided with insights that could now be taken back to the original context in order to provide suggestions that would help both types of participants (teachers and students) enhance their control and agency in the production of discourse in the relevant field (school history). As an example, we draw on another stretch of text from the same discussion that Extract 1 was taken from, in a passage that occurs a little later during the same lesson. The text is marked up to show the appraisal resources the students used in response to the teacher's question. Meanings related to Philip II's CAPACITY, a subsystem of the Appraisal category of SOCIAL ESTEEM, are boxed; meanings related to his PROPRIETY, a subsystem of SOCIAL SANCTION, are **bolded**.

Extract 3. Class discussion on Philip II

T: Ok. Right. So, so, maybe then we can say a bit more about question number two ok? So we could talk about him and about what you think about Philip the Second. Come on. Daniel?

D: He was **a bad ki king** because eh.. he..**he prohibited the Spanish people eh.. study in in fore-foreign universities** and.. I think **he was not very.. very tolerant**

T: Mmm. Ok. Elisa.
E: We think he was [a good monarch] because [he defeated the Turks and he controlled Flandes]
T: Ok. Good. More opinions? Come on!((silence)) Come on, more opinions. Miguel.. José...
J: he was [a good king] but with bad luck because [he suffer a lot of bankruptcies] and.. the Armada was defeated by a storm and... there was ...
T: Great. Excellent appreciation. Good. Ok.

The quantitative findings of our analysis showed that the higher rated texts used significantly more instances of PROPRIETY, when compared to average and lower rated texts, which, on the other hand, used significantly more instances of CAPACITY than the higher rated texts (McCabe and Whittaker, forthcoming). Coffin (2002, 2006) explains that expressions of SOCIAL ESTEEM and SOCIAL VALUATION create an interpreter voice in history texts; when expressions of SOCIAL SANCTION are added to those meanings an adjudicator voice is created. These voices are important in the construction of different types of history text, especially in the move from explanation/interpretation to argumentation. Thus, when judging historical characters, the morality of their actions is something that secondary students need to learn to consider and also need to have the language resources to express.

In Extract 3, the teacher does well to praise the students for their evaluations in response to the prompt. However, in order to make explicit to students the kinds of meanings needed when constructing the past, the teacher could push the students into thinking critically about how the different types of evaluations make different kinds of argument, with questions such as, 'How is Elisa's justification of her evaluation of Philip II different from Daniel's?'. Teachers can make explicit to students that there are overall two types of judgements of people, one based on their capabilities and the other based on ethical behaviour, and highlight the different forms of linguistic expression that these judgements can take. This kind of explicitness in teaching can help raise students' awareness of what they know about history, and why it is important to know it, leading to metacognition, which allows students greater control over and agency in their own learning. Thus, by taking the interpretations of the findings back to the original site of production, we close the circle. Figure 18.5 serves as a visual summary of the whole entextualization and recontextualization process, showing that it is indeed cyclical and that benefits will accrue from closing the circle by initiating a new round of discourse production, entextualization and recontextualization.

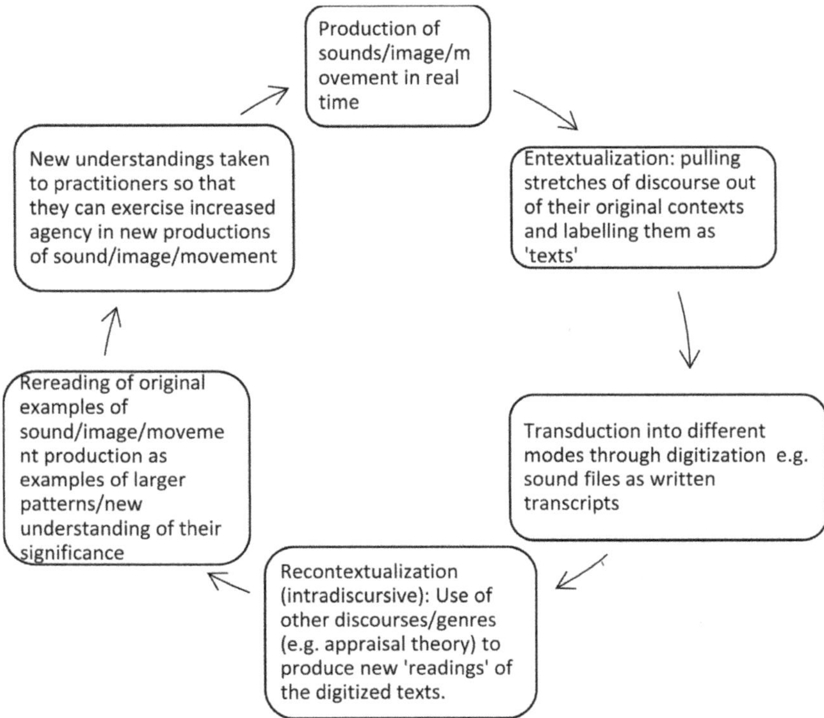

Figure 18.5: The entextualization and recontextualization cycle.

18.6 Conclusion

As researchers, we found the process of reflecting on the journey of these three pieces of discourse extremely beneficial as a reflective and reflexive exercise on our own research practices. As Bauman and Briggs argued, 'A further significant payoff offered by the investigation of the de-contextualization and re-contextualization of texts is a critical and reflexive perspective from which to examine our own scholarly practice' (1990: 78). Such critical reflection enables us as researchers to be more aware of what the processes of entextualization and recontextualization are doing to these student texts. We need to keep these processes in sight as we re-read the texts at successive stages, making sure that the affordances created by digitizing the texts are balanced by a need to triangulate findings by going back to individual texts and performing qualitative analyses. Thus, there emerges a clear argument for the use of corpus-based approaches in combination with other methods, what corpus linguists McEnery and Hardie (2011) describe as methodological pluralism or triangulation. In the type of applied study that the current research is an example of, the use of a small corpus is seen as a method, rather than as belonging to any notion of 'corpus-as-theory', and the strengths of a corpus-based approach can be enhanced if it is used in conjunction with a theory of language (Systemic Functional Linguistics) and appropriate other data analysis methods. In becoming a part of this small corpus, the three texts whose journey this chapter traces had digitality 'thrust upon them' through a process of entextualization and electronic recontextualization, which enabled new readings to made of them, and which, through closing the circle, had the potential to enhance the agency of all concerned, researchers, teachers and students.

About the authors

Tom Morton is Honorary Research Fellow in the Department of Applied Linguistics and Communication at Birkbeck, University of London, UK. His research interests include the application of Systemic Functional Linguistics to second language acquisition, pedagogy and classroom discourse, particularly in Content and Language Integrated Learning (CLIL) contexts.

Anne McCabe is a faculty member of the English Department at Saint Louis University, Madrid Campus, Spain, where she teaches linguistics, ESL and writing pedagogy to undergraduate and graduate students. She has published widely on application of Systemic Functional Linguistics to analysis of educational and media texts.

Endnote

1. This research project was INTER-CLIL – The Interpersonal Function of Language in CLIL Secondary Education: Analysis of a Spoken and Written Corpus, funded by the Spanish Ministry of Economy and Competitiveness (FFI2010-20790/FILO).

References

Bauman, R. and Briggs, C. L. (1990) Poetics and Performance as Critical Perspectives on Language and Social Life. *Annual Review of Anthropology* 19: 59–88.

Bernstein, B. (1996) *Pedagogy, Symbolic Control and Identity: Theory, Research, Critique*. London: Taylor & Francis.

Blommaert, J. (2005) *Discourse: A Critical Introduction.* Cambridge: Cambridge. University Press.

Coffin, C. (2002) The Voices of History: Theorising the Interpersonal Semantics of Historical Discourses. *Text* 22 (4): 503–528.
Coffin, C. (2006) Learning the Language of School History: The Role of Linguistics in Mapping the Writing Demands of the Secondary School Curriculum. *Journal of Curriculum Studies* 38(4): 413–429.
Gouanvic, J. M. (2002) A Model of Structuralist Constructivism in Translation Studies. In T. Hermans (ed.) *Crosscultural Transgressions*, 93–102. Manchester: St. Jerome.
Kress, G. (2003) *Literacy in the New Media Age*. London: Routledge.
Linell, P. (2009) *Rethinking Language, Mind, and World Dialogically: Interactional and Contextual Theories of Human Sense-Making*. Charlotte, NC: Information Age Publishing.
Martin, J. R. and White, P. R. R. (2005) *The Language of Evaluation: Appraisal in English*. London: Palgrave Macmillan.
McCabe, A. and Whittaker, R. (forthcoming) Genre and Appraisal in CLIL History Texts: Developing the Voice of the Historian. In A. Llinares, and T. Morton (eds) *Applied Linguistics Perspectives on CLIL*. Amsterdam: John Benjamins.
McEnery, T. and Hardie, A. (2011) *Corpus Linguistics: Method, Theory and Practice*. Cambridge: Cambridge University Press.
Nicholas, H. and Starks, D. (2014) *Language Education and Applied Linguistics: Bridging the Two Fields*. London: Routledge.
Ochs, E. (1979) Transcriptions as Theory. In E. Ochs and B. Schieffelin (eds) *Developmental Pragmatics*. New York: Academic Press.
O'Donnell, M. (2013) *UAM CorpusTool Version 2.8.12* [online] available from <http://www.wagsoft.com/CorpusTool/> [11/2013].
Silverstein, M. and Urban, G. (eds) (1996) *Natural Histories of Discourse*. Chicago, IL: University of Chicago Press.
Urban, G. (1996) Entextualization, Replication, and Power. In M. Silverstein and G. Urban (eds) *Natural Histories of Discourse*, 21–44. Chicago, IL: University of Chicago Press.
Wodak, R. and Iedema, R. (1999) Introduction: Organizational Discourses and Practices. *Discourse & Society* 10(1): 5–19.

19 Annotating Cohesive Ellipses in an English-German Corpus

Katrin Menzel
Saarland University

19.1 Introduction

The purpose of this chapter is to give an overview of the conceptualization, corpus annotation and cross-linguistic comparison of ellipses used as cohesive ties in English and German. The types and functions of ellipses in an English-German corpus of written and spoken language are analysed in the context of the empirical research project 'GECCo'[1] which uses the Systemic Functional Linguistics (SFL) approach to examine German-English contrasts in cohesion. SFL is a very useful descriptive and interpretive framework for studying the structure of texts and discourse and has a longstanding interest in textual cohesion. The combination of SFL as a theoretical framework with a quantitative analysis of corpus data will lead to insights about the lexico-grammatical properties of English and German and about text-type-specific usage preferences of cohesive devices that would otherwise be missed.

The term 'cohesion' was popularized by Halliday and Hasan (1976) who divided the phenomenon into five main categories: reference, conjunction, lexical cohesion, substitution and ellipsis. Cohesion refers to the text-internal relationship of linguistic elements that are overtly linked via lexical and grammatical devices across text segments in a coherent text. The recognition of textual coherence involves text- and reader-based features and refers to the logical flow of interrelated ideas, thus establishing a mental textual world. There is a connection between these two concepts in that relations of cohesion can be regarded as indicators of meaning relations in a text and hence contribute to its overall coherence. Certain types of ellipsis are an important grammatical means of achieving cohesion in written and spoken discourse. Therefore, one way to hold a text together is by deleting part of it.

Corpus methods allow us to study the language- and register-specific frequencies of cohesive ellipses as they occur in real language use. The main advantage of findings from a corpus is that it is possible to examine the surrounding co-text of examples and to explore contrasts and similarities with regard to frequency and function of ellipsis subtypes across languages, registers and production modes.

The bilingual multilevel-annotated GECCo corpus (ca. 1.69 m. tokens) consists of texts and transcriptions from a broad range of written and spoken registers and text types. It can be used to generate and test various hypotheses and to observe linguistic patterns and discourse phenomena such as ellipsis-antecedent-relations across languages, registers, modes (written vs. spoken) and production types (original texts vs. translated texts).[2] To the best of our knowledge, there are no English or German corpora available so far representing a wide registerial range where cohesive ellipses have been annotated. In general, there is a wide variety of phenomena labelled 'ellipsis', and the term may defy exact classification. The topic of cohesive ellipsis has been less frequently investigated than other discourse phenomena and has probably been neglected in previous studies on cohesive devices due to its complexity. Studies focusing on ellipses as textually cohesive ties are relatively rare and conceptually not always very well defined. In monolingual and cross-linguistic studies on cohesive devices, the topic of ellipsis generally plays a minor role and if it is addressed, Halliday and Hasan's classification (1976) is usually taken as it is and applied to the description of prototypical elliptical constructions. The few quantitative studies on ellipsis from different theoretical approaches have to date been small-scale or tend to be restricted to a very limited set of ellipsis subtypes in monolingual data (e.g. Bos and Spenader [2011] on English lexical-verb ellipsis or Günther [2013] on English nominal ellipsis after adjectives). Clarke (2012) also looked at a variety of functional-structural ellipsis types in an English corpus of about 125,000 words; however, many of the ellipses he described are purely the result of coordination as in Example 1. Such cases will not be dealt with in our analysis of textual cohesion.

Example 1. He was neat and tidy and [he was] determined to get forward at every chance (Clarke, 2012: 168).

Before one can assess the results of previous studies related to ellipsis and annotate and analyse this phenomenon in our corpus data, a conceptual clarification and elaboration of Halliday and Hasan's (1976) work on cohesive ellipses is necessary. This chapter aims to define exactly what is meant by ellipsis as a cohesive device and to show how this phenomenon manifests itself in written and spoken discourse. We will point out some differences in the frequency distribution of ellipses between English and German subcorpora for written and spoken data and how registers and text types in both languages differ in their preference for particular ellipsis types. The written-spoken distinction in the data, however, is not completely unproblematic, as will be shown in the section on the corpus description.

19.2 Cohesive Ellipsis – Conceptualization

Cohesive devices, including ellipsis, are an important topic in SFL. However, apart from Halliday and Hasan (1976), theoretical work on the conceptualization of ellipsis has often been carried out in other theoretical frameworks focusing, for example, on the assumed mechanisms of syntactic, semantic and pragmatic recoverability and interpretation of the ellipsis site. An extensive body of literature on ellipsis has accumulated over time, and it is important to trace the emergence and historical development of 'ellipsis' as a linguistic concept from classical antiquity to modern times to explain some of the reasons behind the complexity and loose definitions of this term (see Menzel, 2014). Several ellipsis typologies have been suggested on the basis of different underlying dimensions. Detailed taxonomies for various ellipsis subtypes in English and German have been proposed by Bühler (1934), Quirk *et al.*, (1985), Zifonun *et al.*, (1997) or Merchant (2001) among others. However, existing typological schemes sometimes do not place ellipsis subtypes on an equal footing and often turn out to have gray areas between categories. Formal, contextual and functional aspects sometimes mix to a certain degree in ellipsis classifications, e.g. in Klein (1985: 3–5) who distinguished between text-type-specific ellipses, ellipses as orders to perform actions, expressive exclamations, elliptical formulaic expressions, lexicalized ellipses, coordinate ellipses, adjacency ellipses, ellipses due to processing difficulties and ellipses due to incomplete linguistic development. In this typology, ellipses categories tend to overlap and are defined on the basis of criteria such as their form, syntactic or textual context, their level of conventionalization and the reason or intention behind their use.

The myriad of fragmentary constructions that have been termed 'ellipsis' in the past usually do not have a focus on textual cohesion. For our purposes, it is important to focus our categories on the potential cohesive function of ellipses in discourse and to sort out other types of non-cohesive sentence fragments, non-clausal units and other omission phenomena that might look similar but actually need different analysis. Forming categories as well as organizing them into coherent systems so that the classification of all examples occurring in the corpus is consistent with theoretical assumptions is a challenge. The sheer diversity of syntactic patterns reflected in large corpora seems to have given people endless options when it comes to economy of expression. It is necessary to subsume the multitude of categories suggested in the literature under more general ones to cover the variety of different omission possibilities in English and German corpus texts from a wide spectrum of communication scenarios on written-spoken and formal-informal continuums.

In the context of textual cohesion, ellipsis can be defined as a phenomenon where the remnant of a syntactic omission is deliberately left grammatically incomplete or deficient to create a sentence fragment or an incomplete phrase as in Example 2.

Example 2. I didn't find it amusing and I don't think they will [find it amusing] either.

The lexico-grammatical content of the ellipsis site can be recovered from its textual antecedent (or, in a few cases, from a postcedent). Certain mismatches and underspecifications are tolerated in both English and German, which has led some linguists to claim that ellipsis is mainly conditioned by semantic, not structural identity. Prosodic parallelism and focus marking also play an important role in the interpretation and processing of ellipses. A recent approach to flawed antecedents supports a 'recycling hypothesis' which combines syntactic, semantic and pragmatic aspects claiming that when a syntactically matching antecedent is not available, the listener or reader creates one using the semantic and pragmatic materials at hand (see Arregui *et al.*, 2006). Being aware of the complexity of the syntax-semantics interface and the impact of pragmatic and prosodic aspects and focus structure on utterance and text processing, we choose to follow the syntactic approach in the current stage. What is important for the classification of our ellipsis categories is the presupposed complete clausal or phrasal structure assuming that ellipsis involves unpronounced linguistic material.

Halliday and Hasan's (1976) distinction between nominal, verbal and clausal ellipses as omissions that function as potentially cohesive devices is taken as a starting point for the development of the theoretical framework for this contrastive study, ensuring the consistent use of SFL terminology within the GECCo project in which all categories and subcategories of cohesive devices suggested by Halliday and Hasan are analysed. These three ellipsis subtypes occur both in written and spoken language in English and German with different register-specific frequencies. Using such general categories precludes many of the flaws of more fine-grained existing typologies. It also helps to avoid the consequences of an overspecified model describing too many small samples in a quantitative analysis, as cohesive ellipsis can be expected to be less frequent than various other types of cohesive devices. In fact, most textual links are lexical, and the resource used most often is lexical cohesion – in many cases repetition of the same item (Taboada, 2004:

172). According to Taboada, who compared English and Spanish, speakers do not favour ellipses to link ideas together in a text as it places 'a heavy burden on the speaker' minds' (Taboada, 2004). However, this is probably not the main reason for the low frequency of ellipses that she observed in her data. Substitution as a cohesive device seems to be even rarer (Taboada, 2004) although it does not need more effort to resolve than elliptical reference. The low number of cases of substitution can be explained by the fact that there are only a few specific constructions of substitution with placeholder elements such as *one, do* or *so*. Ellipsis-antecedent relations are not much more frequent, as they are not independent of the grammatical structure of the text and usually do not span long distances. They are controlled by various syntactic, semantic and stylistic factors and, in contrast to other cohesive ties, represent relations not between two actual text segments, but between an actual passage and a virtual or theoretical complete version (cf. Beaugrande, 1991: 252).

Some clarifications are necessary when working with Halliday and Hasan's tripartite ellipsis typology of nominal, verbal and clausal ellipsis, for which they also give various subcategories. There are a few questions that come to mind when looking at this classification, especially when it is applied to real discourse data of different text types and various communication scenarios in English and German and not only to idealized or prototypical isolated utterance pairs.

A potential overlap of categories might result from the fact that Halliday and Hasan do not keep their five subcategories of cohesive devices strictly separate from each other, and some phenomena of textual cohesion might co-occur in one textual element as a 'double cohesive tie' (Halliday and Hasan, 1976: 157) that is both grammatical and lexical, for instance, when reiterated or omitted words have reference as well. While Halliday and Hasan give detailed subcategories for the distinct phenomena of reference, conjunction, lexical cohesion, substitution and ellipsis, they also claim that ellipsis should be defined in relation to substitution and that omissions are, in fact, a subtype of substitution ('substitution by zero') (Halliday and Hasan, 1976: 143). That would mean that some categories of cohesive devices are on the same level, but some fall under other main categories. Here, we will keep these categories more discrete – either something is left out (ellipsis) or it is replaced by semantically bleached lexical material (substitution).

It has to be kept in mind that there are certain language-specific differences between the internal structures of English and German phrases and clauses. These structural differences that might seem subtle with regard to some aspects and more striking with regard to others (inflectional morphology, word order, features of phrases and structural elements in phrases etc.)

are the reason for some systemic differences relevant to ellipsis, which are addressed in Menzel (2014) and in a project working report[3] in more detail.

To give just two examples, nominal ellipses can be introduced by possessive *-s* in English:

Example 3. His speech lasted longer than the Queen's [ ].

In German, nominal ellipsis after the genitive marker occasionally occurs, but in many cases it is not possible and there are other non-genitive constructions that can be used instead:

Example 4. Seine Rede war länger als die[4] der Königin. (… als der Königin ihre. (colloq.))

German in general will often have only one constituent left in adjacency pairs where English can have a verbal ellipsis.

Example 5. Who was playing the Piano? – Peter [ ]. / Peter was [ ].
Example 6. Wer hat Klavier gespielt? Peter [ ]. / *Peter hat [ ].

Nevertheless, utilizing broad main categories such as nominal, verbal and clausal ellipsis provides a suitable framework for a cross-linguistic analysis of elliptical omissions that potentially refer to textual antecedents, as both English and German have nominal groups, verbal groups and clauses where certain elements can be omitted that are deducible from the co-text.

It has to be determined which cases of nominal, verbal and clausal ellipses establish textual links and are used as text-forming cohesive devices. We have to exclude cases within these categories that formally meet the criteria of incomplete nominal or verbal groups or clauses but, for instance, refer exophorically to the extralinguistic situational context or are rather independent of the context if they have a standard interpretation (cf. Ágel [1991] on lexicalized ellipsis). We will focus on those clear cases of ellipses as syntactic omissions that refer endophorically to preceding or following linguistic items within the text. Ideally, the antecedents or postcedents do not occur in the same clause so that a textual link between different clauses or sentences is created. According to Halliday and Hasan, 'cohesion occurs where the interpretation of some element in the discourse is dependent on that of another' (1976: 4). Although Halliday and Hasan state that 'cohesive relations are the same whether their elements are within the same sentence or not. […]' (1976: 9), all the examples they give are of cohesion across sentence boundaries, assuming that in those cases the effect is more striking. Halliday and Hasan clearly state that cohesion 'is a relation to which the sentence, or any other form of grammatical structure, is […] irrelevant'

(1976: 9) and that cohesive ties between sentences stand out more clearly because they are the only source of texture, whereas within the sentence there are structural relations as well. Therefore, the cohesive effect is less pronounced within the sentence (1976: 9). Although Halliday/Hasan speak mainly of cohesive ties between 'sentences', Halliday later clarified (1994: 216) that he uses the term 'sentence' for graphological units consisting of single independent clauses or clause-complexes. In our analysis of cohesion in GECCo, we specifically look at cases of ellipses across sentences/ clause-complexes, but also at ellipses across clauses and across utterance boundaries although all of these types are sometimes difficult to pin down, particularly in the spoken corpus registers where speech segmentation is more problematic than in written language. These cases have to be distinguished from locally bound omissions referring to antecedents within the same clause or even the same phrase that are mainly the result of intra-clausal grammatical rules.

Let us take a closer look at the main categories of ellipsis relevant to the corpus annotation in this study. Nominal ellipsis is the omission of the head noun within the nominal group, i.e. the omission of a specific element of the noun phrase. Regardless of the specific type of the modifying element after which a deletion of a noun occurs (e.g. after numerals, quantifiers, possessive markers or adjectives), all cases will fall under the broader category of nominal ellipsis in this study. In contrast to other ellipsis types, nominal ellipses can be expected to occur in different written text types such as narrative, technical or business writing as well as in various registers of spoken language. Examples 7–10 demonstrate nominal ellipsis in English and German:

Example 7 This story is interesting. The other two [stories] are even better.
Example 8 Diese Geschichte ist interessant. Die anderen zwei [Geschichten] sind sogar noch besser.
Example 9 Helen is the oldest girl in the class. Julie is the tallest [girl].
Example 10 Helen ist das älteste Mädchen in der Klasse. Julie ist das größte [Mädchen].

In German, the ellipsis remnant has to show strong morphological agreement in order to license the elided noun. In English, nominal ellipses after adjectives are not always possible and mainly restricted to ellipses after some frequently used modifiers (e.g. adjectives describing size, age, material or colour, especially if they express contrast to other modified nominal groups in the immediate context (cf. Günther, 2013) or after comparative and superlative adjectives as those forms have a richer morphology. To avoid explicitly mentioning or repeating a noun, English can use the nominal substitute *one*, which is optional in a few cases.

As has been pointed out above, when analysing ellipsis subcategories with a special focus on cohesion, one has to keep in mind that even Halliday and Hasan's boundaries of the category of ellipsis are not always clear-cut with regard to other very similar phenomena, such as their notion of substitution (cf. Menzel and Lapshinova-Koltunski, 2014). To give just one example to illustrate the overlap between nominal ellipsis and nominal substitution, the distinction of *one* as a nominal substitute from its other cohesive and non-cohesive functions is sometimes not entirely clear due to its multiple word-class membership. Halliday and Hasan state that *one*, apart from its possible use as a nominal substitute (e.g. *the green one*), can function as a personal pronoun (e.g. *One can never know.*), a general noun or 'pro-noun' (e.g. *The one he needs is a lawyer.*), a cardinal numeral + nominal ellipsis (*We saw exactly one [ ].*') or a determiner + nominal ellipsis (e.g. *Will you buy me a bus? I want one [ ].*') where *one* is interpreted as an alternative full form of the indefinite article, which again is different from *I want one with wheels* where the indefinite article and the substitute are fused (Halliday and Hasan, 1976: 98). Therefore, *one* is sometimes used with ellipsis, as a substitute or in another function, and it is not always easy to identify its function without employing grammatical tests. There is also potential ambiguity between different functions that cannot be resolved in certain contexts.

Certain structures subsumed by Halliday and Hasan under nominal ellipsis will not be included in our analysis, such as pronouns with suffixes or non-reduced forms where adding a noun is not possible without changing the form of other sentence elements, e.g. possessive pronouns *mine/yours* or *none* as a pronoun. In analogy, this also concerns certain German pronouns with an agreement suffix, e.g. *keins/meins* and the numeral *eins*. If an inflection paradigm allows the insertion of a noun in only some cases (e.g. after *his/its* in English, but not after other possessive pronouns or *keine/meine/eine* in German), it can be marked as a problematic case in the annotation. Halliday and Hasan do not make a clear-cut distinction between nominal ellipsis after a modifier (Deictic, Numerative, Epithet, Classifier and Qualifier) and noun phrases consisting of certain pronouns that should not be analysed as grammatically defective or incomplete structures because the pronoun replaces the noun. This is complicated by the fact that, particularly in English, there is certain flexibility in word-class membership. We might assume that there is actually no structure within the assumed ellipsis site in some cases that Halliday and Hasan would count as nominal ellipses, e.g. demonstratives that are not followed by nouns as in *I want those* (cf. Halliday and Hasan, 1976: 157). This can be regarded as a determiner-to-pronoun conversion or recategorization.

Verbal ellipsis involves the omission of a verb. Halliday and Hasan divide this category into operator ellipsis (omission of the auxiliary or modal verb) and lexical ellipsis which involves the omission of the lexical verb. In our corpus annotation, we will keep all omissions within the verbal group under the umbrella heading of verbal ellipsis. In general, English has more possibilities than German to leave out verbal group elements due to the different and often longer periphrastic structure of verbal groups in English (e.g. the English progressive or 'expanded form' and the use of *do* as an operator in many cases where German has none). Verbal ellipsis is often accompanied by the omission of related clause elements such as objects. Examples 11–14 show verbal ellipsis in English and German.

Example 11. Has he been crying? – No, [ ] laughing.
Example 12. Hat er geweint? – Nein, [ ]gelacht.
Example 13. Have you eaten? – Yes, I have [ ].
Example 14. Hast du gegessen? Ja, [ ] habe ich.

Clausal ellipsis is the broadest category. It is defined as the omission of a part of a clause ('modal' or 'propositional' element in Halliday and Hasan, 1976: 196). Clausal ellipsis does not take the form of omission of single elements of clause structure (Halliday and Hasan, 1976: 203). Often, it involves the omission of a clause to the exception of a single constituent, and it may co-occur with nominal or verbal ellipsis. The line drawn by Halliday and Hasan between verbal and clausal ellipsis is not very sharp. They state that it is possible to look at verbal ellipsis 'from another angle, taking the clause as the point of departure' (Halliday and Hasan, 1976: 197), and to interpret it as a clausal ellipsis, which means that they do not place their three main ellipsis categories on an equal footing. The classifications used for the corpus annotation should not overlap or involve gradual categories. The aim is to place all cases found in the GECCo corpus clearly in only one category in order to provide the basis for a meaningful quantitative analysis. Therefore, clausal ellipsis is defined here as omissions within clauses that are not covered under nominal and verbal ellipsis.

19.3 Corpus Annotation

This chapter will provide a summary on how the annotation tool MMAX2 (Müller and Strube, 2006) has been used for the manual annotation of ellipsis remnants and, if available, the textual antecedents of omitted elements in the GECCo corpus. Our amended ellipsis typology serves as a theoretical background for the annotation guidelines for the classification and identification of textually cohesive ellipses and their antecedents. Detailed annotation guidelines have been developed on the basis of theoretical discussions about ellipses and examples from the corpus texts providing insights into the process of discussing and deciding on controversial cases in order to develop a consistent annotation standard.

The GECCo corpus is an English-German corpus pre-annotated on various grammatical levels (cf. Hansen-Schirra *et al.*, 2012; Lapshinova-Koltunski *et al.*, 2012) and enriched semi-automatically with information on cohesive devices.[5] The written part is a sentence-aligned parallel corpus consisting of English and German comparable original texts and their translations from the following registers (or text types): fictional texts, political essays, instruction manuals, popular-science texts, letters to shareholders, prepared political speeches, tourism leaflets and corporate websites. The spoken component is a comparable corpus consisting of English and German academic lectures, interviews and the recently compiled corpus registers of talk shows, texts from online discussion sites, medical consultation and religious sermons that are still in the process of being annotated. Each register for each language and production mode contains at least ten texts and ca. 31,250 tokens. Some corpus registers are at the boundary between written and spoken language, according to aspects such as naturalness, communicative closeness, co-spatiality or dialogicity. For instance, we find conceptually spoken language (Koch and Oesterreicher, 1994) in online discussions, which are often more spontaneous, less edited, less coherent and less structurally complex than many other medially written texts. Some corpus registers consist of texts that are written to be spoken (e.g. political speeches in their original language) or include passages that are read out from books or other materials or recited from memory (e.g. sermons and academic lectures).

For the annotation of cohesive devices such as reference, conjunction or substitution, semi-automatic procedures were applied, which involved a rule-based tagging of cohesion candidates and their manual post-correction by human annotators. The corpus can be queried with the Corpus Query Processor (CQP) (Evert, 2005), and the instantiations of the annotated categories of cohesive devices can be easily extracted from the corpus and then evaluated with different statistical methods. Put to the test was whether potentially cohesive ellipses could be queried (semi-) automatically or if manual annotation would be more efficient and reliable. Manual annotation of ellipsis has been found to be not extremely time-consuming, given the comparably low number of cases in the corpus data, and to be much more accurate than automatic methods, as there are numerous theoretical omission possibilities for omissions of nouns, verbs and parts of clauses in different syntactic environments and the part-of-speech tagging is sometimes wrong in ellipsis environments due to deficient or non-standard syntax. Furthermore, checking the contexts of each query result for potential antecedents might generally be time-consuming and complicated with automatic methods. However, the corpus annotations can be used to identify the most frequent patterns of ellipsis contexts to improve semi-automatic annotation methods for certain ellipsis types (e.g. nominal ellipsis after certain triggers such as superlative adjectives or clausal ellipsis in question-answer pairs). Post-correction of automatic annotation methods will always be necessary due to the large variety of omission possibilities and our focus on cases referring to textual antecedents.

The following categories have been annotated by the author of this chapter[6] in MMAX2 with regard to potentially cohesive ellipses: nominal, verbal and clausal.[7] Ellipsis remnants (not the actual omitted elements) and the antecedents of the ellipsis sites were both annotated, with a pointer relation linking a remnant to the antecedent.[8]

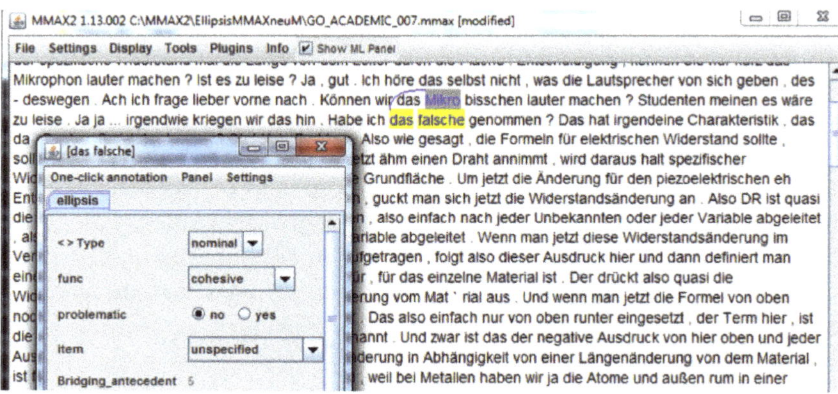

Figure 19.1: Link between elliptical phrase and antecedent in MMAX2.

The function of ellipses without any textual antecedents (e.g. exophoric nominal ellipses) was marked as 'non-cohesive'. Ellipses referring to antecedents within the same clause have been marked as clause-internal. Although these cases do not create a textual link between different clauses or sentences, they have been annotated as well to clearly exclude them and put them under a separate category and to use this information for improving query methods that can also be applied to other corpora. Cases that might initially require further discussion if they seem to be on the borderline to other cohesive devices or raise doubt of whether they should be analysed as ellipses at all – for instance, if there are different opinions in the literature – can be marked as problematic. Therefore, if one wants to narrow the scope of the ellipsis definition, it is possible to consider only the more typical, clear cases for the calculations. If there are chains where several ellipses refer to one common antecedent, the elliptical phrases are all linked with the same antecedent in the annotation. Some cases contain potential ambiguities or might give the reader several plausible options for completing a sentence. In these cases, the annotation is an interpretation by the annotator, who tries to determine an underlying structure that most accurately reflects the author's or the speaker's intended message.

Additionally, it is possible to compare potential and actual cohesive ellipses to certain categories that might superficially look very similar to the categories described above although there are various reasons for treating them as specific separate structures such as autonomous non-clausal units that are not considered to be the result of syntactic omission, text-type-specific block language, abbreviated sentences and non-sentences (cf. Quirk *et al.*, 1985: 833), sentence splits, short yes/no replies where a particle conveys affirmation or negation and other cases. These categories have been annotated as well to clearly distinguish them from cohesive ellipses. It might be worth looking at such cases that have sometimes been called 'ellipsis' in the literature to compare their features to those of endophoric ellipses which can be used as cohesive devices to create textual links. Some cases are on the borderline between a cohesive ellipsis and a sentence split (e.g. by the creative use of punctuation marks as in advertisements or fictional texts), as in most cases more syntactic material might theoretically be added in a way that takes up the structure of the previous environment. However, there is often no actual omission, but a specification is added that may be integrated into the syntax of the previous sentence. The irregular punctuation mark signals a pause for effect, emphasis or reflection (frequent in political speeches in GECCo for instance). German, in particular, uses many of these constructions. Sentence splits, which are mainly forms of extraposition where dislocated sentence elements appear outside the sentence boundary to emphasize certain constituents, have been annotated separately, but the annotation of spoken registers is more difficult for this category. Different transcribers had to make decisions on where to put sentence boundaries, which is already an interpretation of the data. Short yes/no replies, their German equivalent and similar constructions where a particle conveys affirmation or negation (e.g. *OK*, *indeed*) are sentence substitutes, pro-sentences or sentence words that have sentential character (Helbig and Buscha [1994]; Schachter [1985: 32]). Their morphological-syntactic classification as a 'particle' or 'adverb' is unclear (Bussmann, 1996), as is their connection to ellipsis. Cases of aposiopesis (i.e. if a sentence is deliberately broken off), anapodoton (a stand-alone subordinate clause) and anacoluthon (a break in grammatical continuity, where the expected grammatical sequence is absent) and omissions that do not fall under any of the categories described above (e.g. non-rule-based spontaneous omissions in spoken language or ungrammatical ellipses of prepositions or articles) can be annotated as 'other'. Fragments in joint utterance constructions can also be classified under 'other' if a syntactic unit has been completed jointly by two or more participants in interaction. In general, there are only very few examples from the corpus that would fall under this category.

The results of the annotation of those additional categories can be used to make comparisons between incomplete structures and other cases of non-standard syntax or other means of 'Sprachökonomie' and condensed language. The overall syntactic or fragmentary nature of texts and registers and the tendency towards syntactic standardization might be other factors that could be assessed. The annotation does not cover purely semantic implications that are not reflected in incomplete or irregular syntax.

19.4 Corpus Extraction and Analysis

The annotated ellipsis categories can be extracted from the corpus automatically to answer specific research questions. We can, for instance, compare the frequency distributions of particular types of cohesive devices with ellipses used as cohesive ties. Furthermore, it is possible to explore the differences between written and spoken language or between original texts and translations or to analyse the distribution of ellipsis and its subtypes across registers within one language or across languages and to see whether the distinctions along the register dimension may be weaker or stronger in English compared to German. The distance between ellipsis sites and antecedents and the length of antecedents are other aspects that can be measured. As this chapter focuses on demonstrating how concepts from SFL that have been slightly adapted and defined more specifically can serve as the basis for a conceptual description of cohesive ellipsis and a framework for an ellipsis annotation scheme that can be applied to corpus texts, this subsection will confine itself to some illustrative examples of studies that can be carried out based on the annotated corpus data. More details can be found, for instance, in Degaetano-Ortlieb *et al.* (forthcoming) and Menzel and Lapshinova (2014).

There are some interesting differences between registers and text types that reveal systematic differences in the distribution of cohesive ellipsis. Figure 19.2 shows the cross-registerial distribution of nominal, verbal and clausal ellipses. The frequencies in medially and conceptually spoken registers are higher than in other registers, and the contrasts between English and German are not striking. We generally find more elliptical constructions in spoken language, but incomplete sentences, fragments and structural gaps are not just features of spoken language or its representation in written dialogue. Although not shown in this figure, some registers such as instruction manuals, tourism leaflets or corporate websites have a variety of non-cohesive sentence fragments and non-clausal units, and cohesion is principally achieved through lexical means. Spoken texts usually have fewer clause-internal ellipses compared to written texts due to less complex syntactic structures and fewer and shorter nominal groups that occur in the same clause.

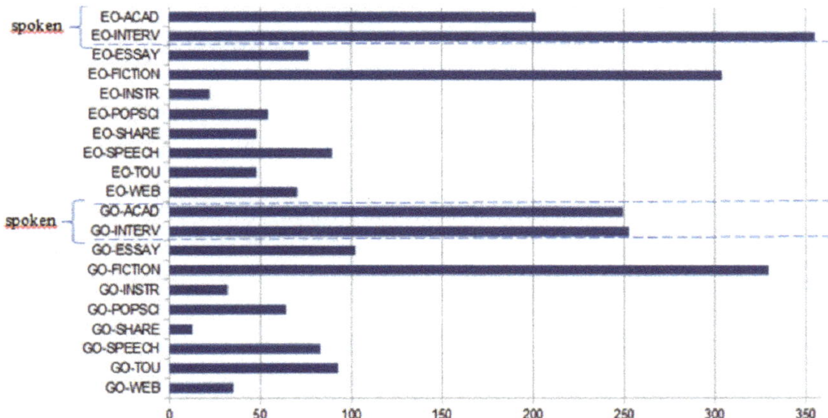

Figure 19.2: Overall number of cohesive ellipses.

Occurrences per 100,000 tokens based on a corpus release from 2013 in English original texts (EO) and German original texts (GO) in academic lectures (ACAD), interviews (INTERV), fictional texts (FICTION), political essays (ESSAY), instruction manuals (INSTR), popular-science texts (POPSCI), letters to shareholders (SHARE), prepared political speeches (SPEECH), tourism leaflets (TOU) and corporate websites (WEB).

Figure 19.3 shows the distribution of nominal, verbal and clausal ellipses without clause-internal and non-cohesive cases (occurrences per 100,000 tokens) in the written and spoken subcorpora and in the translations of the written data. Cross-clausal and cross-sentential verbal ellipses are rarer than other subtypes of cohesive ellipsis in most subcorpora, particularly in the German data, and the frequency differences between ellipsis subtypes in written language seem to be less pronounced than in spoken language.

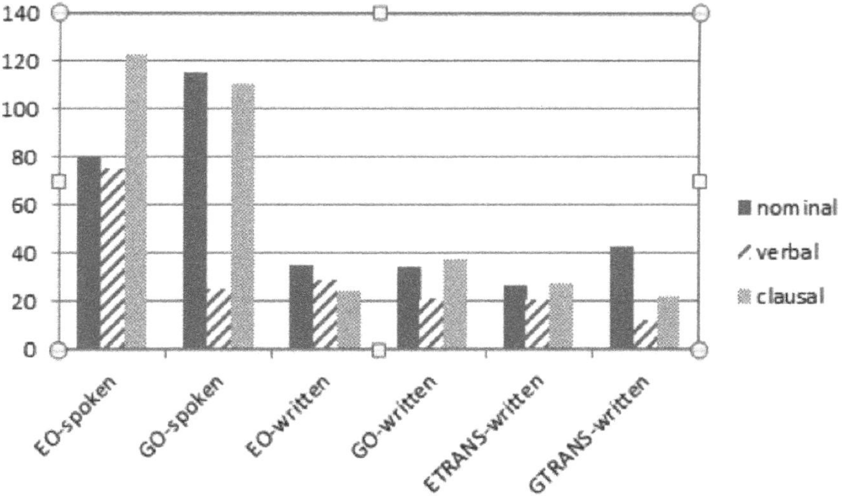

Figure 19.3: Subtypes of cohesive ellipses in written and spoken subcorpora of original texts and translations in GECCo (based on a 2013 corpus release).

The frequency of cohesive ellipses is generally lower in translations compared to that in originals of the same language or the language the texts have been translated from, with the exception of the number of clausal ellipses in ETRANS which is higher than in written English originals and the number of nominal ellipses in GTRANS which is the highest for this subtype in the written subcorpora.

19.5 Conclusion and Outlook

As has been pointed out above, SFL is a useful framework for studying textual cohesion. It provides us with a set of subcategories that can be applied to the description of potentially cohesive ellipses in English and German. Corpus studies are indispensable for a comprehensive approach to ellipsis, as they allow us to analyse the actual distribution of ellipses in naturally occurring language. This is particularly important with regard to ellipsis, as some ellipsis subtypes from other typologies that have been described extensively in the literature are relatively rare in actual language use, even to the point that there are no occurrences of them in our corpus. Many examples in the literature have been mainly constructed for theoretical discussions and acceptability testing. Halliday and Hasan's work on cohesive ellipses needed some conceptual clarification with regard to the potential overlap, ambiguity and vagueness of certain categories. By formulating explicit annotation guidelines, we ensured that all cases found in the bilingual corpus from a wide variety of discourse types were placed clearly in only one category in order to provide the basis for a meaningful and reproducible analysis of ellipsis as a cohesive device. So far, the annotated corpus data in GECCo are mainly available for written registers and only for a few spoken ones. The compilation of spoken registers has been relatively time-consuming, and we have encountered a number of practical problems. Some recorded data had to be transcribed manually, and it is difficult to find cross-linguistically comparable, spontaneous and dialogic material. It would be interesting to see how the recently compiled corpus registers might influence our results, providing a wider base for analysis and generalization, and to evaluate whether the observed differences are merely coincidental or of significance despite the relatively low number of cohesive ellipses in the corpus data compared to other phenomena.

About the author

Katrin Menzel is a teaching and research staff member at the Department of Applied Linguistics, Translation and Interpreting at Saarland University, Germany. Her research in contrastive linguistics and translation studies focuses on text linguistics and cohesion in written and spoken discourse.

Endnotes

1. www.gecco.uni-saarland.de, funded by the Deutsche Forschungsgemeinschaft (STE840/6-2/KU3129/1-2)
2. Searchable online at https://fedora.clarin-d.uni-saarland.de/cqpweb/ (access available for research and educational purposes upon request).
3. Available upon request to k.menzel@mx.uni-saarland.de
4. '*die*' = demonstrative pronoun here replacing the noun.
5. Cf. http://www.gecco.uni-saarland.de/GECCo/Korpus.html and Menzel and Lapshinova (2014) for a more detailed corpus description.
6. Given enough time and resources, ideally more than one human annotator should be used and inter-annotator agreement assessed, but here the complete annotation was performed by the person who also developed the annotation guidelines.
7. In the annotation, no distinction is made between more fine-grained subcategories (e.g. nominal ellipsis after numerals vs. nominal ellipsis after adjectives, lexical verb ellipsis vs. modal verb ellipsis, sluicing as a subtype of clausal ellipsis vs. clausal ellipsis in question-answer pairs, other rejoinder sequences, etc.) in analogy with the annotation of substitution in the corpus data where nominal, verbal and clausal substitutes have been analysed (Kunz and Steiner,

2013). However, it is possible to select only certain specific ellipsis patterns by combining a query for the ellipsis category in combination with other query constraints with regard to other corpus annotation levels (e.g. tokens, lemmas, morpho-syntactic features, parts of speech, phrase chunks and their grammatical functions or sentence boundaries).

8. The annotation does not distinguish explicitly between anaphoric and cataphoric relations, as cataphoric ellipses are quite rare in the corpus data or fall under right-node raising as a separate concept.

References

Ágel, V. (1991) Lexikalische Ellipsen. Fragen Und Vorschläge. *Zeitschrift Für Germanistische Linguistik* 19: 24–48.

Arregui, A., Clifton, C. J., Frazier, L., and Moulton, K. (2006) Processing Elided Verb Phrases with Flawed Antecedents: The Recycling Hypothesis. *Journal of Memory and Language* 55: 232–246.

Beaugrande, R. D. (1991) *Linguistic Theory: The Discourse of Fundamental Works*. London: Longman.

Bos, J. and Spenader, J. (2011) An Annotated Corpus for the Analysis of VP Ellipsis. *Language Resources and Evaluation* 45(4): 463–494.

Bühler, K. (1934) *Sprachtheorie. Die Darstellungsfunktion Der Sprache*. Jena: Fischer [Translated into English by Goodwin, D. (1990) *Theory of Language. The Representational Function of Language*. Amsterdam: John Benjamins Publishing Company].

Bussmann, H. (1996) *Routledge Dictionary of Language and Linguistics*. London: Routledge.

Clarke, B. P. (2012) Do Patterns of Ellipsis in Text Support Systemic Functional Linguistics' 'Context-Metafunction Hook-Up' Hypothesis? A Corpus-Based Approach. PhD thesis, Cardiff University, Cardiff, UK.

Degaetano-Ortlieb, S., Kunz, K., Lapshinova-Koltunski, E., Menzel, K., and Steiner, E. (forthcoming) GECCo – an Empirically-Based Comparison of English-German Cohesion. In G. De Sutter, I. Delaere and M. Lefer (eds) *New Ways of Analysing Translational Behaviour in Corpus-Based Translation Studies*. Berlin: Mouton de Gruyter.

Evert, S. (2005) *The CQP Query Language Tutorial*. Stuttgart: IMS: Universität Stuttgart.

Günther, C. (2013) *The Elliptical Noun Phrase in English: Structure and Use*. New York: Routledge.

Halliday, M. A. K. (1994) *An Introduction to Functional Grammar*. 2nd edn. London and Melbourne: Arnold.

Halliday, M. A. K. and Hasan, R. (1976) *Cohesion in English*. London: Longman.

Hansen-Schirra, S., Neumann, S., and Steiner, E. (2012) *Cross-Linguistic Corpora for the Study of Translations. Insights from the Language Pair English – German*. Berlin and New York: Mouton de Gruyter.

Helbig, G. and Buscha, J. (1994) *Deutsche Grammatik. Ein Handbuch Für Den Ausländerunterricht*. Leipzig: Langenscheidt.

Klein, W. (1985) Ellipse, Fokusgliederung und thematischer Stand. In R. Meyer-Herrmann and H. Rieser (eds) *Ellipsen und fragmentarische Ausdrücke. Vol. 1*, 1–24. Tübingen: Niemeyer.

Koch, P. and Oesterreicher, W. (1994) Schriftlichkeit Und Sprache. In H. Günther and O. Ludwig (eds) *Schrift Und Schriftlichkeit. Ein Interdisziplinäres Handbuch Internationaler Forschung*, 587–604. Berlin: Mouton de Gruyter.

Kunz, K. and Steiner, E. (2013) Cohesive Substitution in English and German: A Contrastive and Corpus-Based Perspective. In K. Aijmer and B. Altenberg (eds) *Advances in Corpus-Based Contrastive Linguistics. Studies in Honour of Stig Johansson*, 201–231. Amsterdam: John Benjamins Publishing Company.

Lapshinova-Koltunski, E., Kunz, K., and Amoia, M. (2012) Compiling a Multilingual Corpus. *Proceedings of the VIIth GSCP-2012 International Conference: Speech and Corpora.* Firenze: FUP. Give in full

Menzel, K. (2014) Ellipsen Als Stil- Und Kohäsionsmittel in Deutschen Und Englischen Politischen Reden. *Germanistische Mitteilungen. Zeitschrift Für Deutsche Sprache, Literatur Und Kultur. Deutsch Kontrastiv* 40(1): 31–50.

Menzel, K. and Lapshinova-Koltunski, E. (2014) Kontrastive Analyse Deutscher Und Englischer Kohäsionsmittel in Verschiedenen Diskurstypen. *Tekst i Dyskurs – Text Und Diskurs. Zeitschrift Der Abteilung Für Germanistische Sprachwissenschaft Des Germanistischen Instituts Warschau*, 247–266.

Merchant, J. (2001) *The Syntax of Silence: Sluicing, Islands, and the Theory of Ellipsis.* Oxford: Oxford University Press.

Müller, C. and Strube, M. (2006) Multi-Level Annotation of Linguistic Data with MMAX2. In S. Braun, K. Kohn and J. Mukherjee (eds) *Corpus Technology and Language Pedagogy. New Resources, New Tools, New Methods (English Corpus Linguistics, Vol. 3)*, 197–214. Frankfurt: Peter Lang.

Quirk, R., Greenbaum, S., Svartvik, J., and Leech, G. (1985) *A Comprehensive Grammar of the English Language.* London: Longman.

Schachter, P. (1985) Part-of-Speech Systems. In T. Shopen (ed.) *Language Typology and Syntactic Description. Vol. 1: Clause Structure*, 3–61. Cambridge: Cambridge University Press.

Taboada, M. T. (2004) *Building Coherence and Cohesion: Task-Oriented Dialogue in English and Spanish.* Amsterdam and Philadelphia: John Benjamins Publishing Company.

Zifonun, G., Hoffmann, L., and Strecker, B. (1997) *Grammatik Der Deutschen Sprache.* Berlin and New York: Mouton de Gruyter.

20 Linguistic Characteristics of Schizophrenia and Mania Computationally Revealed

Ekaterina Shagalov and Jonathan Fine†
Bar-Ilan University

20.1 Introduction

Both schizophrenia and mania are characterized clinically by a number of linguistic features; for schizophrenia in particular: disorganized speech (frequent derailment or incoherence), and for mania: more talkative than usual or pressure to keep talking, flight of ideas, or subjective experience that thoughts are racing and distractibility (attention too easily drawn to unimportant or irrelevant external stimuli). There is thus some overlap in these clinical descriptions.

For clinical research, Likert-type scales have been the main methodological tool (Cohen *et al.*, 2007). The clinical interview is typically carried out by a trained mental health professional. Cohen indicates some of the restrictions of this strategy: it is time-consuming, needs specially trained personnel and multiple sources of information for accurate ratings (2007: 827). Recently, more attention has being given to automated methods in different research fields including diagnosis of mental disorders. Cohen writes:

> Accurate measurement of negative symptoms is crucial for understanding and treating schizophrenia. However, current measurement strategies are reliant on subjective symptom rating scales, which often have psychometric and practical limitations. Computerized analysis of patients' speech offers a sophisticated and objective means of evaluating negative symptoms (2007: 827).

Previous studies (Lott *et al.*, 2002; Morice and McNicol, 1986) show that there is no one language characteristic that can distinguish between groups of schizophrenia patients and unaffected subjects or between groups of speakers with schizophrenia and mania. Notably, deviations in the speech of disordered subjects in a majority of cases are not qualitative, but quantitative. Unaffected speakers also stumble, pause, use neologisms and so on, but less frequently. Across-subject differences within the diagnostic groups are also remarkable. However, this study has found that combinations of features distinguish the diagnostic groups, thus characterizing the disorders.

20.2 Previous Results

In an earlier study of fluency and semantic features in schizophrenia and mania, the semantic features of process types (Material, Mental, Behaviour, Verbal, Relational, and Existential) and logico-semantic relations (including elaboration, extension, enhancement, projection, expansion, etc.) did not show substantial differences between the mania and schizophrenia groups (Shagalov and Fine, forthcoming). Rather, dysfluency measures distinguish the groups. Repetition and pausing, two types of hesitations, have similar functions but the prevalence of repetition in mania and pausing in schizophrenia makes the disorders sound different.

20.3 Research Questions

Though schizophrenia and mania share clinically described language characteristics, our previous study found linguistic markers that give the impression of schizophrenia in contrast to mania. However, with large within-group differences, the question is: how can we identify a new language sample as belonging to the subject with mania or schizophrenia? It is insufficient to discover that one subject makes a lot of silent pauses and another one stumbles a lot.

Examining unique words illustrates the problem. The group comparison shows that the subjects with schizophrenia use fewer unique words compared with the subjects with mania (25.12% vs. 30.31%). However the group score for mania is skewed by the exaggerated use of unique words by one subject (48.16%). The group analysis is therefore not informative in this case.

On the other hand, type-token ratio (TTR) computed as the relation of unique lexemes (types) to the total number of different words (tokens) showed no difference between two diagnostic groups, both with a TTR of 0.27, though it plays a substantial role in the current study. In this study, we present a method of automatically classifying a new language sample using predictors from a linear regression analysis.

20.4 Patients and Method

Informal ten minute clinical interviews were recorded openly with a variety of psychiatric patients (Bartolucci and Fine, 1987). The generally open-ended questions were meant to stimulate spontaneous conversation that would reflect the language of the speaker in the speech community. There were six conversations for schizophrenia from six different speakers and four conversations from three speakers with mania. Diagnosis was made according to the Research Diagnostic Criteria (Spitzer *et al.*, 1978), with the further inclusion criteria of ability to cooperate with the study and English as first language. A range of linguistic measures was used to explore the semantics and discourse fluency of the speakers. The UAM Corpus Tool (O'Donnell, 2008) was used to annotate and analyse the transcripts. For analysis of some research variables (syntactic complexity, amount of talk), the transcripts were entered into Excel or were processed as text files (dysfluencies, type-token ratio, lexical similarity, high- and low-frequency words). The research variables were measured and normalized for the length of the interview depending on the specific variables. SPSS Statistics (version 13.0) was used for analysis.

20.5 Variables

The study exploits the groups of variables that showed greater or smaller importance in our previous research; namely, dysfluency and cohesion variables (5.1), lexical, semantic and richness of description variables (5.2), amount of talk (5.3), and syntactic complexity (5.4). A list of the 46 variables used in this study is given in Appendix A.

20.6 Discourse Variables of Dysfluency and Cohesion

20.6.1 Dysfluency Variables

Dysfluencies encoded as filled and silent pauses have been studied in connection with clinical symptoms of schizophrenia. Rochester *et al.* (1977) argued that the short-term memory problems in schizophrenia underpin longer pauses between clauses compared to healthy controls and disrupt the smooth flow of discourse. Maher (1983) suggested that the attention deficit in schizophrenia results in more probable associative intrusions at clause boundaries.

Filled pauses (FP) as well as silent pauses (SP) have been considered as a signal of speakers' word-finding difficulties (Rohrer *et al.*, 2008). The conventional hesitations (those occurring between clauses) were observed to be longer in the subjects diagnosed with schizophrenia compared to undergraduate students and compared to mania in spite of the fact that the subjects with mania were diagnosed as thought disordered (Resnick and Oltmanns, 1984). Not distinguishing between conventional hesitations and those occurring within clauses, we found that in general the subjects diagnosed with schizophrenia use more silent and filled pauses compared to the subjects with mania (Shagalov and Fine, forthcoming).

Failures to utter an intended lexical item were identified by Chaika (1974) as one of the abnormalities of psychotic speech. These stumbles (Stu) are usually taken to be two or more attempts to pronounce the word. Often, these attempts result in producing the target word. More rarely, subjects do not continue and choose another word.

The increase of adjacent (immediate) repetitions (LI_Re) in speech can convey discourse planning and word finding problems. Beattie and Bradbury (1979) showed that if speakers are conditioned to reduce silent pauses in their speech, they fill the silent gap by increasing the number of word repetitions – the overall speech rate remains constant whereas pauses are changed for word repetitions (in Howell and Sackin, 2001). It was observed that when fluency is disrupted in spontaneous speech, subjects tend to frequently repeat pronouns and conjunctions (Clark and Clark, 1977, in Howell and Sackin, 2001). Later, Au-Yeung, Howell, and Pilgrim (1998) showed that word repetition encompasses functional words in general. Howell and Sackin argue that the repetition of functional words in spontaneous discourse has a role similar to pausing, that is, repetition 'allow[s] more planning time for the up-coming stretches' (2001: 459).

The dysfluency in the speech of the subjects diagnosed with schizophrenia and mania was measured through the following variables: SP, FP, Stu, and LI_Re. The scores were normalized by the number of words (tokens) in the transcript. Filled pauses and stumbles were not identified as words. Thus, they were not counted for the total number of words in the transcripts and were not considered as delimiters between adjacent repetitions (*so however the um .... however the little children would start balking*). For multi lexical units, we counted both the number of times the unit was repeated (NuRe) and the length of the repeated unit (LeRe) (M: *I'm I'mI'm not eating // I'm not eating (.) well // no no (.) I'm not*).

20.6.2 Cohesion

Cohesive ties create dependencies of interpretation across clauses. Halliday and Hasan (1976) classify cohesive ties as: conjunction, reference, ellipsis, substitution, and lexical cohesion (repetition of the same lexical root, synonym, superordinate, general item). Rochester and Martin (1979) reported that subjects with schizophrenia produce less cohesive speech, use more unclear and ambiguous references, more generic references, a higher proportion of lexical cohesion, and fewer conjunctions. Such speakers also experience difficulties in maintaining a discourse plan. Cohesion is violated between sentences at the discourse level whereas syntax within sentences is in general preserved (Leroy *et al.*, 2005).

Several studies documented the abnormally few reference ties in schizophrenia (Harvey, 1983). Rochester, Martin, and Thurston (1977: 102) demonstrate less cohesion in schizophrenia (cohesive ties per clause were 1.91 for thought disordered subjects and 1.96 for non-thought disordered, while normal controls used 2.1 cohesive ties per clause). Chaika and Lambe (1989) found that all groups of speakers use significantly more anaphora than other cohesive ties. However, subjects with schizophrenia use anaphoric references significantly less than either speakers with mania or normals (1989: 416). It has been proposed that impairments in referential cohesion in schizophrenia can be caused by inability to 'maintain multiple referents online for later resolution' or inability to 'use contextual information or real-world knowledge to link the correct anaphor with the correct antecedent' (Ditman and Kuperberg, 2010: 8).

Two cohesive ties were studied: referential markers (RM) and conjunctive devices (CD). The following groups of lexical items were identified as referential cohesive markers (cf. Rochester and Martin, 1979): third person subjective, objective and reflexive pronouns (e.g. *she, him, themselves*); third personal determiners (e.g. *their, his, her, its*); demonstrative references (e.g. *the, this, there, that, those*); relative pronouns (e.g. *who, whom, whose, which*, sometimes *that*). The group of conjunctive devices included: conjunctions (e.g. *after, as, as far, as if, as long as, but, cause, even though, so, so that, still, unless, yet*); complementizers as special subordinating conjunctions that introduce complement clauses (e.g. *whether, that*); interrogative words for indirect questions (*who, when, where, why, while*). The cohesive items that can function in different ways in the discourse were tagged manually.

Because the amount of discourse varies across patients, the conjunctive cohesion was measured as a ratio of cohesive elements to transitivity units (Halliday and Matthiessen, 2004). The number of transitivity units (TU) is equal to the number of processes in the transcript. In speech segment (1) from schizophrenia there are five conjunctions (underlined) and six TU, so the ratio is 5/6, i.e. 0.83.

(1) S: I stayed [TU] with some friends from Vancouver // (.) and I found [TU] work in a factory // (...) then I took [TU] a train home // (.) and when I got [TU] home // then I went [TU] back to school // (...) and stayed [TU] in school for two years

20.6.3 Dysfluencies in Processing Cohesive vs. Non-Cohesive Items, Referential Cohesive Markers vs. Conjunctive Devices, Exophoric Speech Role References vs. Endophoric References

Subjects with schizophrenia experience difficulties in processing cohesion. Incompetent referential strategies (unclear and ambiguous references) were reported in many studies (e.g. Harvey and Brault, 1986; Martin, 1979). We propose that these difficulties in processing cohesive items can be manifested through increasing dysfluencies around them compared to dysfluencies around non-cohesive lexical items. References and conjunctions were identified as cohesive items (CI) and their lists were used as an input for the computational programme. All other items (which are not in the lists) were considered as being non-cohesive (NI). Potentially ambiguous lexical items were tagged manually for their cohesive function. Dysfluencies before and after cohesive and non-cohesive lexical items were studied separately. Dysfluencies were normalized by the total number of cohesive or non-cohesive lexical items for each diagnostic group. We compared also dysfluencies in processing referential cohesive markers (RM) and conjunctive devices (CD).

Subjects diagnosed with schizophrenia, similar to patients with autism or Asperger's syndrome, experience difficulties in interpreting deictic referents (Crow, 2010), perhaps caused by deficits in processing contextual information (Patniyot, 2011). Use of deictic terms, such as 'I' and 'you', requires intact assimilatory functioning because they have no fixed meaning. They are thought to be indexical, that is, their referent meaning is dependent on the context (Patniyot, 2011: 570). The first and second person pronouns in subjective, objective and reflexive forms and corresponding possessive pronouns were coded as exophoric speech role references (SR) whereas the third person pronouns in all forms and corresponding possessive pronouns were coded as endophoric references (Ref3). We compared dysfluencies in processing SR vs. Ref3. The lists of SR and Ref3 were used as an input for the programme. All other lexical items were ignored.

20.7 Lexical Variability and Flexibility, Richness of Description

20.7.1 Type-Token Ratio

A statistical measure typically employed to estimate the lexical diversity of speech is the type-token ratio (TTR) that is computed as the relation of different words (types) to the total number of different words (tokens) in the text. The earliest attempts to distinguish between the speech of psychotic subjects and healthy controls using this measure were made by Fairbanks (1944) who found significantly higher TTR among normals (in Hotchkiss and Harvey, 1986). The TTR of speech samples produced by subjects diagnosed with schizophrenia, especially thought-disordered individuals, is typically less than those produced by healthy subjects (Mann, 1944; in Resnick, 1967). These results have been challenged by other studies that show no difference in counts for subjects with schizophrenia and healthy controls or therapists (Feldstein and Jaffe, 1962).

For this study, a word was defined as a sequence of letters between two spaces. Filled pauses (ah) and stumbles (w- w- would) were not considered as words and were not counted.

20.7.2 Unique Words

Peculiar word use is reported as one of the language abnormalities in schizophrenia (Liddle *et al.*, 2002). Idiosyncratic verbalizations are proposed to represent underlying thought disorder (Johnston and Holtzman, 1979). However, the use of rare words by subjects diagnosed with schizophrenia was interpreted by Pinard and Lecours (1983, in Baskak *et al.*, 2008) as evidence of a large and intact vocabulary.

Lexical flexibility and variability was studied by analysing unique words in the transcripts of the subjects with schizophrenia and mania through: a) within-group comparisons (WGC); b) across-group comparisons (AGC). In WGC, the unique words were calculated as a proportion of unique words (lexemes) in the transcript of the patient to the total number of words (lexemes) in the transcripts of all subjects of the group. As in the earlier study, in AGC, the unique words were counted as a proportion of unique words (lexemes) in the transcript of the patient to the total number of words (lexemes) in the transcripts of all subjects of both groups. All words in the transcripts were reduced to their simple forms (lemmas) – plurals and verbal inflection were removed.

20.7.3 Richness of Description

In addition to the lexical measures of semantic variation, the amount of detail in nominal groups was examined to compare the richness of description of people, places and things (Participants in SFL) in the two diagnostic groups. Nominal groups were analysed in terms of their functions of: Deictic, Numerative, Classifier, Epithet, PostDeictic, Thing and Quantifier (Halliday and Matthiessen, 2004).

Table 20.1: Functions of Nominal Groups (Halliday and Matthiessen, 2004)

Schizo:	**A**	**Bus**	**ride**	**to Michigan**
	Deictic	Classifier	Thing	Qualifier
	Determiner	Noun	Noun	Prepositional Phrase

The richness of description has frequently been estimated by adjective-verb ratio (Rosenberg and Tucker, 1979). Studies that measured this relation have reported that speakers with schizophrenia have low adjective-verb quotient (AVQ). Mann (1944, in Resnick, 1967) compared the adjective-verb quotient measured for the 30 freshmen (0.51) with that for 30 schizophrenic hospitalized patients (0.43). Samokhvalov and Samokhvalova (2011) measured the verb-adjective ratio for subjects with schizophrenia and controls. The scores were higher for schizophrenia (2.5 for men and 2.8 for women with schizophrenia compared to healthy men – 1.4 and healthy women – 1.3). Both these studies show that subjects with schizophrenia demonstrate less description in verbal expression compared to controls.

The adjective-verb quotient (AVQ) was adopted with modification. The description constituent of the relation was measured through the total number of Classifiers and Epithets represented by adjectives and nouns along with PostDeictics, and Qualifiers (D3VQ = Description3-Verb Quotient). The raw scores were divided by the number of processes.

20.7.4 Amount of Talk

Resnick and Oltmanns (1984) reported a negative correlation between verbosity and pausing. Barch and Berenbaum (1997) found that less verbosity was associated with greater pausing and less syntactic complexity both in schizophrenia and mania. In addition, less syntactic complexity correlated with greater pausing. An across-group comparison revealed that subjects diagnosed with schizophrenia demonstrate less verbosity and syntactic complexity than subjects with mania. There were no differences across groups in pausing. The authors highlight that deficits in verbosity, syntactic complexity and pausing are underpinned by a common etiological factor. They hypothesize that all three aspects may be related to language production difficulties.

We measured the amount of talk for each speaker as the relation of the number of utterances to the number of turns. The turn was defined as a stretch of speech produced by one speaker and bounded by the speech of another speaker or by the beginning or end of the conversation (Fine, 1994). Continuers such as *uh*, *um*, *yes*, *yea*, etc. used by the interviewer and signaling his recognition that the patient is in the middle of the expanded turn were not considered as turns. Thus, the speech segments expanding through the continuers were identified as the expanded turn.

The unit of an utterance was defined from the perspective of Systemic Functional Linguistics. The following criteria were used; any of 1) finite or non-finite clause; 2) minor clause – a clause that has no mood or transitivity structure, typically functioning as a call, a greeting, an exclamation or an alarm (*Good morning*!); 3) elliptical clause that can be realized either as anaphoric or exophoric ellipsis or substitution. Anaphoric ellipsis is identified when one or more elements of the clause are presupposed from the previous speech segment(s); for example, a response to a question as in the illustration from schizophrenia: *how long were you out of school? // a year*. In exophoric ellipsis, the clause is 'taking advantage of the rhetorical structure of the situation, specifically the roles of speaker and listener' (Halliday and Matthiessen, 2004: 100). The subject, and often also the finite verb, is extracted from the context: *No idea* instead of *I have no idea*.

Three additional criteria for an utterance were formulated: 4) When 'continuers' divided a clause, that clause was treated as one utterance; 5) Incomplete clauses were treated as separate utterances if the patient aborted an utterance without completing it and started a new one (Adams and Bishop, 1989); and 6) Discourse markers (*well*, *you know*, *I guess*) were not counted as utterances. There is only one utterance in the following example (2). The 'continuers' *oh* and *right* are not considered as separate turns.

(2) M: Oh // yea // my uncle // <u>like he he broke his arm</u>
I: Oh [continuer]
M: a couple of weeks ago

20.7.5 Subordinate Clauses and Depth

It has been proposed that the capacity for conceptual sequencing is impaired in schizophrenia (Docherty *et al.*, 2000). Conceptual sequencing in speech is a process of organizing simple concepts (words and phrases) into an appropriate sequence to express ideas. Conceptual sequencing difficulties can be encoded in unclear and ambiguous referential cohesion as well as in failures of meaning caused by syntactic inadequacy (grammatical unclarities). Syntactic complexity has been reported to be reduced in schizophrenia (Andreasen, 1979; Morice and Ingram, 1982). Morice and Ingram (1982) showed that speech produced by subjects with schizophrenia is syntactically less complex and contains more syntactic errors than the speech of patients with mania.

Syntactic complexity was measured as the number of subordinate clauses per T-unit (SubCl) and the depth of T-units (Depth). The T-unit is a single independent clause with all of its subordinate clauses (Hunt, 1965). Depth of T-units was calculated as mean depth of subordinated embedding per T-unit. There are two subordinate clauses per T-unit in example 3 (*if I had gone* and *if I had a breakdown*), but the depth is only one, because one subordinate clause is not embedded into the other. These two subordinate clauses are paratactically connected.

(3) M: But if I had gone and had a breakdown // I might have not been such a pleasant environment

20.8 Classifying a Language Sample as Belonging to Schizophrenia or Mania

20.8.1 Best Combination of Variables for Distinguishing Two Diagnostic Groups

Linear regression analysis (LRA) was used to find combinations of variables (predictors) that can distinguish the diagnostic groups and classify a new language sample as belonging to schizophrenia or mania. The aim is to identify the predictors that reflect the clinical judgements and may well be the bases for those judgements. Linear regression estimates the coefficients of the linear equation, involving one or more independent variables that best predict the value of the dependent variable. Disorder (schizophrenia or mania) is the dependent variable in our analysis. All other variables are independent.

The first goal was to choose an invariant set of variables that can be applied to new language samples and distinguish the two groups in diagnostic practice. For the first phase, the best subset of variables (from all 46 research variables listed in Appendix A) for distinguishing between two diagnostic groups was determined. In ten trials, one sample of the ten speech samples was 'held out' and was to be classified as either schizophrenia or mania using the predictors chosen by applying LRA to the training set of the nine remaining samples.

The variables that were chosen as the best predictors in more than four of the ten trials are: repetitions of endophoric references (10 trials), stumbles on exophoric speech role references (7), filled pauses after endophoric references (6), conjunctions per 100 transitivity units (5), filled pauses after speech role references (5), depth of hypotactic embedding (5), subordinate clauses per T-unit (5), type-token ratio (5).

Five of eight best predictors involved cohesion, that is, text-forming devices in the textual metafunction. This finding further supports an underlying difficulty in schizophrenia of interpreting and producing textness. Subjects with schizophrenia experience difficulty interpreting deictic reference because deictic terms (e.g. 'I' and 'you') have no fixed meaning since their referential meaning changes depending on the context (Crow, 2010; Patniyot, 2011). In our study, there are filled pauses after speech role references: *I didn't discuss it with* ***my*** *<u>ah</u> (.) with the Dean of Studies.* Difficulties in processing cohesive items including references in schizophrenia can result in unclear references (Rochester and Martin, 1979) and dysfluencies when processing anaphoric references (Shagalov and Fine, forthcoming). In our study, there are filled pauses after anaphoric references: *the man <u>...</u> was taking care of her (.)* ***he*** *<u>um</u> (.) he's a I think it is or (.) and uh (.) he's had an awful time.*

At this first research stage, the error rate was 0.4; that is, only six of ten cases were classified correctly (Table 20.1). The false-negative classification error rates were 33% for schizophrenia (two schizophrenia samples from six were incorrectly classified as belonging to mania) and 50% for mania (two mania samples from four were incorrectly classified as belonging to schizophrenia). In the linear regression analysis, we assigned to all subjects the number of the group of the disorder: 1 to the subjects with schizophrenia and 2 to the subjects with mania. The hyperplane that divides the subjects into two groups passes through 1.5 on the correspondent ace (the mean for these two numbers). So, the results were compared with this score: < 1.5 – schizophrenia, > 1.5 – mania.

Table 20.2: Predictors. Classifying a New Sample

Speaker	**Predictors**	**Results**	**1.5**
Sch-Al	*TTR, Depth, NuRe, Cl_SP_B, CD_FP_A, SR_Stu, Ref3_SP_A, Ref3_Re*	1.22	Schizo
Sch-Ch	*D3VQ, SubCl, RM_FP_A, RM_SP_A, SR_FP_A, SR_Stu, Ref3_SP_A, Ref3_Re*	0.77	Schizo
Sch-Du	*TTR, Depth, Conj, RM_SP_A, CD_Re, SR_FP_A, SR_Stu, Ref3_Re*	-0.21	Schizo

Sch-Ja	*D3VQ, Depth, CD_FP_A, SR_FP_B, SR_SP_B, Ref3_FP_A, Ref3_SP_A, Ref3_Re*	1.60	Error
Sch-Man	*TTR, SubCl, Cl_SP_A, RM_SP_B, SR_FP_A, SR_Stu, Ref3_FP_A, Ref3_Re*	0.57	Schizo
Sch-McD	*AGC, Depth, Conj, NI_FP_A, NI_SP_B, SR_LI_Stu, Ref3_FP_A, Ref3_Re*	2.14	Error
M-Mu1	*TTR, SubCl, RM_FP_A, RM_SP_A, CD_Re, SR_FP_A, SR_Stu, Ref3_Re*	1.55	Error
M-Mu2	*Depth, Conj, Cl_SP_B, CD_FP_A, SR_Stu, Ref3_FP_A, Ref3_SP_A, Ref3_Re*	1.47	Error
M-Ra	*TTR, SubCl, Conj, Cl_SP_A, RM_SP_B, SR_FP_A, Ref3_FP_A, Ref3_Re*	2.68	Mania
M-Re	*AGC, SubCl, Conj, NI_FP_A, NI_SP_B, NI_Stu, Ref3_FP_A, Ref3_Re*	4.30	Mania

20.8.2 Classifying a New Language Sample Using the Best Subset of Variables

The question was: Whether the combination of variables formed from the best subset of predictors can minimize the errors in classifying new language samples as spoken by a speaker with schizophrenia or mania. With only the eight best predictors (namely, repetitions of endophoric references [Ref3_Re], stumbles on exophoric speech role references [SR_Stu], filled pauses after endophoric references [Ref3_FP_A], conjunctions per 100 transitivity units [Conj], filled pauses after speech role references [SR_FP_A], depth of hypotactic embedding [Depth], subordinate clauses per T-unit [SubCl], type-token ratio [TTR. 1.5 – Error 0.1]) entered into LRA, only one speech sample, belonging to mania, was not classified correctly (Table 20.3). The false-negative classification error rates were 0% for schizophrenia (all six samples were classified correctly) and 25% for mania (one mania sample from four was classified as belonging to schizophrenia).

Table 20.3: Best Predictors: Classifying a New Sample

Speaker	Result	< 1.5	> 1.5
Sch-Al	0.29	Schizo	
Sch-Ch	1.13	Schizo	
Sch-Du	0.68	Schizo	
Sch-Ja	1.08	Schizo	
Sch-Man	0.89	Schizo	
Sch-McD	0.82	Schizo	
M-Mu1	0.58		Error
M-Mu2	1.84		Mania
M-Ra	2.30		Mania
M-Re	2.38		Mania

20.9 Discussion

This computational investigation of the language of schizophrenia and mania has revealed a rather complex picture of the differences. There are differences in the various categories of syntax, cohesion, semantics and fluencies. However, it is the combination of measures from these categories, rather than striking differences in single dimensions that characterizes the differences between the diagnoses. In syntax, there is less syntactic depth in schizophrenia; there is less cohesion in schizophrenia; the semantics in schizophrenia seems more deviant and there is less detail about participants, yet there are more unique words in mania; and there is generally more dysfluency and especially more pausing in schizophrenia but more repletion and false starts in mania. These findings often accord with other studies of schizophrenia on its own and in comparison to mania. For many variables, schizophrenia and mania seem the same.

When variables were considered together, the differences between mania and schizophrenia became clearer. Two measures of dysfluencies, when combined with exophoric speech role references and when combined with endophoric (anaphoric) references, were two of the eight best predictors of the difference between the diagnostic groups. It is not just that there is a difference in dysfluency, with more pauses in the language of schizophrenia and more repetitions and false starts in mania, but crucially, the differences are in the different co-occurences of dysfluencies with kinds of reference. Five of the eight best predictors involved cohesion, strongly implicating the nonstructural text-forming devices that link the language to itself (endophoric reference and conjunction) and to the physical context of the speech event (exophoric reference). These variables of text-formation are essentially relational and so their important role in predicting differences between the groups suggests that mania and schizophrenia are heard as relating differently to the verbal and non-verbal contexts. Furthermore, the eight best predictors of the difference in schizophrenia and mania involve the simultaneous occurrence of dysfluency variables, cohesion variables, a lexical variable (type-token ratio) and syntactic variables. The disorders, and their differences, thus appear across several aspects of spontaneous language.

20.10 Conclusion

The computational analysis of a variety of variables captures the combinations of features that distinguish the language of mania and schizophrenia. Since diagnosis is largely based on language data, both in the speech community when the individual is identified as being atypical and in the clinical setting where clinical interviews and diagnostic instruments are the main tools, the language characteristics of a disorder largely define what we mean by the disorder and what the pathological phenomena are. The investigation of language in the disorders is thus importantly an investigation of the nature of the disorders themselves. The outcome that shows that the language characteristics of the disorders are interrelated and cut across various kinds of linguistic characteristics suggests that we should think of the disorders as rather complex entities that appear clinically in rather complex combinations of language features. Clinicians perhaps intuitively form a gestalt of schizophrenia and mania that are made up of a range of types of linguistic phenomena.

Although it is outside the scope of this chapter, the combination of variables for schizophrenia and mania could suggest common or different underlying mechanisms. For example, the processing issues discussed by Kuperberg (Ditman and Kuperberg, 2010; Ditman *et al.*, 2011) may underlie one or more of the linguistic variables. In addition, just in terms of the linguistic variables themselves, some variables could influence other variables. For example, less detail in nominal groups in schizophrenia could be related to increased pausing. Cause and effect in either direction is possible. Similarly, syntactic depth and dysfluency could be causally related in either direction. These issues obviously need more detailed exploration. At present, the findings of this study can be seen as phenomena that need to be accounted for by neuro-cognitive theories of schizophrenia and mania.

A clear limitation in this study is the rather small number of subjects and language samples. However, viewed as a series of case studies, some essential issues are captured. Clinical disorders are often defined as non-overlapping sets of criteria such that two individuals with the same diagnosis may have no specific diagnostic criteria in common (see Fine, 2006 for a discussion of the problem). The limitation of power in this study is also a limitation in the power of all studies that are based on heterogeneous groups. Discovering real differences is hampered in both cases by the a priori heterogeneity of the groups.

About the authors

Ekaterina Shagalov holds a PhD degree from Bar-Ilan University, Ramat Gan, Israel. In her doctoral study, she used computational means to distinguish mania and schizophrenia on the basis of linguistic characteristics that coincide with clinical descriptions of the disorders. She works as a linguist in Dixilang Company which has developed speech recognition technology.

† **Jonathan Fine** was Professor of Linguistics in the Department of English Literature and Linguistics at Bar-Ilan University, Ramat Gan, Israel. His research focuses on the language of psychiatric disorders in children and adults (including schizophrenia, autism, hyperactivity) from a functional perspective.

References

Adams, C. and Bishop, D. V. M. (1989) Conversational Characteristics of Children with Semantic-Pragmatic Disorder. I: Exchange Structure, Turntaking, Repairs and Cohesion. *British Journal of Disorders of Communication* 24: 211–239.

Andreasen, N. C. (1979) Thought, Language, and Communication Disorders: Clinical Assessment, Definition of Terms, and Assessment of their Reliability. *Archives of General Psychiatry* 36: 1315–1321.

Au-Yeung, J., Howell, P., and Pilgrim, L. (1998) Phonological Words and Stuttering on Function Words. *Journal of Speech, Language, and Hearing Research* 41: 1019–1030.

Barch, D. M. and Berenbaum, H. (1997) Language Generation in Schizophrenia and Mania: The Relationships among Verbosity, Syntactic Complexity, and Pausing. *Journal of Psycholinguistic Research* 26(4): 401–412.

Bartolucci, G. and Fine, J. (1987) The Frequency of Cohesion Weakness in Psychiatric Syndromes. *Applied Psycholinguistics* 8: 67–74.

Baskak, B., Ozel, E. T., Atbasoglu, E. C., and Baskak, S. C. (2008) Peculiar Word Use as a Possible Trait Marker in Schizophrenia. *Schizophrenia Research* 103: 311–317.

Beattie, G. W. and Bradbury, R. J. (1979) An Experimental Investigation of the Modifiability of the Temporal Structure of Spontaneous Speech. *Journal of Psycholinguistic Research* 8 (225): 248.

Chaika, E. and Lambe, P. (1989) Cohesion in Schizophrenic and Normal Narration Revisited. *Journal of Communication Disorders* 22: 407–421.

Chaika, E. O. (1974) A Linguist Looks at Schizophrenic Language. *Brain and Language* 1: 257–276.

Cohen, A. S., Alpert, M., Nienow, T. M., Dinzo, T. J., and Docherty, N. M. (2007) Computerized Measurement of Negative Symptoms in Schizophrenia. *Journal of Psychiatric Research* 42: 827–836.

Crow, T. J. (2010) The Nuclear Symptoms of Schizophrenia Reveal the Four Quadrant Structure of Language and its Deictic Frame. *Journal of Neurolinguistics* 23: 1–9.

Ditman, T., Goff, D., and Kuperberg, G. R. (2011) Slow and Steady: Sustained Effects of Lexico-Semantic Associations Mediate Referential Impairments in Schizophrenia. *Cognitive, Affective and Behavioral Neuroscience* 11(2): 245–258.

Ditman, T. and Kuperberg, G. R. (2010) Building Coherence: A Framework for Exploring the Breakdown of Links across Clause Boundaries in Schizophrenia. *Journal of Neurolinguistics: "Language in Schizophrenia" Special Issue,* 23 (3): 254–269.

Docherty, N., Hall, M. J., Gordinier, S. W., and Cutting, L. P. (2000) Conceptual

Sequencing and Disordered Speech in Schizophrenia. *Schizophrenia Bulletin* 26: 723–735.

Feldstein, S. and Jaffe, J. (1962) Vocabulary Diversity of Schizophrenics and Normals. *Journal of Speech and Hearing Research* 5(76): 78.

Fine, J. (1994) *How Language Works: Cohesion in Normal and Nonstandard Communication*. Westport, CT: Ablex Publishing.

Fine, J. (2006) *Language in Psychiatry: A Handbook for Clinical Practice*. London: Equinox.

Halliday, M. A. K. and Hasan, R. (1976) *Cohesion in English*. London: Longman.

Halliday, M. A. K. and Matthiessen, C. M. I. M. (2004) *An Introduction to Functional Grammar*. 3rd edn. London: Hodder Arnold.

Harvey, P. D. and Brault, J. (1986) Speech Performance in Mania and Schizophrenia: The Association of Positive and Negative Thought Disorder and Reference Failures. *Journal of Communication Disorders* 19: 161–173.

Harvey, P. D. (1983) Speech Competence in Manic and Schizophrenic Psychoses: The Association between Clinically Rated Thought Disorder and Cohesion and Reference Performance. *Journal of Abnormal Psychology* 92: 368–377.

Hotchkiss, A. P., and Harvey, P. D. (1986) Linguistic Analyses of Speech Disorder in Psychosis. *Clinical Psychology Review* 6: 155–75.

Howell, P. and Sackin, S. (2001) Function Word Repetitions Emerge when Speakers are Operantly Conditioned to Reduce Frequency of Silent Pauses. *Journal of Psycholinguistic Research* 30 (5): 457-474.

Hunt, K. (1965) Grammatical Structures Written at Three Grade Levels. *NCTE Research Report No. 3*. Champaign, IL: National Council of Teachers of English.

Johnston, M. H. and Holtzman, P. S. (1979) *Assessing Schizophrenic Thinking*. San Francisco, CA: Jossey-Bass.

Leroy, F., Pezard, L., Nandrino, J., and Beaune, D. (2005) Dynamical Quantification of Schizophrenic Speech. *Psychiatry Research* 133: 159–171.

Liddle, P. F., Ngan, E. T. C., Caissie, S. L., Anderson, C. M., Bates, A. T., Quested, D. J., White, R., and Weg, R. (2002) Thought and Language Index: An Instrument for Assessing Thought and Language in Schizophrenia. *The British Journal of Psychiatry* 181(4): 326-330.

Lott, P. R., Guggenbühl, S., Schneeberger, A., Pulver, A. E., and Stassen, H. H. (2002) Linguistic Analysis of the Speech Output of Schizophrenic, Bipolar, and Depressive Patients. *Psychopathology* 35(4): 220–227.

Maher, B. (1983) The Education of Health Psychologists: Quality Counts – Numbers are Dangerous. *Health Psychology* 2(5): 37–48.

Mann, M. B. (1944) The Quantitative Differentiation of Samples of Written Language. *Psychological Monographs* 56.

Morice, R. D. and McNicol, D. (1986) Language Changes in Schizophrenia: A Limited Replication. *Schizophrenia Bulletin* 12(2): 239-251.

Morice, R. D. and Ingram, J. C. (1982) Language Analysis in Schizophrenia: Diagnostic Implications. *Australian and New Zealand Journal of Psychiatry* 16: 11–21.

O'Donnell, M. (2008) The UAM Corpus Tool: Software for Corpus Annotation and Exploration. *Proceedings of the XXVI Congreso De AESLA*. Almeria, Spain.

Patniyot, N. S. (2011) Thought Disorder in Schizophrenia: Impairment in Contextual Processing Via Integrative Failures in Cognition. *Medical Hypotheses* 77(4): 568-572.

Pinard, G. and Lecours, A. R. (1983) The Language of Psychotics and Neurotics. In A. R. Lhermitte, F. Bryans and B. Bryans (eds) *Aphasiology*, 313–335. London: Ballie`re Tindall.

Resnick, H. S. and Oltmanns, T. F. (1984) Hesitation Patterns in the Speech of Thought-Disordered Schizophrenia and Manic Patients. *Journal of Abnormal Psychology* 93(1): 80-86.

Resnick, R. W. (1967) 'Personality Patterns and Psycholinguistic Differences in Response to Music'. Unpublished PhD thesis. University of Florida, Florida.

Rochester, S. and Martin, J. R. (1979) *Crazy Talk: A Study of the Discourse of Schizophrenic Speakers*. New York: Plenum.

Rochester, S., Martin, J. R., and Thurston, S. (1977) Thought-Process Disorder in Schizophrenia: The Listener's Task. *Brain and Language* 4(95): 114.

Rohrer, J. D., Knight, W. D., Warren, J. E., Fox, N. C., Rossor, M. N., and Warren, J. D. (2008) Word-finding Difficulty: A Clinical Analysis of the Progressive Aphasias. *Brain* 131(8): 38.

Rosenberg, S. D. and Tucker, G. J. (1979) Verbal Behavior and Schizophrenia: The Semantic Dimension. *Archives of General Psychiatry* 36(12): 1331-1337.

Samokhvalov, V. P. and Samokhvalova, O. E. (2011) Toward a Neuroethology of Schizophrenia: Findings from the Crimean Project. In M. S. Ritsner (ed.) *Handbook of Schizophrenia Spectrum Disorders. Vol. 2. Phenotype and Endophenotypic Presentations*, 121–164. Dordrecht; Heidelberg; London; New York: Springer Science.

Shagalov, E. and Fine, J. (forthcoming) Fluency and Semantics of Language in Schizophrenia and Mania. *LACUS Forum 39*.

Spitzer, R. L., Endicott, J., and Robins, E. (1978) Research Diagnostic Criteria. *Archives of General Psychiatry* 35(6): 773-782.

Appendix A: Research Variables Entered into LRA

1	Lexical Variability and Flexibility	*TTR*	Type-token ratio
2		*WGC*	Unique words in within-group comparison
3		*AGC*	Unique words in across-group comparison
4		*D3VQ*	Description-verb quotient (Classifiers/Epithets/PostDeictics/Qualifiers)
5	Amount of Talk	*AT*	Amount of talk
6	Syntactic complexity	*SubCl*	Number of subordinate clauses per t-unit
7		*Depth*	Depth of t-units
8	Cohesion	*Conj*	Conjunctions
9	Dysfluencies	*SP*	Silent pauses
10		*FP*	Filled pauses
11		*Stu*	Stumbles
12		*LI_Re*	Lexical item repetitions
13		*NuRe*	Number of repetitions of multi lexical units
14		*LeRe*	Length of repeated multi lexical units
15	Dysfluencies around Cohesive Lexical Items	*CI_FP_B*	Filled pauses before cohesive items
16		*CI_FP_A*	Filled pauses after cohesive items
17		*CI_SP_B*	Silent pauses before cohesive items
18		*CI_SP_A*	Silent pauses after cohesive items
19		*CI_LI_Re*	Repetitions of cohesive lexical items

20	Dysfluencies around Non-Cohesive Lexical Items	*NI_FP_B*	Filled pauses before non-cohesive items
21		*NI_FP_A*	Filled pauses after non-cohesive items
22		*NI_SP_B*	Silent pauses before non-cohesive items
23		*NI_SP_A*	Silent pauses after non-cohesive items
24		*NI_LI_Re*	Repetitions of non-cohesive lexical items
25		*NI_LI_Stu*	Stumbles for non-cohesive items
26	Dysfluencies around Referential Cohesive Markers	*RM_FP_B*	Filled pauses before referential markers
27		*RM_FP_A*	Filled pauses after referential markers
28		*RM_SP_B*	Silent pauses before referential markers
29		*RM_SP_A*	Silent pauses after referential markers
30		*RM_LI_Re*	Repetitions of referential markers
31	Dysfluencies around Conjunctive Cohesive Devices	*CD_FP_B*	Filled pauses before conjunctive device
32		*CD_FP_A*	Filled pauses after referential markers
33		*CD_SP_B*	Silent pauses before referential markers
34		*CD_SP_A*	Silent pauses after referential markers
35		*CD_LI_Re*	Repetitions of referential markers

36	Dysfluencies around Exophoric Speech Role References	*SR_FP_B*	Filled pauses before speech roles references
37		*SR_FP_A*	Filled pauses after speech roles references
38		*SR_SP_B*	Silent pauses before speech roles references
39		*SR_SP_A*	Silent pauses after speech roles references
40		*SR_LI_Re*	Repetitions of speech roles references
41		*SR_LI_Stu*	Stumbles for speech roles references
42	Dysfluencies around Third Person References	*Ref3_FP_B*	Filled pauses before third person references
43		*Ref3_FP_A*	Filled pauses after third person references
44		*Ref3_SP_B*	Silent pauses before third person references
45		*Ref3_SP_A*	Silent pauses after third person references
46		*Ref3_LI_Re*	Repetitions of third person references

Subject Index

academic writing 3, 126, 134, 148, 284–5, 287–8, 291
affect – see appraisal: affect
affective alignment 62, 65–6, 69, 74
annotation 6–7, 14, 16, 232, 245–55, 263, 310, 316–22, 324–6
appraisal 2, 5, 7, 30, 35–8, 41–2, 63, 66–7, 69, 73–5, 78, 173, 175, 211, 213–5, 219–23, 225, 230, 241, 251, 261, 296–9, 302–5
  affect 35–41, 43, 65–7, 70–1, 73–4, 76–7, 173–4, 180, 220, 223
  appreciation 32, 36–41, 67, 74, 173–4, 220–2, 224, 226, 305
  judgement 35–41, 50, 52, 66–7, 73–4, 173, 175, 220–4, 271, 298, 306
appreciation – see appraisal: appreciation

blog/s 1–2, 8, 13–16, 18–19, 21–3, 25–6, 30, 45–6, 48, 50–59, 206; blogger/s 2, 22, 23–5, 46, 49–55, 56–7, 59–60; blogging 13–15, 45–46, 48, 57

Coriolanus (see also Shakespeare) 5, 211, 216–224
corpora (see also State of the Union, EU Debt Crisis) BNC 14, 16, 18–21, 27, 104, 217; COBUILD 121; CoHAE 3, 105–7, 110–12, 117; GB-News 113–116; GECCo 7–8, 310–11, 313, 316, 318–9, 321, 324–5; ICE-GB 276, 280, 283, 286; ICE-Ireland 86–88; LiveJournal 14, 16, 26; Shakespeare Corpus 226; Time Magazine 107; UKWaC 109, 112–15, 117
corpus tools: AntConc 87; Corpus Query Processor 319; Halliday Centre Tagger 6, 246, 251–4; Sketch Engine 6, 104, 116, 264, 266, 273; SPSS 330; UAM Corpus Tool 6, 246, 251–4, 297, 330; WordSmith Tools 18, 27, 187, 217, 226, 230, 232, 237; XAIRA 254
corpus-assisted 5–6, 211–14, 243, 247, 260, 263, 272
corpus-based 2, 6, 13–14, 102, 248, 297, 307–8

diachronic 3, 6, 86, 99, 102, 105, 107, 110–11, 113, 225, 227, 230, 232, 240
digital 1–8; digital actions 32; digital artefact/s 13, 32, 64–5, 68, 70, 76–7; digital article 29; digital assemblages 163; digital citizenship 2, 45; digital commemorative artefacts 63; digital communication 1, 3, 9, 37; digital context/s 3, 30, 68, 186; digital document 207; digital editions 184; digital environment/s 70, 93, 151, 162–3, 186; digital ethnography 68 (netnography); digital genres 1; digital image 163; digital language 2; digital media 5, 45; digital memorial/s 62, 65; digital networks 45; digital pedagogy 134–5, 144; digital performance 64; digital platforms 19, 22; digital portals 50; digital practices 19–20; digital reference 122; digital research article 151; digital science 186; digital settings 29–31, 42; digital social actions 32, 42; digital sources 184; digital space/s 31, 62, 64, 68, 76–7; digital still frame 167; digital surgery 120; digital technologies 29, 32; digital text/s 4–5, 25, 36, 93, 132, 163, 166, 170, 180, 184, 192, 201; digital textuality 30–1; digital video images 299; digital world 299

engineering 4, 9, 134, 136, 146–7
entextualization 7, 296–9, 301, 304, 306–8

Facebook 1, 19, 29, 33, 35, 37–8, 43, 45, 81
fandom 2, 13–20, 22–25, 73, 76
financial crisis 6, 260, 264, 268, 271; EU/European debt crisis 6, 246, 252

Google+ 43, 68

hotel websites 4, 198–9, 201–2, 204–8
hyperlink/s 3–5, 86, 139, 198–9, 203, 205–7; hypertext/s 4, 138, 153, 198, 200–1, 207

imagined community 2, 62–4, 70, 78; imagined audience 64, 70, 71–2

judgement – see appraisal: judgement

lecture/–r/s 4, 9, 142, 163, 166–7, 171–80, 319, 323

material process/es 20, 55, 72, 90–1, 103, 108, 110, 116, 121, 177, 180, 220–1, 243, 253, 329
medic/–al/–ine 3–4, 9, 153, 156–7, 120–5, 127–32, 193, 292, 319; medical discourse 122, 319; online medicine 121, 123, 131; medical research 153, 156–7; medical sites 120; medical textbook 156; medical texts 131
mental process/es 3, 20, 38, 57–9, 72, 90–2, 99, 102–5, 107–13, 116–7, 121, 169, 177, 220, 253, 265, 329
metaphor/ical 4, 6, 43, 100, 109, 122–5, 129, 131, 178, 198, 220–1, 236, 260
Mood/ MOOD 70, 100, 223, 251, 261–2, 277, 280, 336
multimodal/ity 2, 4, 8, 13–4, 22, 26, 29, 31, 37, 41–2, 69, 76–7, 81, 84, 86, 134–5, 151, 166–71, 175, 177, 179, 202, 304; multimodal analysis/es 4, 22, 26, 171, 175, 179; multimodal ensembles ensemble/s 31, 37, 41–2; multimodal text/s 2, 29, 81, 166, 168–9, 304

news 1–4, 20, 31, 43, 45–6, 48, 50, 55–6, 59, 81, 85–6, 93, 99, 111–6, 123–4, 128–9, 160, 202, 246–7, 260, 271, 272, 281–3, 285–6, 289–90; editorials 279; electronic news 264; online news 81, 93; news webpage 186
newspaper/s 2, 9, 66, 81, 84, 93, 113, 184–7, 191, 264, 269, 279

persuasive technologies 2, 29–32, 35, 37–9, 42
practices 3, 14, 19–20, 29–32, 35, 38–9, 42, 47, 62, 64–5, 152, 298, 307

recontextualization 3, 7, 31, 70, 77, 135, 151–4, 156, 160, 163–4, 185–6, 296–9, 301, 304, 306–8
Rheme 7, 276–80, 282, 293

science 123, 156, 281–2, 284–5, 288–291; popular science 3, 4, 184–9, 191, 194–5, 319, 323; scientific text 122–4, 136, 142, 169, 184, 229; science writing 4, 7, 123, 131, 134, 136–7, 152.
semantic space 120, 131–2
Shakespeare 1, 5, 8, 216–219, 226; Shakespeare's *Coriolanus* 5, 211, 216–224
social action/s, social actor/s 2–3, 29–32, 34, 39, 42, 45–6, 48–52, 58, 152
social distance 4–5, 120, 131–2, 169
social media 2, 8, 29, 31, 42, 64–5, 78; channels 65, 68; contents 37; discourse 65, 71, 78; interactions 30; platforms 64–5; practices 62; shrines 64–5; site/s 65–6, 78
site/s (see also website/s) 1–2, 29, 48, 62, 65–6, 68–9, 75–8, 81, 120, 123–4, 126–7, 130–1, 135–6, 141–3, 144, 147, 158, 160, 162, 199, 230, 299, 306, 312, 319–20, 322
social semiotic/s 1, 81, 134–5, 148, 166, 168, 170, 179
State of the Union 6, 8, 229–31, 234–5, 244

terminal illness 4, 120, 122, 130–1
Theme 5–7, 123, 126, 251, 262, 269, 276–80, 282, 294
transitivity 2, 4, 6, 69, 71, 73, 102–3, 184–6, 220, 251–4, 332, 336, 338–9
Twitter/–ing 19–20. 29, 43, 48, 66, 81
tweet 19, 30

US Presidents 6, 229–31, 234–6, 242

verbal art 5, 162, 211, 214–6, 225
verbal process/es 20–1, 71, 91–3, 103–4, 169
video/s 15–16, 29, 30, 33, 38, 63, 65, 67–72, 75–7, 86–7, 156–61, 163, 166, 170, 180–1, 291, 293, 299–300; videochat 29; video commentary 69; video files 86; video texts 166; video tribute/s 63, 65, 67–72, 75–7
vlogs 25
weblog/s 32, 156–7
website/s (see also site/s) 1, 3–4, 19, 31, 38, 81, 108, 113, 120–1, 123, 126–7, 141–6, 149, 157–163, 198–208, 244, 252, 319, 323
wiki/s 1, 8, 29, 32
Wikipedia 29, 48, 120, 123–5, 130

YouTube 2, 8, 29, 45, 62–70, 77, 121, 157–161, 163

Author Index

Aarts, B. 295
Adami, E. 31, 43
Adams, C. 336, 342
Ágel, V. 315, 326
Aguilera Carnerero, C. 256
Alba-Juez, L. 44, 214, 228
Allen, G. 169, 181
Alpert, M. 342
Alsop, S. 9–10
Amoia, M. 327
Anderson, B. 63, 78
Anderson, C. M. 343
Andreasen, N. C. 337, 342
Arancibia, M. C. 48, 51
Aristotle 260, 273
Arizzi, C. 94
Arregui, A. 313, 326
Askehave, I. 200, 201, 207
Atbasoglu, E. C. 243
Augustin, A. 202, 207
Au-Yeung, J. 331, 342

Bache, C. 103, 117
Baisa, V. 118
Baker, P. 230, 244
Bakhtin, M. 81, 94, 167, 169, 181
Baldry, A. P. 81, 84, 86, 94, 166, 167–69, 181, 201, 207
Balint, M. 128, 133
Banks, D. 252, 256, 265, 273
Barch, D. M. 335, 342
Baroni, M. 118
Barthes, R. 99–101, 117, 155, 164, 203, 207
Bartlett, T. 103, 117
Bartolucci, G. 330, 342
Barton, D. 48, 61
Baskak, B. 334, 342
Baskak, S. C. 342
Bateman, J. 207–8, 247, 249, 258
Bates, A. T. 343
Bauman, R. 297, 298, 299, 307, 308
Bayley, P. 213, 228–30, 232, 241, 245, 247, 257–8, 263
Beattie, G. W. 331, 342
Beaugrande, R. D. 314, 326
Beaune, D. 343
Bednarek, M. 81, 94, 214, 226, 246–7, 257
Bell, A. 112, 115, 117
Berber Sardinha, T. 263, 273
Berenbaum, H. 335, 342
Bernardini, S. 118
Bernard, G. R. 153–55, 157, 163, 164
Bernstein, B. 15, 151–54, 156, 165, 299, 308
Bevitori, C. 230, 232, 245, 247, 257–58, 263
Bezemer, J. 134–36, 149, 151–56, 164, 165, 178, 181
Biber, D. 113, 117, 279, 295
Bishop, D. V. M. 336, 342
Blommaert, J. 298, 305, 308
Blood, R. 13, 27
Bolter, J. D. 30, 43
Bondi, M. 88, 94
Bonus, S. 27, 61, 95
Booth, P. 71, 78
Bortoluzzi, V. 49, 61
Bos, J. 311, 326
boyd, d. 42–43, 64, 70, 76, 78–79
Bradbury, R. J. 331, 342
Brault, J. 333, 343
Briggs, C. L. 296, 298–9, 307–8
Brown, P. 108, 117
Bruce, B. 32, 43
Bruns, A. 31, 43
Bühler, K. 312, 326
Bultnick, B. 121, 133
Burnard, L. 16, 27
Buscha, J. 321, 326
Bussmann, H. 321, 326

Butler, C. S. 246–7, 250, 256–7
Byrne, P. S. 128, 133

Caissie, S. L. 343
Caldas-Coulthard, C. R. 184–5, 195
Calsamiglia, H. 185, 195
Cambria, M. 81, 85, 94
Cammaerts, B. 46, 61
Caple, H. 81, 94
Cardoso, G. 51, 61
Carpentier, N. 46, 61
Castells, M. 51, 61
Chaika, E. O. 331–2, 342
Charteris-Black, J. 263, 273
Chow, I. C. 259
Ciapuscio, G. 185, 196
Clarke, B. P. 99, 105, 108–9, 113, 117, 311, 326
Cléirigh, C. 141, 150, 172–3, 183
Clift, R. 185, 196
Clifton, C, J. 326
Coccetta, F. 94
Coffin, C. 213, 226, 247, 257, 298, 306, 309
Cohen, A. S. 328, 342
Conboy, M. 81, 94
Conrad, S. 279, 295
Cope, B. 167, 179, 181
Coppa, F. 16, 27
Costechi, E. 251, 258
Crawford Camiciottoli, B. 175, 182
Crompton, P. 279, 295
Crow, T. J. 333, 338, 342
Crystal, D. 100, 117
Cummings, M. 278–9, 295
Cutting, L. P. 342

Davidse, K. 102, 108, 117
Davies, M. 105, 117
Degaetano-Ortlieb, S. 256, 257, 322, 326
Deignan, A. 263–4, 273–4
Delwiche, A. 13, 27
Derewianka, B. 273, 275
Dhainaut, J. F. 164
Dinzo, T. J. 342
Ditman, T. 332, 341–2
Docherty, N. 336, 342
Domingo, M. 205–6, 208
Doss, E. 62, 75, 78
Döveling, K. 62, 65, 75–6, 78
Downing, A. 277, 295
Drury, H. 134, 136, 144–6, 149
Dwyer, P. 183

Eckles, D. 43–4
Eggins, S. 84, 87, 94
Ellison, N. 42–3
Elorza, I. 187, 196
Ely, E. W. 164
Endicott, J. 344
Evert, S. 319, 326

Fairclough, N. 46, 48, 61, 112, 117, 170, 182
Fawcett, R. P. 103, 117–8
Feldstein, S. 334, 343
Ferraresi, A. 118
Fernandez, E. C. 122, 133
Figueroa, J. P. 61
Fillmore, C. 216, 226, 242
Fine, J. 329–31, 336, 338, 341–4
Finnemann, N, O. 200, 208
Firth, J. R. 101, 118
Fisher, C. J. 164
Flowerdew, L. 247, 257
Fodor, J. A. 103, 118
Fogg, B. J. 32–4, 43–4
Fox, N. C. 344
Francis, G. 187, 196, 247–8, 258
Frazier, L. 326
Fries, P. H. 277, 295
Fusari, S. 232, 246, 251–2, 257–8

Gabrielatos, C. 229, 244–5
Galtung, J. 112, 115, 118
Garber, G. E. 164
Garcia Riaza, B. 187, 196
Gardner, S. 9–10, 247, 257
Gaventa, J. 46, 61
Getz, D. 200, 208
Ghadessy, M. 84, 95
Giannoni, D. S. 184, 187, 196
Gibbs, R. W. 273–4
Gibson, J. J. 29, 44
Gibson, M. 62, 78
Gillmor, D. 13, 27
Gledhill, C. J. 123, 133
Goff, D. 342

Goffman, E. 167, 182
Goldsmith, K. 151, 163, 165
González, M. 61
Gordinier, S. W. 342
Gotti, M. 184, 196
Gouanvic, J. M. 305, 309
Greenhalgh, T. 128, 133
Groote, P. D. 79
Grusin, R. 30, 43
Guggenbühl, S. 343
Günther, C. 311, 316, 326
Guzmán, J. 47, 52, 61

Haarman, L. T. 228, 245
Hall, M. J. 342
Halliday, M. A. K. 3, 5, 10, 14–5, 27, 37, 44, 50–2, 59, 61, 87, 91, 95, 99, 101–3, 110, 112, 118, 121–2,125, 131, 133–4, 149, 151–2, 156, 161–2, 165–8, 174, 180, 182, 185–6, 196, 211–6, 226, 229, 238, 245–8, 257–8, 260–2, 267, 269, 273–4, 276–7, 294–5, 310–8, 326, 331–2, 335–6, 343
Hansen-Schirra, S. 319, 326
Hård Af Segerstad, Y. 62, 79
Hardie, A. 263, 274
Harju, A. 62, 65, 79
Harvey, P. D. 332–4, 343
Hasan, R. 99, 100, 113, 118, 151–2, 161–2, 165, 214–5, 226–7, 310, 312–8, 326, 331, 343
Havelock, P. 133
Heer, J. 64, 76, 78
Heilman, K. 184, 196
Helbig, G. 321, 326
Helterbrand, J. D. 164
Heritage, J. 185, 196
Herring, S. C. 13, 27, 48, 61
Hiippala, T. 201, 208
Hjelmslev, L. 100, 118
Ho-Dac, L. M. 187, 196
Hoey, M. 187, 196
Hoffmann, L. 327
Hogan, M. 32, 42
Holtz, M. 263, 274
Holtzman, P. S. 334, 343
Honnibal, M. 250, 255, 258
Hood, S. 172–3, 182
Hotchkiss, A. P. 334, 343
Howell, P. 331, 342–3
Hundt, M. 105, 119
Hunston, S. 173, 183, 185, 187, 196, 211, 213–4, 227–8, 246–8, 258–9
Hunt, K. 337, 343
Hurtwitz, B. 128, 133
Hyland, K. 173, 180, 182, 184, 196

Iedema, R. 296, 299, 209
Ingram, J. C. 337, 343

Jaffe, J. 334, 343
Jarvis, L. 62, 76, 79
Jaworski, A. 176, 182
Jenkins, H. 16, 28
Jewitt, C. 135, 149, 205, 208
Johnson, J. H. 214, 228, 230, 245, 247, 258, 274
Johnson, M. 122, 133, 260, 274
Johnson, T. 111, 118, 270, 272
Johnston, M. H. 334, 343
Jones, J. 134, 150

Kalantzis, M. 167, 179, 181
Kaltenbacher, M. 201, 208
Kaltenbacher, T. 201, 208
Kappagoda, A. 251, 258
Karagevrekis, M. 181
Karppi, T. 65, 79
Kasperowski, D. 62, 79
Katz, J. J. 103, 118
KhosraviNik, M. 244
Kilgarriff, A. 104, 116, 118, 264, 274
Kim, C. K. 187, 196
Klaassens, M. 62, 79
Klein, W. 312, 327
Knight, N. K. 174, 182
Knight, W. D. 344
Knox, J. S. 86, 95
Koch, P. 319, 327
Kok, A. K. C. 201, 208
Kouper, I. 27
Kozinets, R. V. 68, 79
Kress, G. 3, 10, 23–5, 28, 31–2, 44, 82, 95, 134–9, 141, 144, 149–56, 160, 162–5, 167–9, 174, 177–82, 202–3, 205, 208, 297, 299, 309
Krzyzanowski, M. 244

Kunz, K. 325–7
Kuperberg, G. R. 332, 341–2

Lagerkvist, A. 62, 79
Lakoff, G. 122, 133, 260, 274
Lam, M. 165, 245
Lambe, P. 332, 342
Langrish, T. 149
Lapshinova-Koltunski, E. 256–7, 317, 319, 322, 325–7
LaRosa, S. P. 164
Lasica, J. D. 13, 28
Laterre, P. 164
Lecours, A. R. 334, 344
Lee, C. 48, 61
Leech, G. 99, 105, 108, 110, 115–6, 118–9, 327
Lemke, J. 105, 118, 141, 150, 156, 165, 198, 207–8, 213, 227
Leroy, F. 332, 343
Levin, M. 105, 107–8, 111, 119
Levinson, S. C. 108, 117
Liddle, P. F. 334, 343
Linell, P. 296, 299, 309
Lombardo, L. 247, 257
Long, B. E. L. 128, 133
López Ferrero, C. 185, 195
Lopez-Rodriguez, A. 164
Lott, P. R. 328, 343
Louw, B. 225, 227, 264, 274
Luporini, A. 216, 228, 258, 263, 273–4
Lyons, J. 103, 119

MacDonald, M. N. 156, 165
Maher, B. 330, 343
Mahlberg, M. 187, 196, 247, 257
Mair, C. 105, 119
Malcolm, K. 167, 182
Malinowski, B. 78–9, 152, 165
Mann, M. B. 334, 335, 343
Marchi, A. 229, 244–5
Martin, J. R. 30, 35–7, 41–2, 44, 50–1, 54–5, 61, 63, 66–7, 69–71, 74, 76, 79, 84, 94–5, 102–3, 119, 122, 133, 135, 150, 152, 155, 165, 173, 175, 178, 182–3, 185, 196, 213–4, 225–7, 236, 241, 245, 262, 274, 276–8, 294–5, 297, 299, 309, 332–3, 338, 344
Marwick, A. E. 64, 70, 79
Maton, K. 156, 165
Matthiessen, C. M. I. M. 3, 5, 10, 50–1, 59, 61, 91, 95, 102, 110, 116, 119, 121, 125, 131, 133, 152, 165–8, 174, 177, 180, 182, 186, 196, 212–3, 215, 226–7, 229, 231, 245–6, 248, 258, 260–1, 262, 267, 274, 276–7, 294–5, 332, 335–6, 343
Mayol, A. 46, 61
McCabe, A. 184, 196, 297, 306, 309
McDaid, D. 120, 133
McEnery, T. 244, 263, 274, 307, 309
McNamara, D. S. 185, 197
McNicol, D. 328, 343
Menzel, K. 312, 315, 317, 322, 325–7
Merchant, J. 312, 327
Miller, D. R. 214, 216, 225, 227–8, 230, 245, 247, 250, 258, 263, 270, 272, 274–5
Mindt, D. 108, 110, 119
Moisander, J. 63, 79
Montecino, L. 47–8, 51, 61
Moon, R. 110, 119
Morice, R. D. 328, 337, 343
Morley, J. 213, 228–9, 245
Mort, P. 134, 144–5, 149–50
Moulton, K. 326
Muir, M. 145, 149
Müller, C. 318, 327
Muntigl, P. 168, 174, 182
Mushin, I. 186, 197
Myers, G. 184, 197

Nandrino, J. 343
Neighbour, R. 128, 133
Nelson, G. 279, 295
Neumann, S. 326
Ngan, E. T. C. 343
Nicholas, H. 297, 299, 302, 309
Nielsen, A. E. 200–1, 207
Nienow, T. M. 342

O'Donnell, M. 162, 165, 187, 196, 212, 228, 246–7, 249–51, 254, 258, 296, 309, 330, 343
O'Halloran, K. A. 213, 226, 247, 257
O'Halloran, K. L. 84, 86, 94–5
Ochs, E. 300, 309
Oesterreicher, W. 319, 327

Oltmanns, T. F. 331, 335, 344
Ozel, E. T. 342

Pachler, N. 32, 44, 134, 150
Page, R. E. 42, 44, 65, 79
Painter, C. 119, 273, 275
Palmer, F. R. 99, 115–6, 119
Pantti, M. 64–5, 79
Paolillo, J. C. 27
Papacharissi, Z. 42, 44
Park, A. 120, 133
Park, D. 13, 28
Partington, A. 213, 227–9, 245
Patniyot, N. S. 333, 338, 343
Pendleton, D. 128, 133
Petroni, S. 31, 44
Pezard, L. 343
Pilgrim, L. 331, 342
Pinard, G. 334, 344
Potter, L. 264, 274
Pounds, G. 187, 197, 271, 275
Pulver, A. E. 343
Pyysiäinen, J. 77, 79

Quested, D. J. 343
Quirk, R. 99, 105, 108, 115, 119, 312, 321, 327

Rayner, K. 201, 208
Reicher, S. 77, 79
Resnick, H. S. 331, 335, 344
Resnick, R. W. 334–5, 344
Riquelme, G. 61
Robins, E. 344
Rochester, S. 330, 332, 338, 344
Rohrer, J. D. 330, 344
Rokka, J. 63, 79
Rose, D. 50–1, 54–5, 61, 63, 66, 79, 135, 150, 155, 165, 173, 175, 178, 182–3, 185, 196, 213, 227
Rosenberg, S. D. 335, 344
Rossor, M. N. 344
Ruge, M. H. 112, 115, 118
Rychlý, P. 118, 265, 274–5

Sackin, S. 331, 343
Sailor, L. 200, 208
Samokhvalov, O. E. 335, 344
Samokhvalov, V. P. 335, 344
Santamaria Garcia, C. 37, 42, 44
Santana, A. D. 78–9
Schachter, P. 321, 327
Scheidt, L. A. 27, 61, 95
Schneeberger, A. 343
Schofield, T. 133
Scott, M. 16, 18, 28, 87–8, 95, 187, 196–7, 217, 228–9, 232, 245
Semino, E. 122, 133
Shagalov, E. 329, 331, 338, 344
Shepherd, M. 207–8
Silverstein, M. 298, 209
Silvia, T. 111, 118
Simpson, P. 263, 275
Sinclair, J. 225, 247–9, 258
Sindoni, M. G. 15–6, 22, 25–6, 28, 42, 44, 87, 95
Sloman, J. 166, 178, 183
Smirnova, A. V. 195, 197
Smith, N. 105, 119
Smitterberg, E. 105, 119
Smrz, P. 274
Spenader, J. 311, 326
Spevack, M. 216, 228
Spitzer, R. L. 330, 344
Starks, D. 297, 299, 302, 209
Stassen, H. H. 343
Steiner, E. 325–7
Steingrub, J. S. 164
Strecker, B. 327
Strube, M. 318, 327
Sumiala, J. 62
Sumiala, M. 64–5
Svartvik, R. 119, 327

Taboada, M. T. 313–4, 327
Tan, S. 166, 183
Tandon, R. 46, 61
Tate, E. 128, 133
Tate, P. 128, 133
Taverniers, M. 100, 119, 260–1, 275
Teich, E. 14, 28, 256–7, 259
Teruya, K. 165, 231, 245
Thibault, P. 84, 94, 166–70, 181, 201, 207
Thompson, G. 35, 44, 173, 183, 185–7, 192–4, 196–7, 211, 213–4, 228, 246, 259, 260, 262, 269, 270, 275
Thurlow, C. 182
Thurston, S. 332, 244

Tognini Bonelli, E. 247–9, 259
Tolkien, J. R. R. 277, 295
Torr, J. 273, 275
Tribble, C. 16, 28, 87–8, 95
Tucker, G. 211, 228, 255, 259
Tucker, G. J. 335, 344
Tugwell, D. 274
Tyworth, M. 27

Unsworth, L. 141, 150
Urban, G. 296, 298, 309

van Dijck, J. 64, 65, 80
van Dijk, T. 76, 80
van Leeuwen, T. 23–5, 28, 32, 44, 49, 51, 61, 137–40, 141, 143, 150, 155, 160, 165, 167–9, 177–9, 182, 202–3, 208
Vanclay, F. M. 79
Vincent, J. L. 164

Wallis, S. 295
Walter, T. 62, 64–5, 80
Warren, J. D. 344
Warren, J. E. 344
Watson, C. B. 217, 222, 228
Watters, C. 207–8
Webber, P. 175, 183
Webster, J. J. 259
Weg, R. 343
Welsch, P. 27
White, P. R. R. 30, 35–7, 41, 44, 63, 66–7, 69, 70–1, 79, 214, 227, 236, 241, 245, 297, 299, 309
White, R. 343
Whittaker, R. 297, 306, 309
Whorf, B. L. 103, 119
Williams, G. 113, 119, 229, 244–5
Williams, J. 185, 197
Wodak, R. 244, 296, 299, 309
Wolfsfeld, G. 45–6, 61
Wong, B. T. M. 246, 251–2, 259
Wright, E. 27, 61, 95
Wright, S. 45–6, 61
Wu, C. 14, 28

Yan, H. 259
Yanning, Y. 263, 275
Yarbus, A. L. 201, 208
Yu, N. 27
Yus, F. 51, 61

Zanchetta, E. 118
Zappavigna, M. 2, 10, 42, 44, 64–6, 71, 74, 78, 80, 173, 183
Zifonun, G. 312, 327